Mobbing

Mobbing

CAUSES, CONSEQUENCES, AND SOLUTIONS

MAUREEN DUFFY

AND

LEN SPERRY

OXFORD
UNIVERSITY PRESS

Oxford University Press, Inc., publishes works that further Oxford University's
objective of excellence in research, scholarship, and education.

Oxford   New York
Auckland   Cape   Town   Dar es Salaam   Hong Kong   Karachi
Kuala Lumpur   Madrid   Melbourne   Mexico City   Nairobi
New Delhi   Shanghai   Taipei   Toronto

With offices in

Argentina   Austria   Brazil   Chile Czech   Republic   France   Greece
Guatemala   Hungary   Italy   Japan   Poland   Portugal   Singapore
South Korea   Switzerland   Thailand   Turkey   Ukraine   Vietnam

Copyright © 2012 by Oxford University Press, Inc.

Published by Oxford University Press, Inc.
198 Madison Avenue, New York, New York 10016
www.oup.com

Oxford is a registered trademark of Oxford University Press, Inc.

Library of Congress Cataloging-in-Publication Data

Duffy, Maureen P.
  Mobbing: causes, consequences, and solutions / Maureen Duffy and Len Sperry.
      p. cm.
  Includes bibliographical references and index.
  ISBN 978-0-19-538001-9
  1. Bullying. 2. Harassment. 3. Intimidation. 4. Organizational behavior. I. Sperry, Len.
II. Title.
BF637.B85D85 2012
302.3'3—dc23   2011018641

ISBN 978-0-19-538001-9

To our life partners, Patrick and Patti

Foreword

This book would be a pleasure to introduce if it were only a thorough, up-to-date, easy-to-read summary of research on a serious problem of human relations at work. This book is more than that.

Mobbing is a new concept, a new word that has crept into the vocabularies of employees and employers over the past thirty years in all countries of the Western world. The word already existed, of course, but in the sense of violent eruption of political unrest. In its new meaning, the word refers to an outpouring of intense but usually nonviolent collective hostility toward a workmate. This linguistic innovation began in Scandinavia, where Swedish psychologist Heinz Leymann coined the term *workplace mobbing*, drawing on earlier research in ethology by Nobel Laureate Konrad Lorenz. News of Leymann's studies spread across northern Europe, to Italy and Spain, and finally, over the past dozen years, to the Americas and Australia.

What you hold in your hands is the first book on workplace mobbing from a major publisher in the United States. In 1999, a small company in Iowa released the deservedly popular paperback on this subject by Noa Zanolli Davenport and her colleagues. Mellen Press then published a long series of scholarly research reports. Meanwhile, articles about mobbing have been coming out in dozens of academic journals, as well as leading newspapers and magazines. Now, at last, one of the most respected publishers in the English-speaking world is releasing a comprehensive book on mobbing. It is careful and comprehensive enough to win academic kudos, yet fluent and readable enough to deserve the broadest public readership. Publication of this book is something to celebrate, a landmark event in the development of a body of knowledge that substantially deepens our understanding of what happens to people in their jobs.

The word *mobbing*, even if sometimes hazily defined, has caught on throughout the world simply because it fits with what ordinary people can see happening in their workplaces. It resonates with their experience. They have themselves witnessed interruptions of business as usual, breaks from the office routine, occasions wherein managers, peers, or some combination thereof gang up on a co-worker and make that person's life a living hell, toward eliminating the target one way or another from the workplace. Leymann's gift to all of us was to put a name on this extraordinary process, exhilarating for the perpetrators, terrifying for the target, momentous in the lives of all concerned. Having the word *mobbing* in our lexicon lets us recognize and understand bizarre events in our working lives that would otherwise be incomprehensible. It is a "necessary word," as British litterateur John Sutherland has recently opined.

I would highlight six strengths of the present book.

First, the understanding of mobbing with which the book begins is not facile or mechanical, but rich in depth and insight, and informed by a wide reading of history and current affairs. These authors are not narrow, superficial specialists. They are mature, broadly educated scholars able to situate their specific subject matter in the larger contexts of social science and humane learning. They appropriately include lucid discussion of similarities and differences between workplace mobbing and other impassioned outbursts of collective hostility, from witch hunts in seventeenth-century New England to hysteria over Satanic ritual abuse of children in late twentieth-century California.

Second, the exposition here of what mobbing means is enhanced immeasurably by analysis of real-life examples, case studies of the process in varied kinds of workplaces. This leaves the reader with an understanding of this phenomenon more complex than can be gained from any measuring instrument or checklist of indicators.

Third, these authors steer shy of the self-help genre that already encompasses too high a proportion of trade books in social science. They write less as experts dispensing recipes for how to cure what ails you, than as teachers providing resources for readers' respective journeys in self-education. There is no quick fix for mobbing as a personal tragedy or organizational pathology. Duffy and Sperry wisely disclaim "one size fits all" remedies. They do not give readers ideas to swallow, but insights to reflect on and apply creatively to the widely discrepant situations in which readers find themselves.

Fourth, this book appropriately treats mobbing in schools, whether of administrators, teachers, or students, not as a separate field of study but as categorically similar to mobbing in the public service, hospitals, condo corporations, or wherever else. Schools are one kind of workplace. The general principles for understanding the nature, techniques, stages, causes, and consequences of mobbing in schools are the same as for workplaces of whatever other kind.

Fifth, while avoiding overgeneralization and sweeping statements, Duffy and Sperry do not mince words about the basic findings researchers of mobbing have come up with. A good example is what they say about departments of human resources. The blunt truth is that notwithstanding the good intentions of many functionaries in these departments, they are structurally branches of administration, subject to the organization's overall hierarchy of authority. A mobbing target who expects HR professionals to challenge that hierarchy for the sake of higher standards of justice and fairness is, as a rule, barking up the wrong tree. Duffy and Sperry talk straight. They do not give false hopes.

Sixth and finally, I applaud the attention in later chapters to the effects of mobbing on targets' families. Duffy and Sperry are among those few researchers who have published studies on the family health consequences of husband or wife or son or daughter being mobbed at work. It is good to see that they have included this earlier research in this book. Mobbing is a debilitating stressor not only for the target but for all those with whom he or she shares domestic life.

In North America, research on mobbing has burgeoned since the dawn of the twenty-first century. So has dissemination of knowledge in this area to an ever larger public. Psychologists, psychiatrists, sociologists, anthropologists, and professors of law, medicine, nursing, library science, and social work are all contributing to development of the field from the points of view of their respective disciplines. It is wonderful that two scholars as capable as Maureen Duffy and Len Sperry have pulled the existing knowledge together within the covers of a single book, and that Oxford University Press has decided to publish it. This is a foundational piece of work, one that will be read for decades to come.

Kenneth Westhues
Professor Emeritus of Sociology and Legal Studies
University of Waterloo, Canada

Preface

Mobbing is a form of persecution, of humiliation, of degradation. It is the dark side of organizational life in workplaces, universities, schools, religious organizations, the military, the judicial system, correctional institutions, and community organizations like condominium and homeowners' associations. For it to be successful, mobbing must include multiple players—leaders and followers (we'll call them perpetrators), a single or multiple targets (we'll call them victims), a group or community of participants who are involved by virtue of their witnessing of the events (we'll call them witnesses or bystanders), and organizational members with the power and status to stop the mobbing but who, instead, participate in it either actively or by turning a blind eye to it (we'll call them the organization). In a mobbing, a sequence of events unfolds over time in which the victim is disparaged and belittled by the perpetrators who are acting within the legitimacy of the organizational domain (we'll call this the ritual or social process). The effects of mobbing are always loss—loss of dignity, loss of respect, loss of status, loss of personal identity, loss of professional identity, loss of job, loss of money, loss of friendship and social networks, loss of family support, loss of health insurance, loss of health, loss of life. These losses may be partial or they may be total, as in the case of loss of life. A reasonable person might be forgiven for thinking that this kind of thing couldn't possibly happen today, in the 21st century. But it does and frequently.

Hugo Meynell (2008) has called mobbings "mini-holocausts" because of their devastating and, not infrequently, totalizing effects on a victim. In a mobbing that, by definition, takes place within the shelter of an organization, the organization provides maximum deniability for wrongdoings visited on employees, students, or other organizational members. The claims of "I didn't know what was going on," "I was in the dark and didn't have all the facts at my disposal," and "I didn't do anything" are commonly heard responses by organizational representatives in positions of responsibility. Organizational deniability combined with the moral righteousness of perpetrators in a mobbing makes for a very dangerous cocktail.

Victims of mobbing go from insiders to outsiders, from confidantes to pariahs, from competent to incompetent, from persons with integrity to persons who are untrustworthy, and from comfortable organizational members to those who have had the rug pulled out from under them. The social process of mobbing is an example of what the classic sociologist Harold Garfinkel (1956) called a "degradation ceremony." In a degradation ceremony, the denouncers must meet the challenge of demonstrating that the person or persons denounced in fact never were who they were thought to be—that they were always less than their reputations and that they didn't share their community's values and, therefore, should rightly be denounced and excluded. In a degradation ceremony, such as a mobbing, the perpetrators claim not that the victim was once good and now is bad, but that the victim was never any good in the first place.

Over the last 3 years, we published a number of articles in various academic journals about understanding mobbing and its individual and organizational consequences. As we mentioned in our acknowledgments, we were involved in a special issue of the *Consulting Psychology Journal* entitled: "Workplace Mobbing and Bullying: Organizational Consultation Strategies." One of us (LS) was the special issue editor and was awarded the Elliott Jacques Memorial Publication Award from the *Consulting Psychology Journal* editorial board at the 2010 American Psychological Association 118th Annual Convention for "the most outstanding publication of 2009."

Our articles generated a great deal of response from readers. We got calls, e-mails, and letters from people inside and outside of the country who said that they had experienced what we had written about. Friends of people who had been mobbed sent copies of our articles to their friends, hoping that the articles would be of help to them. People who had been mobbed told us that they carried one or more of our articles around with them because the articles helped them to deal with what was currently happening to them at work. The articles seemed to serve as a kind of talisman for some of our readers. The topic had touched a nerve—that was clear to us. Many people who contacted us knew that what was happening to them at work was wrong and demoralizing, but they didn't have a name for it until they read our articles. People sent us articles they had been working on themselves about bullying or mobbing and asked for feedback.

We found ourselves hearing and thinking in a different way about the numerous accounts in the newspaper and media about people who had been fired from work or kids who had been bullied. Some of the accounts were public scandals, and we found ourselves researching every piece of information we could about them. We wanted the back stories, and we reached out to people who had clearly undergone painful work or school experiences. In this book, we describe and use two types of illustrations. The first type are public stories about abuse in schools, workplaces, and other institutional settings that have become a part of the national consciousness and that, as citizens, we have followed in the media and in our national history. The second type are illustrations derived from the perspectives of mobbing "insiders." Mobbing insiders include victims, perpetrators, witnesses or bystanders, and those holding organizational authority when a mobbing occurs. The roles are not necessarily discrete, and a single individual could, for example, be a victim of mobbing, a witness to the mobbing of others, and hold organizational authority.

We also became immersed in the literature on mobbing and saw that at least two different threads of research had begun and diverged. One line of research pursued the concept of "mobbing" and the other line pursued the concept of "bullying." As we write this preface to our book, there exists no consensus on the meaning of the two terms, and that lack of consensus has complicated research. We see this lack of consensus more as an ongoing opportunity for developing greater conceptual clarity than as a problem, and as an indicator that more research and discussion across disciplines must continue to take place to tease out the differences between the two constructs.

Mobbing is a serious and demanding topic. We stand in the light that researchers, practitioners, and scholars from multiple disciplines have already shed on mobbing, and we feel both privileged and humbled to join in their ongoing conversation. We would like to acknowledge them and their contributions to understanding mobbing and abuse by naming them individually but, we fear, by attempting to do so, we might inadvertently leave someone out. You will know who they are by virtue of our citing and crediting of their work in our book.

By training and profession, we both are mental health clinicians, even though we wear and have worn many different hats over the years; namely, that of educator, researcher, administrator, and consultant. Our training compels us to look at the consequences of mobbing for both individuals and organizations and to bring our full attention to bear on the development of effective interventions for remedying and preventing mobbing and for helping those who have suffered its devastating consequences. In this book, you will see the fruits of our efforts to do just that and you will see our conceptualization of the differences and similarities between bullying and mobbing. It is our hope that our book will contribute additional perspectives to the professional conversation about mobbing. Although this book is primarily intended for researchers, consultants, educators, and clinicians, it will also appeal to other interested readers.

Acknowledgments

We extend our profound appreciation to Kenneth Westhues, Ph.D., whose pioneering and elegant research has advanced our understanding of mobbing and sensitized those of us who study mobbing to the dangers of reproducing mobbing-like behaviors in efforts to eliminate it. We would also like to acknowledge and honor the late Heinz Leymann, M.D., for building such a strong and generative foundation of organizational and clinical research. Dr. Leymann's commitment to the study of mobbing and his compassion for its victims has continued to inspire and renew us. We also wish to recognize Gary Namie, Ph.D., and Ruth Namie, Ph.D.,untiring consultants, researchers, and advocates who have given so much of their lives and energy to increasing awareness of bullying and workplace abuse among both professionals and the public in the United States.

During the course of completing this book, we also had occasion to edit and contribute to a special issue of the *Consulting Psychology Journal* entitled: "Workplace Mobbing and Bullying: Organizational Consultation Strategies." We are particularly appreciative of the collegial sharing with some extraordinary professionals. These included Gary Namie, Ph.D., Ruth Namie, Ph.D., Patricia Ferris, Ph.D., Suzy Fox, Ph.D., Lamont E. Stallworth, Ph.D., Laura Crawshaw, Ph.D., and Richard Kilburg, Ph.D.

I (MD) would like to acknowledge my colleagues at the International Institute for Human Understanding, for their support of my work and their commitment to the prevention and elimination of mobbing: Patricia Munhall, Ed.D., Torben Riise, Ph.D., Kelley Rowan, M.A., and Vineeth John, M.D. I also wish to thank Ronald J. Chenail, Ph.D., Dr. Dora Fried Schnitman, and Patricia Cole, Ph.D., for their enthusiasm and support of this project, and to express my appreciation for the perspectives of Joan Friedenberg, Ph.D. I cannot say enough about what the encouragement and support of my husband, Patrick, and my sister, Eileen Alexander, has meant to me throughout this project.

I (LS) would like to recognize some present and past colleagues on the GAP Committee on Work and Organizations: David Morrison, Josh Gibson, Brian Grant, Steve Heidel, Barbara Long, Daven Morrison, Duane Hagen, Jerrold M. Post,

Barrie Greiff, Alan McLean, and Peter Brill. Special kudos goes to my long-time colleague and editor, Rodney Lowman, Ph.D.

This book is an outgrowth of a number of scholarly articles about mobbing that we have published in various academic journals over the last 3 years. As a result of these articles, we have received and continue to receive e-mails, letters, and calls from many, many individuals who have experienced mobbing and who were informed and reassured by what we had written. We want to recognize their struggles, and we trust that this book may in some small way assist them and the professionals with whom they are working to foster their continued recovery.

Finally, the staff at Oxford University Press deserve special recognition, particularly our editor, Abby Gross, for her discernment and support; Joanna Ng, editorial assistant, for her careful attention to so many details; and Karen Kwak, for her meticulousness in overseeing the production process.

Contents

Part Four   RECOVERY, SOLUTION, AND PREVENTION

Part One

AN INTRODUCTION TO MOBBING

1

Introduction

*It was amazing . . . how the truth could be just a little skewed
so that it sounded sinister.*
—Ken Follett (2007, p. 486)

There is a chilling but instructive scene, midway through Ken Follett's best-selling novel, *World Without End* (2007), in which one of the novel's main characters is put on trial for witchcraft by an ecclesiastical court. Set in England during the Middle Ages, the character is bright, resourceful, and asks too many questions. In short, she is an upstart who gets in the way of the Prior's ambition and lust for power, given that it is he who controls the town and its wealth. She is more interested in creating business that would benefit the townspeople rather than benefit the Prior. She was on the brink of being elected alderman of the town and, were that to have happened, the old ways of doing things would have quickly been challenged.

The Prior, her cousin, whom she didn't particularly like, but whom she never thought would go to the lengths that he did, secretly schemed with a few other family members and townspeople to get rid of her and end her influence. Given the time and place, the easiest way for the Prior to be rid of her was to accuse her of being a witch and have her hanged. On the day before she was to be married, the Prior beckoned everyone to church and, to the gasps of the assembly, opened the witchcraft trial of Caris Wooler.

Although Follett (2007) never refers to it as such, his character, Caris Wooler, was mobbed. Her story illustrates the intricacies of mobbing and the way in which any fact set can easily be distorted and reframed as sinister or otherwise unacceptable by those intent on targeting someone in the interests of disposing of them or of ending their influence. Caris Wooler escaped the gallows but at the cost of the life she had been planning to live. Seemingly overnight, she was catapulted into a whole new set of circumstances that initially devastated her and that, for many, would have been a crushing final blow. Some people survive being mobbed, others do not. Injury, illness, suicide are fairly common outcomes. Homicide is not unknown. Mobbing is a much more sophisticated way of doing someone in than murder, and in most countries it has the advantage of being entirely legal.

Mobbing is frequently confused with bullying, and, although it shares some of the characteristics of bullying, it is a distinct form of interpersonal abuse. Mobbing occurs in all forms of organizations and can potentially impact anyone. It is a common occurrence in workplaces, universities, schools, the military, religious organizations, the judicial system, and correctional institutions, and even rears its lethal head in other kinds of organizations like condo boards and homeowners' associations. Unlike bullying, mobbing is a systemic phenomenon that involves the interplay of organizational, group, and individual dynamics and behavior. Mobbing always includes organizational dynamics and involvement, whereas bullying does not. It results in injuries to its victims, and the nature of the injuries is such that mobbing is an unrecognized public health problem. Recovery from mobbing does not follow the same process as recovery from bullying. Therefore, distinguishing mobbing from bullying is critical in helping mobbing victims recover and in identifying effective prevention strategies. At the end of this chapter, we describe the layout of this book and the sequencing of the chapters that will illustrate the differences between mobbing and bullying, the causes and risk factors for mobbing, and recovery and prevention strategies.

Here, however, we want to continue our introduction of mobbing in a more phenomenological way. We want to provide comprehensive examples of what it might look and feel like to experience mobbing and its consequences. To that end, we provide one example of mobbing in the workplace and another in a school setting, describe the effects of mobbing, and analyze what might be learned about mobbing from each case. We then situate mobbing historically and socially in the United States by referring to two sets of events—one in fairly recent times and one in the distant past—and examine the significance of each for our understanding of the social process of mobbing.

Mobbing in the Workplace

In this book, we use the term "victim" purposefully to refer to the target of mobbing. We do so to underscore that mobbing results in victimization, which in turn results in injury. The use of the term "victim" should in no way be understood as a reference to weakness or inability to cope. In some quarters in popular culture, the use of the term "victim" is eschewed as politically incorrect because of the erroneous thinking that victimization implies a posture of self-pity or helplessness. Victimization has nothing to do with whether a person feels sorry for oneself or not, or whether the person survives injuries or not, or whether the person learns to adapt and cope or not.

The following example can be viewed through the interaction of individual, group, and organizational behaviors involved in the mobbing. Additionally, it can be viewed through the analysis of the series of abusive acts, many covert and insidious, leading to the final outcome for the victim.

Mobbing in the Workplace: Lee, Too Good for His Own Good

In Taiwan, where he was born, Lee was raised to respect authority and, in particular, to never challenge his bosses. When Lee emigrated to the West, he felt that respecting authority had served him well as he worked his way up through the ranks to finally become certified as a control room supervisor in a nuclear power plant. It was to his surprise and dismay that he found himself in a situation in which he was frequently at odds with his manager over following technical procedures in the control room. One of Lee's occupational strengths, in a nuclear power plant environment that required constant attention to safety, was his ability to concentrate and focus. Lee could spend hours at a stretch watching the wall-size computer displays showing the status of the internal environment in the nuclear power plant and the external power environment in the field. He was not easily distracted and could spot an out-of-range indicator within seconds of its appearance on the display. In the technical procedure manual, such out-of-range indicators were referred to as *deviations*. All deviations were required by procedure to be logged in the control room journal. Lee was meticulous about entering the time and nature of each deviation into the journal. His training by the nuclear regulatory agency under which he worked emphasized safety, safety, safety.

A deviation logged in the control room journal triggered a report by the control room manager, who then passed a copy of the report to the quality assurance (QA) supervisor, who was in turn required to initiate a safety investigation. Lee logged more deviations during his control room supervisor shifts than did any other supervisor. Both the manager and QA supervisor had been badgering Lee for months to stop writing up every deviation, notwithstanding the fact that their power plant had been cited for multiple safety violations in each of its last two compliance inspections by the nuclear regulatory agency. The manager and QA supervisor deliberately piled on the pressure by frequently reminding Lee that all of their bonuses were linked to the number of deviations reported—the fewer the deviations, the higher the end-of-year bonuses. The manager and the QA supervisor had also been complaining to a couple of the night field workers about how Lee was creating problems for them by causing unnecessary work and that he was jeopardizing all their bonuses. What the manager and QA supervisor had left out of their gossip with the field workers was that Lee was following procedure by logging deviations. Unknown to him, Lee had unwittingly developed a coterie of coworkers who were out to get him.

Lee was under a lot of pressure. It went against everything he had been taught to ignore recommendations from his bosses, yet he also felt obliged to follow the technical procedures for handling deviations that had been drilled into him during all of his training. Lee made the decision to follow the technical manual because it contained the safety guidelines. Tension in the control room continued to build. His coworkers intensified their campaign against him. Lee's diligence and concentration were creating way too much work for them, and they had decided to look for opportunities to deep six him.

Their chance came one night when Harry, a field worker, who needed two levels of authorization to shut down a series of operating devices for what he had termed "minor maintenance," got his second-level authorization from Lee. During routine maintenance, Harry had noticed a piece of deteriorated equipment that he thought he could take care of by himself, even though protocol required a minimum of two certified technicians to work on that particular piece of equipment. Harry figured he could take care of it by himself, but knew that Lee would not give him authorization to go ahead without another worker. So, Harry called the manager, who had buddied up to him in complaining about Lee. The manager told Harry to call Lee for authorization but to tell him the problem piece of equipment was a different one than it really was—one only requiring a single certified worker for specialized maintenance. The manager thought it was no big deal and that Harry could take care of it himself.

After questioning Harry about the nature of the problem with the equipment and checking that protocol allowed a single technician to conduct maintenance on that particular equipment, Lee authorized Harry to conduct extended maintenance on it. Of course, Lee had no way of knowing that he had been lied to by Harry and that Harry was actually conducting maintenance on a different piece of equipment. Out in the field that night, Harry ran into problems. His maintenance activities on the operating devices caused a chain reaction of equipment failures and sequential plant shutdowns that ran from one end of the power plant campus to the other before it was over.

Immediately after this accidental and expensive series of shutdowns, an internal investigation was initiated, and Lee was the only one involved to get fired. Harry, the field worker, admitted to making a mistake but never told his supervisors that he had given Lee false information about which piece of equipment he was working on. Harry also kept quiet about the fact that it was the manager's suggestion to lie to Lee to get authorization that they both knew Lee would not have given had he been told the truth. In the investigation, Harry swore that he had told Lee about the actual piece of equipment he had been working on and concealed the lie he had fabricated with the manager's input. The manager and QA supervisor both told the investigators that Lee was difficult to work with and that his perfectionist standards got in the way of a smoothly functioning workplace. Lee told the investigators which piece of equipment that Harry had told him he would be working on. Based on the input from the manager, QA supervisor, and Harry, the investigators rejected Lee's account of the episode. Half-truths and lies about Lee had become part of the culture of the control room.

Ultimately, Lee was fired. Lee did his job the way he was supposed to and, in the process, caused others to have to do their jobs as they were supposed to—and they didn't like it. The nuclear power plant was a lot safer when Lee was working there. The manager and QA supervisor went back to taking those same old short-cuts that weren't so easy to get away with when Lee was around. Lee didn't appeal the decision of the nuclear power plant investigation to fire him. Lee left the power plant never knowing that a number of his coworkers had been actively conspiring against him and that a couple of them, especially Harry, had lied out-right during the investigation. Lee was too ashamed to tell his family that he had lost his job. He did not want to worry them or bring shame on them. Lee did not know what to do to get another job. He had loved being responsible for monitor-ing the power plant operations in the control room and following detailed proto-cols. Lee figured he was not going to get decent references from his now former employer and saw his options as very limited.

At some point, months before the final incident, Lee had been faced with a choice—to turn a blind eye to following protocol and logging plant deviations, or to carry on doing what he was supposed to do. Lee made his choice to follow pro-tocol and log all deviations. It was "the right thing to do," but he paid for that choice with his job.

ANALYSIS AND KEY POINTS

Although Lee never knew it, and never had a name for it, he was a victim of work-place mobbing. In going through the facts of Lee's case, a number of clear identi-fiers of workplace mobbing stand out. In this section, we analyze those identifiers and discuss how and why they are indicators of victimization from workplace mobbing. In Chapter 3, we will describe the technical aspects and definitions of workplace mobbing. In this chapter, we describe its phenomenological character-istics—what it is like to live through a workplace mobbing in all of its covert and destructive manifestations. In reviewing Lee's case, several clear identifiers of workplace mobbing stand out:

1. Lee was different—not so much because he was from Taiwan but, most impor-tantly, because he diligently carried out the responsibilities of his job. In terms of job performance, Lee raised the bar for the group of coworkers with whom he interacted daily. Lee had enviable focus and concentration, and he relished the challenge and responsibility of spotting deviations on the computer dis-play. It was very difficult to distract him, and he took seriously what he was charged to do.

   • The targets of workplace mobbing are often different in some way from the majority of the workers and are often among the most competent in the organization (Bultena & Whatcott, 2008; Gates, 2004; Hillard, 2009).

2. If Lee's job had been simply to produce widgets, his entire department would have been cheering him on. The problem was that Lee's "widgets" were finding system errors or other deviations on the nuclear plant's computer display of feedback for the internal and external plant environments. In simple terms,

Lee's job was to find problems, and the whole organization was double-bound because it was trying to reduce systemic errors, safety violations, and other kinds of problems. The organization was so determined to reduce safety violations and other problems that it had introduced significant rewards in terms of end-of-year bonuses, in the hopes of motivating personnel to improve their safety and performance records. Lee thought that the way to improve safety and performance records was to identify problems and correct them. Unfortunately, some of Lee's coworkers, such as his manager, the QA supervisor, and Harry, thought that the way to improve safety and performance was to deny real problems, take shortcuts, and lie, when expedient. If the widgets you are supposed to produce are identifying problems, and reducing the number of problems is tied to increased pay, workers tasked with identifying problems are at very high risk.

- Workplace mobbing is not an interpersonal situation between one or a few mobbers and a victim. It involves the interplay of group dynamics with organizational dynamics (Liefooghe & Mackenzie Davey, 2001; O'Moore & Lynch, 2007; Vanderckhove & Commers, 2003).
- In Lee's case, a number of coworkers targeted Lee because his job performance was requiring them to increase theirs, thus disturbing their previously comfortable and settled routines.
- In the initial gossip about Lee started by the manager and QA supervisor, they deliberately created a negative impression of Lee by passing on partial information and half-truths to coworkers, including to Harry, the field worker.
- The entire group of coworkers participating in the mobbing of Lee lied a number of times about Lee's behavior and performance, and continued to do so at a particularly critical juncture; namely, when Lee was being investigated for his role in authorizing maintenance that led to a series of accidental and expensive equipment shutdowns.
- No one who knew the truth of the situation came forward and spoke up for Lee—a common witness or bystander response in workplace mobbings.
- The power plant as an organization was complicit in Lee's mobbing at a number of levels. They fostered a culture of competition to reduce errors by offering financial incentives that, in fact, promoted cheating. Incentives should not have been based on reducing the number of reported deviations but should, instead, have been based on the number of usable strategies developed for improving overall safety and performance (Salin, 2003). Additionally, the internal investigation was geared toward placing blame on an individual worker, rather than on problem-solving by reviewing and examining system-wide procedures.

3. Throughout the mobbing, Lee was increasingly ostracized and isolated from his coworkers. At the beginning stages of the mobbing Lee probably didn't

notice that his coworkers were distancing themselves from him because he was so focused and task-oriented. When his manager and the QA supervisor began to explicitly badger him about logging fewer deviation reports, Lee would have become consciously aware of the "ganging up" on him.

- Mobbing victims are typically ostracized and isolated by their coworkers and/or supervisors (Rayner & Hoel, 1997).
- Mobbing behaviors are carried out by a group that targets an individual or several individuals. Other coworkers and/or supervisors are inducted into the group of mobbers through the control of information about the target; namely, by spreading false information, by withholding accurate information, and by failing to correct information known to be false about the target (Davenport, Schwartz, & Elliott, 1999). Mobbers are masters of impression management, and they deliberately create a negative and misleading image of the target victim. When the image of the target victim becomes sufficiently negative and damaging, it is easy to recruit others into the group of mobbers. The mobbers become the "ingroup" and the victim(s) become the "outgroup." The control of information by the core mobbing group is central to the creation of an "in" and an "out" group.
- Mobbing victims, like Lee, are often unaware of the coordinated network of coworkers and/or supervisors and organizational involvement leading to their exiting the organization through termination or constructive discharge (Westhues, 1998, 2002).

4. Lee was fired after an internal investigation aimed at placing blame rather than solving problems.

- In mobbing prone organizations, genuine due-process is lacking. Since the focus is on fault-finding and placing blame (Davenport et al., 1999), investigatory procedures are skewed in the direction of protecting the organization and finding a scapegoat. The notion of "kangaroo courts" comes to mind.
- Lee's experience of being mobbed left him feeling shamed and further isolated (Lewis, 2004). His personal and professional identities had been assaulted (Lutgen-Sandvik, 2008). His future, in terms of reemployability, looked grim. Culturally, he was even further isolated because he could not bring himself to tell his family what had happened.
- Like most mobbing victims, Lee was at risk for a host of physical and psychological sequelae to the mobbing (De Vogli, Ferrie, Chandola, Kivimäki, & Marmot, 2007).

As a result of the frequency (see Chapter 2) and severity of the negative health consequences from mobbing (see Chapter 8), mobbing has become an urgent public health problem. Lutgen-Sandvik (2003), referencing Hornstein (1996), states that "there will be no meaningful change in either the occurrence or consequence of abuse unless the structure of the workplace is reformed according to a new social and legal contract, one that encourages cooperation, justice, and a heightened and broadened sense of community" (p. 498). The case of Lee bears out her statement. Lee was at the mercy of organizational forces that he did not even know existed, yet those forces profoundly reshaped Lee's life, his views about himself, and his relationships with his family members in ways that continued to unfold over time. The individual and collective cruelty of the manager, QA supervisor, and field worker cannot be ignored either. Hugo Meynell (2008), who delivered the second Hector Hammerly Memorial Lecture at the University of Waterloo in Canada, referred to mobbings as "little holocausts," reflecting the depth of organizational involvement and evil, and the shattering of mobbing victims' lives.

Mobbing in Schools: Rachel Fannon at School

Rachel Fannon was interviewed by Connie Chung (2001) in a segment on bullies for the ABC broadcast news program *20/20*. Rachel's story is also told in Garrett's (2003) book on bullying in American schools. Rachel was from Littleton, Colorado, a Denver suburb, that 2 years prior to her ABC news interview had dealt with the tragedy of the Columbine High School massacre. In her interview with Connie Chung, Rachel described herself as always having been shy and never having many friends. Rachel reported being tormented for over 5 years on a daily basis by a group of other students who verbally abused her by thinking up words for "ugly" and then high-fiving each other when they did. She reported that they also kicked her behind the knees and stuck their legs out to trip her. She finally broke down and told her mother about the abuse because she said she was no longer able to bear it.

Connie Chung's (2001) skillful interview included questions to Rachel about whether she had ever thought of ending her own life and whether she had ever told any teachers or administrators at school about the abuse. Rachel said that she thought of ending her life just to make the abuse stop and that teachers regularly saw the abuse happening. Rachel visibly stiffened and appeared to become angry when she reported that one teacher's intervention was telling her to toughen up, ignore it, and learn to be like an Amazon woman. As the abusive behavior continued, Rachel, who already had a heart problem, began to experience tachycardia and a decline in her academic performance. Rachel, a beautiful and articulate girl, cried softly on a number of occasions throughout the interview. She acknowledged that she had emotional scars when Chung asked her if she had any lasting effects from the abuse. A final note in Chung's profile of Rachel Fannon was her report from the principals of Rachel's schools that the complaints about Rachel's bullying never got to them and that, despite their schools' anti-bullying policies, Rachel had fallen through the cracks. Rachel's abuse by her peer tormentors was carried out in more than one school, presumably as the students moved up in grades and transferred from middle to high school.

ANALYSIS AND KEY POINTS

It doesn't take much looking behind the reported facts of Rachel Fannon's case to see the combination of individual, group, and organizational dynamics, so characteristic of mobbing, at work. It is clear to us that Rachel was the victim of mobbing, not bullying. Here is why. At the individual level, Rachel was self-described as shy and without many friends. A group of other students had been abusing her for the extraordinary period of over 5 years on a daily basis. This group, whose composition probably changed somewhat over that length of time, was clearly able to act with impunity within the schools and remained free to carry on its campaign of terror against Rachel (and who knows what other students). The group constituted itself as an ingroup and Rachel was plainly a member of the outgroup. The group's viability and long-term survival are prima facia evidence of its support organizationally within the schools. Finally, school personnel witnessed the abuse, according to Rachel, and yet it continued. That the abuse reportedly never reached the principals of the schools involved suggests that the communication flow between teachers and administrators about incidents of harm to students was impaired, or that the teachers who apparently witnessed Rachel's abuse either turned their backs on it or did not consider it significant enough to move the information up the chain of command.

1. Nature of the group of offenders and their negative acts:

   - The offenders consisted of a group, not just one or two individual bullies. They acted in concert with one another, and their abusive behavior toward Rachel was coordinated. Their abusive behavior was a form of group activity in which, for example, the object was to think up as many names for "ugly" as they could. They congratulated themselves with high-fives and, presumably, other celebratory rituals.
   - The abusive behavior was systematic, intentional, and protracted. It was designed to humiliate and devalue Rachel.
   - The protracted nature of the interpersonal abuse is highly characteristic of mobbing, as is the frequency of the negative abusive acts. When Rachel finally told her mother about the abuse, she reported that physical and verbal abuse had been occurring on a daily basis for 5½ years.

2. Responsibility for resolution of the mobbing:

   - The teacher's advice to ignore the abuse and to be like an Amazon woman placed the responsibility for management and resolution of the situation on Rachel, not on the offenders, a characteristic response by authority in many mobbings. This is a version of "blame the victim," in which victims who are already suffering as a result of interpersonal abuse are then expected to solve the problem themselves and make the abuse go away. Rachel did consider one solution—suicide—to make the abuse stop.
   - That it took Rachel so long to finally tell her mother should not surprise anyone. She had very likely internalized the damaging belief that she was somehow responsible for making the abuse stop, if not for its occurrence in the first place. As a result, she would have been filled with shame and humiliation. Teachers who witnessed the abuse and told her to just ignore it and be tough would have reinforced this belief that she was responsible for ending the abuse.
   - That a group of offenders was able to survive and carry out their abusive behavior over such a long period of time suggests to us that those with the authority and power to stop them turned a blind eye to their behavior or minimized it. Doing nothing is an act of omission that effectively aligns authorities with the offenders.

3. Student bystanders:

   - The group of offenders was not reported as cornering Rachel in places around the schools where no one else was present. Other students would have witnessed their aggressive and abusive behavior, and there is no indication from the reports that any came to Rachel's aid.

4. Organizational involvement:

   - That the principals reportedly commented that complaints about the bullying of Rachel never reached them and that she "fell through the cracks" suggests that the power to act was centralized in the hands of high-level administrators and that first-responders—teachers—were either not empowered or not trained to act to protect Rachel.
   - That teachers reportedly saw what was happening and failed to act to protect Rachel involves the culture, structure, and strategies of the school as an organization.
   - That the teachers would have such little knowledge about how to intervene or what to do when witnessing the kind of torment that Rachel was subject to on a daily basis speaks to the failure of the schools' anti-bullying policies and also points to a school-wide lack of training about recognition and effective intervention.
   - If the schools Rachel attended were public schools, the organizational involvement extends beyond the individual schools to the entire school system and represents a system-wide failure to provide teachers with

specific intervention skills and tools to respond to both offenders and victims. Teachers in the trenches are most likely to be called on as first-responders in the event of complaints of mobbing or bullying in schools. If the schools Rachel attended were private ones, the organizational involvement and responsibility extends to the Boards of Advisors and all school community stakeholder groups.

Although colloquially referred to as "bullying," what happened to Rachel was mobbing, not bullying. The key distinctions between bullying and mobbing that are present in Rachel's case, and that we will examine in detail in Chapters 3 and 4, are the group dynamics of the offender students and the organizational dynamics also involved. That parents of students who have been "bullied" and who have suffered subsequent injuries have a felt sense that what happened to their children is more than bullying is apparent in the increasing number of lawsuits being filed by them against school systems for failure to protect their children from harm while at school and for failure to provide an emotionally and physically safe environment. Although parents may not be familiar with the meaning of the term "mobbing," they are giving voice to their awareness of organizational dynamics through their lawsuits against schools and school systems.

Understanding Mobbing through Recent and Past Historical Events

Although the idea of mobbing or ganging up on someone is not new to most of us, the idea of mobbing as a social process that occurs with surprisingly high frequency in schools, workplaces, and other kinds of organizations may well be a new idea. Mobbing is not a rare occurrence in society, and much of it goes unaddressed. However, past and recent U.S. history provides more than a few examples of mobbings (even though not referred to as such) that have riveted our collective attention while its victims suffered multiple crippling losses, including death. Mobbings are not individual acts, and Leymann (1990, 1993, 1996) recognized that fact clearly. These examples are presented to provide a larger context within which to understand the significance of mobbing in schools and in workplaces, and to demonstrate the complex interplay between individuals, groups, organizations, and larger social systems.

THE SALEM WITCH HUNT MOBBINGS

Between June 10 and September 22, 1692, 19 accused witches were hanged at Gallows Hill in Salem, Massachusetts. One man, over 80 years old, was pressed to death under heavy stones for failing to enter a plea to the charge of witchcraft. Pressing was a particularly vicious form of torture and death reserved for those who defied the legitimacy of the court. Failure to enter a plea was considered contempt for the court, and the brutality of pressing was intended to force a recalcitrant accused to enter a plea. At least four other accused witches died in prison, and about 150 had been imprisoned altogether.

Challenging the credibility of the accusers was a sure way to end up accused oneself, but accusing others was a fairly sure way to end up safe from the gallows. Speaking out was a high-risk activity. John Proctor protested against the investigation of his wife, Elizabeth, for witchcraft and, on the day of her investigation, he was also charged with witchcraft. Proctor was later executed but his wife escaped that fate. The local justice system completed its work in just 3 months. Within so short a period, a few hundred persons had been accused of witchcraft in and around Salem, about 150 of them had been imprisoned, and 19 were executed (Boyer & Nissenbaum, 1974). Five years later, the General Court ordered a day of self-examination. A judge in the trials admitted wrongdoing and apologized, as did many others involved in the Salem witch trials. Very few public events conjure the imagination the way the Salem Witch Hunts do even to this day.

Salem at the time of the witchcraft trials was a Puritan community in conflict. There were power struggles between prominent families and anger over loss of status and social standing among some members of the community, political questions about how independent Salem Village should be from Salem Town, a preoccupation with the supernatural and the devil, land disputes, changes of ministers, and the development of alliances and coalitions (Boyer & Nissenbaum, 1974). The triggering event was the emergence of convulsion-like symptoms in the daughter of the relatively new minister. Other children began to manifest similar symptoms, and the town became enveloped in hysteria after the local doctor finally raised the suggestion that the convulsion-like symptoms might be related to witchcraft. The local ministers then leaped into action and went on literal witch hunts. The penalty for witchcraft was death by hanging. The trial courts admitted what was called "spectral evidence" into the hearings.

Spectral evidence was evidence that the devil had taken on the shape of the accused witch and appeared to others in the community, in particular, to the accusers (Boyer & Nissenbaum, 1974). The form that the evidence took was basically stories that the accusers, largely children, had visions or dreams of the accused. In these dreams, the accused witches were doing fantastic things like flying on brooms through the mist. The accused were asked to prove that they were not witches and asked impossibly leading questions, such as "Why do people act the way they do when in your presence?" Most of the accusers were children who were behaving outrageously by any standards. However, one pathetic accused was also a child, 4-year-old Dorcas Good, who was imprisoned in Boston and who remained in heavy irons for the entire period (Boyer & Nissenbaum, 1974). Her mother, Sarah, was one of those executed.

Boyer and Nissenbaum (1974), through their study of primary data, uncovered some fascinating patterns related to the acceleration of the accusations and the division of the community into accusers and accused, or, into what we might call an ingroup and an outgroup. In the context of the Salem Witch Hunts during the summer of 1692, the outgroup was comprised of those accused, although at other times, this same group of accused was very much part of the higher social strata and hence Salem's ingroup. During the summer of 1692, a period of bizarre collective behavior overcame a growing number of children in the Salem area. The children's behavior was deviant and irrational, and their hysteria accelerated over the summer. Many of Salem's adults, caught up in their own collective frenzy (in part, about the operation of the devil in the life of their community), participated in witch hunting and ended up accusing hundreds. The adults ostensibly were trying to save and protect their afflicted children. Only a few of the adults questioned the behavior of the children. In fact, according to Boyer and Nissenbaum, most of the accused were not even known to the accusing girls. It is difficult, if not impossible, to believe that ten accusing girls, who demonstrated outrageous, uncensored behavior and who accused people whom they did not even know could have been acting on their own. It is inconceivable that these girls were acting independently without encouragement from their parents or other adults in the community. (As an updated parallel, in a recent academic mobbing, some individuals signed grievances against faculty members without having first read them, such was the frenzy and lust to inflict harm.)

The initial three accused of witchcraft were low on the social scale. After they were accused, however, something striking happened. Accusations were leveled at those considered to be of high social standing within the Salem community; namely, churchgoers, land owners, and well-educated community members. Even the wife of the governor himself was accused of witchcraft and "by the end of summer some of the most prominent people in Massachusetts and their close kin had been accused if not officially charged" (Boyer & Nissenbaum, 1974, p. 32). Boyer and Nissenbaum studied the original maps of Charles Upham, who lived in the 1800s and who spent his life studying the Salem Witch Hunts and Trials. One of the strategies Upham used was to plot the home of just about every resident of Salem in 1692 and to further plot whether the home contained an accuser, an accused witch, or a defender. What Upham's map revealed was remarkable. The vast majority of accusers lived in the west part of Salem, and the vast majority of the accused witches and those who either defended them or questioned the legitimacy of the witch hunts lived on the eastern side of Salem. By and large, the mobbers lived on the west side of town and the victims on the east. Salem's mobbers lived in proximity to one another on the west side of town and must certainly have known each other and helped each other out. Those who were to become accused lived on the east side of town and were generally wealthier and more influential.

In 1692, work was conducted within the container of community, not in organizations, as largely occurs today. Such work was agricultural, maritime-related, or small business and was monitored by community and religious leaders.

The same leaders within the existing community structures were expected to manage predictable disputes surrounding issues of commerce and land ownership. Boyer and Nissenbaum (1974) stated:

> It is altogether possible that the level of internal bickering in Salem Village was, at least to begin with, no higher than that in many other New England communities of the late seventeenth century. What made Salem Village disputes so notorious, and ultimately so destructive, was the fact that structural defects in its organizations rendered the Village almost helpless in coping with whatever disputes might arise. (p. 51)

Defective organizational structures, as they interact with the external social environment, remain to this day a significant risk factor for mobbing. One useful aspect of analyzing the Salem Witch Hunt mobbings today is that no one takes seriously the idea that the accused were, in fact, witches—the most serious attribution of individual evil and wrongdoing that could have been applied at the time. The equivalent labels of today would be "difficult," "troublemaker," "mentally unstable," and even a "bully." Analyzing Salem helps us to understand both the pervasiveness of the fundamental attribution error and its wrongheadedness. Using the individual as the explanatory framework and ignoring group, organizational, and community dynamics leads to thin, impoverished explanations that, in the Salem mobbings, led to death for some, suffering for many, and a community in chaos for all. This same attitude continues to result in more or less the same outcomes today. How little have we learned since 1692?

Analysis and Key Points
The following list proposes some important lessons that can be learned from the Salem Witch Hunt mobbings:

- Ganging up and proffering multiple accusations against a target or targets can become a rapidly escalating process and, when it occurs, should function as a red light and an indicator of a need to slow down and examine the larger context.
- The *ad numerum fallacy* still holds sway. Just because many people believe something to be true does not make it so. The skeptics among us and those who question provide essential balance.
- It is very difficult, if not impossible, to prove that one is innocent of something that is difficult to prove one way or another in the first place (e.g., that one is not a team player or that one is not over-reactive or that one is not a witch).
- Moral righteousness and moral superiority are extremely dangerous characteristics. Crusades usually result in bloodbaths, not in righting wrongs.
- The content of rumor, gossip, and innuendo should be analyzed carefully and corrected when inaccurate. Slowing down the wildfire of character assassination

by gossip and rumor campaigns is essential to an early burn-out of a potential mobbing, and it can be accomplished by challenging suspicious or false information.

THE MCMARTIN PRESCHOOL SEXUAL ABUSE MOBBINGS

About 300 years after Salem, in the affluent enclave of Manhattan Beach, California, it took the justice system not 3 months but about 7 years to consider its work complete in the McMartin Preschool Sexual Abuse case. By March 1984, within 5 months of initiating their investigations of the children of the McMartin Preschool, the Children's Institute International had diagnosed 384 of current and former McMartin Preschool students as having been sexually abused (Linder, 2003). Seven McMartin teachers were accused and charged with committing over 500 sex crimes against 40 children. The first person charged in the case, Ray Buckey, spent 5 years in jail before going to trial. By 1986, charges were dropped against five defendants, and only Peggy Buckey and Ray Buckey remained under indictment. Peggy Buckey was acquitted in 1990 on all counts, and after two trials, the jury deadlocked in the case of Ray Buckey, although the majority of the jurors voted in favor of his acquittal (Linder, 2003).

The McMartin Preschool Sexual Abuse Case occurred during the height of national fears about child sexual abuse. Twenty-five years later, for many who lived through the trials of the people involved and watched the case unfold on national television, hearing the name of the McMartin Preschool still elicits shudders of revulsion—in spite of the fact that no one was found guilty, in spite of the fact that the children's accounts of the sexual abuse that allegedly occurred grew more and more fantastic over time and were associated with little or no substantiating evidence (Linder, 2003), and in spite of the fact that the investigatory interviews of the children by the Children's Institute International were highly leading and suggestive (Ceci & Bruck, 1995; Garven, Wood, & Malpass, 2000; Schreiber et al., 2006)—so leading that mental health professionals have expressed concern that some of the children will live the rest of their lives with false memories of abuse generated through the investigatory process. Going forward with the prosecutions was based on the untested and now disproved premise that children do not fabricate or are not suggestible (Leichtman & Ceci, 1995) about sexual abuse and that everything they say must be believed.

Even though the targets of the McMartin Sex Abuse Case mobbing were all employees of the McMartin Preschool, the mobbing was initiated by "a person served," Judy Johnson, a parent of one of the preschool students. Johnson filed a police report stating that Raymond Buckey, a McMartin preschool employee had molested her son. Ms. Johnson followed up with a letter to the district attorney saying that her son told her he went to an armory behind her house where Ray flew through the air and where the "goatman" was present and where a ritual-like atmosphere prevailed. The police department, in its zeal to protect children, sent out a letter to all of the parents of children at the McMartin School and asked them to notify the police if their children had ever observed Ray Buckey tie up a child or leave the classroom during naptime. The letter further indicated that the police were concerned that criminal acts had taken place at the school including sodomy, handling of genitals, and oral sex (Reinhold, 1990a). That the children were subjected to leading and suggestive questions during interviews by the examiners from the Children's Institute International has been studied and established by multiple scholars (Ceci & Bruck, 1995; Garven et al., 2000; Schreiber et al., 2006). The role of the letter from the police department to the parents in setting off a frenzy of fear and panic, while noted, has been less studied in terms of its suggestibility.

Almost immediately, the parents of the preschool students, the police department and its investigators, and a child abuse examiner from Children's Institute International were involved in the case and actively soliciting evidence to support initial fantastic claims of abuse. Some of these claims were reminiscent of Salem, like the claim that Ray Buckey flew through the air. Other fantastic claims included that the children were taken to other locations by airplanes or helicopters where they witnessed a horse being killed with a baseball bat (Garven et al., 2000). The mobbing would widen however and soon also included the prosecutor's office and the media, with a criss-crossing of relationships between media representatives, the prosecutor, and the key child abuse investigator. The primary child abuse interviewer in the case and the newsman who first broke the McMartin Preschool Sex Abuse case began a romantic relationship. A prosecutor in the case became engaged to the city editor of the *Los Angeles Times* (Reinhold, 1990a).

Such boundary crossings between people charged with investigatory, prosecutorial, and reporting responsibilities, and possessed of almost limitless power to influence others, raise significant questions about their ability to remain objective and unbiased. Whether all of those involved in such boundary crossings should have recused themselves from participation in the case raises important ethical questions. The print and broadcast media in Los Angeles maintained a decidedly uncritical stance in their reporting of the case and, in so doing, gave the allegations full credibility in spite of their fantastic nature (Reinhold, 1990a,b).

Analysis and Key Points

The organizations and institutions arrayed against the indicted teachers and employees of the McMartin Preschool were the parents, the police department, the child abuse investigators, the office of the prosecutor, the media, and a nation consumed with fear of child sexual abuse. Interpol and the Federal Bureau of Investigation also became involved, looking for evidence of child pornography that never turned up (Reinhold, 1990a). With such an array of organizational and institutional power determined to find evidence of guilt, who could stand against it? At the end of the day, the only group who did stand against such powerful forces was the jury. As in the Salem Witch Hunt mobbings, the McMartin Preschool Sexual Abuse Case mobbings also provides an opportunity for analyzing what could have been done, but wasn't, to stop a relentless social process that hurt everyone in its wake, especially the children, and destroyed the lives and reputations of those indicted. The following list proposes some important lessons that can be learned from the McMartin Preschool Sex Abuse mobbings:

- Workplace mobbings can be initiated not just by supervisors or coworkers but also by people served, such as students, parents of students, customers, and any other stakeholder group (Serantes & Suárez, 2006).
- Premises and propositions upon which arguments are based cannot be taken for granted but must themselves be questioned. In the McMartin mobbings, the premise upon which irrational adult behavior was based was that the children's stories of sexual abuse must be believed at all costs, with or without supporting evidence.
- Alliances, coalitions, and close interpersonal relationships among people charged with the responsibility of being independent and dispassionate investigators should be thoroughly questioned and scrutinized.
- Moral righteousness created a dichotomous heroes-and-villains scenario in which the heroes were the media and the army of investigators, and the villains were the teachers and staff of the McMartin Preschool, in particular, Raymond Buckey. Buckey and the others were segregated, demonized, and identified as "other." They were objectified and dehumanized. When this process of dehumanization and demonization occurs, no punishment is too severe.
- The more incredible and fantastic an allegation, the more it must be subject to scrutiny and corroborated by evidence. The fantastic and extraordinary nature of the allegations of sexual abuse (i.e., the children were taken on airplane and helicopter rides where they witnessed animal abuse and were sexually abused themselves) required equally extraordinary evidence that never materialized.
- Mobbing victims are often forced to live for the rest of their lives with the taint of shame and revulsion from disproved and/or unproven allegations, without remedy for making them whole.
- Polarized win–lose contexts admit no uncertainty and push proponents of particular positions to "prove" their positions at all costs. That persons in positions of power and authority should shift and change their viewpoints in light of the accumulation of new information must be encouraged as a moral good rather than be regarded as a failure to prove a particular point.
- All organizations exist and interact within external environments that can be powerfully influential. In the McMartin case, the influential external environment included a developing social awareness of child sexual abuse and the institutions of the police, legal system, and media.

Conclusion

It is much easier to look at instances of school or workplace mobbing with the advantage of hindsight than it is to name a mobbing in process. Infamous examples of mobbings that have been described in this book so far, like those at Salem and McMartin, can be carefully analyzed and lessons can be drawn from these cases to help us understand the complex interplay of individual, group, organizational, and community dynamics at work. From these instances, we can identify critical errors in thinking and decision-making that led what we will assume to be otherwise reasonable people to act in highly unreasonable and irrational ways. We can also identify critical take-away lessons that can both inform our understanding of these devastating events and, if we use the lessons, help us to prevent them from happening again.

But from the in-the-moment, insider's perspective, Salem was about witches and witches were bad and must be eliminated. From the same insider's perspective, McMartin was about child molesters who must be identified and eliminated. From this same perspective, Lee's case was about a conscientious worker who was too perfectionist and who caused organizational problems as a result. Similarly, Rachel Fannon, however appealing she may be, needed to learn to toughen up and be like an Amazon woman. In these explanations, the individual is the focal point, and group and organizational dynamics have been ignored. When teased out one after the other, the individually focused explanation ceases to be satisfying and more importantly ceases to provide a useful explanation for the events described.

Individually focused explanations are biased toward accounts and analyses that emphasize personal and psychopathological factors. Social psychologists refer to this bias or viewpoint as the *fundamental attribution error* (Jones, 1979, 1990; Jones & Harris, 1967). Simply put, the fundamental attribution error is the tendency for individuals to overemphasize personality-based explanations in others while underemphasizing the role and power of situational and organizational influences. Accordingly, individuals assume that the actions of others are indicative of the type of person they are, rather than indicative of the social and organizational forces that influence them. Not surprisingly, this assumption can result in erroneous explanations for behavior.

Systemic and organizational involvement in each of these tragic episodes was clearly present, as we have described in detail. But, until the recent failures of a number of our financial institutions, organizational ineptitude and wrongdoing has been much harder to pin down, has become more clinical and bureaucratized, and has elicited a muted response when compared with the outrage generated by individual wrongdoing. A basic premise of this book is that three sets of dynamics influence an individual's behavior in a school, workplace, or other organizational setting; namely, personality or individual dynamics, situational or group dynamics, and systemic or organizational dynamics. To fully comprehend and explain behavior in an organizational or community setting, all three sets of dynamics must be considered, not just one or two. A related assumption is that individual, group, and organizational dynamics can either foster or reduce the likelihood of mobbing in organizations.

Mobbings are devastating events for individuals and costly at multiple levels for organizations. We cannot take effective action to prevent mobbings or effectively help victims of mobbings until we can fully grasp the nature of the group and organizational involvement in mobbing episodes.

Plan of the Book

Mobbing: Causes, Consequences, and Solutions is divided into four sections. In the first section, the social process of mobbing is introduced and is distinguished from bullying. Chapter 2 provides a history of the study of mobbing, from its origins in the 1980s to the present day. In Chapter 3, similarities and differences between mobbing and bullying are presented and analyzed. Chapter 3 provides a framework for recognizing mobbing in organizational contexts, especially in workplaces and schools. We have tried to go beyond the descriptive presentation of examples of mobbing by examining the underlying assumptions, organizational strategies, and implications for intervention and prevention that the examples suggest. In addition, we have made every effort to identify and cite the most current relevant research from around the world.

In the second section of the book, we provide an explanatory framework for how mobbing in organizations develops. In Chapter 5, we describe four different theoretical frameworks that can account for the emergence of mobbing in organizations, and we provide a detailed analysis of the components of organizational dynamics and the relationships among them. In Chapter 6, we look at the group, leadership, and individual antecedents of mobbing, and provide an assessment of the strength of the existing research about them. Chapter 7 looks longitudinally at the process of organizational development and summarizes mobbing risk factors that incline an organization either toward or away from a state of mobbing-proneness.

The consequences of mobbing is the focus of the third section of the book. In Chapter 8, we examine the health consequences of mobbing and provide a summary chart of the most current research about the impact on health and well-being of mobbing victims. As a result of the weight of the research evidence, we propose that mobbing is an unrecognized public health problem requiring public health actions to address it. In Chapter 9, we look at how mobbing affects family and social relationships, and in Chapter 10, we examine the effects of mobbing on career and work performance. In this section on the consequences of mobbing, we provide a novel application of trauma research for understanding why victims respond the way they do when mobbed.

The last section of the book focuses on recovery, solutions, and prevention. Chapter 11 provides mental health professionals with evidence-based information for effective practice and intervention with mobbing victims and their families. As a part of this chapter, we provide a template for developing a personalized recovery plan for clients who are mobbing victims. In Chapter 12, we look at the organizational support systems that may afford help to mobbing victims, and we look at ways in which human resources (HR), for example, can be either helpful or hurtful. In so doing, we hope to promote thoughtful reflection about how organizations can improve their internal support systems for victims of mobbing. In Chapter 13, we build on the previous two chapters and examine the systemic intervention skills that professionals and organizations need to develop to provide platforms for sustained individual and organizational recovery from mobbing. Chapter 14 addresses organizational mobbing prevention strategies, and Chapter 15 extends this discussion by looking at issues in anti-mobbing policy development and at legislative efforts to prohibit school and workplace abuse. No solution attempts are without the risk of unintended adverse consequences. In our discussions of intervention and prevention strategies, we do not ignore these risks.

2

The Emergence of the Study of Mobbing

Frankly, it can be dangerous to write about what goes on in
organizations.
—Margaret H. Vickers (2002, p. 614)

Early research on mobbing and bullying began in the 1960s and 1970s (Brodsky, 1976; Heinemann, 1972; Lorenz, 1963, 1965, 1968; Olweus, 1973). The foundational research on mobbing expanded in the 1980s with the work of Heinz Leymann (1990, 1993, 1996; Leymann & Gustafsson, 1996). Thirty years or thereabouts is a short period of time in the development of any discipline. Because of the worldwide interest in the topic, a considerable body of theoretical and research literature has been developed by practitioners and researchers in multiple fields. The study of mobbing or bullying is a good example of a multidisciplinary study.

Mobbing or bullying is studied in the fields of business and management, organizational studies, sociology, psychology, conflict resolution, law, nursing, medicine, traumatology, and occupational health, to name the major disciplines involved. The benefits of a multidisciplinary approach to an emerging field include the rapid development of a body of research and theoretical literature. The difficulties of a multidisciplinary approach are that disciplinary vocabularies and research methods vary considerably. A number of vocabularies exist for nonphysical interpersonal abuse. Although our focus is on mobbing and presenting the emergence of mobbing research, we cannot ignore very closely related research that uses other vocabularies, especially that associated with bullying.

In this chapter, we review the important "moments" in research on mobbing and related vocabularies of nonphysical interpersonal abuse. Our approach begins with the early years, with the introduction of the term "mobbing" in the 1960s and 1970s, and moves through the intervening decades to the present. Our interest is in presenting an overview of critical research and critical issues in research on mobbing. However, it is beyond the scope of this book to comprehensively analyze the many conceptual issues involved in the use of various terminologies used to describe interpersonal abuse in organizations or to classify them. Such a task would require at least an entire volume unto itself. Our hope is to highlight the critical "moments" in the research on mobbing and to provide signposts for both students and researchers who are interested in adding to the rapidly accumulating knowledge base in the many fields in which mobbing and nonphysical interpersonal abuse are studied.

The 1960s and 1970s

Austrian ethologist Konrad Lorenz (1963, 1965, 1968) used the term "mobbing" to describe animal behavior in which prey animals gang up on usually larger and stronger predator animals to scare them away. The behavior of birds is probably the most commonly used example of mobbing in the animal world, although fish, seals, squirrels, chipmunks, chimpanzees, and monkeys, among many other animals, are also known to participate in mobbing. When birds mob a perceived predator, often a larger bird, one or two birds start by pursuing it and flying toward it. Soon, other birds are attracted to the mobbing calls and respond by participating in mobbing the predator. The size of the group of birds involved in the mobbing increases rapidly, with the endgame being the driving off of the predator. Animal mobbing is a highly confrontational, overt social process aimed at the removal of a threat. A good example, from Lorenz's work, is geese ganging up on a fox to scare it away. Lorenz noted that mobbing served two functions: to scare away the stronger animal, and to serve as intraspecies education about where predator animals may be found and what must be done to repulse them. Lorenz (1968) also described examples of mobbing in school children and in soldiers. Human mobbing is also a social process aimed at removal of a threat, but it is usually not nearly as overt as in the animal kingdom.

Around the same time, Dr. Peter-Paul Heinemann (1972), a Swedish school physician, used Lorenz's term "mobbing" to refer to aggression by children against children and its potential lethality. In 1973, Dan Olweus, who later developed one of the most widely known school bullying prevention programs, used the term "mobbing" to explore aggression among children—aggression being his original field of research. Olweus (2001) began to have concerns about using the term "mobbing" and abandoned it for "bullying" instead. Where children were concerned, Olweus feared that the use of the term "mobbing" overlooked the role of individual perpetrators and risked a "blaming the victim" mentality if the victim came to be regarded as the one provoking the attack. Olweus (1977, 1978, 1979) extended his research on childhood aggression in the 1970s by studying a variety of issues related to aggression and peer acceptance in adolescent boys, and to aggressive reaction patterns in males. From his original use of the term "mobbing" to describe childhood aggression, he switched to use of the term "bullying" to describe research on aggression among schoolchildren. Far from Austria and Scandinavia, Dr. Carroll Brodsky (1976) published what is probably the first comprehensive book on workplace harassment in the United States. He addressed the consequences of workplace harassment, the psychological and systemic issues in workplace harassment, and used case examples to illustrate his ideas.

The 1960s and 1970s gave us the term "mobbing," initially in ethology, followed rapidly by its adoption to describe aggression primarily in schoolchildren (Heinemann, 1972; Lorenz, 1963, 1965, 1968; Olweus, 1973). Heinemann, however, also talked about mobbing as group violence among adults as well as among children. In the workplace, Brodsky (1976) introduced the concept of the "harassed worker." With these research strands coming from different disciplines and different countries, mobbing, bullying, and workplace harassment were placed on the table as compelling areas for ongoing research and conceptualization.

The 1980s and 1990s

The original work on workplace mobbing was done by Heinz Leymann, psychiatrist and industrial psychologist, who conducted his research in Sweden in the 1980s and 1990s, and who purposefully used the term mobbing to describe abusive workplace behavior. Leymann (1986, 1990, 1993, 1996) adopted the term mobbing from the study of animal behavior and, in particular, from the work of ethologist Konrad Lorenz (1963, 1965, 1968).

THE FOUNDATIONAL WORK OF HEINZ LEYMANN

The work of Heinz Leymann (1986, 1990, 1993, 1996; Leymann & Gustafsson, 1996, 1998) laid the foundations for worldwide interest in the phenomenon of mobbing or workplace abuse. Leymann developed a model for understanding the typical phases in a mobbing episode, beginning with a triggering event or critical incident and, usually, ending with the expulsion of the mobbing victim from the workplace. Leymann combined two skill sets and professional bodies of knowledge to analyze workplace mobbing, integrating his organizational research with his therapeutic acumen. As an industrial psychologist, he was keenly attuned to the organizational dynamics involved in mobbings and, in particular, to what happened when the victim began to complain to management or administration and the mobbing became a "case." Once the mobbing achieved the status of a case, and victims complained or protested to management, they usually found themselves in a rapidly escalating situation in which they were recast—no longer seen as victims, but now as the source of the workplace problems.

It is hard not to be impressed by the carefulness of Leymann's observations and the astuteness of his analysis. His research enabled him to identify the repeated pattern in which organizations opposed the resistance of mobbing victims by reframing victims as the problems, adding insult to injury by labeling victims as difficult or unstable, and frequently imposing punitive psychiatric evaluations upon them. In analyzing organizational responses to mobbing cases that had been called to the organization's attention, Leymann (1990) said that "usually, in cases where the conflict has gotten completely out of hand, the employer representative demands some form of total capitulation to his demands" (p. 124). It is this polarization and freezing of the organizational response that tips many workplace mobbings into highly destructive events for both the organization and the victim.

As a psychiatrist, Leymann (1990, 1993) was keenly attuned to the devastating impact of mobbing on victims and found that approximately 15% of suicide victims in Sweden had experienced workplace mobbing as a part of their backgrounds in the months prior to their suicides. Leymann also noted the high rate of posttraumatic stress disorder in mobbing victims and the high rate of psychosomatic symptoms. It is clear from Leymann's writings that he was sensitive to the pain and suffering of mobbing victims and worked to develop effective strategies for dispute resolution at the organizational level and for psychological intervention at the individual level. In fact, he and Gustafsson (Leymann & Gustafsson, 1996) set up a clinic for mobbing victims in Sweden. It is hard not to be moved by Leymann's obvious compassion and understanding of the plight of mobbing victims. Leymann (1990) said this about assigning psychiatric labels to mobbing victims:

> It is remarkable how central is the feeling of violation of rights in all the cases which have been examined. From the psychiatric point of view this observation is highly interesting. A logically justified experience of being gravely violated in connection with the typical (and logical) behavior pattern in this situation—namely, a struggle for moral redress against forces which portray the victim as someone with personality problems, is frequently misinterpreted by psychiatrists as a sign of paranoia. (p. 125)

Leymann captured the distortion involved in interpreting resistance to perceived injustice as psychopathological. In pointing out this distortion, Leymann shed light on the fact that one of the only means left for mobbing victims to act autonomously and retain some semblance of dignity was through acts of protest and resistance. Unfortunately, as Leymann also pointed out, such protest was typically restoried as simply more evidence of the victim's instability.

In Germany, Zapf (1999a,b) and his colleagues (Zapf, Knorz, & Kulla, 1996) initially followed Leymann in the use of the term "mobbing" to study workplace abuse. As the decade ended, Zapf began to use the term "bullying" to describe his research into workplace abuse.

LEYMANN'S WORKPLACE MOBBING FIVE-PHASE MODEL

In their foundational work, Leymann (1990) and Leymann and Gustafsson (1996) provided a clear and descriptive model of the five phases of a mobbing episode. Phase 1 is the initial conflict phase, in which an interaction, event, situation, or new or preexisting difference of opinion functions as the tipping point and becomes the catalyst for mobbing. Phase 2 is the period during which the victim is subject to continuing abusive and aggressive acts by the mobbers. This is also the recruitment phase, in which other workers are recruited into the mobbing, and the process of devaluation and discrediting of the victim accelerates. Phase 3 represents a critical turning point, in which administration or management enters into the mobbing, often as a result of the mobbing victim's request for help. Until this point, management and administration may have been aware of the mobbing but ignored or minimized it, thus fueling it by their aggressive passivity. The entrance of management and administration into the process does not typically result in a good outcome for the victim but usually results instead in revictimization. Phase 4 is the full revictimization period, in which administration or management align themselves with the mobbers, and the mobbing is again accelerated as a result of management's labeling of the victim as "difficult," "hard to get along with," "not a team player," "unstable," "a bully," "under extreme stress," or the ultimate revictimization—being labeled as "mentally ill." Phase 5 is the final or expulsion phase, in which the victim is terminated from the workplace, either proactively by administration or management, or through constructive dismissal because the working conditions have become intolerable for the victim and leaving is the only choice available to preserve health.

MOBBING RESEARCH IN NORTH AMERICA

In 1998, Ken Westhues picked up the threads of Leymann's work and published his first of many books on the topic of academic mobbings. Westhues continued to develop his work on mobbings in academia in the next decade. Around the same time, Davenport, Schwartz, and Elliott (1999) published their book *Mobbing: Emotional Abuse in the American Workplace*, based on Leymann's work and with a foreword written by him in 1998. With these contributions, research, scholarship, and public awareness about mobbing were introduced to Canada and the United States.

WORKPLACE BULLYING RESEARCH

In 1992, the British journalist Andrea Adams wrote a book entitled *Bullying at Work: How to Confront and Overcome It*. Her book popularized the term "workplace bullying," and that term was quickly adopted in the United Kingdom and elsewhere by researchers and activists alike. In the United Kingdom, Charlotte Rayner (1997) published an important article on the incidence of workplace bullying and, with her colleague Helge Hoel, also published a summary of the review of the extant literature on workplace bullying (1997). The nature of bullying and victimization at work was studied in Norway (Einarsen, 1998, 1999) and in Ireland (O'Moore, Seigne, McGuire, & Smith, 1998a). Studying prevalence and risk groups (Einarsen & Skogstad, 1996), stress and health consequences (Einarsen & Raknes, 1991), and bullying and the quality of the work environment (Einarsen, Raknes, & Matthiesen, 1994) were part of a large research agenda on workplace bullying in Norway. In Finland, Vartia (1996) studied work stressors and identified bullying as a significant issue. In Australia, Sheehan and Barker (1999) were also focusing on workplace bullying and published a paper addressing strategies for dealing with it. Concerns about bullying in Australia also resulted in a more popular book addressing bullying from the backyard to the boardroom (McCarthy, Sheehan, & Wilkie, 1996).

In the United States, Baron and Neuman (1996, 1998) were addressing workplace abuse under the headings of workplace violence and workplace aggression. Keashley introduced the concept of *emotional abuse* to distinguish it from physical violence, and investigated the phenomena independently (1998) and with her colleagues (Keashley, Harvey, & Hunter, 1997; Keashley, Trott, & McLean, 1994). In the 1980s and the 1990s, the stage had been set in Europe, Australia, and the United States to tackle issues associated with nonphysical forms of abuse in the workplace. Different terms were used to describe psychological and emotional abuse in the workplace and, rather than a consensus emerging, the opposite occurred.

SCHOOL BULLYING RESEARCH

In the 1980s and 1990s, a basic task was documenting the prevalence of school bullying and developing a basic understanding of its dynamics. The contributions to the research literature on school bullying owe a debt to the work of Olweus (1993a,b) in Norway and to Rigby (1994, 1996) in Australia, among many others in many other countries. As complex as it had been to conceptualize workplace psychological abuse, it was much easier to understand and conceptualize the impact of the psychological abuse of children and youth in school settings through bullying. Farrington (1993), a British criminologist, advanced the discussion of school bullying by indicating that oppression was a common feature of it. Besag (1989) in the United Kingdom wrote one of the early books attempting to understand and manage bullies and victims. In Finland, analysis of school bullying was focusing on the need to move beyond looking primarily at the offender–victim relationship to include looking at the multiple roles that schoolchildren play in bullying, such as that of bystander or witness (Salmivalli, Lagerspetz, Bjorkqvist, Osterman, & Kaukiainen, 1996). In the United States, an early paper examined the perceptions of adolescent victims of school bullying (Hoover, Oliver, & Hazler, 1992).

It was the school shootings in cities and towns across the nation that substantially elevated interest and research in the phenomenon of school bullying in the United States. The Columbine High School massacre on April 20, 1999, in which 12 students, one teacher, and the two shooters were killed, mobilized attention to schools, school culture, isolation, bullying, and the individual antecedents of aggressive behavior among youth.

The 2000s

In the 2000s, the foundations that had been set for research into nonphysical workplace abuse in the preceding decades since the 1960s flourished, producing sophisticated research in the areas of workplace mobbing, bullying, and emotional abuse of workers. Additionally, where schoolchildren were concerned, the focus shifted to developing prevention programs that included the whole school and the multiple stakeholders within a school community. We review some of the highlights of this decade of burgeoning research. We do so with recognition that a continued lack of clarity exists in the naming of constructs to define the particular nonphysical interpersonal abuse under investigation. It is not an accident that many, if not most, articles about workplace abuse begin with the discussion of the issues involved in naming the construct under study.

WORKPLACE MOBBING RESEARCH

The 2000s saw a range of research from multiple countries expanding on the discourse of mobbing in workplaces. Vandekerckhove and Commers (2003), from the perspective of the Netherlands, described downward mobbing (supervisor to subordinate) and suggested that such forms of mobbing were a sign of the economic times and of globalization. Sheehan (2004) also contributed to the discourse of mobbing from Australia; he presented ideas for working toward cooperative workplace organizations and considered legislation as another possible solution. Sheehan's efforts are both important and interesting in that he has authored multiple papers (cf., Sheehan & Barker, 1999) in which he uses "bullying" as the framework for analysis. In another paper, Shallcross, Sheehan, and Ramsay (2008) study the experiences of mobbing among public sector workers in Australia and deliberately elect to use the term "mobbing" as the basis for their analysis, stating that "the term 'mobbing' is preferred in this study to distinguish the behaviour as a form of group behaviour, instead of, for example, the term 'bullying' that implies 'individual acts' of physical aggression" (p. 57).

Westhues (2004, 2005a,b) continued and expanded his research and analysis of academic mobbing. In Spain, López-Cabarcos and Vázquez-Rodríguez (2006) looked at academic mobbing from the Spanish perspective, and, in Turkey, Tigrel and Kokalan (2009) described the nature and impact of academic mobbing there. The focus on the unique quality of academic mobbing to which Westhues first called attention has been picked up by researchers in western and eastern Europe.

The impact of mobbing on nurses, physicians, and other healthcare workers has been studied in Taiwan (Chen, Hwu, Kung, Chiu, & Wang, 2008) and in Turkey (Yildirim & Yildirim, 2007; Yildirim, Yildirim, & Timucin, 2007). Health consequences of mobbing are the focus of Chapter 8 in this volume. A sample health impact study from Chapter 8 that merits mention here is a joint study between Harvard University's Massachusetts General Hospital and the hospital of the University of Rome, in which workplace mobbing victims were assessed for their risk of suicide (Pompili et al., 2008); 52% were found to have some risk of suicide, with 20.6% identified as having a medium to high risk of suicide. Nolfe, Petrella, Blasi, Zontini, and Nolfe (2008) studied the subjective perceptions of mobbing victims and the psychopathological effects of the experience of having been mobbed.

In addition, the study of mobbing's impact on victims' beliefs about justice in the world in general and in their lives in particular was the focus of a fascinating study from Croatia about victims of mobbing and its impact on their general and personal just-world beliefs (Adoric & Kvartuc, 2007).

This brief review of workplace mobbing research in the 2000s illustrates the increasing growth and specialization of mobbing research into areas that include general workplace mobbing, and the focus on specific types of work settings, such as academia and health care. The health consequences of mobbing are a significant focus area, and we are beginning to see work that identifies helpful treatments for mobbing victims. For example, Hillard (2009), a psychiatrist, recommends investigating patients' claims of mobbing before writing patients off as paranoid.

Types of Workplace Mobbing and Organizational Settings

Workplace mobbing is a set of abusive interpersonal behaviors involving work groups and the organization, and it can occur in any direction within the workplace hierarchy and across any set of workplace relationships. Workplace mobbing can be top-down, in which supervisors and/or managers or administrators mob a supervisee or someone holding a lower rank within the organization. Workplace mobbing can be bottom-up, in which workers of lower rank mob a supervisor. Both of these forms of workplace mobbing can be referred to as *vertical mobbing*. *Horizontal* or *lateral mobbing* occurs when workers mob other workers at more or less the same level in the organization. Workplace mobbing can also include people served; namely, customers, clients, students, or patients. People served typically become involved in workplace mobbing when they are recruited by someone within the organization to join in a mobbing that is already in progress. An example would be a faculty member in a school or university recruiting students to join in the mobbing of another faculty member.

No sector of the workplace is immune from mobbing. Workplace mobbing, bullying, and the emotional abuse of workers has been identified across multiple sectors of the workplace including in education (Lewis, 2004; Westhues 2005a,b), health care (Kivimaki, Virtanen, Vartia, Elovainio, Vahtera, & Keltikangas-Järvinen, 2003; Yildirim & Yildirim, 2007), the legal system (see Chapter 1, the McMartin Preschool mobbings), the nonprofit sector (Bultena & Whatcott, 2008), civil service (De Vogli, Ferrie, Chandola, Kivimäki, & Marmot, 2007), the public sector

(Shallcross et al., 2008), libraries (Hecker, 2007), the arts (Quigg, 2003), and manufacturing industries (Mikkelsen & Einarsen, 2001).

Prevalence of Workplace Mobbing

Although different researchers use different methods for identifying prevalence rates of workplace abuse and different terminology in reporting those rates, Lutgen-Sandvik, Tracy, and Alberts (2007), based on their study of workplace abuse in the United States, found the following: "Given the data available, we can speculate that approximately 35–50% of U.S. workers experience one negative act at least weekly in any 6–12 month period, and nearly 30% experience at least two types of negativity frequently" (p. 854). The Workplace Bullying Institute/ Zogby International U.S. Workplace Bullying Survey (2007), in the largest survey of its kind, found that 37% of American workers had experienced workplace abuse at some time in their working lives. In the United Kingdom, Quine (2003) reported that 37% of the participants in her study had experienced workplace abuse in the previous year and that a disturbing 96% had experienced abuse by more than one person. A workplace study in Taiwan (Chen et al., 2008) identified a 1-year prevalence rate of 51% for verbal abuse and 16% for mobbing. These workplace abuse prevalence figures, although arrived at through different research methods, indicate that workplace mobbing and abuse are significant global problems.

Workplace Bullying Research

In the United States, the campaign against workplace bullying was initiated by Drs. Gary and Ruth Namie through the founding of their Workplace Bullying Institute and through the publication of their book, in 2000, *The Bully at Work*, and its second edition in 2009a. In 2007, their Workplace Bullying Institute partnered with Zogby International in conducting the largest survey of its kind about the prevalence and nature of workplace bullying in the United States. The sample size was 7,740 respondents (The Workplace Bullying Institute/Zogby International U.S. Workplace Bullying Survey, 2007). The Namies have combined research and activism and, as a result of their work, have brought workplace bullying to the awareness of people in the United States and around the world. They have also partnered with David Yamada, a law professor, in advocating the passage of the Healthy Workplace Bill which he crafted (Yamada, 2004).

Also in the United States, Lutgen-Sandvik (2006, 2008) and her colleagues (Lutgen-Sandvik et al., 2007) have taken a communication flow perspective in conducting their research and have developed fascinating findings about the experience of dealing with bullying in the workplace and the toll that bullying takes on personal and professional identity. She has also examined responses to being bullied and has conceptualized them within the frame of resistance (Lutgen-Sandvik, 2006). Her work is insightful and original. Still in the United States, Keashley, already mentioned in the section covering research in the

1980s and 1990s, has continued to develop her work on emotional abuse by examining the topic from the perspective of the target (2001), its impact on management (Keashley & Neuman, 2004), and the effect of bullying on service delivery (Keashley & Neuman, 2008). Fox and Stallworth (2009) have developed frameworks for preventing workplace bullying through alternative dispute resolution and training. In Canada, Ferris (2004, 2009) has continued to develop her practice-based evidence work in developing conceptual frameworks for understanding workplace bullying and for developing intervention and prevention strategies.

A foundational book presenting research from many parts of Europe, Australia, South Africa, and the United States was edited by Einarsen, Hoel, Zapf, and Cooper (2003a). The book brings together sophisticated analyses and multiple perspectives about the problem of bullying and includes sections on explaining and managing the problem and on remedial actions. The book provides an excellent review of the empirical literature on workplace bullying through 2003.

SCHOOL MOBBING RESEARCH

In 2003, Gail Elliott wrote a popular book on school mobbing entitled *School Mobbing and Emotional Abuse: See It—Stop It—Prevent It with Dignity and Respect*, presumably drawing from her collaborative efforts on workplace mobbing (Davenport et al., 1999). Hers is the only book of which we are aware that deals with the topic of school mobbing as distinct from school bullying. In distinguishing mobbing from bullying, one of the key factors that Elliott (2003) identified is the covertness of mobbing behaviors. Anyone who is looking can see one child kick or hit another—such forms of aggression are clearly overt and available for observation. Golden (2003), in his foreword to Elliott's book on school mobbing, says that "passive violence is a type of violence that has no overt aggression and can be hidden. We could call it 'stealth violence' because the original source is so often unseen" (p. xvi). The mobbing case of Megan Meier described in Chapter 3 is a good example of the terrorism inflicted by such covert, stealth violence. Although our definition of school mobbing is concerned with the interplay of individual, group, and organizational dynamics, the distinction between overt and covert aggression is an important one in terms of identification, prevention, and treatment.

School Bullying Research

Because most of the research on interpersonal abuse at school is conducted under the heading of "bullying," we are left to utilize that research in assessing the pervasiveness of the problem even though our own position and model holds that what is referred to as school bullying is more often a description of school mobbing. Our reasons for taking this position were discussed in relation to a case in

Chapter 1, and will be discussed in relation to our conceptual model, which we describe in Chapter 3.

Prevalence of School Bullying

Assessment of the frequency of school bullying/mobbing is usually conducted through surveys of self-identified victims. Another method of assessing the frequency of school bullying/mobbing is through the use of surveys of self-identified perpetrators. The research below may be surprising, given the high rate at which individuals admit to being a perpetrator of bullying at school.

ASSESSING FREQUENCY THROUGH SCHOOL BULLYING/MOBBING
VICTIM REPORTS

School bullying is a phenomenon that is described throughout the world. In the United States, the National Center for Educational Statistics (2007) reported that 28% of students between 12 and 18 years of age reported being bullied during the previous 6 months. In terms of types of bullying experienced, the report from the National Center for Educational Statistics indicated that 19% of the bullied students said they had been made fun of, 15% reported that they had been the subject of rumors, and 9% said that they had been the subject of physical abuse. Another U.S. study found that 60% of children aged 8–15 years ranked bullying as a significant concern or problem in their lives (Kaiser Family Foundation and Children Now, 2001).

ASSESSING FREQUENCY THROUGH SCHOOL BULLYING/MOBBING
PERPETRATOR REPORTS

In a fascinating study by Williams and Guerra (2007), researchers looked at prevalence rates for bullying by asking students whether they perpetrated any particular forms of bullying rather than by asking if they were victims of any form of bullying, which, to date, has been the most common means of collection of prevalence data. Williams and Guerra surveyed 3,339 students in Colorado in 5th, 8th, and 11th grades in 2005, and followed-up in 2006 with a survey of 2,293 of the original respondents. The findings across all grade levels indicated that 71% of the sample reported participating in verbal bullying, 40% reported participating in physical bullying, and 9% reported participating in bullying through e-mail or instant messaging (IM).

SUMMARY OF SCHOOL MOBBING/BULLYING FREQUENCY RATES
IN THE UNITED STATES AND AROUND THE WORLD

These high rates of exposure to bullying in school are also supported by the work of Juvonen, Nishina, and Graham (2001), who report that close to 75% of adolescents have experienced bullying in the forms of name-calling, rumor-mongering, and public ridicule or humiliation, and that approximately one-third of adolescents have experienced more coercive physical bullying, such as unwanted touching. In Canada, Beran and Tutty (2002), who conducted research about bullying among students in the Calgary area, found that approximately 15%–25% of the student population experienced peer harassment at least some of the time. The frequency of peer harassment found by Beran and Tutty in Canada is in range with the frequency found in the United Stated by the much larger survey reported by the National Center for Educational Statistics referred to above.

A recent study in the Netherlands by Fekkes, Pijpers, and Verloove-Vanhorick (2005) surveyed 2,766 children between ages 9 and 11 about their exposure to bullying and what happened after disclosure of bullying to an adult. Sixteen percent of the children reported being bullied on a regular basis. Almost half of the children did not tell their teachers. However, when they did tell their teachers and the teacher tried to help, the bullying either stayed the same or got worse. Particularly interesting was that the majority of teachers and parents who knew about the active abusive behavior of alleged bullies did not attempt to talk with them about it. McGuckin and Lewis (2006) conducted a survey of students in Northern Ireland about their experiences of bullying and were dismayed to find that students reported that 76.8% of other students were bullied either a little or a lot. This finding is high in comparison with other studies of the frequency of bullying in Northern Ireland (Collins, Me Aleavy, & Adamson, 2002, 2004) and in relation to frequencies of exposure to bullying from around the world. McGuckin and Lewis raise the question of whether living in a context of sectarian and political violence affects the rates of bullying and recommend further research as a matter of urgency.

Dussich and Maekoya (2007) state that "in many schools around the world, bullying is sometimes thought of as a normal part of school life. However, studies are demonstrating that significant numbers of students are being injured while at school" (p. 495). Based on a study of 1,893 U.S. students in grades 8 through 12, Harris (2004) identified what she referred to as these "dismal conclusions" about bullying:

- Three out of four students are aware of name-calling, students being left out of activities, and teasing at least some times at school.
- Bullying happens at many places on the campus, even locations where there is teacher supervision, such as in the classroom.
- Nearly one-third of students admit that being bullied causes them to feel sad and miserable, or angry.
- A small percentage of students tell school faculty about being bullied; when they do tell, for more than one-third, nothing changes, and for a small but significant number of students, things get worse.
- Over one-half of students are not convinced that administrators or teachers are interested in stopping bullying. (pp. 13–14)

What Young People Think about Bullies and Bullying

One of the more interesting recent studies about children's perceptions of bullying comes from the work of Bosacki, Marini, and Dane (2006). Recognizing that
much of the research on school bullying comes from quantitative research studies
which, by their nature, don't allow participants to provide full descriptions of
their own experiences, Bosacki et al. designed a qualitative study in which they
encouraged children to draw pictures and construct narratives about bullying that
had the most significance for them. The sample consisted of 82 boys and girls
between 8 and 12 years old. The children were simply asked to draw a bullying
incident and then to provide their responses to several open-ended questions
about the incident. One interesting finding was that, whereas most of the children drew two characters, a bully and a victim, the older the children were, the
more likely they were to draw pictures that included up to four participants, suggestive of the group nature of much bullying. Another interesting finding was the
emotional depiction of the bullies by the children. Bosacki et al. found that

> The children's drawings and narrative accounts of bullying suggested
> that some of the bullies they have encountered seemed to enjoy inflicting
> harm on a peer rather than experiencing the negative emotions that one
> would expect to drive reactive aggression. For example, in 78% of the
> children's drawings of a bullying experience, the bully was depicted as
> smiling. Along similar lines, when asked what the bully might have been
> feeling, 51% mentioned positive feelings, whereas only 39% indicated
> negative emotions such as anger. Thus, the majority of bullies are depicted
> as enjoying themselves. (p. 241)

The smiling faces of the vast majority of the children's drawings indicated that
almost all of the children perceived bullies as proactive or instrumental rather
than as reacting to provocations against them. *Proactive bullying* is unprovoked
(Juvonen & Graham, 2004) and is suggestive of someone acting with intent to
harm another. *Reactive bullying* is behavior that is responsive to a perceived provocation by another and that may be understood as self-defense by the person
engaging in such behavior. It's fairly clear from the Bosacki et al. study that most
of the children thought their bullies were engaging in bullying behavior deliberately and without provocation.

Conclusion

New findings about mobbing behaviors among birds point to a level of cooperation and reciprocity that had previously not been thought possible (Wheatcroft &
Price, 2008). The purpose of Wheatcroft and Price's research was to contribute to

the understanding of the development of cooperation in living systems—what they describe as a poorly understood process. Their findings suggest that birds are more likely to help each other out in mobbing a target if they have assisted each other in the past. Although we are not suggesting the direct application of animal models to human ones, the research is tantalizing and underscores the role of cooperation in any mobbing event—be it animal or human. It's easy to forget that, in gangs, for example, even though the level of violence directed toward targets or outsiders may be extreme, cooperation among the gang members or insiders is necessary to carry out the violence against the target. In human mobbings, the elements of cooperation and reciprocity among the mobbers has, to our knowledge, not been addressed at either the theoretical or research levels. To eliminate someone in the workplace through mobbing does require cooperation and reciprocity among the group of mobbers, and often the organization itself is a cooperative participant in the mobbing. School and workplace mobbers must band together for a period of time to accomplish their aim of discrediting, humiliating, and not infrequently, eliminating their targets.

As we will describe in Chapter 3, we think it is important to attend seriously to the conversation about terminology for the sake of developing theoretical sensitivity. The more theoretically sensitive we are to the meanings embedded in labels, the more easily we will be able to distinguish one construct from another. Additionally, the interests of research are better served with a unifying construct to describe a phenomenon because hypothetical inferences and operationalization of terms for research become more coherent. As it stands, the term "bullying" still suggests top-down abuse to many, and the existence of an a priori power relationship (which we will discuss further in Chapter 3). The term "mobbing" suggests neither top-down bullying exclusively nor the existence of an a priori power relationship. Use of the term "bullying" is further complicated theoretically because it is used in ways that both include and exclude organizational involvement. However, we have reviewed important "moments" in the research of both mobbing and bullying here because both strands have contributed heavily to our current understanding of nonphysical interpersonal abuse.

Since, in this chapter, we have attempted to review and situate an enormous body of research literature on mobbing, bullying, and related constructs like nonphysical interpersonal abuse and emotional abuse, it would be an error to leave the subject of research without mentioning those areas in which we believe more mobbing research needs to be done. Given our focus on group and organizational involvement as central to the etiology of mobbing, we would like to see more organizational research examining the roles of management, supervisors, coworkers, and bystander/witnesses when mobbing occurs. We would also like to see significantly increased attention and research about effective interventions for individuals and program and policy outcome studies for organizations that have made efforts to implement anti-mobbing strategies. We would also like to see research in areas for which almost none currently exists in the field of mobbing; namely, mobbing's impact on family and friends—this research could fall under the heading of co-victimization research, and we would also like research to address issues of reemployability and reemployment experiences subsequent to an initial mobbing. In the field of mobbing, calling for more research in the areas we have just named is of critical importance. Although our knowledge of mobbing, its characteristics, prevalence, and consequences has increased dramatically, the presence of good research in a number of areas serves to underscore the absence of it in those areas we have just listed.

3

Understanding and Defining Mobbing

*The sad truth of the matter is that most evil is done by people
who never made up their minds to be or do either evil or good.*
—Hannah Arendt (1978, p. 180)

In this chapter, we provide comprehensive definitions for school and workplace mobbing and distinguish the more commonly used term "bullying" from the term "mobbing." We present a conceptual framework for understanding bullying and mobbing as occurring along a continuum related to the degree of involvement of group and organizational dynamics and to the severity of the negative consequences for the victims.

Mobbing is a social process in which people get hurt, often very badly hurt. Mobbing happens in schools and in workplaces. It happens in religious organizations, the military, the judicial system, correctional institutions, and in community-based organizations such as homeowner and condominium associations. Mobbing also occurs within wider community contexts, as we have discussed in Chapter 1, as in the cases of the Salem Witch Hunt and the McMartin Preschool Abuse Scandal. All instances of mobbing leave a trail of hurt, injury, multiple losses, and collateral damages. When workers get mobbed in the workplace, their physical and psychological health suffers, marriages suffer, relationships with children suffer, and a cascade of reputational and financial losses can quickly follow. When kids get mobbed at school, their physical and psychological health suffers, their family relationships suffer, their parents who stand up for them may become secondary mobbing targets, academic performance suffers, friendships suffer at a time in life when friendships are critical to identity formation, and, depending upon the severity of the mobbing and responses to it, future academic admissions and achievement may be compromised.

Bullying or Mobbing: Issues in the Naming of a Construct

A number of terms are used to describe workplace abuse, and there is little consensus among researchers about which term is the most descriptive and useful.

The debate in the literature centers largely around the use of the terms "bullying" and "mobbing" and whether they are different or essentially synonymous (Bultena & Whatcott, 2008; Davenport, Schwartz, & Elliott, 1999; Einarsen, Hoel, Zapf, & Cooper, 2003b; Namie & Namie, 2000, 2009a; Westhues, 2005a, b). However, other general terms have also entered the descriptive and research lexicon to refer to workplace abuse. The generalized terms in use to describe workplace abuse include *workplace harassment* (Brodsky, 1976), *workplace aggression* (Neuman & Baron, 1998), *emotional abuse in the workplace* (Keashley, 1998, 2001), *workplace incivility* (Andersson & Pearson, 1999; Cortina, Magley, Williams, & Langhout, 2001), and *abusive supervision* (Tepper, 2000). In cases in which children are concerned, most researchers agree that abusive behavior by children and students falls under the heading of "bullying." However, in the case of children and students, we raise the question of whether using the term "bullying" to describe abusive behaviors is always the best choice or whether the term "mobbing" also applies within school contexts.

It is understandable how both researchers and consumers of the literature on bullying, mobbing, workplace abuse, or whatever term is being used to describe workplace hostility can become confused and frustrated by the variety of terms used to refer to it. The range of terms used to describe workplace abuse is also loosely geographically associated with researchers in different parts of the world (LaVan & Martin, 2008). The term "bullying" tends to be used by researchers and writers in the United Kingdom, Australia, Ireland, and Northern Europe. The term "mobbing" tends to be used in Scandinavia, Germany, and Germanic-speaking countries, whereas in North America, a variety of more generalized terms like workplace aggression, emotional abuse, or workplace trauma are used.

Developing Theoretical Sensitivity

Our rationale for continuing the conversation about the differences in meaning between "mobbing" and "bullying" and other generalized terms used to refer to workplace abuse hinges on the importance of developing theoretical sensitivity. The current body of literature about bullying and mobbing has more than sufficient breadth and depth, so that immersion in it reveals distinctions between bullying and mobbing that are critical to understanding their different natures, manifestations, and consequences. In addition, theoretical sensitivity to differences between bullying and mobbing will be useful in developing effective interventions for victims and prevention models for organizations. Corbin and Strauss (2008) provide a good description of theoretical sensitivity in the process of conducting qualitative research that is also applicable to immersion in a body of research literature:

> It takes being immersed in the materials for some time before the significance of what is being said comes through. Sensitivity grows with

exposure to data. I might say that analyzing data is like peeling an onion. Every layer that is removed takes you that much closer to the core. This is what is meant by "theoretical sensitivity," being more in-tune with meanings embedded in data. (pp. 230–231)

Immersion in the existing literature about bullying and mobbing provides an opportunity for the development of theoretical sensitivity. The teasing out of similarities and differences between the concepts of "mobbing" and "bullying" is far from a semantic exercise. Such analysis has the potential for advancing our understanding of the continuum of behaviors, differing group and organizational dynamics, and differential consequences from both bullying and mobbing.

Defining "Bullying" and "Mobbing": What's Already in the Literature?

Reviewing existing definitions of "bullying" and "mobbing" in the research and theoretical literatures is a good place to begin an analysis of the differences between the concepts. Since we are looking at school and workplace abuse, the definitional categories in which we are interested are school bullying, workplace bullying, and workplace mobbing. There is no category for school mobbing because interpersonal abusive behavior among school-aged children and students is over-whelmingly referred to as "bullying" and almost no definitions of school mobbing are currently in use.

Leymann's (1990) definition, given below, of workplace mobbing has formed the basis for most of the definitions of either bullying or mobbing in use by researchers and scholars today. Several examples of other widely used definitions of school and workplace bullying and workplace mobbing will also be presented. In an effort to develop greater theoretical sensitivity to the embedded meanings in the definitions, we will analyze them and discuss their implications.

DEFINITIONS IN USE: A QUALITATIVE CONTENT ANALYSIS

In this section, we have provided a set of definitions that are widely in use for school bullying, workplace bullying, and workplace mobbing. The purpose of gathering these definitions was to provide the data for a qualitative content analysis of the definitions in terms of their constituent elements and in terms of the meanings of those elements in relationship to how they were embedded within the larger context. Each category of definition was analyzed separately and then a cross-case analysis of the sets of definitions was conducted to discern whether any important distinctions in definitions and meaning were apparent between school bullying, workplace bullying, and workplace mobbing. In the following sections, we provide three commonly used examples of definitions of "school bullying," "workplace bullying," and "workplace mobbing." Since the construct "school mobbing" has been used so infrequently, we have no working definitions of it to analyze.

DEFINITIONS OF SCHOOL BULLYING

We selected the following three definitions of school bullying for the content analysis. They were selected because they are widely used in the research and theoretical literature and are free-standing definitions without other reference citations within them:

> Bullying is a specific type of aggression in which (1) the behavior is intended to harm or disturb, (2) the behavior occurs repeatedly over time, and (3) there is an imbalance of power, with a more powerful person or group attacking a less powerful one. This asymmetry of power may be physical or psychological, and the aggressive behavior may be verbal (e.g., name-calling, threats), physical (e.g., hitting), or psychological (e.g., rumors, shunning/exclusion). (Nansel, Overpeck, Pilla, Ruan, Simons-Morton, & Scheidt, 2001, p. 2094)
>
> A student is being bullied or victimized when he or she is exposed, repeatedly and over time, to negative actions on the part of one or more other students. . . . Bullying is characterized by the following *three criteria*: (1) It is aggressive behavior or intentional "harm-doing" (2) which is carried out "repeatedly and over time" (3) in an interpersonal relationship characterized by an imbalance of power. (Olweus, 2003, pp. 62–63)
>
> Bullying is commonly defined as an aggressive behavior (words, actions, or social exclusion) which intentionally hurts or harms another person; the behavior occurs repetitiously and creates a power imbalance such that it is difficult for the victim to defend him or herself. (MacNeil & Newell, 2004, p. 15)

DEFINITIONS OF WORKPLACE BULLYING

The following two definitions of workplace bullying by well-known researchers were selected for content analysis. These definitions are widely used in the field:

> Bullying at work means harassing, offending, socially excluding someone or negatively affecting someone's work tasks. In order for the label bullying (or mobbing) to be applied to a particular activity, interaction or process it has to occur repeatedly and regularly (e.g., weekly) and over a period of time (e.g., about 6 months). Bullying is an escalating process in the course of which the person confronted ends up in an inferior

position and becomes the target of systematic negative social acts. A conflict cannot be called bullying if the incident is an isolated event or if two parties of approximately equal "strength" are in conflict. (Einarsen et al., 2003b, p. 15)

Bullying [occurs] when an individual experiences *at least two negative acts, weekly or more often, for 6 or more months in situations where targets find it difficult to defend against and stop abuse.* (Lutgen-Sandvik, Tracy, & Alberts, 2007, p. 841)

DEFINITIONS OF WORKPLACE MOBBING

These three definitions of workplace mobbing reflect the perspectives of foundational scholars in the field. Like the definitions above for workplace bullying, they are widely used and commented upon by other researchers:

Psychical terror or mobbing in working life means hostile and unethical communication which is directed in a systematic way by one or a number of persons mainly toward one individual. There are also cases where such mobbing is mutual until one of the participants becomes the underdog. These actions take place often (almost every day) and over a long period (at least for 6 months) and, because of this frequency and duration, result in considerable psychic, psychosomatic and social misery. This definition eliminates temporary conflicts and focuses on the transition zone where the psychosocial situation starts to result in psychiatric and/or psychosomatic pathological states. (Leymann, 1990, p. 120)

A malicious attempt to force a person out of the workplace through unjustified accusations, humiliation, general harassment, emotional abuse, and/or terror. It is a "ganging up" by the leader(s)—organization, superior, co-worker, or subordinate—who rallies others into systematic and frequent "mob-like" behavior. Because the organization ignores, condones, or even instigates the behavior, it can be said that the victim, seemingly helpless against the powerful and many, is indeed "mobbed." The result is always injury—physical or mental distress or illness and social misery and, most often, expulsion from the workplace. (Davenport et al., 1999, p. 40)

Workplace mobbing is the collective expression of the eliminative impulse in formal organizations. It is a conspiracy of employees, sometimes acknowledged but more often not, to humiliate, degrade, and get rid of a fellow employee, when rules prevent achievement of these ends through violence. It is a shared outpouring of irrationality upon the mundane bureaucratic landscape of modern work. (Westhues, 2005a, p. 42)

SAMPLE SELECTION AND ANALYSIS

The intent in any cross-group or cross-case analysis is to identify similarities and differences and to provide theoretically sensitive interpretations of those similarities and differences—in this case, similarities and differences in definitions of school bullying, workplace bullying, and workplace mobbing. The definitions selected are representative of each category of definition and are widely used. They are not, however, an exhaustive set of definitions of the phenomena of school bullying, workplace bullying, and workplace mobbing, nor were they randomly selected. They were purposefully selected because of their widespread use and the excellent reputations of the scholar-researchers who authored them. Additionally, the selected definitions did not include citations to other work within the definition itself. Many definitions of workplace bullying or workplace mobbing contain citations within the definition, and those were excluded. This sample of definitions of school bullying, workplace bullying, and workplace mobbing is intended to be illustrative only of the elements and features of definitions in use and is not intended to suggest that these definitions include all of the elements of the phenomena being described, nor is it intended to be definitive in any sense. What the content analysis is intended to do is to examine the features of each definition in terms of their meaning and to analyze the elements of the definitions to promote greater theoretical sensitivity.

We analyzed the above exemplars of definitions of school bullying, workplace bullying, and workplace mobbing according to conventions of qualitative content analysis. The first step in the analysis was the segmenting of the selected definitions into their constituent elements by class of definition (i.e., school bullying, workplace bullying, or workplace mobbing). The second stage in the analysis was open coding of each of the segmented definitional elements and labeling of them. The third step in the analysis was the creation of categories of labels within each definitional group and then comparison of those categories across the three definitional groups. The fourth stage in the content analysis was the interpretation of meaning in the constituent elements of the definitions and the comparison of meanings across the three definitional categories.

IMPLICATIONS AND DISCUSSION

Central to each of the categories of definition (i.e., school bullying, workplace bullying, and workplace mobbing) is the exposure to and experience of a set of negative actions or aggressive behaviors directed at a target by one or more others. In both the categories of bullying (i.e., school and work), the notion that the aggressive behaviors must occur repeatedly—with "repeatedly" operationalized as once or twice a week—appears as a prominent definitional feature. Leymann (1990) was the first to designate a number of times per week that the negative behaviors must occur, but he did so in an effort to differentiate occasional, expectable workplace conflict from the very different and sustained process of mobbing. In the workplace mobbing definitions, other than Leymann's own, the repeated nature of the negative acts was a central feature, but not their precise duration. The frequency of occurrence of negative actions is useful for researchers in that it can be used as a screening tool to operationalize bullying or mobbing and distinguish those phenomena from other kinds of workplace conflict. The use of frequency of events of negative actions is problematic in that it largely relies on the self-reports of targets or victims. Those self-reports can be both under- or overestimated, although current research suggest that there is a higher probability of under-reporting or under-acknowledging hostile work behavior (Myers, 1996; Serantes & Suárez, 2006).

The duration of the experience of negative acts is a part of each category of definition, but appears more strongly in the definition of workplace bullying. The concept of duration is useful again insofar as it distinguishes transient, expectable workplace conflict from the more sustained processes of bullying and mobbing. However, the notion of 6 months as a minimum period seems highly arbitrary and more reflective of the criteria sets in the American Psychiatric Association's *Diagnostic and Statistical Manual of Mental Disorders* (2000) than it is of a process definition for bullying or mobbing. If a person is the victim of sustained and repeated acts of humiliation and degradation for 3 or 4 months and suffers negative health consequences, what, then, do we call that process?

"Intention to do harm" was a prominent feature of both the school bullying and workplace mobbing definitions, although it was missing from the workplace bullying definitions. It makes sense that "intention to do harm" would show up strongly in school bullying definitions. The image of the school bully is that of a bigger, stronger aggressor looking for a soft target or "easy mark" to intimidate and harass. In the case of workplace mobbing, the definitions are clear that the elimination of the worker perceived as the threat is the goal of the process. In the set of definitions of workplace bullying used in this sample (albeit a small set), the definitions are silent on the issue of intent to do harm and therefore leave open both possibilities—that bullying could happen inadvertently, without conscious intent, or that workplace bullying could be a conscious process involving a primary intent to harm.

The idea of bullying without conscious intent is not as far-fetched as it might seem at first glance. The philosopher Hannah Arendt (1963) famously coined the phrase "the banality of evil," and meant by it that evil emerges where thoughtlessness and inability or refusal to carry on interior dialogue occurs. In the sense in which Arendt described "the banality of evil," workplace bullying could happen in contexts in which concern for the other, a capacity for compassion, and the ability of putting oneself in another's shoes are absent. Arendt's "banality of evil" also has an organizational underpinning in that failure to engage in interior dialogue also extends to uncritical acceptance of and alliance with organizational norms—going along to get along.

Those who mob others always do so with insufficient information about the victim—about the victim's point of view, intentions, and hopes and dreams. By casting the victim as "other," those who mob do not have to engage in the messy business of trying to understand another's position or motivation. They have rendered judgment in advance, and that judgment is revealed in actions in which they have moved to strip a victim of status and influence or to eliminate the victim from the organization or community. Such is the absence of reflection and compassionate engagement. Such is the banality of evil.

All three of the categories of definitions included a definitional element related to power imbalance. Upon closer scrutiny, an important distinction in the meanings of the notion of "power imbalance" in the definitions became clear. The distinction was whether the power imbalance preceded the bullying or mobbing, or whether the process of bullying or mobbing created a post factum power imbalance. In the school bullying definition by Nansel, Overpeck, Pilla, Ruan, Simons-Morton, and Scheidt (2001), power imbalance precedes bullying. We are referring to this type of power imbalance as an *a priori power imbalance*. The construction of the power imbalance in Olweus' (2003) definition is most suggestive of a preexisting or a priori power imbalance; however, Olweus leaves open the possibility of the power imbalance being created through the social process of bullying, as in the example of a student being targeted through anonymous letters or notes. In the MacNeil and Newell (2004) definition of school bullying, a power imbalance "is created" by virtue of the process of bullying. We are referring to this type of power imbalance as an *a posteriori power imbalance*. In the workplace bullying definitions, Einarsen, Hoel, Zapf, and Cooper (2003b) include an a posteriori power imbalance as an element of their definition. Lutgen-Sandvik, Tracy, and Alberts (2007) suggest such an a posteriori power imbalance when they state that "targets find it difficult to defend themselves and stop abuse." In the workplace mobbing definitions of Leymann (1990) and of Davenport, Schwartz, and Elliott (1999), an a posteriori power imbalance is said to be created through the process of mobbing. Westhues' (2005) definition is suggestive of the same understanding.

What is so interesting about the analysis of the meaning of "power imbalance" in the three sets of definitions is the fine distinction made between a power imbalance preexisting before the bullying or mobbing and is therefore "a priori" and one that emerges through the processes of bullying or mobbing and is therefore an after-the-fact or a posteriori power imbalance. Only in the school bullying category is there a definition in which an a priori power imbalance is asserted as a criteria for bullying. To create a power imbalance through a process of bullying or mobbing suggests that the erosive effects of the process itself are significant and have alarming effects on the victim. The effects of a power imbalance generated as a result of bullying or mobbing can be severe and can extend to feelings of helplessness and defenselessness by the victim. A reading of existing definitions of bulling/mobbing may, at first glance, lead one to think that the power imbalance is preexisting. The connotative image of a "bully" in Western culture reinforces the idea of an individual who is bigger and stronger and who is willing to push others around, thus supporting the notion of a preexisting power imbalance. Our analysis of definitions in use suggests the contrary—that the majority of the definitions indicate that power imbalance arises as a *result* of the bullying or mobbing process itself. The question of whether a power imbalance precedes or is generated by workplace mobbing is an important one that requires further research and analysis.

In the sample of definitions of school bullying, workplace bullying, and workplace mobbing, the issue of organizational complicity only appears in the workplace mobbing category. In their study of patients who had been victims of workplace mobbing, Albini, Benedetti, Giordano, Punzi, and Cassito (2003) found that dysfunctional organizational practices played a significant role in each case. The organization is the context for what is referred to in these definitions as either workplace bullying or workplace mobbing. With repeated negative actions directed toward a target, occurring over a period of time, with the intention to harm, and resulting in the victim experiencing a sense of helplessness, it is inconceivable that the organization is not involved at some level in the bullying/mobbing.

Negative consequences relating to work is an element in one of the definitions of workplace bullying. By contrast, in the workplace mobbing definitions, negative consequences are a focus in each of the definitions but are considered more broadly and include damage to health and welfare as well as damage to job. Workplace bullying and mobbing have become a focus of research interest, legal interest, and medical interest primarily because of their severe impact on the health and welfare of victims. What is surprising and disconcerting is that the definitions of school bullying do not include a focus on the effects of school bullying. Srabstein, Berkman, and Pyntikova (2008) are advocating the recognition of the serious effects of bullying on physical and mental health and on long-term academic performance as a basis for declaring it a public health problem. Table 3.1 provides an overview of the core elements of the definitions of school bullying, workplace bullying, and workplace mobbing, and comparisons across the three definitional categories.

Proposed Definitions of Bullying and Mobbing

From the content analysis of a sample of definitions of school bullying, workplace bullying, and workplace mobbing, three conclusions are evident: the definitions include specific dimensions and features of the bullying and mobbing phenomena, the definitions overlap across some but not all dimensions, and only the definition of workplace mobbing includes organizational involvement and a spectrum of negative consequences for victims. The conclusions that we draw from our review and study of the workplace mobbing literature are that bullying and mobbing are

Table 3.1 **Content Analysis of Elements of Definitions of Bullying and Mobbing**

Core Elements of Definition	School Bullying (n = 3)	Workplace Bullying (n = 2)	Workplace Mobbing (n = 3)
Presence of Aggressive Behavior & Negative Acts	Aggressive behavior/ Negative actions (× 3)	Aggressive behavior/Negative actions (× 2)	Aggressive behavior/ Negative actions (× 3)
Types of Aggressive Behavior & Negative Acts	Verbal, physical, or psychological negative acts (× 2)	Harassing, offending, excluding, negatively affecting one's work tasks (× 1)	Hostile, unethical communication, ganging up, conspiracy, mobbing to eliminate victim (× 3)
Duration of Aggressive Behavior	Negative actions occur over time (× 3)	Duration of 6 months (× 2)	Duration of 6 months (× 1)
Frequency of Negative Acts	Aggressive behavior occurs repeatedly (× 3)	Aggressive behavior occurs repeatedly (× 2)	Aggressive behavior occurs repeatedly (× 2)
Intent to do harm	Intention to do harm (× 3)		Intention to do harm (× 3)
Power imbalance: A priori	Imbalance of power (a priori) (× 2)		
Power Imbalance: A posteriori	Power imbalance (a posteriori) (× 1)	Power imbalance (a posteriori) (× 1)	Power imbalance (a posteriori) (× 2)
Power Imbalance: Origin unspecified		Victims cannot easily defend self (× 1)	Results in victimization (x 3)
Negative Consequences for Victims		Negative work consequences (× 1)	Negative consequences related to health, welfare, and job (× 3)
Organizational Complicity			Organizational complicity (× 2)

distinct phenomena, and that both bullying and mobbing can occur in school settings and in the workplace. Organizational involvement is the distinguishing factor between bullying and mobbing, and it is a critical factor. The factor distinguishing bullying from mobbing is the absence of organizational involvement in cases of bullying and the presence of organizational involvement in cases of mobbing.

Leymann (1990) stated that, from use of the mobbing assessment instrument he developed (the Leymann Inventory of Psychological Terrorization; LIPT), it was clear to him that individuals do not suffer from degrees of mobbing—they are either a victim of mobbing or they are not. His conclusion is based on the consequences of a mobbing process and whether a person is traumatized or not. Consequences as a result of a mobbing process have huge import for victims, their families, and for those in a number of professional capacities who treat and interact with victims. In identifying the presence of organizational involvement as the critical distinguishing factor in mobbing, we are proposing that the degree of organizational involvement as manifested through the frequency and intensity of negative and hostile actions, including acts of both commission and omission, can be assessed across a continuum.

Bullying as a distinct phenomena identifiable by its lack of organizational involvement is nevertheless a set of aggressive and hostile behaviors directed toward a target, and it occurs with considerable frequency in school settings and in the workplace. A major indicator of school and workplace health is the absence of bullying and mobbing. Bullying, by our definition, can occur within school and workplace contexts but when it does, it is suggestive of individual and/or group dynamics without organizational involvement. The presence of mobbing, on the other hand, is an indicator of abuse-prone organizations and is conceptualized in terms of the frequency and intensity of hostile and negative interactions that include the organization. Our conceptualization, therefore, is a systemic one and includes individual, group, and organizational dynamics across a continuum from a healthy, nonabusive organizational context to a very abusive organizational context, identified as *mobbing II*. The graphics in Figures 3.1 through 3.5 illustrate the continuum of school and workplace health and abusiveness that we are proposing based on the interface of individual, group, and organizational dynamics. The severity of mobbing in our conceptualization is related to the frequency and intensity of negative organizational involvement.

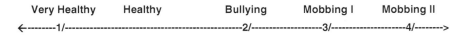

| Very Healthy | Healthy | Bullying | Mobbing I | Mobbing II |

←--------1/--2/--------------------3/--------------------4/-------->

1. Non-Abusive Workplace or School Setting: Productive and Healthy
2. Abusive Behavior in a Workplace or School Setting: **Bullying**
3. Abusive Workplace or School Setting: **Mobbing I**
4. Very Abusive Workplace or School Setting: **Mobbing II**

*Adapted from Sperry (2009b)

Figure 3.1 Continuum of Workplace and School Health and Abusiveness.*

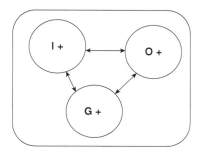

LEGEND:

☐ = ***Workplace or School***

O = ***Organizational Dynamics*** which can be (+) healthy, (-) abusive, (--) very abusive, ***or*** (+ /-) mixed

G = ***Group Dynamics*** of team or school grouping which can be (+) healthy, (-) abusive, (--) very abusive, ***or*** (+ /-) mixed

I = ***Individual Dynamics*** which can be (+) healthy, (-) abusive, (--) very abusive (in mobber or bully), ***or*** (+ /-) mixed

V = ***Victim*** or target of **Mobbing** or **Bullying**

➡ = **Abusive actions**

→ = **Healthy or neutral actions**

Figure 3.2 Nonabusive Workplace or School Setting.

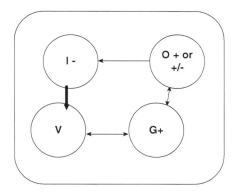

Figure 3.3 Abusive Behavior in a Workplace or School Setting: Bullying.

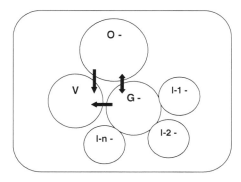

Figure 3.4 Abusive Workplace or School Setting: Mobbing I.

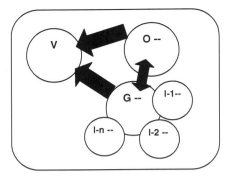

*Adapted from Sperry (2009b)

Figure 3.5 Very Abusive Workplace or School Setting: Mobbing II.*

In qualitative research, to understand a phenomenon as thoroughly as possible, research questions are often presented in the form of a generalized overarching question intended to focus on the main area of the research with a few subquestions designed to zero in on specific and differential aspects of the research project. Mirroring that format, we will present an overarching description of mobbing that encompasses both school and workplace events. We will then provide separate definitions of mobbing specific to school and to the workplace, together with illustrative examples of each.

General Definition of Mobbing

Mobbing is the targeting of an individual or group of individuals within an organization or school and the subjecting of that individual or group of individuals to a series of abusive and humiliating behaviors designed to cast them in a negative light, destabilize them, create suspicion about their worth as members of the organization, and, ultimately, to either force them out of the organization or to render them as suspect and unworthy while remaining within the organization. The results of this typically protracted traumatizing experience are significant psychosocial losses or other negative consequences, including adverse health effects. Much as organizational officials might like to say, mobbing is not about a lone individual or a small group of people acting alone and targeting others within a school, workplace, or other organization. Group dynamics and organizational involvement are always present to varying degrees. Mobbing can never be understood by seeking out explanatory frameworks in terms of individual psychopathology alone. Psychopathology may be present, but more critical is the group and organizational dynamics that operate within the contexts in which mobbing takes place. The variability of individual responses to mobbing is related to factors of personal vulnerability to injury and resilience.

Specific Definition of School Mobbing

School mobbing involves the harassment of an individual student or group of students by one or more other students. Mobbing involves individual, group, and organizational dynamics. It predictably results in humiliation, devaluation, discrediting, and degradation; damage to personal and/or academic reputation; and, often, removal of the target from the school through transfer, illness, or expulsion. The results of this typically protracted traumatizing experience are significant academic, health, and psychosocial losses or other negative consequences. School mobbings may include direct face-to-face harassment; the spreading of rumors, innuendo, and destructive "whispering campaigns" behind the victim(s) back; and/or *cyber-mobbing* through the use of the same type of harassing behaviors on the web, and, in particular, through Web 2.0 interactive social networks. Because of the centrality of sexual identity development during childhood and adolescence, school mobbing may include sexual harassment of both a verbal and nonverbal direct, physical nature. Mobbing has different levels of severity. In contrast to mobbing, bullying is abusive and harmful behavior directed at a specific victim or victims by a single offender. Unlike mobbing, there is little or no direct organizational involvement in the abusive behavior. In short, school mobbing and bullying can be conceptualized along a continuum of health and abusiveness, on which bullying is a less severe and encompassing form of abusiveness than mobbing.

The following is a brief example of an episode meeting the criteria of our definition of school mobbing. The illustration is notable, as are so many mobbing cases, by the failure to act on the part of those in authority. Organizational accountability and responsiveness to the harm done to the boy was nonexistent. School personnel aligned with the offender boys by virtue of their brushing off the hostile and exclusionary behavior as normal and to be expected for boys of their age.

"BOYS WILL BE BOYS"

Boys singling out another boy at an intensive summer football training camp and ostracizing, belittling, and otherwise humiliating the target boy cannot be brushed off under the widely used rubric of "boys will be boys." Let's take the case of Reginald, who was at the football training camp for the first time and who was there on a scholarship. He was targeted by a group of other boys with whom he went to school in his home town and who locked him out of the dorm for the first 2 nights of the week-long camp. In spite of Reginald's frantic banging on the door to be let back in, the other boys only laughed and tossed out a dirty sleeping bag to him. On the third night, the boys let Reginald back in, after 2 nights of exposure to rain and mosquitoes and the humiliation of having to urinate and defecate outside.

There were too many adults around for the "boys will be boys" explanation to make any sense. There were parents acting as chaperones and camp house parents in rooms adjacent to the boys' dormitory. There were coaches and assistant coaches working with the boys all day long and often eating with them; these adults had to notice that Reginald was looking worse for the wear. Back at Reginald's home school, other coaches, school administrators, school staff members, and teachers were told stories of what happened to Reginald at the football training camp. Other children at the camp brought home the stories of what happened to Reginald to their own parents. The stories of Reginald's mistreatment and abuse by a group of boys at the summer football camp became known to a number of adults, many of whom were part of larger organizational systems like the school and the camp administration.

Even though Reginald was too humiliated and fearful to tell his own story, his story was known and told by others, many of whom were adults acting within a larger organizational context and responding to organizational culture and norms. It's a lot less trouble to brush off incidents like Reginald's as typical "boys will be boys" behaviors than it is to examine the organizational complicity in the psychological injuring of Reginald and the failure of agents of the organization to intervene on his behalf and to take initiatives to prevent such behavior in the future.

Specific Definition of Workplace Mobbing

Workplace mobbing is nonsexual harassment of a coworker by a group of members of an organization for the purpose of removing the targeted individual(s) from the organization or at least a particular unit of the organization. Mobbing involves individual, group, and organizational dynamics. It predictably results in the humiliation, devaluation, discrediting, and degradation; loss of professional reputation; and, often, removal of the victim from the organization through termination, extended medical leave, or quitting. The results of this typically protracted traumatizing experience are significant financial, career, health, and psychosocial losses or other negative consequences. Mobbing has different levels of severity. In contrast to mobbing, bullying is abusive and harmful behavior directed at a specific victim or victims by a single offender. The bully may be a peer or supervisor, but other members of the work group are not involved, although others may have observed the abuse. Unlike mobbing, there is little or no direct organizational involvement in the abusive behavior. In short, workplace mobbing and bullying can be conceptualized along a continuum of health and abusiveness, on which bullying is a less severe and encompassing form of abusiveness than mobbing.

The following is a brief example of an episode meeting the criteria of our definition of workplace mobbing. Dr. J. was a threat to both the culture and delicate equilibrium of his workgroup unit, in this case, the microbiology department. Dr. J. did not fit in, and his colleagues were intent on keeping it that way. He was different, and he was a threat. He threatened the way in which the credentials of the existing members of the workgroup were viewed, and he threatened their incrementally productive but not stellar work accomplishments. Because he was passionate about his work, the easiest solution was to sabotage Dr. J.'s work and make the workgroup so unpleasant that no one, least of all Dr. J., would want to stay.

IVY LEAGUE OR POISON IVY

Dr. J. had been hired by the microbiology department of a medical and research center in a mid-size city directly after his postdoctoral work at an Ivy League institution in the northeast. His undergraduate and graduate education had all been obtained at other Ivy League institutions. Even before Dr. J. arrived at his new workplace, and before he met his colleagues, jokes were making the rounds about the "Ivy League boy" and how affectation and superiority would not be tolerated in their department. The jokes included the "silver spoon in his mouth" compared to the hard-working, often hard-scrabble ways in which many of the other scientists had made their way up the educational and career ladder. When Dr. J. finally arrived, to make sure he understood his place in the pecking order of the department, he was assigned additional tasks by the department head befitting a research assistant, not a scientist. Dr. J. was hired to participate in the genome sequencing of microbes that withstood extreme conditions, such as survival in extremes of heat and cold. Others in the department were also working on the project and resented Dr. J's involvement.

In the small world of genome sequencing of "extreme" microbes, Dr. J. had already made something of a name for himself and was regularly invited to speak at international conferences. Some in the department complained to the head of laboratory that Dr. J.'s overseas trips were taking him away from his work; work that then had to be done by others who were not "microbial rock stars" like Dr. J. The scientist who headed the laboratory also began to hear the "silver spoon in mouth" comments and the mimicking of Dr. J.'s Boston accent. The laboratory head simply laughed and added a few wisecracks of his own at Dr. J.'s expense. While Dr. J was away, months' worth of his data disappeared and several of his computer files had been corrupted. Dr. J. would return from his conference presentations to decide that he could not function as a scientist in such an environment and that, although his work was not irretrievably lost, it had been set back by several months. In Dr. J.'s case, his mobbing had begun before he even arrived on the job and before he had met all of his co-workers and administrative supervisors. Although Dr. J. thought the negative comments would die down after a short time, they in fact accelerated, ending with the sabotage of his work.

Conclusion

In this chapter, we have looked closely at the constructs of bullying and of mobbing. We have identified the primary difference between them as the presence of organizational involvement in mobbing and its absence in bullying. Organizational involvement in cases of school mobbing, as in the case of Reginald described above, often takes the form of acts of omission—not taking action when action is required. In workplace mobbing, as in the case of Dr. J. above, workgroup members and supervisors took proactive actions to harass and make Dr. J.'s life miserable. They also deliberately sabotaged his work. In Dr. J.'s case, his doctoral colleagues resembled a group of school bullies intent on showing the new kid on the block who's in charge. However, no one from the upper levels of administration came to Dr. J.'s aid or launched an investigation to find out who may have committed the acts of work sabotage until after he had resigned—again, acts of omission by those in authority, not taking action when action is required. In most but not all instances of workplace mobbing, however, acts of omission and acts of commission by organizational authority comingle in such a way that organizational behavior is made to appear impersonal through the use of formal channels that are rigged against the victim.

In this chapter, we have provided a view of workplace abuse that includes a continuum of organizational health and abusiveness, with mobbing emerging at the end of the continuum representing organizational abusiveness. When researching mobbing, victims and their experiences have been most studied and most documented. Researchers have also called for more investigation of the roles and dynamics of perpetrators. We support this call for gathering data that represent the perspectives and behaviors of perpetrators. In addition, we urge focused study on the role of the organization in the emergence of mobbing and, in particular, on the study of how official organizational channels and procedures are utilized in the service of elimination of workers who have been mobbed. We also urge equal attention in research to acts of omission and commission and to the study of the emergence of power differentials in mobbing episodes. We are quite unconvinced that power differentials preexist in mobbing episodes. We are more inclined to the view that power differentials arise during conflicts that then result in relative disadvantage for the mobbing victim, no matter the victim's previous status in the organizational hierarchy. More study on this issue of power is clearly needed to understand how power operates during mobbings.

4

Recognizing Mobbing

*Mobbing can be understood as the stressor to beat all
stressors. It is an impassioned, collective campaign . . . to
exclude, punish, and humiliate.*
—Kenneth Westhues (2004, p. 4)

In the previous chapter, we provided comprehensive definitions of mobbing and specific definitions of workplace and school mobbing. We provided the specific definitions of workplace and school mobbing because schools and workplaces are the two organizational types in which almost everyone will spend significant portions of their lives. In this chapter, we examine the specific components of our definitions of mobbing and illustrate through discussion and case illustrations how they are manifested and performed in everyday organizational life. The illustrations we use to recognize mobbing in light of our definition of it are the cases of Tatum Bass at Miss Porter's School and the Megan Meier story, two cases that have received widespread media coverage in recent years, and a case involving a condominium association.

In looking at our comprehensive definition of mobbing from Chapter 3, eight characteristic features of mobbing, listed below, are included. We have grouped these features into four categories; namely, perpetrator behaviors, purpose or intent, involvement of group and organizational dynamics, and consequences for victims.

PERPETRATOR BEHAVIORS

1. The targeting of an individual or group of individuals within an organization.
2. Subjecting of that individual or group of individuals to a series of abusive and humiliating behaviors.

PURPOSE OR INTENT

1. Designed to cast them in a negative light, destabilize them, create suspicion about their worth as members of the organization.
2. Ultimately, to either force them out of the organization or to render them as suspect and unworthy while remaining within the organization.

INVOLVEMENT OF GROUP AND ORGANIZATIONAL DYNAMICS

1. Mobbing is not about a lone individual or a small group of people acting alone.
2. Group dynamics and organizational involvement are always present to varying degrees.
3. Mobbing can never be understood by seeking out explanatory frameworks in terms of individual psychopathology alone.

CONSEQUENCES FOR VICTIMS

1. Variability of individual responses to mobbing is related to factors of personal vulnerability to injury and resilience.

Workplace
Humiliation, devaluation, discrediting, and degradation; loss of professional reputation; and, often, removal of the victim from the organization through termination, extended medical leave, or quitting. The results of this typically protracted traumatizing experience are significant financial, career, health, and psychosocial losses.

School
Results of this typically protracted traumatizing experience are significant academic, health, and psychosocial losses or other negative consequences.

Recognizing School Mobbing

Most readers will be familiar with the concept of school bullying, and many will have experienced it. In this chapter, however, our focus is on the concept of school mobbing. In fact, most of what passes for school bullying is, in fact, school mobbing. School mobbing includes many of the characteristics of school bullying, especially, the ganging up on another student by one or more students with the intent to humiliate and degrade the student through the commission of a range of hostile acts directed toward the target.

What distinguishes school mobbing from school bullying are the group dynamics of those involved in perpetrating the mobbing and the organizational involvement of the school through either its acknowledgment or denial of the problem. Victims of school mobbing are key figures in the process because they are the ones most hurt by it. Mobbing and bullying are public health problems because of the serious health consequences associated with them. Many families and school communities are already tragically familiar with these health consequences, which can be physical, psychological, or both.

The school community consists of a network of administrators, teachers, coaches, staff members, students, parents, parent advisory boards, and members of the wider school community. Local businesses, social service agencies, police departments, and local faith-based organizations are examples of wider school community members. We demonstrate how much of what is called school bullying is, in fact, school mobbing because of the importance of group and organizational dynamics in the aggressive episodes, and, in some cases, the involvement of the wider school community. In school settings, because of the involvement of parents and community volunteers, the school as an organization is more properly understood as a school community consisting of students, staff, teachers, coaches, administrators, parents, and volunteers.

Where the school as an organization begins and ends is a very blurred line, given the role of parent advisory boards and parent–teacher associations and the influence and power that these groups typically yield. Bullying or cyber-bullying behaviors that move beyond the conventional understanding of a one-to-one aggressive interaction between a stronger, more powerful perpetrator and a weaker, more vulnerable victim and begin to encompass the targeting of victim(s) by a group of other students and the active or passive involvement of the school organization and wider school community are no longer acts of bullying—they are acts of mobbing. The organization, most often the school, may become involved in efforts to address the aggressive behavior or may become involved in a complicit way by ignoring and/or denying the hostile behavior of some students toward other students and minimizing or denying its damaging effects. Through the use of case illustrations, we explore the dynamics of school mobbings and demonstrate the involvement of larger systems acting beyond the perpetrators and victims.

Types of Hostile Acts in Mobbing: Physical, Verbal, Written or Electronic, and Performative

Hostile and aggressive acts directed toward a victim can be physical, verbal, written or electronic, or performative. Physical acts of mobbing include hitting, kicking, punching, slapping, hair pulling, spitting, tripping, and hiding, stealing, vandalizing, or destroying the personal property of another. Verbal acts of aggression include name-calling, use of verbal slurs against the victim, gossip, rumor mongering, spreading false information and malicious lies, and all other verbal means of attacking one's personal or academic reputation. Written and electronic aggressive acts include all of the same types of abusive behaviors as in the verbal category but are communicated in written or electronic form rather than verbally. Examples of aggressive written and electronic acts are writing offensive and abusive notes to the victim anonymously or with a signature. Signed notes may be nondeceptive and include the signature of the actual note-writer and sender, or they may be deceptive and be "signed" fraudulently with the name of a third party who did not write the note, implicating a third party as a perpetrator who may or may not be involved. Such notes may be sent directly to the victim, or they may be circulated to others who are involved in the abusive ganging up and mobbing.

Electronic mobbing is often called *cyber-bullying* and includes abusive e-mailing, text messaging, and the posting of offensive and abusive names, stories, and/or images on the Internet, in particular, on Web 2.0 social networking sites like Faceboook and MySpace that are commonly used by teenagers and young people.

Performative acts of aggression toward another include ignoring the victim, walking away from the victim, turning one's back on the victim, refusing to talk with the victim, not sitting with the victim in a social setting like the lunchroom or gym, and essentially excluding and isolating a victim from the normal social life of the workplace, school, or other organization. Performative acts of aggression toward a victim can also take the form of abusive hand gestures, eye-rolling, and other facial gestures signifying disgust and contempt. Performative acts of aggression in mobbings are signifiers of social distance and of intent to socially ostracize a target.

The Case of Tatum Bass and Miss Porter's School in Farmington, Connecticut

In November, 2008, the family of Tatum Bass filed a federal lawsuit on her behalf against the prestigious Miss Porter's School and the school's headmistress (Santos, 2009). At the time, Tatum Bass was a 17-year-old high school senior. Her lawsuit claimed that she was cruelly bullied for months by a clique of girls at the school who referred to themselves as the "Oprichniki" (Reitz, 2008; Santos, 2009), the same name as the group that protected the 16th-century Russian Czar, Ivan the Terrible, and who tortured and killed those who opposed him. The suit alleged that the bullying consisted of months of tormenting on Facebook and abusive name-calling within the school. The name-calling reportedly included public humiliation about her attention-deficit disorder and repeated slurs like "you're retarded" and "you're stupid" (Reitz, 2008). Bass's lawsuit also claimed that she suffered overwhelming anxiety and emotional distress (Reitz, 2008; Santos,

2009). At some point during the episode, Bass cheated on an art history test, turned herself in to the headmistress, and was given a 3-day suspension (Reitz, 2008; Santos, 2009).

THE EARMARKS OF A SCHOOL MOBBING

This case has been reported in newspapers around the United States (cf. de la Torre, 2009; Reitz, 2008; Santos, 2009) and is the subject of multiple Internet blogs and bloggers. For example, on "Topix," an Internet forum (2008, December 10–July 20, 2009, 27), there are 604 comments listed between December 10, 2008 and July 27, 2009 about the Tatum Bass incident and Miss Porter's school. Our interest is in analyzing the information reported in the news accounts and in comparing that information with the criteria we have established to distinguish bullying from mobbing.

It is instructive to compare the news reports of Tatum Bass's alleged bullying with the elements of our definition of school mobbing. In the news accounts referenced above, Bass's lawsuit charges that she was the target of repeated abusive and aggressive behaviors by a group of other students who curiously referred to themselves as the "Oprichniki." In this case, those accused of bullying are a group rather than an individual. The dynamics of a group during a mobbing are qualitatively different from the dynamics of an individual bully. Olweus (2003) suggests that, when several young people participate together in bullying, a number of unique outcomes occur related to the processes of the group. Among those processes is a form of collective behavior or social contagion. Being a part of a group involved in bullying increases the likelihood that students will actually carry out aggressive acts. Olweus also cites the disinhibition in a group setting against acting aggressively. In other words, the individual's regulatory mechanisms against acting in an aggressive way are weakened in the context of a group. Additionally, Olweus identifies the "diffusion of responsibility" (2003, p. 69) that occurs in group bullying. If everyone in the group is involved, the sense of personal responsibility and accountability is less strong because "others are doing it too."

News reports of her lawsuit indicate that Tatum Bass stated she was also harassed on Facebook (Reitz, 2008; Santos, 2009). The viral nature of Web 2.0 social networking sites makes it difficult, if not impossible, to limit the damage to one's reputation and sense of personal identity once abusive or harassing comments are posted. When an abusive comment, story, or image is posted, the original sender no longer has any control over the dissemination of the product, and the same comment, story, or image is initially seen by up to hundreds or even thousands of people. It can be resent hundreds of times, in seconds, by any of the original recipients with just the click of a mouse. The same news accounts (Reitz, 2008) indicate that Tatum Bass claimed she was harassed for months by girls at Miss Porter's School and that she suffered overwhelming anxiety and emotional stress. Additionally, other news reports (de la Torre, 2009) indicate that Ms. Bass was ultimately expelled from Miss Porter's School and that she and her family were worried about the impact of the expulsion on her admission opportunities to selective colleges and universities. Such health and academic consequences are characteristic of a school mobbing.

The final issue, and the most important for understanding and ultimately doing something to prevent mobbing, is the role of the larger organization in a school mobbing—meaning the school itself with its network of administrators, teachers, coaches, and parents. Miss Porter's is a relatively small school with an enrollment of approximately 330 students, two-thirds of whom are boarders (Reitz, 2008). In a school of this size, it is difficult to imagine that at least some of the official network of responsible adults did not know that Tatum Bass perceived herself as the victim of protracted harassment and bullying. Indeed, the family's lawsuit alleges that the headmistress did nothing to intercede to stop the harassment of Tatum Bass and bears responsibility (Peretz, 2009; Santos, 2009). It is also curious that a group in the school, whether school sanctioned or not, would name itself the "Oprichniki," given its primary association with torture and death squads. Questions left unaddressed in the news accounts are what efforts, if any, were made by the school to protect Ms. Bass from the alleged abusive behavior of her schoolmates, and what anti-bullying programs and policies the school had in place.

Peretz (2009), in her *Vanity Fair* article about Tatum Bass and the culture of Miss Porter's School, suggests that Tatum Bass was most guilty of violating the school's ingrained norm against weakness even though she was allegedly expelled for unexcused absences and cheating. In other words, Peretz points toward the conclusion that Tatum Bass was punished for complaining about the abuse she received rather than "bucking up" and toughing it out.

The case of Tatum Bass, as reported in the news accounts, has the characteristic earmarks of a school mobbing. Indeed, the mobbing of Ms. Bass is ongoing in a variety of blogs and forums online dedicated to the topic. As in many mobbings, leaving the school or workplace does not end the attacks on the target. On the internet forum "Topix," the early postings after the story about Tatum Bass was published in newspapers around the country were running about two to one against Tatum Bass and in favor of protecting the reputation of the school. Ms. Bass is apparently from South Carolina, and there were a number of postings deriding her Southern origins. There were also postings that perpetuated the misguided and dangerous position that bullying is basically normal and that her parents should have kept out of it and left her to fight her own battles—again, placing the responsibility on the victim rather than on the perpetrators. Although wanting to protect the reputation of a school seems legitimate, launching insulting and inflammatory personal characterizations seems highly illegitimate.

The tragic fact of the matter is that bullying and mobbing are associated with severe and enduring negative health consequences. Among young people, bullying is associated with increased risk of loneliness, depression, and suicidal ideation (Nansel et al., 2001; Van der Wal, De Wit, & Hirasing, 2003). Victims of bullying in early adolescence have also reported ongoing psychological, social, and physical negative effects after the cessation of the bullying (Ando, Asakura, & Simons-Morton, 2005). In addition to these serious health consequences, victims of peer abuse and peer harassment have more absences from school, lower grades, and, not surprisingly, they are more likely to develop a generalized dislike for school (Eisenberg, Neumark-Sztainer, & Perry, 2003; Juvonen, Nishina, & Graham, 2000). It is only through rapid and effective intervention by adults in leadership and responsible positions within the school setting that such negative health and academic consequences can be mitigated.

A challenging irony that is infrequently addressed in most mobbings, including both school and workplace mobbings, is the fact that the victims are basically blamed for the sequence of negative events and are labeled as "difficult" or "troubled" and as the primary cause of the damaging consequences that have befallen them (Leymann, 1990, Leymann & Gustafsson, 1996). Such constructions of the victim as perpetrator in mobbings are similar to the experiences of women in the past, when they first began reporting rapes. In those early days of consciousness-raising about the need to protect women from being sexually victimized, rape victims who dared to report the crimes against them would have to defend themselves against suggestions that "they asked for it." In mobbing cases, when victims dare to speak out against the abusive behavior directed toward them, they can still expect to be vilified and either directly or indirectly labeled as the "cause" of their own problems. In exactly this way, in one of the early postings on Topix (2008, December 10 [Msg. 478]), Tatum Bass was blamed for what happened to her. The writer, who went by the handle "1catlover" stated, "Bullies and retards are just part of school life; public or private. Sounds like she is a spoiled cheater with no backbone (to me)!"

In summary, our definition and criteria for school mobbing seem to be fully met based on the stories of what happened to Tatum Bass as reported in the various news accounts summarized above. In the template below, we organize the events, based on these cited news accounts, into their respective component of our definition of school mobbing.

PERPETRATOR BEHAVIORS

1. The targeting of an individual or group of individuals within an organization.
   Tatum Bass was an individual targeted within her school, Miss Porter's.

2. Subjecting of that individual or group of individuals to a series of abusive and humiliating behaviors.
   Tatum Bass reportedly experienced months of tormenting on Facebook and abusive name-calling within the school.

PURPOSE OR INTENT

3. Designed to cast them in a negative light, destabilize them, create suspicion about their worth as members of the organization.
   The offensive names Tatum Bass was reportedly called included "You're retarded," and "you're stupid." Such names are designed to degrade, humiliate and inflict hurt—especially to developmentally vulnerable adolescents and to those with learning disabilities. Tatum Bass reportedly had been diagnosed with attention deficit disorder.

4. Ultimately, to either force them out of the organization or to render them as suspect and unworthy while remaining within the organization.
   Tatum Bass was reportedly both suspended and expelled from the school.

INVOLVEMENT OF GROUP AND ORGANIZATIONAL DYNAMICS

5. Mobbing is not about a lone individual or a small group of people acting alone.
   The mobbing was reportedly carried out by the group of senior girls known as the "Oprichniki."

6. Group dynamics and organizational involvement are always present to varying degrees.
   The "Oprichniki" were reputedly an elite group of senior girls whose function was to carry on the school's traditions. By recommending a multischool dance, Tatum Bass violated a school tradition and, apparently, became their target. School administration allegedly did not intercede on behalf of Tatum Bass, even though they reportedly were aware of the harassment to which she was being subjected.

7. Mobbing can never be understood by seeking out explanatory frameworks in terms of individual psychopathology alone.
   Tatum Bass turned herself in for using notes to cheat on a test, claiming that the months of emotional abuse had worn her down. Although cheating is an unacceptable behavior, it does not account for the reported behavior of the alleged perpetrators in subjecting Tatum Bass to months of verbal and cyber-abuse or in the perception by the student and her family of lack of administrative involvement in efforts to protect Tatum Bass from further harassment.

CONSEQUENCES FOR VICTIMS

8. Results of this typically protracted traumatizing experience are significant academic, health, and psychosocial losses or other negative consequences. Variability of individual responses to mobbing is related to factors of personal vulnerability to injury and resilience.

Tatum Bass took medical leaves, was suspended from school, and was ultimately expelled. She also reportedly suffered from overwhelming anxiety and emotional distress.

Group and Organizational Processes in School Mobbings: Where Are the Teachers and Administrators?

In school mobbings and, indeed, in many school bullyings, although the conventional wisdom holds that bullying is a dyadic relationship, the research does not bear this out. Because of the many locations in which bullying occurs across the school campus, including in the presence of teachers (cf., Harris, 2004) bullying is hardly a private affair. Almost always, bystanders are present who may be directly or indirectly involved in the bullying or mobbing. In a study by O'Connell, Pepler, and Craig (1999), the behavior of bullies was found to be reinforced by the passive looking on of their peers. This passive reinforcement occurred 54% of the time in their study. Twenty-one percent of the time, they found that other student observers of the bullying took on the behaviors of the bully and modeled the bullying behaviors, adding insult to injury. In almost three-quarters of the cases, bystander students played either a direct or indirect role in continuing the bullying or the mobbing. In only a quarter of the cases did observing peers try to do something— either to intervene on behalf of the victim or to distract the bully. Fekkes, Pijpers, and Verloove-Vanhorick (2005) stated that "bullying does not only occur between children who bully and those who are bullied, but is considered a group phenomenon in which other children participate" (p. 82). A similar view has been put forward by Juvonen and Graham (2004).

Among the most unsettling data relates to students' perceptions that administrators and teachers are not really interested in doing anything about the problem of bullying (Harris, 2004) and that if students did risk telling their teachers about being bullied, the situation would either remain unchanged or would get worse (Fekkes et al., 2005; Harris, 2004). Administrators and teachers represent the organizational component in school mobbing. They also are the potential first-responders in protecting children and adolescents from school mobbing and bullying.

There are both benign and callous reasons why a teacher or administrator might not be responsive when bullying is brought to his or her attention. A fascinating qualitative research study was conducted by Mishna in 2004. She conducted 15 interviews with five children in 4th and 5th grades who had experienced some form of bullying, and she conducted further interviews with one of their parents, their teachers, and a vice-principal and principal to obtain multiple perspectives about the experience of bullying. Mishna's findings are significant in helping to understand why school personnel and parents respond in ways that may look like they are ignoring the problem. Two teachers revealed their beliefs-in-action when one said "It's hard to know whether somebody constantly picked on is doing something to cause it." Another believed, "In some cases, victims seem to thrive on being victims" (Mishna, 2004, p. 238).

Mishna (2004) interprets these responses as instances of teachers having difficulty in defining bullying. An alternative and equally plausible explanation is that these responses are just another version of "blame the victim." The issue of power imbalance arises in Mishna's findings when one teacher states "It can be very hard to decide whether it really is a bullying situation, whether it's one up, one down, or 50–50" (p. 238). In this instance, the teacher seemed to be attempting to determine whether the incident was simply predictable conflict or something more serious, based on a possible power imbalance. The difficulty the teacher had was in trying to define what a power imbalance looked like in a real-world situation as opposed to in a hypothetical or training situation. A possible outcome of such uncertainty is doing nothing. The teachers' responses in Mishna's study seemed to be skewed in the direction of minimizing or normalizing the problem. Another example from her study was the teacher who believed that some children "make themselves victims by seeing bullying where it isn't" (p. 238).

A question that arises from Mishna's (2004) study is whether teachers receive training in how to respond to bullying and mobbing, and how effective the training is in helping teachers to stop it. In the case of the Mishna study, teachers were impeded from taking effective action by their embedded beliefs that they had to sort out who the victim and bully were before doing anything to help. Sorting out who is victimizing whom in a school bullying or mobbing situation may be straightforward, but it also may be quite complicated. The primary goal of timely intervention should be ensuring the safety of students who are perceived by themselves or others as victims of bullying or mobbing, without harming other students by prematurely labeling them as bullies or offenders. The territory is potentially treacherous, and mistakes can be made both by minimizing or ignoring the situation in the hopes that it will resolve itself or by prematurely labeling a student as a perpetrator. Existing research supports a rational basis for children believing that little or nothing will be done if they report bullying to their teachers (Fekkes et al., 2005; Harris, 2004; Mishna, 2004) and that victimization from bullying is under-reported, not over-reported (Hanish & Guerra, 2000; Sharp, 1996).

The Mishna (2004) study illustrates the responsibility that is placed in teachers' hands to determine whether and how to intervene in suspected cases of bullying. Failure to take action when action is required is a common organizational response (Atlas & Pepler, 1998; Batsche & Knoff, 1994). The involvement of the bully, the bystanders who are fueling the bullying (O'Connell et al., 1999), and the involvement of representatives of the adult school community who have moral, if not legal responsibilities to protect children from bullying, create multiple layers of group and organizational involvement well beyond the dyad of bully and perpetrator. For this reason, most school bullying is in fact school mobbing. That is not to say, however, that teachers and school administrators are lacking in concern about the problem of bullying. In most cases, teachers do not know what to do, do not know how to interpret and evaluate instances of alleged bullying or mobbing, initiate failed solution attempts that make matters worse by trying to assess and apportion blame, have little or no awareness of the seriousness of the consequences of bullying or mobbing, have little or no training in how to respond effectively to charges of bullying or mobbing, have little or no support from supervisors, and are members of school communities without school-wide anti-bullying and anti-mobbing programs.

Shifting from a Blaming to a Helping Standpoint

Teachers and school administrators, like parents, are at the vortex in instances of school mobbing and bullying. They are the first-responders. The research cited above suggests that teachers and school administrators are in urgent need of up-to-date information about school bullying and mobbing, and that they also need new skill sets that will allow them to address these problems by shifting from a "who is at fault here" position to a "how can we help the victim and prevent mob-bing/bullying in the future" position. Such a shift in mindset parallels the shift in public policy about drug crime scenes that has occurred in a few forward-thinking states. Under the old mindset, when police arrived at a crime scene involving illegal drugs, they would first ask "Who can we arrest here?" However, in New Mexico, which has high death rates from heroin abuse, a new mindset requires police arriving at the same crime scene involving illegal drugs to first ask "Whose life can we save here?" before moving on to the question "Who can we arrest here?" This change in viewpoint still includes accountability, but it places helping and saving lives first. It's a change that has made a life-saving difference, and we recommend that it be introduced into schools so that teachers, the first-responders in school settings, can likewise shift from first asking "Who is at fault?" to "What do I need to do to protect the victim?"

The Cyber-Mobbing and Death of Megan Meier

News of the Megan Meier story circulated rapidly around the world through print and broadcast media and through the Internet about a year after Megan's death by suicide, once family members began to tell her story in public. Megan was a 13-year-old teenager who hanged herself in her closet on October 16, 2006, and died the following day. Megan was a vulnerable young adolescent, who had been diagnosed with depression and attention deficit disorder a number of years earlier. She was also concerned about being overweight, and her mother reported that she had been bullied in school. Central to the event was the creation of a fake MySpace account in the name of "Josh Evans," a 16-year-old boy who, as it turned out, never existed. This fake MySpace account was created by the mother of a friend with whom Megan had had a falling out; and a young woman who worked for the friend's mother; Megan's former friend was also involved with the communications from the fake account (Pokin, 2007). For a month, the fake "Josh Evans" posted warm, caring messages to Megan on MySpace—messages like "You're beautiful," and "Your eyes are beautiful" (Tuchman, 2007). Almost as quickly as these warm, fuzzy messages began, enthralling to a vulnerable 13-year-old, their tone and content began to change. Messages like "Megan is fat," and "Megan is retarded" began appearing on MySpace. More nasty messages were sent to Megan on MySpace, and the ganging up had escalated to the point at which Megan was responding with foul language that upset her mother. Megan's father believes the last message that Megan read before she ran upstairs and hanged herself was the one from the fake "Josh Evans" claiming that he had heard she was not nice to her friends. Her father remembered the message as this: "Everybody in O'Fallon knows how you are. You are a bad person and everybody hates you. Have a shitty rest of your life. The world would be a better place without you" (Pokin, 2007).

Megan's mother and father were in the kitchen talking about the hostility toward Megan on MySpace when Megan's mother reported that she had a bad feeling, froze, ran upstairs, and found her daughter had hanged herself in the closet (Pokin, 2007). Within an hour of receipt of the final message, Megan had committed suicide (Patrick & Currier, 2008). It is a gut-wrenching experience to watch Megan's parents talking about those moments when they found their daughter and to hear her mother say that tears were rolling down Megan's cheeks while her father was trying to cut her down and give her CPR (Tuchman, 2007). Megan died the following day from the injuries she sustained.

The mother of Megan's friend who created the fake MySpace account, the friend herself, a temporary employee of the mother who carried out instructions to post messages from the fake "Josh Evans" account, and at least one other of Megan's peers, were all aware of the vicious hoax that was being perpetrated on Megan. Yet, it was not until 6 weeks after Megan's death and funeral that Megan's parents found out that "Josh Evans" never existed, that the whole MySpace account was a fraud, and that the messages were sent by the mother of Megan's friend and her employee. A neighbor, the mother of the other peer who had access to the "Josh Evans" account, coordinated a meeting at a counselor's office in which Megan's parents were told of the vicious hoax. That neighbor's daughter, Megan's peer, had access to the account; she sent one message to Megan from it and ultimately disclosed the whole sordid tale to her own mother (Pokin, 2007). A federal fraud statute was used to indict the woman who had masterminded the "Josh Evans" hoax (Patrick & Currier, 2008). In November, 2008, a federal jury convicted the woman who created the fake "Josh Evans" MySpace page of three misdemeanor charges of accessing computers without authorization (Weich, 2008). As a result of the Megan Meier tragedy, a Missouri law was enacted in 2008 that makes Internet stalking and harassment a felony when committed by adults aged 21 and over and a misdemeanor for those under 21 (Currier, 2008). The collateral damage from the Megan Meier tragedy is ongoing. Ron and Tina Meier have divorced. He has difficulty concentrating and maintaining focus; she is filled with guilt and blames herself (Pokin, 2007). Presumably, for those involved in the creation of the fake MySpace account and for those who knew about it and did nothing, the tragedy of Megan Meier also continues in some form.

The question must be raised about what schools in the area where Megan lived had been doing about the problem of bullying. In an interview reported on the popular website for young women "Jezebel," the Jezebel (2007, November 15) reporter called the school she believed Megan Meier had been attending and asked for confirmation if Megan Meier had attended the school, explained that her readers were very interested in the case, and asked what the schools were doing to teach kids how to stand up to bullies and what the schools were doing to help parents help their children deal with bullies. To each question, the school secretary reportedly answered that she couldn't say anything. Exasperated, the Jezebel reporter exclaimed "Don't you care?" The questions posed by the Jezebel reporter were critical ones. After the tragic cyber-bullying case of Megan Meier, the community needed more satisfying answers than "I can't say anything" to questions about what the school was doing to help prevent bullying.

There were certainly clear and powerful group dynamics involved in the mobbing of Megan Meier, including the involvement of adults. In her case, the school community was represented by those adults who involved other children in the mobbing and who were connected to the school as parents. The question of the role of the formal school organizations in the case of Megan Meier is unclear. There seems to be insufficient information about whether the schools and their representatives were aware of Megan Meier's vulnerability and the horrific abuse being perpetrated against her, although the alleged refusal of one school to answer questions about what it was doing organizationally to address bullying is puzzling. The collective accounts of the Megan Meier story also reveal a culture within the school community that overvalued popularity and undervalued concern for others, especially concern for vulnerable young people.

COMMENTARY ON SCHOOL MOBBING

Over 20 years have passed since Heinz Leymann's (Leymann, 1990; Leymann & Gustafsson, 1996) original work on mobbing. Through his astute observations and research, he noted how victims of mobbing ended up being labeled as troublemakers or the cause of their own problems. Labeling a mobbing victim as "difficult," "mean," or as "the proximate cause of their own problems" is a particularly pernicious aspect of mobbing, setting up a social double-bind from which escape is extremely difficult. Mobbing usually goes on for an extended period of time, and it has an erosive effect on the victim's personality—wearing the person down, inspiring mistrust of others, and increasing hypervigilance associated with continuously being on the lookout for further acts of aggression and abuse. Such reactions are not paranoid—they are rational, self-protective responses to ongoing physical and/or psychological abuse.

A young teenager who is being taunted and mocked by peers at school and over the Internet is already isolated and ostracized, even when at home. Thinking about going to school raises the unanswerable question of who is involved in the abuse. Is everyone? Only some people? How can he know or find out? Because the question is unanswerable, he takes the safest position: He assumes that many people are involved and he keeps to himself even more, thus providing "evidence" of his loner status and difficult personality, and thus promoting further abuse against him.

In the cases of Tatum Bass and Megan Meier described above, both were taunted with slurs based on their having been diagnosed with psychological disorders. Both Tatum Bass and Megan Meier had been diagnosed with attention deficit disorder previous to their experiences of school mobbing. Megan Meier had also been previously diagnosed with depression. Both were called "retarded," and Tatum was called "stupid" in spite of her excellent academic record. The abuse of information received either from the victim directly or through other sources about the victim's psychological or psychiatric history is repugnant. The use of psychiatric or psychological labels by peers to attack and damage another child's reputation during bullying and mobbing demonstrates the continuing cultural stigma associated with psychological problems and mental illness, even when the particular diagnoses used are quite common. Information that children share with each other about their own psychological diagnoses can become weapons of abuse during bullying and mobbing, leading to profound experiences of shame and humiliation in vulnerable victims. The words attributed in the police report (Pokin, 2007) to the mother who created the fake MySpace account also point to the ongoing cultural stigma associated with mental illness. The mother reportedly said that she didn't feel as guilty about what happened to Megan when she found out that Megan had tried to commit suicide before.

It should also be instructive in a cautionary way that both Tatum Bass and Megan Meier were effectively labeled as "bullies" during their mobbings. In the aftermath of all the publicity about Tatum Bass, she continued to be mobbed on Internet postings. The posting on the Internet forum Topix (2008, December 10 [Msg. 478]) quoted above labels Tatum as a bully. In some of the hateful messages crafted by the mobbers of Megan Meier, she was labeled as "mean," not an uncommon synonym among children and teens for a bully. Westhues (2005b) points out that calling someone a "bully" is a common form of mobbing in the academic world.

Mobbing includes both direct and indirect forms of aggression. We have arrived at a point in time when awareness of bullying is increasing, but understanding of its manipulative and contorted nature is still in the early stages. Most teachers and students have some concept of what "bullying" means. Very few will have been exposed to the term "mobbing" to describe a severe form of bullying that includes the relationship among individual, group, and organizational dynamics. In the cache of hostile behaviors that can be utilized to bully or mob someone, the act itself of labeling another as a "bully" is a highly potent and damaging hostile act that injects chaos and confusion into any search for understanding within a particular bullying or mobbing episode. It is a bitter irony that labeling someone a bully in the current climate will mobilize organizational responses in schools and workplaces more quickly than will detailed behavioral descriptions of the range of hostile acts perpetrated over time against a victim to hurt and wear them down. Thus, the act of calling another a bully must itself be scrutinized in terms of its potential use as a calculated and devious act of aggression.

ANALYSIS AND KEY POINTS

From our analysis of school mobbing and the cases of Tatum Bass and Megan Meier, any number of take-away lessons can be learned. The following list includes those that we consider compelling in any effort to more fully understand the nature of school mobbing.

- Mobbing is different from bullying, is more severe, and includes the interplay of individual, group, and organizational dynamics.
- Mobbing includes a range of hostile acts, some direct and overt, but many that are covert, devious, highly manipulative, and cumulative in their erosive effects over time.
- The consequences of school mobbing are potentially so severe that it is irresponsible for adults to dismiss bullying and mobbing behaviors as something that kids have to work out for themselves.
- Victims of school mobbings are frequently targeted by information they have shared with their peers about their psychological problems or psychiatric disorders. This is particularly true for adolescents.
- As in adult mobbings, children who are mobbed are doubly injured by being blamed as the cause of their own problems.
- Calling someone a "bully" may itself be an aggressive act of bullying or mobbing designed to rapidly mobilize organizational responses.
- An ethic of caring requires that adults with any knowledge of a mobbing or bullying of a child or adolescent take immediate and appropriate action to try and stop it.

We will discuss the implications of these lessons learned about school mobbings for intervention on behalf of victims, policy development, and school-wide intervention programs in later chapters.

Recognizing Mobbing in Community Organizations

In Chapter 1, and in many other chapters in this book, we provide detailed examples of workplace mobbing. We have looked at examples of school mobbing in Chapter 1 and in this chapter, and we will look at more examples of school mobbing in later chapters. In Chapter 1, we also looked at mobbing within the judicial system, in our discussion of the McMartin Preschool Abuse Scandal case. To illustrate the ubiquitousness of mobbing within organizations, the next case presented for consideration is one of a mobbing in a condominium association. Condominium and homeowners associations are generally established under state law as private, not-for-profit organizations (McCabe, 2005) governed not by an organizational chart but by the covenants, conditions, restrictions, and bylaws of the organization (Natelson, 1989). Voting rights in a condominium association are tied to property rights. Only those who are unit owners may belong to the condominium association and vote. A condominium association is an interesting organization in that its structure is informal, yet the leadership and organizational strategies have the potential for significantly impacting the daily lives of every resident. In short, a condominium association can be very powerful.

CONDO BOARD MATTERS

In a 20-year-old luxury condominium, the current condominium association board had been in office for a long time. Most of the 300 unit holders were retired and had multiple homes, although some still worked at their businesses or professions. After Hurricane Wilma cut a wide swath of destruction from west to central Florida to the lower Keys, some of the owners wanted to upgrade their windows to the new standards requiring a thicker, impact-resistant glass than was previously required. Because of its age, the condominium was grandfathered in and residents were not obliged to upgrade. When a resident applied to the board for approval to upgrade to the stronger, impact-resistant glass, the board found reasons to stall and delay approval even though, by law, they could not refuse the unit owner's request to meet the upgraded standards. When she received board approval, the unit owner went ahead and installed the new windows and doors at a cost of around $125,000. The board then found fault with the installation and harassed both the unit owner and installer. The whole experience was so unsettling and disturbing to the unit owner that she and two other residents decided to run for the board—the long-standing board—and they won, unseating three of the board members.

The original board members, together with a number of other unit holders, were not happy with the change in board composition and coalesced into a disgruntled group. The new board members had also been elected officers and therefore had the obligation of running board meetings. The disgruntled group disrupted board meetings by yelling, hollering, and proffering personal insults against the officers during the meetings, rendering it difficult or impossible for board business to be discussed. Many meetings had to be suspended and, on several occasions when contentious issues were on the agenda, police were hired to provide security during board meetings. Fewer and fewer residents attended the meetings, presumably wanting to minimize their exposure to the conflicts that were growing increasingly hostile. The new board wanted to institute board procedures that emphasized transparency and respect for good business practice, as well as respect for neighbors. For example, they wanted to institute a three-bid process for every board purchase of goods and services over a predetermined minimum. The new board also wanted to systematically identify problems with the building and have them repaired, in order to protect everybody's investments.

The members of the disgruntled group took turns waiting in the lobby area and, over a period of several weeks, told every resident they could find that the new board members were going to require every unit owner to install the thicker, impact-resistant windows and that the cost to the unit owners collectively would be approximately $40,000,000. This group also told the residents that the board members were going to fire the current management company and hire a much more expensive full-service one.

The problem was that none of this information was true. The new board members had no interest in imposing the upgraded hurricane window standard on all unit owners, nor did they have any interest in hiring new management. They were satisfied with the current management. The three board members were subject to a months long campaign of rumor mongering and personal and business-related attacks on their characters. None of them had ever experienced anything like it in their highly successful business lives. One of the new board members took it particularly hard—the board member who was still working and had not retired. The campaign against them culminated with a drive to recall the three board members. The disgruntled group was able to gather the required number of signatures to launch the recall drive and, after several more months, came within a few votes of success. The group was not successful in overthrowing the targeted board members through a legitimate election despite their campaign of spreading misinformation, scare-mongering, innuendo, and character assassination. In the end, however, they were successful for different reasons. Two of the board members quit in disgust and the third became too ill to continue her duties as a board member.

COMMENTARY ON CONDOMINIUM ASSOCIATION MOBBING

McCabe (2005), citing statistics from the Community Associations Institute, points out an under-reported fact; namely, that some 50 million people in the United States live under the rule of a homeowners or similar association and that homeowners associations outnumber cities 13 to 1. Condominium and homeowners associations are corporate entities operating like mini-governments and affecting the lives of increasing numbers of people each year. The sheer numbers of people living under the rule of condominium and homeowners associations makes them an important focus of analysis at many levels. Mollen (1999) acknowledges the magnitude of the problem of conflicts within condominium and similar associations and states:

> Conflicts arising from "occupancy relationships" ("occupancy conflicts") often evoke emotions of extreme hostility, bitterness, and frustration. Many parties to such disputes erupt into diatribes of emotionally charged words which exponentially expand and intensify the conflict. The printable vocabulary of occupancy conflicts often includes words like "livid," "vicious," "revenge," "fraud," "arrogant," "pompous," "power crazy," "breach of fiduciary duty," "self-dealing," "favoritism," "insensitive," "litigious," "stupid," and "troublemaker." Not only are occupancy conflicts extremely intense, but they are propagating with alarming rapidity. (p. 75)

The above list of terms used in occupancy conflicts contains a number of words commonly used in all kinds of mobbings to devalue and discredit the target/victim. The other words are the language of conflict and sometimes of mobbing that are more specific to condominium association mobbings. In utilizing our template to analyze the case of the condominium association mobbing, we find the following:

PERPETRATOR BEHAVIORS

1. The targeting of an individual or group of individuals within an organization.
   Three recently elected board members were targeted by a group of other condominium association members, including some who lost a recent board election. The conflict escalated into a mobbing when the focus shifted from the issue of upgrading windows to attacks on the persons of the board members.

2. Subjecting of that individual or group of individuals to a series of abusive and humiliating behaviors.
   The three individuals were subject to an orchestrated campaign of misinformation, personal slurs, and innuendo about their motives. They were also prevented from performing their job functions at board meetings by deliberate disruption and abusive name-calling.

PURPOSE OR INTENT

3. Designed to cast them in a negative light, destabilize them, create suspicion about their worth as members of the organization.

Scare tactics were used by the disgruntled group to cast the three targets in the most negative light possible. In addition, personal and professional slurs and innuendo were also used to devalue the victims and their contributions to the board.

4. Ultimately, to either force them out of the organization or to render them as suspect and unworthy while remaining within the organization.
   The disgruntled group led a recall campaign (which was perfectly legal) to remove the three board members. They came within a handful of votes of succeeding legitimately. The mobbing succeeded in removing two of the victims from the board, who quit in disgust. The other board member became too ill to continue in her role, leaving an open question about the impact of the stress of being mobbed on her health.

INVOLVEMENT OF GROUP AND ORGANIZATIONAL DYNAMICS

5. Mobbing is not about a lone individual or a small group of people acting alone.
   The disgruntled group acted in concert, planning their activities in a strategic way.

6. Group dynamics and organizational involvement are always present to varying degrees.
   The group actively sought to influence and involve as many other condominium association members as they could, some of whom later expressed regret about being taken in by the disgruntled group and believing them.

7. Mobbing can never be understood by seeking out explanatory frameworks in terms of individual psychopathology alone.
   An analysis of the personalities of both the perpetrators and victims would have yielded almost nothing of value in understanding the condominium mobbing and its consequences.

CONSEQUENCES FOR VICTIMS

8. Variability of individual responses to mobbing is related to factors of personal vulnerability to injury and resilience.
   The victims had a difficult time believing what had happened during the mobbing. As highly successful business owners and professionals, they all said they had never experienced anything like it before. They were disgusted. One felt more personally assaulted and hurt than the others. One became seriously ill during the mobbing.

In a community-based organization, such as in this condominium association, all of the elements of our definition of a mobbing were fully met. Although mobbings occur frequently in workplaces and schools, they also occur in community-based organizations like homeowners and condominium associations, demonstrating that mobbings can and do happen in wide array of organizations.

Conclusion

Although mobbing is most frequently described in workplaces, it is not limited to them. Schools and a wide variety of other organizations, such as condominium and homeowners associations, are also at risk for the emergence of mobbing. Mobbing is recognizable by its consistent set of characteristic elements. The targeting of an individual or group of individuals within an organization and the subjecting of that individual or group of individuals to a series of abusive and humiliating behaviors are the characteristic perpetrator behaviors. The intent of mobbing is to cast the target/victims in a negative light, destabilize them, and create suspicion about their worthiness as members of the organization. The ultimate goal in many mobbings is the removal of the target/victim from the organization or the neutralizing of the target/victim's influence within it. Unlike bullying, mobbing takes place within a context of group and organizational dynamics and is not the behavior of a lone individual or a small group of people acting alone in the absence of organizational complicity.

The case of the condo association mobbing is an excellent example of how mobbing can never be explained or understood in terms of individual psychopathology alone. In the case of Megan Meier, in which the involvement of the formal school organization was unclear from published accounts, what is not unclear is the inference that can be drawn from the horrific events about the premium placed on the value of popularity within the culture of the school and school community. Although individual factors may have predisposed Megan Meier to greater vulnerability in her responses to being mobbed, those factors do not account for her being abused, nor do they mitigate the power of the value of popularity under whose influence a number of members of the school community operated. The case of Tatum Bass also appears to meet the elements of our definition of mobbing, leaving her expelled from her school and apparently traumatized by the alleged sequence of abusive events. In subsequent chapters, additional case examples from workplaces and schools will be described to continue the process of illustrating what mobbing is and how it unfolds. Later chapters will also address individual and organizational recovery from mobbing and prevention strategies.

Part Two

HOW MOBBING DEVELOPS

5

Organizational Dynamics

Effective mobbing requires, eventually, the collaboration of a person's coworkers with the workplace managers.
—John Bolt (2005, p. 100)

In this section, we turn our attention from understanding, defining, and recognizing mobbing to looking at its causes. Understanding the causes of mobbing is a relatively new area of scholarship, but one that is being addressed by researchers and other scholars interested in developing meaningful frameworks for understanding how mobbing develops and proceeds within an organization. In this chapter, we review several antecedents of mobbing at the organizational level. We also refer to them as potential risk factors for mobbing. In Chapter 6, we will review the group, individual, and leadership antecedents of mobbing and the characteristics of organizations that are not mobbing-prone. In Chapter 7, we will examine organizational development longitudinally and identify the stages of development that exist when the organization and corresponding leadership style are most conducive to the emergence of mobbing.

Although still in its early stages, the development of theoretical frameworks for explaining mobbing serves to emphasize the complexity of the social process of mobbing and encourage dialogue and theory development that accounts for it. These models and the ensuing discussion of organizational antecedents of mobbing can be utilized to understand workplaces, schools, and, indeed, any institution. Lutgen-Sandvik and McDermott's (2008) communication flows model was developed to understand employee-abusive workplace organizations, but it also provides a framework that we believe could be used as an analytic model for understanding schools and other institutions.

Models of Mobbing

We begin our discussion of the causes of mobbing by reviewing four theoretical models from different disciplines that offer sound possibilities for understanding the complex phenomenon of mobbing, irrespective of the type of organization or institution within which mobbing takes place. In the first model, we utilize a recent study of bullying victims in the public service sector (Strandmark, Lillemor, & Hallberg, 2007) to demonstrate a conflict model of mobbing. *Conflict models* are most associated with sociological perspectives. The second model we present is a *cybernetic model* of mobbing that draws from the richly explanatory frameworks provided by the field of cybernetics to explain how systems, including complex systems like organizations, maintain and reproduce themselves. In the third model, we look at the *communication flow framework* of Lutgen-Sandvik and McDermott (2008). This model arises from communications theory and focuses on how discursive patterns within an organization reciprocally shape both the organization and its members. The fourth model we examine is the *antecedent, behavior, consequences or A-B-C model* used frequently in psychology to identify antecedents of behavior and the consequences of that behavior. Model building is an important step in theory development, and we present these models with the intention of summarizing current explanatory frameworks for understanding how mobbing develops and proceeds and for encouraging further investigation and discussion of how mobbing unfolds and what causes it.

Conflict Model of Mobbing

A recent qualitative study (Strandmark et al., 2007) examined how mobbing was initiated in the workplace. It found that workplace reorganization gave rise to conflict over values, which resulted in power struggles. Characteristics of the abuse-prone workplaces studied were lack of decisional control, weak or passive leadership, betrayed expectations, and role confusion. Together, these conditions created a work environment in which deep professional and personal values conflicts arose. These values conflicts further compounded ongoing cognitive and affective conflicts.

So, what were these values conflicts? These conflicts often involved differing ways of viewing or relating to customers, patients, clients, or students. For example, most members of a sales team might view customers as basically exploitable, whereas another team member might find such a standpoint offensive and want all customers to be treated with genuine respect. Or, most teachers on a faculty might believe that students learn best when the environment is structured with specific expectations, whereas one or two other faculty members are convinced that kids learn best in an unstructured environment without overly determined learning objectives and expectations. A values struggle may then arise among these individuals, in which both sides believe that its ways of thinking and working are the best ones, thus further escalating conflicts within the work group.

The research (Strandmark et al., 2007) identified two differing profiles of workers who were likely to become mobbing targets. The first profile included individuals self-described as strong, competent, and driven, while the second profile included individuals self-described as vulnerable and sensitive. Both perceived that they were out of compliance with the norms and values of their work teams. They disregarded the unspoken expectations and rules of their workgroups. As a result of differing values and deviation from team norms, these individuals were regarded as threatening to other team members and became targets. A struggle for power began when efforts to resolve these values conflicts failed. The fights that followed were attempts to decide who would prevail. It was found that when values conflicts were solved, the power struggle ebbed, but when these values conflicts remained unsolved, the gap widened between the targeted individual and that person's opponents. Although the targeted individual occasionally would gain power over his or her opponents, it was more likely that opponents overpowered the targeted individual. The researchers found that if the conflict remained unsolved, the gap widened between the targeted individuals and opponents, resulting in the beginning of the mobbing process. If the struggle continued, systematic and persistent mobbing ensued. Only after the target left or was forced from the organization did the mobbing cease within that organization, at least temporarily.

The model that resulted from this study is characterized as a conflict model, in which a conflict over basic values results in a power struggle that, if continued, leads to mobbing. An important finding of this study was that, if and when the values conflicts were "resolved," either by the individual capitulating to group pressure or because a compromise was reached, mobbing did not occur. In other words, mobbing began and continued until the conflict was ultimately resolved, usually with severe, deleterious consequences to the mobbing target.

In his original and classic research, Leymann (1990) also identified work conflict as the triggering factor in cases of mobbing. He said, "as regards the investigated situations, it is known that the triggering situation most often observed is a conflict (usually over work)" (p. 121). Leymann then described the predictable stages resulting from the escalation of the original work conflict. Those stages were discussed earlier in Chapter 2. It is important to note, however, that Leymann saw the initial conflict resulting in a mobbing as widening to include multiple layers of the organization, in particular, administration or management.

Cybernetic Model of Mobbing

Although they do not characterize it as such, Strandmark, Lillemor, and Hallberg (2007) have provided a theoretical basis for a cybernetic view of mobbing. In their escalating conflict model, mobbing can be understood as a difference or deviation-minimizing strategy to return the workgroup or organization back to the status quo by eliminating the perceived source of the threat or conflict. In cybernetics, negative feedback is information fed through a system, such as an organization, that results in minimizing deviations from a baseline. In a difference- or conflict-averse organization, mobbing can be a successful strategy to return an organization to its baseline position of intolerance of conflict, dissent, or questioning. Understanding an organization's baseline requires understanding how it balances its strategies, structure, culture, leadership, members, and the external environment. These organizational elements are discussed in detail in this chapter.

An important concept in cybernetics that can be applied to organizations is the concept of *autopoiesis* (Maturana & Varela, 1998). Autopoiesis refers to the way that the parts of a system—for example, strategies, structure, culture, leadership, members, and the external environment—interact with each other and define each other. Autopoiesis also refers to the way in which a living or social system reproduces itself. As it maintains and regenerates itself, the organization as an autopoietic system is always pulling itself back to its baseline or status quo through negative (deviation-minimizing) feedback. What this essentially means for mobbing-prone organizations is that they are most likely to reproduce themselves as mobbing-prone because of the interrelationships among their core elements and the difficulties involved in changing both the element itself and the relationships among them.

Hostile organizations in which employees consistently experience lack of transparency and openness, fear of job loss, favoritism and unfairness, few opportunities for advancement, and fear of the consequences of speaking out or taking a stand will reproduce themselves over long periods of time as hostile organizations with the same features. Negative feedback that pulls an organization back toward its baseline or status quo and engenders reproduction of itself is very powerful. That is not to say that change is impossible, but change is difficult and requires an understanding of systemic interrelatedness and identification of high leverage points at which intervention is most likely to help a system move in a new direction.

Without effective intervention, therefore, hostile organizations will reproduce themselves as hostile organizations. For mobbing-prone organizations, intervention at the leadership level is a high leverage point, given that the function of leadership is that of directing an organization. Strategies and structure are also potential high leverage points. Culture is a low leverage point because it so powerfully reflects the other organizational elements. Members are a very low leverage point because of the constraints on members provided by other interacting organizational elements. Successful interventions at high leverage points in an organization have the effect, analogously, of pushing an organization out of an existing orbit into another orbit, ideally a more member-tolerant and supportive one.

Communication Flows Model of Mobbing

Lutgen-Sandvik and McDermott (2008) have developed a communication flows model of what they refer to as "employee-abusive organizations." Their model is based on the reciprocally constitutive nature of human communications and how such communications generate shared meanings within particular conversational domains, including those of organizations. Their model provides the means of tracking abusive and hostile messages within the communications networks of members of organizations and illustrates how those communications shape the organization's culture into an abusive one.

Lutgen-Sandvik and McDermott's (2008) model consists of the following seven basic propositions:

- Two or more abusive message flows are indicative of employee-abusive organizations.
- Employee-abusive organizations are more likely to develop when leadership participates in or condones hostile communications.
- When civility in discourse is widely breached by multiple members within the organization, employee-abusive organizations are more likely to develop.
- When cultural norms of competition, individualism, and aggression are embedded in the dominant discourse of the organization, it is more likely to be an employee-abusive one.
- The longer hostile communications persist over time, the more hostile an employee-abusive organization is likely to become.
- Employee-abusive organizations always produce negative outcomes for members and stakeholders.
- Employee-abusive organizations can change, but only with the commitment and leadership of upper management.

Consider this example, which is relevant to most of Lutgen-Sandvik and McDermott's (2008) propositions above. Gossip is a primary form of hostile communications within organizations and can ultimately have a significantly erosive effect. Gossip is insidious in that it often begins with light-hearted jokes or barbs about another person but can progress into outright defamation. For example, in a hostile organization that supported gossip, a member publicly called another member an execrable name and made an abusive nonverbal gesture when the target member passed in the hallway. When the target reported the hostile behavior to the supervisor in charge, the supervisor made a note on the memo from the target who had requested help to tell the offender to just ignore the target, revealing the supervisor's bias, favoritism, and tolerance for such abuse. In effect, the abusive communication was condoned, and the offender's behavior reinforced. That an organizational employee would feel free to act with impunity and publicly refer to another employee using execrable language along with making an abusive physical gesture is astounding enough. That the offender would simply be told by the supervisor to ignore the target without being counseled about the difference between appropriate and inappropriate communications is illustrative of the condoning of uncivil discourse by an organization's leadership.

Commitment to positive organizational change requires acknowledging the problem as an organizational one and rejecting the "bad apple" or "asshole in the workplace" stance (Sutton, 2007)—first-order solutions that do not work. Lutgen-Sandvik and McDermott (2008) provide an intriguing framework for looking at the discursive practices of an employee-abusive organization and for using an analysis of them to understand the degree and complexity of an organization's hostile and abusive culture. The model, in its current formulation, emphasizes top-down forms of abusiveness. We believe that it could be expanded to also include bottom-up and lateral forms of abusiveness.

ABC Model of Mobbing

A simple process model of individual and organizational behavior, called the A-B-C model (Boyce & Geller, 2001), offers another view of the process of mobbing. In this model, an antecedent (A) is a trigger or stressor that precedes a behavior (B). A consequence (C) is an event that follows a given behavior and that strengthens, maintains, or extinguishes the behavior. Another way of saying this is that antecedents trigger specific behaviors while consequences motivate those behaviors. This three-component model has been found to be helpful in conceptualizing and predicting mobbing behavior and in designing interventions to respond to incidents of mobbing and in preventing them (LaVan & Martin, 2008).

Chapters 2, 3, and 4 have already described the B or mobbing behavior component of this model. This chapter and Chapters 6 and 7 focus on the antecedent component of mobbing, while Chapters 8, 9, and 10 will focus on the consequence component of mobbing. In addition to our account of organizational antecedents of mobbing, Hoel and Salin (2003) also take the view that organizational abuse is complex and multidimensional and provide a review of research addressing organizational antecedents. We begin with the organizational antecedents, given that each of the four models of mobbing described above focuses primarily on the organizational level, thus reinforcing the notion that the "bad apple" view of organizational abusiveness is oversimplistic, atomistic, and fails dismally to account for the key elements at work in the social process of mobbing.

Organizational Dynamics

Organizational dynamics refers to the interplay of influences among an organization's subsystems or dynamics. An organization can be visualized as a set of five overlapping, concentric circles, wherein each circle represents the dynamics of an organization: structure, culture, strategy, leaders, and members within a larger circle representing the organization's external environment (Sperry, 1996b). Each of these six dynamics is briefly described.

STRATEGY

Strategy refers to the organization's overall plan or course of action for achieving its identified goals. Corporate strategy is based on the organization's core values, vision, and mission statements. The organization's statement of core values answers the question: "What are the basic values that guide the organization?" The vision statement answers the question "What can the organization become, and why?" whereas the mission statement answers the question "What business are we in, and who is our customer?" Strategy answers the "how do we do it" question (Sperry, 1996b). Strategic planning and implementation is essential for organizations in achieving their goals by effectively organizing their people. A major challenge is to link their business strategies with the ways in which personnel are managed. Just as a business plan describes targeted business goals and results in measurable terms, "people plans" project people "results" in measurable terms. Organizations with people plans generally utilize "high-commitment" strategies (Pfeffer, 2007) that emphasize ongoing training and development of personnel, job security, and decentralized decision-making to allow for greater control.

Targeted people goals can be specified just as targeted business goals are specified. An example of a targeted business goal is, "We will increase our market share by 15%." An example of a targeted people goal is, "90% of our employees will rate their supervisors as good or excellent on showing respect to subordinates." Whether organizational people goals are achieved can be articulated, quantified, and assessed through surveys, interviews, or formal third-party observations. For organizations that attend to people goals, outcomes will be manifested in increased job productivity, satisfaction, and morale instead of complaints of mobbing or bullying. Pfeffer (2007) states that "a truly enormous body of research from a number of countries shows that how people are managed affects quality, profitability, productivity, and total return to shareholders" (p. 119).

By attempting to incorporate both a "people plan" and a "business plan" in the corporate strategy, corporate leadership may need to change past management practices that resulted in high levels of stress, distrust, dissatisfaction, or abusive behaviors. The goal of integrating both plans is to achieve a reasonable balance and synergy between people and production. A basic axiom is that structure should follow strategy, which is to say that the structure of an organization should be designed to be compatible with its strategy. Today, the strategy of most corporations is geared toward increased productivity and competitiveness. Needless to say, such a strategy—and a compatible structure—is a recipe for increased abusiveness in the workplace.

STRUCTURE

Structure refers to those mechanisms that aid an organization in achieving its intended task and goals. The task is divided into smaller person-sized jobs or roles that are grouped and clustered into larger units labeled teams, departments, or divisions. Structure specifies the reporting relationship of all roles, their span of control and scope of authority, and their location in a hierarchy of roles (i.e., an organizational chart). It also specifies the expectations of each role along with policies, procedures, and routines for interacting and communicating with others in the performance of the task. Roles prescribe the boundaries of acceptable behavior for a particular job, while norms define group behavior. Norms are the unwritten but widely shared expectations about what constitutes appropriate behavior in an organization (Sperry, 1996b).

A key component of an organization's structure is its policies and procedures. Unlike norms, policies and procedures are written documents that specify how the day-to-day duties of the organization are carried out and by whom. Having an adequate set of organizational policies and procedures is like flying on autopilot— most situations encountered by organizational personnel are automatically covered by policies and related procedures and therefore render formal decision-making by personnel unnecessary. Because the internal and external environment of the organization continues to change, new policies or revisions of existing policies are needed. For example, federal laws pertaining to sexual harassment led to the addition of anti–sexual harassment policies in employee handbooks throughout corporate America.

Another element of structure involves the hierarchical layers or levels within an organization. Bureaucratic organizations may have four or more hierarchical levels ranging from entry-level workers to top management or the executive level, whereas flatter and nonbureaucratic organizations may have as few as two layers. Certain types of abusiveness are more likely to occur at given levels of an organization. For example, although teasing and goading, name-calling, physical contact, or overt accusations may occur at any level of the organization, it is more common at lower levels. In the middle levels of the organization, abusiveness tends to manifest as attacks on professional or managerial skills and abilities, and is often accompanied by political maneuvering to discredit others. On the other hand, abusiveness at the executive level tends to be much more subtle and exclusionary (Sperry, 1998; Tigrel & Kokalan, 2009). Depending on the level of the organization, abusiveness can function as a means of degrading, controlling, discrediting, or eliminating an individual.

In addition, abusiveness is a means by which coworkers test and determine their status relative to one another. For instance, the new worker joining an organization is generally an unknown entity. He or she usually arrives via the personnel department, knowing few, if any, coworkers. Seldom have these workers been interviewed or selected by those coworkers. In some instances, abusiveness is part of a workgroup's "initiation rite." Often, an "initiation ritual" is deeply ingrained in established workgroups. Such abusiveness and harassment unifies them as the "ingroup" and makes them feel stronger and more secure (Brodsky, 1976).

One of the most tangible structural components of an organization is a given job. Several aspects of a job that can trigger abusiveness include occupational selection, standards of productivity, work and job pressure, and stress, as well as role conflict, ambiguity, and overload. Certain occupations and organizations are inherently more abusive or aggressive than others. This is particularly the case with police officers and police departments, or for that matter with football players and football teams. One does not become a police officer by mere chance. Becoming socialized in a career involves a process of self-selection as well as group selection. Accordingly, a young male with lower-middle-class roots who is both aggressive and conventional is more likely to seek a position on the force than is a shy, intellectually oriented middle-class college student. The nature of police work allows for the expression of a certain amount of abusiveness in the service of the law, and at the same time encourages the containment of abusiveness through a highly structured organization that respects lawfulness and order. Police work fits the psychological needs of the more aggressive and conventional individual, and such persons quite naturally gravitate toward it. Should individuals find during police training and early duty that the work is not satisfying or that they are somehow incompatible with fellow officers, they will either be weeded out or quit. The result is that a police force is a relatively homogeneous group of individuals who have much in common with each other and who are distinctly different from other occupational groups, such as clerical workers (Sperry, 1998).

Defined standards of productivity can also foster abusive behavior. Increased demands for productivity lead to work pressure that can result in abusiveness. Productivity standards are utilized in business because they provide an objective standard against which to measure an employee's work behavior or a work team's outputs. Accordingly, a worker may be slow or sloppy and become a target for abusiveness by supervisors (Brodsky, 1976). Or, a worker may be too productive and become a target for abusive behavior by coworkers for being a rate buster. It is easy to forget that characterizations of worker output as slow or as rate busting are relational or systemic phenomena, not individual characteristics—they can only be understood in relation to the organization's standards and norms for productivity.

Work pressure refers to externally imposed work demands or pressures exerted on employees to achieve maximum productivity. Increasingly, the private sector is based on maximization of profits through high productivity. The demand, therefore, is for workers to increase production so that the organization can become even more competitive. Work pressure results and is an inherent tension within a production system. Work pressure is experienced as threatening because workers realize that they may lose rewards or control over their environment and that punishment may be imposed if they fail to measure up. Such punishments might be threats, reprimands, transfers to lesser jobs, dismissal, or disruption of friendship patterns (Brodsky, 1976).

Job Strain

An individual's job may be the source of incredible satisfaction and challenge, or it can be the source of dissatisfaction and debilitating distress. Job demand and decisional control are two factors in the job strain model developed by Karasek and Theorell (1990). Job strain is defined as the short-term physiological, psychological, and behavioral manifestations of stress resulting from a job in which psychological demands are high and control over the job is low. All job classifications can be thought of in terms of the degree of demand and control. Essentially, the demand–control model articulates two levels of high and low demand and two levels of high and low control.

Low-strain jobs are those characterized by low demand and high control. Telephone linemen and machinists would be considered low-strain jobs. In contrast, high-strain jobs are characterized by high demand and low control. Assembly workers and telephone operators would be considered high-strain jobs. However, even though job demands are high, the extent to which workers can make decisions about how to plan and execute their jobs "attenuates the extent of stress" and impairment they experience. For example, a study of over 5,000 Swedish and American men found that the lower tenth of workers in terms of having low job control, were five times more likely to develop heart disease than were the top tenth of the workplace hierarchy who had the greatest control over their job (Karasek & Theorell, 1990).

Job strain is reported among occupants in a wide range of jobs and professions. Let's take the example of school teachers and counselors. Although some school systems permit teachers and counselors some degree of decisional latitude with their high-demand job duties, other school systems allow little or no decisional latitude. The result is that school personnel in high-demand/low-control settings are more likely to experience significant physical and emotional symptoms (Santavirta, Solovieva, & Theorell, 2007). Sleep disturbances are also more common in teachers with high job strain (Cropley, Derk-jan, & Neil, 2006).

What about job strain and mobbing? In a large national sample of 24,486 French workers, it was found that job strain and mobbing had significant effects on the health and well-being of workers. Specifically, high job strain, low levels of social support, and workplace mobbing were found to be risk factors for poor health, long sickness absence, and work injury (Niedhammer, Chastang, & David, 2008).

CULTURE

Culture refers to the constellation of shared experiences, beliefs, assumptions, stories, customs, and actions that characterize an organization. The major determinants of culture are the values manifested by senior executives, the history of the corporation, and the senior executive's vision of the organization. These translate into culture through the shared experiences, memories, stories, and actions of employees. The corporate culture provides a guide to action for new situations and for new employees. Culture is to the organization what personality and temperament are to the individual (Sperry, 1996b). Thus, culture defines an organization's identity both to those inside and outside the organization. In their classic work, Deal and Kennedy (1982) list five aspects of culture: corporate relations or business environment, manifestation of corporate values, corporate heroes, corporate rules and rituals, and the "secret" network—the rumor mongers, spies, cliques, and whisperers that form the "hidden hierarchy of power" in the organization. The culture of a corporation may be difficult to describe in words, but everyone senses it. It gives an organization its unique "flavor" and essentially it's "just the way we do things around here."

The culture subsystem subtly controls workplace behavior. Accordingly, management can significantly influence employee behavior by effectively managing the organization's culture. Stable organizations have strong, clear cultures that are consistent with other subsystems. Although the general character of an organization's culture tends to remain the same, its manifestations may be healthy and functional or unhealthy and dysfunctional. In a fascinating analysis of postcommunist countries, the cultural avoidance of uncertainty or ambiguity, and collectivist cultures that emphasized group loyalty and ingroup/outgroup formations rather than valued individuality and difference, and cultures with high power distances between those with power and authority and those without it (i.e., high bureaucratized, vertical cultures) were associated with the emergence of dark or destructive leaders (Hofstede, 1991; Luthans, Peterson, & Ibrayeva 1998; Padilla, Hogan, & Kaiser, 2007). We suggest that this same analysis translates directly to organizations that are mobbing-prone and accurately describes certain types of military, religious, and educational organizations.

Sometimes, corporate culture is relatively easy to detect, as with the Microsoft Corporation. Microsoft is located on the outskirts of Seattle on an outwardly serene campus that belies the hard-core, driven professionals that work there. 8 AM on any morning of the week will find the parking lots nearly full. "Ten hours later, as many people will be going into their offices as out. The cafeterias are open until midnight on a discount meal plan. 'Anything with caffeine is free'" (Meyer, 1994, p. 40). At Microsoft, coworkers are likely to be one's best friends because Microsoft is more a way of life than a job. People work hard because they want to and because they find it exciting.

But, at other times, corporate culture is much more difficult to detect. The reader might wonder why core values are being discussed as part of corporate culture when they were previously described as part of corporate strategy. It is important to distinguish between "stated" core values and "actual" core values. Unfortunately, too often there is a disconnect between stated and actual or manifested core values; between what an organizations says it values and what values are actually experienced by the organization's personnel and its customers. The greater the discrepancy between stated and actual values, the greater the confusion and distress for personnel. For instance, a new employee who joined an organization thinking that the organization's stated values of integrity and putting employees and customers first may become quickly disillusioned to find that the organization is primarily profit-driven and that some managers are being investigated for corruption. In mobbing-prone organizations, the gap between espoused and actual values is wide. This gap creates troubling cognitive dissonance for organizational members who hear their leaders saying one thing and see them doing the opposite.

The culture and climate of an organization may be sufficiently offensive, intimidating, or hostile that it interferes with the ability of certain workers to perform their jobs effectively. Some organizations that have been traditionally male, such as fire and police departments, as well as construction, mining, and forestry companies, have been the subject of sexual harassment and job discrimination litigation. Usually, this occurs in organizations in which male employees have resented the forced introduction of women or minorities into their job ranks as a result of legislation or policy change. These organizations often have cultures that have acquired characteristics that are offensive to women or minorities. These may include the posting of calendars with pictures of nude women, the telling of off-color or ethnic jokes, or the use of offensive language. Such an atmosphere would be considered hostile by most women or minorities, and as such creates an additional burden of stress and anxiety for them (Friedland & Friedland, 1994).

Sometimes, the culture of the organization is downright deadly. In early 2009, the Department of Defense and the armed services reported that the suicide rate of servicemen and -women had risen sharply in the past few years. At least 128 Army soldiers took their own lives in 2008, an estimated suicide rate of 20.2 per 100,000, which represented a sharp increase from the 2007 rate of 16.8 per 100,000. This was the first time in nearly 30 years that the Army rate had exceeded the civilian suicide rate of 19.5 per 100,000. What was the explanation given for this increase? Cindy Williams, an expert on military personnel systems, said that reporting a mental condition is inconsistent with the military culture that says soldiers don't ever get ill, the so-called "I'm okay" culture. "Even if the Army wants to change the culture, it is hard for a soldier to go to a supervisor and say 'I am thinking suicidal thoughts,'" she reported (Barnes & Chong, 2009).

Performativity versus Creativity Culture
The federal government and a number of states are endeavoring to increase accountability in public school systems through such initiatives as the No Child Left Behind Act and mandatory achievement testing programs such as the FCAT in Florida. Basic to these initiatives is what can be called the *performativity culture*. The performativity culture seeks to raise standards in schools and to develop a highly skilled workforce that can compete in the world economy. It relies on the learning and assessment of basic academic skills and competencies through incentives, control, and rewards and sanctions. The *creativity culture*, by contrast, seeks to involve young people as both spectators and participants in creativity and to enable all young

people to "find their talent." It relies on exposure to the arts and on teachers who utilize innovation in teaching all content areas. A necessary tension arises among those involved in learning and teaching when a school district requires both performativity and creativity. The tension in attempting to include creative learning with performative policies finds some teachers frozen, as if blinded by headlights, unsure whether they should innovate, take risks and foster creativity, or emphasize skills and accountability (Duffy, Giordano, Farrell, Paneque, & Crump, 2008).

LEADERSHIP

Leadership refers to a process of influence whereby a leader persuades, enables, or empowers others to pursue and achieve the intended goals of the organization (Sperry, 1996a; Sperry, 2002). Leadership and management are similar, but differ. Management involves the five functions of planning, organizing, staffing, directing, and controlling, whereas leadership emphasizes the directing function (Sperry, 2004). An effective leader can create a vision that tells members where the corporation is going and how it will get there, and then galvanizes members' commitment to the vision by being ethical, open, empowering, and inspiring (Bennis & Nanus, 1986). Needless to say, good leaders must be good managers and vice versa (Jaques & Clement, 1991). Furthermore, the leadership subsystem plays a critical role in shaping themes that harmonize the subsystems of structure, culture, and strategy (Kets de Vries & Miller, 1984).

It has been said that the personality of a strong leader can significantly influence all aspects of an organization (Sperry, 2002). Bill Gates, the founder of the Microsoft Corporation, and Microsoft is a good illustration of this principle. Gates has been described as an empire builder with unbridled ambition rather than as an innovator or technology expert (Meyer, 1994). He is portrayed as obsessed with the technology industry and Microsoft's place in it, and is a person of extraordinary intensity. Not surprisingly, Gates' personality has significantly shaped the strategy, structure, and culture of the Microsoft Corporation. "Microsoft is made in Gates' image: raw, confrontational, aggressive, fast, creative, organized, and impatient" (Meyer, 1994, p. 40).

For abusiveness to occur in an organization, the aggressive elements must exist within a culture that permits and rewards abusiveness, and leadership must allow or permit the abusiveness. Accordingly, both the type and degree of abusiveness are a function of the extent to which there is a pervading sense of "permission to act abusively" on the part of the abuser(s) (Sperry, 1998). Abusiveness in the work setting requires some level of acquiescence by management. Typically, supervisors tacitly support one worker's abuse of another by looking the other way or failing to discipline the perpetrator(s). Other times, supervisors participate in or initiate the abusive behavior. Occasionally, a superior may know of a lower-level supervisor's harassment of employees, but will not intervene, believing that to put an end to it would undermine that supervisor's authority (Brodsky, 1976).

Consider the following example of leadership condoning hostile communications. An anonymous letter sent to the chief operating officer of an organization scurrilously attacked an employee by stating that the person was known to drink heavily and be prone to violent and unpredictable behavior and that the employee lived out of wedlock. The letter was disseminated widely within the upper leadership of the organization and was then sent to a middle manager who was charged with responding to it. The middle manager said that there was no evidence of workplace drunkenness or violence and that who the employee lived with was not known. When responding, the middle manager also included a statement expressing concern that such anonymous, scurrilous correspondence was addressed and attended to by the organization and that the distribution of the anonymous letter multiplied the original defamation. The outcome was that the middle manager was chastised verbally by the chief operating officer for "lecturing" the organization and, unbeknownst to the middle manager, the written response was placed in his personnel file as evidence of unacceptable outspokenness and "uppitiness." Such communication flows are illustrative of leadership participating in hostile communications and, further, of branding and punishing an organizational member who challenged their practices—the quashing of dissent. The degree to which an organization's leadership is invested in creating files of alleged negative behaviors about employees and communicating informally to managers that they should save materials that could later be used against an employee is indicative of rampant organizational hostility.

Because of the nuanced nature of mobbing, organizational abusiveness can also be directed toward the highest levels of leadership within an organization. Mobbing, as we have already described, is not only a top-down phenomenon, although top-down mobbing is among its more common forms. Mobbing is multidirectional and includes lateral and bottom-up forms. In Chapter 11, we describe the health outcome of the mobbing of a university president. In another instance of high-level mobbing, the president of the board of a nonprofit organization that shared goods and services with a private organization was mobbed and demoted as a result of insisting that business negotiations between the two entities be open and transparent. Although more top-down mobbing than lateral or bottom-up mobbing occurs, it is an error to think that mobbing does not also occur to targets at the highest levels of organizational leadership, and our theoretical models need to have adequate explanatory power to encompass all forms of mobbing, not just top-down.

MEMBERS

Since a leader's success is largely a function of the productivity and behavior of the members who report to him or her, personnel or members is an important subsystem in any organization. Personnel function best when leadership style best corresponds with their needs and style (Uris, 1964). For example, a subordinate with an affinity for the autocratic approach will respond favorably to an autocratic leadership style. The lack of match between leadership style and member needs can account for conflict, stress, decreased productivity, and performance (Sperry, 1996b).

Furthermore, individuals do not typically work or learn in isolation, but more likely perform in small work teams or learning groups. These groups can either increase or decrease the group's or team's outcomes, and either support or harm individual members. The behavior of such groups will be discussed in Chapter 6, in the section on group dynamics.

EXTERNAL ENVIRONMENT

The five organizational subsystems described above interact and mutually influence one another. The configuration of these subsystems is also greatly affected by an organization's external subsystem, the environment. The environmental subsystem refers to those factors outside an organization's internal subsystems that influence it and interact with it (Sperry, 1996b). The environment includes economic, legal, political, and sociocultural factors. It also includes other factors such as community relations, workforce availability, competitors, shareholders and

Table 5.1 **Organizational Dynamics***

Dynamic	Description
Strategy	The organization's overall action plan for achieving its mission and goals; includes the organization's stated core values
Structure	Framework and mechanisms (roles, reporting relationships, policies and procedures, reward and sanctions) for achieving the strategy
Culture	Reflection of actual core values, customs, and actions that characterize and define its identity to those inside and outside of the organization
Leadership	The process of inspiring, guiding, and coordinating others to achieve the organization's strategy; includes supervisors at all levels of the organization
Members	Individuals and work teams in the organization who, with guidance from leadership, attempt to accomplish its strategy
Environment	Factors outside the organization (competitors, customer demands, community, government regulations) that influence and interact with it

*Based on Sperry (1996b).

other stakeholders, market saturation, customers' demands and changes, government statutes, environmental policies, other regulatory requirements, and standard industrial practices. In times of turbulence and rapid social and technological changes, the environmental subsystem may exert as much or more influence on organizational direction and functioning as other subsystems. Federal legislation or its absence, in the case of mobbing and bullying, has and will continue to significantly impact the health and well-being of an organization's personnel (see Table 5.1).

Conclusion

Clearly, these organizational dynamics are systemically interrelated. For example, it has been said that "structure follows strategy" in effective organizations, meaning that, to fulfill its mission an organization develops a strategy and modifies or puts in place the corresponding structures that will facilitate the accomplishment of that strategy. Also, earlier in this section, we noted the link between leadership and culture in the example of how Gates' hard-working, creative, and confrontational style was reflected in similar behavior of Microsofters.

Research (Karasek & Theorell, 1990) indicates that when a structure characterized by high job strain (i.e., one in which workers have little or no decisional control) combines with an autocratic leadership style, the result is the compounding of adverse medical and psychological symptoms and conditions. Each of the four explanatory models for understanding organizational abusiveness; namely, the conflict model, the cybernetic model, the communication flows model, and the A-B-C model, incorporate either an explicit or implicit understanding of the interrelatedness of the organizational dynamics of strategy, structure, culture, leadership, members, and the external environment. To influence and change mobbing-prone organizations, it is necessary to analyze which elements in particular organizational contexts are most likely to function as high-leverage intervention points.

6

Group, Leadership, and Individual Antecedents of Mobbing

It almost goes without saying that the sort of people who want to
shake things up, to change things, can get under other people's skins.
It goes with the territory, the breed, the trade.
—John Elkington and Pamela Hartigan (2008, p. 24)

Awareness of abusiveness in the school and the workplace and its impact is increasing in the United States and worldwide (Chappell & Di Martino, 2006). This abusiveness not only includes mobbing and bullying, but also sexual harassment, homicide, and threats by psychologically unstable coworkers. Abusiveness is a form of inappropriate aggression that can and does negatively impact health and productivity (Duffy & Sperry, 2007; Sperry & Duffy, 2009; Sperry & Larsen, 1998). In a June 15, 2006 press release, the International Labor Office (ILO) noted that such abusiveness has reached epidemic levels in a number of countries. It indicated that the global cost of workplace violence is enormous, amounting to untold millions of dollars in losses in other countries from medical expenses, absenteeism, and sick leave. It also concluded that professions that were once regarded as sheltered from workplace violence, such as teaching, social services, library services, and health care, are being exposed to increasing acts of violence, in both developed and developing countries. Data reported in this press release published by the ILO were cited in Chappell and Di Martino (2006).

Statistics provided earlier in this book indicate that about 30% of youth in the United States are estimated to be involved in bullying (Nansel et al., 2001), while approximately 37% of U.S. workers report being the target of bullying (Workplace Bullying Institute, 2007), and that these prevalence rates have increased. So, why is abusive behavior increasing? Some have pointed to the current economic downturn, while others suggest that the explanation lies with the decrease in everyday civility in many cultures. Although such explanations are reasonable, researchers have yet to reach consensus on why these prevalence rates are increasing.

In the previous chapter, we provided explanations for how mobbing develops by presenting theoretical frameworks sophisticated enough to account for complexity and for the interrelatedness of multiple causal factors. We examined organizational dynamics and their interaction in some detail and presented a variety of brief illustrative examples. Although attempting to understand causation can be theoretically helpful and can provide avenues for continued research to test proposed models, causal frameworks do not guarantee easy solutions.

In this chapter, we continue our focus on factors that influence or support and reinforce abusiveness even though definitive causes are yet to be determined. We build on the perspective of the previous chapter and incorporate a discussion of how individual and group dynamics interact with organizational dynamics and must also be considered in the analysis of the social process of mobbing. Additionally, we devote a special section to those leadership styles and dynamics that seem to foster mobbing. We describe individual and group dynamics that influence and reinforce abusive organizational behavior. We do this to consider smaller units than the organization as a whole in the analysis of mobbing, but remind our readers that the individually based "bad apple" theory of mobbing is a woefully inadequate one, even though we recognize the importance of looking at individual factors and how those factors are mutually influenced by the larger organizational ones. We then turn our attention to organizations in which mobbing is less likely to occur and look at how those organizations differ from mobbing-prone ones.

Individual and Group Dynamics and Mobbing

As noted in the Chapters 1 and 4, media accounts have brought the consequences of mobbing and bullying into our collective consciousness. Interestingly, the first impulse of the general public, many managers, some psychologists and psychotherapists, and particularly the media, is to attribute mobbing and bullying in school and workplace settings to psychopathology of the individual offender(s). In terms of explanatory power, this "bad apple" explanation or view is quite limiting; however, it is consistent with the individualism, autonomy, and personal responsibility ethos reflected in the American Dream, the justice system, and even mental health practice.

On the other hand, there are others who appreciate the power of groups and organizations in influencing student and worker behavior. In fact, taken together, these three views—the individual dynamics or "bad apple" explanation, the workgroup dynamics or the "some bad apples" explanation, and the organizational dynamics or "bad barrel" explanation—provide a reasonably coherent and compelling account of the causes of workplace or school mobbing behavior. A basic premise of this book is that three sets of dynamics influence an individual's behavior in a school and workplace settings: personality or individual dynamics, situational or group dynamics, and systemic or organizational dynamics. A related assumption is that individual, group, and organizational dynamics can either foster or reduce the likelihood of mobbing (Sperry, 2009a). These three sets of dynamics do not work independently of each other but are inextricably interconnected and exert reciprocal influence. Hence, our model is best thought of as a systemic one.

Individual Dynamics

That individual factors (i.e., personality traits, experiences, motivations, and other psychological factors) are sufficient to cause aggressive and abusive behavior has been challenged by considerable research on situational factors, such as group dynamics (Milgram, 1974; Zimbardo, 1974, 2008). Although many clinicians and psychotherapists favor this individual dynamics orientation, research strongly suggests that an individual's behavior in an organization is more likely to be influenced by powerful situational and organizational determinants. In fact, in specific circumstances, otherwise morally good individuals engage in abusive behaviors because of situational and systemic factors (Milgram, 1974; Zimbardo, 1974, 2008). Because society is overly invested in the individualistic view of abusive behavior, it should not be surprising that it attempts to treat or manage such behavior by subjecting individuals to therapy, rehabilitation, or incarceration, rather than addressing situational or systemic factors. However, if the principal cause is group and/or organizational dynamics, such individual interventions are likely to fail or be less effective than if the interventions included these other causal factors (Sperry, 2009b). We begin our discussion of the individual antecedents of mobbing by examining individual dynamics in relation to victims and perpetrators of mobbing and leadership styles of managers.

ADULT VICTIMS/TARGETS OF MOBBING

Personality
Because organizational dynamics have an effect on individual behavior, a worker's or student's personality style and level of psychological maturity interacts with the organization's dynamics and differentially influences that individual's behavior (Mantell, 1994). Although some find this organizational–personality interactional perspective useful, others would hold that mobbing can be explained largely in terms of the individual dynamics of both perpetrator and victim. It has been observed that hostile, nonsupportive organizational cultures are more likely to foster interpersonal violence in immature and personality-disordered employees than in more psychologically healthy employees (Sperry, 1998). Research also suggests that personality factors play a role in mobbing (Matthiesen & Einarsen, 2001). There is relatively little research profiling the victim, and what exists is briefly reviewed here.

Limited research has portrayed the victim's personality as having a tendency to psychological disturbance on a wide range of personality factors (Matthiesen & Einarsen, 2001). Three different profiles were reported. One profile indicated an extreme range of severe psychological problems and personality disturbances—that is, a personality profile characterized as depressive, anxious, suspicious, uncertain, and confused. A second profile was characterized by depression and suspiciousness, whereas the third profile reflected a quite normal personality, despite having experienced bullying behaviors. The researchers concluded that specific vulnerabilities and hardiness factors exist among the range of victims. Specifically, those with psychological problems, low self-confidence, and a high degree of anxiety may be more likely to feel bullied and harassed and find it difficult to defend themselves from such behavior (Matthiesen & Einarsen, 2001). Given the small sample sizes, methodological limitations, and absence of replication of results, the findings of this study are quite preliminary. In another study examining psychopathology among 146 mobbing victims, exposure to mobbing was associated with depression, difficulty in making decisions, anxiety about change, passive-aggressive behaviors, psychosomatic symptoms, and the need for attention and affection. Since the study was a cross-sectional one, cause and effect could not be determined. Without further research, it is unknown whether the mobbing caused such a personality profile or if the personality profile existed prior to the mobbing or if there was an interaction effect between the two (Girardi et al., 2007).

What do these studies and speculations tells us about the role of personality in workplace mobbing? The answer is "relatively little." Meaningful answers to the question of how personality factors are operative in workplace mobbing and bullying requires that research study personality style in relationship to group and organizational dynamics. At present, research seldom if ever accounts for these interactive relationships, thereby limiting both the theoretical and clinical utility of the results of such studies.

Work Orientation

Besides personality, a more germane type of individual dynamics is work orientation. Work orientation refers to an individual's attitude toward work, as reflected in an individual's thoughts, feelings, and behaviors about work (Wrzesniewski, McCaukley, Rozin, & Schwartz, 1997). Three work orientations have been identified: job, career, and calling orientations. Those with a job orientation view their work as simply a job. For them, work is a means to a financial end, so they can engage in nonwork activities like hobbies and other interests. Those with a career orientation value pay, prestige, promotion, and status, and these are the main focus of their work because they lead to higher self-esteem, increased power, and higher social standing (Bellah, Madsen, Sullivan, Swidler, & Tipton, 1985). For these individuals, personal identity is closely tied to their career and their work. For many professionals, their professional identity becomes their personal identity.

In contrast, for those with a calling orientation, work is their passion and they value the sense of fulfillment it provides them, while at the same time laboring to make the world a better place (Davidson & Caddell, 1994). Research demonstrates that most professionals adopt a career orientation, and those with a calling orientation report higher job satisfaction and higher life satisfaction than do those with either job or career orientations (Wrzesniewski et al., 1997).

So, what does work orientation have to do with mobbing? The extent to which a victim is physically and psychologically impacted by mobbing is a function of his or her attitude about work. Victims with a career orientation typically experience considerably more distress and disability than do those with other work orientations. Because their personal-professional identity is so closely tied to their work, victims with career orientations may view the abusive attacks of others, and particularly the threat of or actual job loss, as a total invalidation of their personal-professional identity (Sperry, 2009a). As a result, they conclude that they have no remaining purpose in life, and may die or suicide soon afterward. Westhues (2005a) describes a number of such cases. Thus, awareness of a victim's work orientation is useful in understanding his or her reaction to mobbing.

INDIVIDUAL CHARACTERISTICS OF CHILD AND ADOLESCENT VICTIMS OF MOBBING

Rigby (2004) summarized the research about child victims of bullying that suggested child victims were more likely to be physically weak, introverted, and have low self-esteem. That bullied or mobbed child and adolescent victims are most likely to become depressed, socially isolated and withdrawn, and have negative self-images was supported by Juvonen and Graham (2001). Among children who were victims, physical weakness and having fewer friends have consistently been identified as characteristics of victims of bullying for two decades (Olweus, 1993a; Pellegrini, 1994; Perry, Kusel, & Perry, 1988). Gay, lesbian, and bisexual adolescents have also been identified in the research as being at greater risk of being bullied and mobbed (Garofalo, Wolf, Kessel, Palfrey, & DuRant, 1998), as have overweight and obese adolescents (Janssen, Craig, Boyce, & Pickett, 2004).

Most troubling, children and adolescents victimized by bullying had higher rates of participation in violence and violence-related behaviors than did nonbullied children and adolescents (Nansel, Overpeck, Haynie, Ruan, & Scheidt, 2003), although Juvonen and Graham (2004) found that bullied children and adolescents were more likely to suffer in silence than to lash out in violence. This disparity in findings may be related to the fact that there is a category of child or adolescent involved in bullying who is referred to as a *bully-victim* (Kokkinos & Panayiotou, 2004). This child or adolescent is victimized by bullying and also engages in bullying behavior. The distinction between proactive and reactive aggression is important here (Price & Dodge, 1989). Proactive aggression is intentional aggression designed to hurt or dominate others. Reactive aggression is defensive aggression in the interests of self-protection in the face of a threat. It is a "fight-back" response. There is no research of which we are aware that incorporates the variable of time in relation to how soon or how long after a bullying or mobbing threat a child or adolescent victim may fight back. (Refer to Chapter 11 for further discussion of the role of time and the "fight response" to threat.) Salmivalli and Nieminen (2002) found that child and adolescent victims were less likely to engage in aggressive behavior, and when they did, the aggression was of the reactive type. Fanti, Frick, and Georgiou (2009) determined that bullies and bully-victims engaged in both proactive and reactive aggressive behavior. There is also little research about the nature of combined proactive and reactive aggression. We suggest that, under certain circumstances, reactive aggression could be as deadly as proactive aggression in its consequences, even though intent and neurophysiological arousal states may be quite different.

Rather than having a preexisting psychopathological profile, one reason that Juvonen and Graham (2004) believed children who have been bullied or mobbed experience emotional problems is because they end up blaming themselves for their situations. Indeed, based on their extensive review of the research, Juvonen and Graham (2004) challenged the notion that a child mobbing/bullying victim personality type actually exists. They believe that situational and social factors play important roles in determining what children get mobbed or bullied, and that those factors include situational ones like moving to a new school, for example, or not having friends. Juvonen, Nishina, and Graham (2000) found that mobbing or bullying victim status among schoolchildren tended to be a temporary rather than a permanent status. Children who accommodated to a new school situation or who developed a friendship group were then less likely to be mobbed or bullied.

Children with categorical attributes, such as homosexuality, or semicategorical attributes, such as being overweight, may experience more sustained bullying and/or mobbing. These findings have implications for parent and school interventions and provide little to no support for the existence of a child or adolescent victim personality profile. In the case of children who are mobbed and bullied, there is less research on victims and victimization than there is on bullies and bullying (Prinstein, Boergers, & Vernberg, 2001). For adults, the reverse is the case. There is more information on the experience of victimization than on the experience of participation in adult mobbing.

OFFENDERS/PERPETRATORS OF MOBBING

Personality

Unfortunately, there is also little research on the psychological profile of those engaging in mobbing. In one study of 2,200 Norwegian employees, 5% were bullies who described themselves as being high on aggressiveness and hostility (Einarsen, Raknes, Matthiesen, & Hellesoy, 1994). Based on survey data and clinical observation, Namie (2003) suggested that all bullies are narcissistic and egocentric. Although these individuals may not meet all criteria for an American Psychiatric Association's *Diagnostic and Statistical Manual of Mental Disorders* (DSM-IV-TR) diagnosis of narcissistic personality disorder, they do exhibit some narcissistic features.

Still others speculate that some bullies exhibit malignant narcissism (Glad, 2002, Vaknin, 2001). *Malignant narcissism* is a variant of the narcissistic personality with the additional feature of sadism (i.e., taking of pleasure from another's pain). In the workplace, malignant narcissists achieve and get promoted by abusing and exploiting peers and underlings. Although they get ahead by terrorizing their subordinates, they act reverentially and obsequiously (i.e., kiss up) to their superiors (Vaknin, 2001). They are convincing "yes men" to their superiors, while at the same secretly despising them, convinced that they are far superior and more important than their bosses.

Seigne, Coyne, Randall, and Parker (2007) conducted a study in an effort to identify personality types in bullies. In a very small sample (n = 34), they found that bullies were more aggressive and independent than nonbullies. The limitations of research about the personalities of bullies are significant and, at present, it is probably best to heed the advice of Zapf and Einarsen (2003), who stated that "empirical evidence indicates that bullying cases differ in the degree to which personality is involved as a potential cause" (p. 166). As we have been saying, to approach an understanding of the causes of mobbing, it is much more useful to examine the interactional effects among the individual, group or workgroup, and larger organization. The weakest and least likely place to find meaningful explanations of mobbing is within the individual.

INDIVIDUAL CHARACTERISTICS OF CHILD AND ADOLESCENT OFFENDERS/PERPETRATORS OF MOBBING

Attempting to describe the personality characteristics of child and adolescent perpetrators of mobbing and bullying is beset with difficulties. The difficulties center on whether the perpetrator or bully is a "pure" bully or a bully-victim and the nature of the aggression—proactive or reactive—not to mention complex methodological issues in attempting to develop personality profiles. Because of these difficulties, we recommend caution in drawing conclusions or making interpretations based on available date. Much more work and research needs to be done. Nonetheless, some interesting research findings are available that, if nothing else, provide direction for future research.

Randall (1997) reported that school bullies lack empathy and have little to no awareness of how other children perceive them—a clear deficit in interpersonal and social awareness. A number of scholars have linked bullying to social anxiety, depression, and low self-esteem (Salmon, James, & Smith, 1998), and to behavioral problems (Farrington, 1993). Conversely, Sutton, Smith, and Swettenham

(1999) found that bullies were cool and collected and displayed high levels of social competence. Other scholars identify bullies as using aggression to get what they want at the expense of others (Carney & Merrell, 2001; Griffin & Gross, 2004).

The focus on personality traits of bullies has been expanding because of hypotheses linking bullying behavior in childhood to conduct-disordered and/or criminal behavior in later life. The focus of a number of recent studies (Fanti et al., 2009; Frick & White, 2008) is on whether childhood bullies exhibit the callous and unemotional traits that are regarded as the core features of psychopathy (Cleckley, 1976). In their study, Fanti, Frick, and Georgiou (2009) found that the combination of proactive and reactive aggression in their study sample of adolescents was associated with higher levels of callous and unemotional traits, and that callous unemotional traits were linked to severe forms of aggression. These traits were found in the pure bullies and in the bully-victims. Although their work needs to be replicated and extended, one of the implications of the Fanti, Frick, and Georgiou (2009) study is that co-occurring or combined forms of proactive and reactive aggression are possible indicators of more serious pathology and higher risk.

Although the findings on callous unemotional traits are intriguing, existing research to develop a bully profile remains conflicting. It seems wise to bear in mind the systemic perspective of the authors of a recent study of bullying and victimization in a Scottish secondary school: "More recent research regards bullying and victimisation as the manifestation of the unique interaction between bully and victim rather than as the result of any individual characteristics that bullies and victims might have" (Karatzias, Power, & Swanson, 2002, p. 47).

Abusive or Toxic Leadership Styles

As with victim and perpetrator profiles of mobbing and bullying, research about what constitutes an abusive or toxic leader is in its early stages, and no personality profile of a toxic leader is empirically supported at this time. Process and outcome have been used as one set of dimensions through which to evaluate leaders. In evaluating military leadership styles, Reed (2004) indicated that:

> A loud, decisive, demanding leader is not necessarily toxic. A leader with a soft voice and a façade of sincerity can also be toxic. In the end, it is not one specific behavior that deems one toxic; it is the cumulative effect of demotivational behavior on unit morale and climate over time that tells the tale. (p. 67)

In this example, Reed is using outcome as the primary measure, not process, by which to evaluate leadership. In another example that used outcome as a leadership measure, Padilla, Hogan, and Kaiser (2007) pointed to Mother Teresa as a constructive leader because of the good she did for the poor around the world.

If we look at process as a variable by which to evaluate the quality of leadership, then we turn our attention to how leaders behave and do what they do. The state of the current research on destructive leadership involving process variables, or how leaders act, seems to crystallize around narcissism and its behavioral by-products of exploitation for personal gain, personal self-interest, and aggrandize-ment at the expense of others, ignoring the concerns and welfare of others in a workgroup, manipulative and self-serving behavior, self-centered focus on personal power and ambition, and pushing grandiose and unrealistic organiza-tional visions (Conger & Kanungo, 1998; Glad, 2002; Maccoby, 2000; Reed, 2004; Rosenthal & Pittinskya, 2006; Vaknin, 2001). In addition, Padilla, Hogan, and Kaiser (2007) stated that "a comparison of destructive and constructive leaders suggests that the rhetoric, vision, and worldview of destructive leaders contain images of hate—vanquishing rivals and destroying despised enemies" (p. 182). The leadership qualities that we describe here apply to all kinds of organizations, be they business, educational, religious, or other types.

Understanding leadership, like understanding all of the other domains of organizational functioning, is important for understanding how mobbing develops. In attempting to generate a nuanced model of what constructive and destructive leadership looks like, Einarsen, Aasland, and Skogstad (2007) point out that destructive leaders may behave constructively in some domains— that such leaders are not necessarily all good or all bad. Their model is based on leadership behaviors and outcomes and includes behaviors related to the legitimate interests of the organization and those related to the support and well-being of subordinates. Constructive leaders engage in behaviors that support both the legitimate interests of the organization and the well-being of subordinates. The model encompasses a range of other leadership behaviors that include pro-organization, anti-subordinate behaviors or pro-subordinate, anti-organization behaviors or some combination of the two, allowing for a more nuanced and less dichotomous way of depicting leadership behavior. Top-down mobbing is more likely to develop when a leader participates in anti-subordinate behaviors. However, this model is useful in calling attention to the fact that destructive leaders may also be simultaneously engaging in behaviors supportive of the organizational mission and goals. This both/and modeling of leadership—the manifestation of destructive and constructive leadership behav-iors simultaneously—mirrors the insidiousness of mobbing, in which a target is mobbed by organizational leadership under the mantra of "the best interests of the organization."

Individual leadership factors and styles interact with other organizational features to produce mobbing and other forms of destructive leadership. Whatever their personality characteristics, leaders who are viewed with suspicion and mistrust by followers, and whose ostensible good intentions are not widely believed, foster a culture of mistrust, insecurity, and doubt within an organization, and this contributes to making the organization ripe for mobbing. Current scholarship is moving away from an analysis of the individual leader as the cause of organizational problems to an analysis of the interaction effects of destructive leadership styles. These include the narcissist and hate-filled leader interacting with susceptible followers who are conformers or who want to pursue their own personal agendas and therefore ignore negative leadership within unstable and ineffective institutions in which members feel threatened at any number of levels (Padilla et al., 2007). Tierney and Tepper (2007) endorse this view in concluding that "there seems to be a strong indication that what accounts for destructive leadership may be situational as well as dispositional. Focusing exclusively on the leader as the agent of destruction may, therefore, provide an incomplete depiction of how and when such leadership emerges" (p. 172).

In perhaps one of the most striking examples of dichotomous leadership, Bueno de Mesquita (2009) described the story of Belgium's builder king, Leopold II, who oversaw dramatic progress in economic development, worker and individual rights, and economic help for the poor at home in Belgium. Leopold did all this while also reigning over the Congo, where he acquired massive personal wealth through the exploitation of the country's resources and people, and freely encouraged slavery, torture, and murder to achieve his ends. Leopold was the leader in both countries during the same period. The difference was the context—in this case, the context being the country—and the difference in structure and constraints between the two could not have been greater. Although Bueno de Mesquita's tale of Leopold is compelling in its own right and could be analyzed from multiple perspectives, we introduce it to again point out the power of context.

Abusive Managerial Behavior

Supervisors and managers are the most likely perpetrators of mobbing. The U.S. Workplace Bullying Survey conducted by Zogby International (Workplace Bullying Institute, 2007) found that 72% of bullies or perpetrators of mobbing are managers. So, what is the behavior of such managers, and how are they different from managers who do not engage in mobbing? To answer that question, Crawshaw (2007), utilizing practice-based evidence, distinguished five types of managers or bosses.

- *Adequate.* These managers relate to workers in socially acceptable ways that promote effective and smooth working relationships, and are perceived by workers as respectful.
- *Annoying.* These managers relate to workers in ways that result in mild, temporary irritation to workers, but do not damage work relationships or organizational functioning.

- *Avoidant.* These managers avoid interpersonal contact with workers by isolating themselves physically or emotionally. This neglect reduces worker morale and motivation.
- *Aberrant.* These managers relate in a personality-disordered ways (psychopathic, paranoid, or narcissistic) that negatively affect worker and organizational functioning.
- *Abrasive.* These managers relate to workers in a harsh or abusive manner that damages work relationship sufficiently to disrupt organizational functioning.

The abrasive managers exhibit five characteristic behaviors: overcontrol, threats, public humiliation, condescension, and over-reaction in relating to workers. Basic to each of these five behaviors is intimidation (Crawshaw, 2007). Crawshaw contended that these abrasive managers are not evil or mentally ill, but rather that they view themselves as supercompetent and fear being perceived as inadequate, incompetent, or as failures. These managers tend to view the world as a constant threat to their survival and "defend against this unconscious fear with abrasive behavior designed to protect their self-perception of supercompetence" (Crawshaw, 2007, p. 63). Furthermore, they view incompetence displayed by workers as the result of character flaws. Consequently, they are more likely to react to instances of incompetence with aggression and intimidation in the forms of overcontrol, threats, public humiliation, condescension, and over-reaction. Such abusive strategies ensure the manager's dominance and continued survival. Not surprisingly, they are not empathic, and see no need to empathically understand why a worker is performing below standards, because the abusive manager follows a mental schema that explains workers' incompetence as stemming from stupidity, laziness, or defiance. Crawshaw (2007) maintains that an abusive manager's empathic blindness is learned early in life as a result of caregiver modeling of aggressive rather than empathic responding.

In terms of our conceptualization of mobbing, abrasive and aberrant managers, using Crawshaw's (2007) schema, would be more likely to participate in mobbing. However, we agree with Crawshaw that the number of aberrant managers is rather small compared to the number of abrasive ones.

Group Dynamics

In contrast to the emphasis placed on individual dynamics in clinical psychology, social psychology presumes that situational factors are the primary determinants of people's behavior. In the workplace, employees function either as members of formal work teams or groups that are led by a supervisor or manager, or they may function as members of an "informal group." In either case, work group dynamics can powerfully influence the expression of mobbing.

GROUP COHESIVENESS

A group of individuals in the workplace typically behaves as a unit or as an "ingroup" because of group cohesiveness and other powerful forces that keep its individual members together and focused on the same goals. When these forces of cohesion fail, the group begins to disintegrate and ceases to be a group. Narcissism and dependency form some of the more powerful of these group cohesive forces (Mantell, 1994). In its simplest and most benign form, narcissism is manifested as group pride. As the members feel proud of their group, so the group feels proud of itself. A less benign but universal form of group narcissism is the creation of an enemy (i.e., animosity toward an "outgroup"). A sure-fire way of cementing group cohesiveness is to ferment the group's hatred of an external enemy. Deficiencies within the ingroup can be easily and painlessly overlooked by focusing attention on the deficiencies of the outgroup.

The phenomenon of dependency is also central to group cohesion, as well as to leader–follower dynamics. Dependency on a leader occurs because some individuals are more fit—or have more desire—to lead than others. Furthermore, it is much easier to be a follower than a leader. The role of the leader involves making complex decisions, exercising initiative, developing and overseeing the implementation of a plan, risking unpopularity, motivating others, and demonstrating courage and foresight. On the other hand, the role of the follower, to varying degrees, requires submission of one's personal authority and maturity as a decision-maker to the leader. In work organizations, leaders are not elected by followers in a work team or division, but are designated from above and deliberately cloaked with symbols of authority. Accordingly, the team leader or supervisor exercises considerable control over the behavior of followers or employees with regard to the type and amount of abusiveness that will be sanctioned.

Padilla, Hogan, and Kaiser (2007) identified strong ingroup/outgroup formation within an organization or culture as a factor associated with the development of strong leaders who are not always constructive. They viewed the function of strong leaders in these contexts as building identity and solidarity while also releasing members from having to sort out conflicts for themselves more directly.

It should be noted that ingroup versus outgroup distrust or animosity is sometimes relatively amenable to change. For instance, in middle school settings, in which there is a noticeable division among students based on financial advantage (i.e., wealthier students wearing designer clothes compared to other students in the school), school boards have found that a mandatory dress code can greatly reduce ingroup–outgroup differences.

FORMAL VERSUS INFORMAL GROUP

These groups may be formal work teams, or they may be informal groups. The "informal group," also called the "informal organization" (Leavitt & Bahrami, 1987), is formed by personnel usually coalescing around a workplace issue or an outside activity. Actually, these groups accomplish much of the organization's work. Chance meetings at the coffee machine, impromptu lunch meetings, and informal telephone calls go a long way toward defining and achieving the organization's strategy.

On the other hand, these informal groups may have an agenda that is antithetical to the organization's stated goal. It may be to disrupt the production of the organization or a given unit within the organization, or it could be to degrade or eliminate a particular employee, as occurs in cases of mobbing. The dominant cultural discourse within organizations flows through the organization's subgroups. In mobbing-prone organizations, such communications are marked by organizational subsystem jockeying for dominance and impunity in negatively characterizing organizational members on the basis of presumed personal characteristics. Organizational members are then cast into ingroups or outgroups.

For example, a recent study of academic mobbing in Turkish universities (Tigrel & Kokalan, 2009) illustrates the formation of a hostile subgroup that included faculty members organizing students to target another faculty member. Tigrel and Kokalan reported a mobbed professor's experiences, who said that "his/her department associates organized the students and got them to mob him/her. The same participant stated that he/she was ignored by the university management although the management was aware of his/her talents and that the duties she should have been assigned were assigned to some others" (p. 97). Needless to say, the presence of a disaffiliative, disgruntled, or hostile informal group can wreak havoc within a workgroup and seriously undermine the organization's strategy (Mantell, 1994).

Organizations in Which Mobbing Does Not Occur

In the sections above, we looked at the interplay of individual and group dynamics in the formation of organizational culture and behavior, and in the development of destructive organizational behaviors like mobbing. It is also instructive to pay attention to the characteristics of organizations in which mobbing is unlikely to occur and to analyze how they differ from mobbing-prone organizations.

In some organizations, mobbing has not occurred and is unlikely to occur, whereas other organizations seem predisposed to this phenomenon. What makes some organizations immune to mobbing and others predisposed to it? To understand the answer to this question, we begin our discussion with a description of organizations that are free of mobbing. This discussion provides a perspective for understanding mobbing in an organizational context.

Among promising studies that are attempting to answer the question is a qualitative study of 148 organizations (Hodson, 2001; Hodson, Roscigno, & Lopez, 2006). In this in-depth study, the researchers found that job security and organizational coherence differentiated workplace organizations that had supported bullying and mobbing and those that did not. They defined "job security" as security from layoffs and limited susceptibility to supervisory abuse. "Organizational coherence" was defined as the extent to which an organization's production procedures were smoothly functioning and well integrated. By contrast, organizational incoherence was manifested by a lack of clarity and confusion about procedures, roles, and expectations, which reflected inadequate or arbitrary work processes and leadership. Results indicated that some 64% of the organizations studied had good to exceptional organizational coherence.

Overall, this research found that employees in workplaces with high levels of job security and organizational coherence were more protected from mobbing and bullying. Job security and organizational coherence are aspects of an organization's strategy, structure, and culture. In combination, organizational coherence and job security—in which the mutual expectations for long-term employment are reciprocally honored by both the organization and its membership—contribute to a climate conducive to productivity and antithetical to the development of mobbing. In the context of the global economic downturn, such a combination of organizational coherence and job security is hard to find. Hodson, Roscigno, and Lopez (2006) also found that the most likely places for bullying and mobbing were those with high levels of job insecurity and low levels of coherence. They concluded that organizations with high job security and coherence had "no need for bullying and . . . find it inconsistent with the effective working of well-defined operation procedures that are already in place" (p. 408).

In a recent large study conducted in Canada (Soares, 2010), seven separate quantitative research studies of organizational life and management practices were completed. The seven studies were conducted among diverse groups of unionized workers; namely, professionals in education, office workers, stevedores, health workers, blue collar workers, technical workers, and engineers. Using Maslach and Leiter's (1997) model, Soares' team analyzed six areas of organizational life and three sets of management activities. The areas of organizational life examined were workload, control, reward, community, fairness, and values. The management activities studied were supervision, communication, and skills development. The findings from Soares' work are important in developing an understanding of the kinds of organizations in which mobbing and bullying are less likely to occur. Based on these studies, he concluded that work overload or intensification, lack of control, insufficient reward, breakdown in the workgroup or community, absence of fairness, conflicting values, supervision that is nonparticipative, and lack of managerial communication and skills development are indicative of more abuse-prone workplaces and that, when these indicators are not present, workplaces are likely to be less abuse-prone. Soares identified work load, organizational justice or fairness, and group cohesion as being especially important organizational dimensions in predicting workplace abuse. His findings echo our systemic model for understanding mobbing, given that workload and organizational justice and fairness are organizationally determined while group cohesion is a critical aspect of group dynamics.

Conclusion

Research, as indicated in our discussion of individual factors, does not provide much support for the "bad apple" explanation of mobbing. That is not to say that individual factors are not relevant, but rather that their effects within the development of mobbing-prone organizations are complex and reciprocally constituted. The group dynamics or "some bad apples" explanation provides an understanding of subgroup formation in the pursuit of identity and solidarity within an organization. When subgroups are factionalized to become ingroups and outgroups, conditions are favorable for the development of mobbing. As with individual factors, group dynamics within an organization are inextricably linked to the organization itself. In looking at organizations that either foster or inhibit the development of mobbing, it is the organization itself and its strategies, structure, culture, leadership, members, and external environment that determine proneness or resistance to mobbing. The "bad barrel" needs to replace the "bad apple" as the explanatory metaphor for how mobbing develops.

7

Organizational Development and Risk Factors

Allowing a victim to suffer a mobbing case and then just letting the employee go should be recognized as a major management failure.
—Charles Bultena and Richard Whatcott (2008, p. 662)

This chapter continues the discussion of those factors that cause or influence mobbing, which we began and expanded in Chapters 5 and 6. In the previous chapters, we focused our attention on conceptual models for understanding the development of mobbing and on organizational subsystems and how those subsystems interact with individual and group variables within the organization and with the external environment outside the organization. The analysis of organizational subsystems provides a cross-sectional view of an organization but reveals little about an organization's developmental or longitudinal history. Just as a person grows and develops and then declines, so do organizations. We begin with a discussion of the organizational life cycle and its importance as another perspective through which to view organizational life. We then provide an overview of the organizational stages of change and go on to review various risk factors associated with mobbing that involve individual, group and organizational dynamics from a longitudinal rather than cross-sectional perspective as in Chapters 5 and 6.

Organizational theorists have noted the relative abundance of cross-sectional analysis and research on organizations and the relative lack of such literature on longitudinal perspectives of organizations (Kimberly & Miles, 1980; Quinn & Cameron, 1983). As Bateson (2000), the classic systemic theorist about human systems suggested, "binocular vision" or multiple perspectives are essential for obtaining the fullest view possible of a phenomenon. By itself, a cross-sectional view of organizational dynamics is insufficient to understand organizational behavior and potential risk factors for mobbing. When it is combined with the longitudinal view of organizational life cycle theory, a fuller and richer understanding of organizational strengths and vulnerabilities becomes available and is much more useful in assessing the likelihood and risks for mobbing, including when in the organizational life cycle risks for mobbing are greatest.

A strong body of theoretical and research literature suggests that organizational life cycle theory is valuable in understanding and even predicting organizational behavior (cf. Jawahar & McLaughlin, 2001; Milliman, Von Glinow, & Nathan, 1991; Quinn & Cameron, 1983). The value of looking at organizations from a life cycle perspective is the identification and understanding of changes that organizations are likely to go through over time and at different stages in their development (Beverland & Lockshin, 2001; Lester, Parnell, & Carraher, 2003). Transitions in organizational life cycles, as in all human systems, are periods of both opportunity and vulnerability that depend on leadership, the external environment, and the interface of the other organizational subsystems already discussed in previous chapters. Longitudinal organizational perspectives provide a basis for analyzing organizations as they shift and change over time and for identifying potential periods of greatest risk for mobbing and mobbing-related behaviors.

We conclude this chapter with two exemplars of mobbing, one involving a school setting and organization and the other involving a workplace setting and organization. In these exemplars, we integrate the cross-sectional and longitudinal perspectives in order to analyze organizational vulnerabilities likely to give rise to mobbing incidents. We also look at leaderships styles associated with organizations at various stages of development and their relationship to the emergence of mobbing.

The Organizational Life Cycle

Over the last several decades, a number of organizational researchers have developed life cycle stage models that distinguish the structures, strategies, activities, and interactions with the external environment that occur differentially over the course of an organization's life (Adizes, 1979, 1999; Chandler, 1962; Churchill & Lewis, 1983; Dodge, Fullerton, & Robbins, 1994; Kazanjian, 1988; Miller & Friesen, 1984; Mintzberg, 1984; Quinn & Cameron, 1983; Torbert, 1974). These organization life cycle models vary in the number of stages they identify (typically between three and ten), and researchers suggest that this variance is a function of whether the stages are relatively more elaborated or condensed (Lester et al., 2003). The organization life cycle model that we describe below consists of six stages encompassing organizational birth, expansion and consolidation, and decline.

An example of recent research utilizing an organizational life cycle perspective is that of Beverland and Lockshin (2001), who sought to "examine the developmental patterns of profit-driven wineries in New Zealand" (p. 354). They studied 20 wineries in New Zealand, wanting to understand the developmental experiences of business owners within that nation's growing wine-making industry, which has established a solid reputation for producing fine wines. Their findings resulted in the mapping of a life cycle model for New Zealand wineries with specific stages through prebirth or the entrepreneurial stage to start-up, expansion, and growth. Associated with each stage were a specific business focus, particular structures and strategies involving production, marketing, distribution, and staff functions, and challenges unique to that stage. Their model, using a growing industry with an already established global good reputation, added support to the already sizable organizational life cycle literature and theories while also incorporating contextual uniqueness. As in the case of New Zealand wineries, life cycle models and theories that are validly derived can offer roadmaps to help organizations anticipate needs and resources and avoid common pitfalls that they are likely to encounter as they grow in complexity and develop. These roadmaps are best understood and used as templates or frameworks for understanding the terrain, rather than as precise directions for getting from one point to the next.

Organization life cycle analysis affords decision makers with opportunities to anticipate possible threats and weaknesses that must be addressed at various stages of organizational development in order to maintain organizational strength and vitality and to address changing stakeholder needs. In common parlance, we refer to actions based upon this type of anticipatory analysis and scenario planning as being proactive. Jawahar and McLaughlin (2001), in referencing organizational life cycle analysis, specified the context within which the advantage of proaction is available to organizational members, in particular, to decision-makers. They stated that the "strategy of proaction involves anticipating and accepting responsibility and, therefore, can only be used when threats are forecasted. If a threat currently exists, then it will be too late for proaction, and firms can at best only use accommodation" (p. 405). The organizational conditions for the development of mobbing, as we discuss below, are likely to be more prevalent during certain periods in the organization's life cycle and are therefore subject to anticipation and proaction to prevent and/or thwart the emergence of mobbing in the interests of reduction of harm to the organization, its members, and its stakeholders.

In recent years, efforts have been made to develop longitudinal models that have broad explanatory power. For example, Lester, Parnell, and Carraher (2003) proposed an empirically derived five-stage organizational life cycle model that they identified as applicable to all organizations, both large and small. Jawahar and McLaughlin (2001) stressed that "theory and research suggest that the pressures, threats, and opportunities in the external and internal environment of an organization vary with the life cycle stages" (p. 405), highlighting the usefulness of organizational life cycle analysis, anticipation, and forecasting in the service of proactive leadership behavior. Examining organizations both cross-sectionally and longitudinally provides systemic binocular vision (Bateson, 2000) to enhance the understanding of organizational life. Such life cycle analysis affords distinct opportunities for looking at how organizational subsystems (from a cross-sectional perspective) and organizational stages of development (from a longitudinal perspective) interface with their environments to give rise to mobbing threats that, when acknowledged and anticipated, are much more easily managed.

Systemic Openness and Organizational Life Cycle Models

It is worthwhile to consider, however briefly, the concept of "openness" in systems and its applicability to understanding organizational development, change, and responsiveness to risk factors. Systems can be conceptualized along a continuum from closedness at one end to openness at the other end. Closedness and openness are systemic characteristics that refer to the degree to which the system allows or prohibits information from within or outside of itself to be incorporated as input back into the system. A frequently used example of a closed system is that of a thermostat. A thermostat functions based on its own mechanism and the input of the temperature in the environment it is set up to regulate. It can function effectively with only the temperature as the primary input.

Open systems, on the other hand, take in multiple inputs or pieces of information from the environment and utilize or transform those inputs in the creation or generation of the products the open system is designed to produce or reproduce. The human body, couples, families, organizations, and social institutions are all examples of open systems. Their viability and survivability require ongoing input from the environment, whether that input is food and oxygen (as in the case of the human body) or beliefs, values, meaning systems, practices and strategies, mission statements, and other ongoing information (as in the case of larger human systems). Becvar and Becvar (2000) stated that "all living systems are open to some extent, so openness and closedness are a matter of degree. An appropriate balance between the two is desirable for healthy functioning" (p. 70). In summary, the critical defining characteristic of an open system is the interface and permeability between it and its total environment.

Although not all organizational models use the language and terminology of systems theory or cybernetics, all organizational models that attend to the relationship between the organization and its internal and external environments include the important construct of systemic openness in their modeling. Organizational life cycle models are based on the concept of growth over time, development, and change—concepts integral to open systems theory. Growth, development, and change represent the outcomes from multiple inputs into a system from its environment that have been utilized by the system in ways that are productive or counterproductive, effective or ineffective. A good example of the explicit use of open systems concepts within the framework of organizational life cycle models can be seen in the work of organizational life cycle theorists and researchers who map differential threats, opportunities, and pressures from both the internal and external environments, according to the particular life cycle stage of the organization (Anderson & Zeithaml, 1984; Dodge et al., 1994; Dodge & Robbins, 1992).

Open Systems Models of Organizations

Traditional or classical models of organizations are focused on standardized role performance, tasks, and uniformity of function. Two such theories are Weber's *theory of bureaucracy* (Weber, 1947) and *scientific management theory* (Taylor, 1911). Although useful in several respects, these closed systems models also have significant shortcomings. The main critique of these models is that they fail to account for interactions between the organization and its environment. This failure effectively denies organizations any viable means for change (Katz & Kahn, 1966) and for recognition of external threats. Open systems models of organizations were developed as a reaction to earlier organizational models that failed to account for the contextual relationship between the organization and its environments, both external and internal. Since the 1960s, almost all organizational theorists and researchers have embraced an open systems perspective, either explicitly or implicitly.

Katz and Kahn (1978) developed one of the earliest explicit open systems organizational models. It encompasses four factors: energic inputs into the organizations, transformation of those inputs within the system, energic outputs, and recycling. Energic inputs, or external influences, include familiar resources like employees, raw materials or services, and capital. They also include intangible external influences, such as status, recognition, satisfaction, or other personal rewards. The transformation process involves using energies, or inputs, to create products or services. Energic outputs are simply the products or services that are provided back to consumers as a result of the use of these energic inputs. Finally, *recycling* refers to the process by which outputs and the information about them are recycled back into the organization. For example, when an organization provides a service, the revenue generated becomes an input into the organization that is used to pay workers and develop other programs.

In addition to identifying these four phases, Katz and Kahn (1978) cataloged a number of systemic characteristics of successful organizations. These include entropy, homeostasis, and equifinality. They recognized the cybernetic and biological principle of *entropy*, which holds that all living systems move toward disorganization or death, and applied this principle to organizations. Nevertheless, an open system can continue to thrive by importing more energy from the environment than it expends, thus achieving negative entropy or *negentropy*. For instance, a failing organization might be able to revitalize itself by hiring a new chief executive officer who improves the way the organization transforms energic inputs.

Another systemic characteristic is dynamic *homeostasis*, which suggests that all successful organizations must be able to achieve balance between subsystems. For example, a sales department might grow very quickly if it is very successful or if demand for its products jumps. But, if the manufacturing arm of the organization is unable to keep pace with sales activity, the entire organization becomes at risk. Thus, subgroups must maintain a rough state of balance as they adapt to external influences. For a system like an organization to be in a state of negentropy (or tending toward maximal order and vitality), it must be in a state in which it is maintaining balance among its subsystems. Katz and Kahn also explained open systems by using another systemic principle, that of *equifinality*. This concept suggests that organizations can reach the same end state by a number of different paths. In fact, the course is not fixed and may develop organically as both internal and external influences intervene.

As an open systems organizational model, the Katz and Kahn (1966, 1978) open systems model is also regarded as an organizational life cycle model (Gupta & Chin, 1994; Quinn & Cameron, 1983), suggesting that organizations as open, living systems must balance openness and closedness among all of their subsystems and across all of their stages of growth and development if they are to survive and flourish. Three stages are included in Katz and Kahn's (1978) open systems life cycle model: a primitive collective response to common problems, the assurance of stability of organizational structure (i.e., informal norms, rules, and authority structures), and the development of elaborated supportive structures (i.e., differentiated subsystems and adaptive systems to respond to environmental changes). From an open systems perspective, mobbing is a social process occurring within organizations when the organization becomes overly closed to information about its environment—typically, about its internal environment, but potentially about both its internal and external environments.

Quinn and Cameron (1983) have developed a highly regarded integrative model of organizational growth and change. It is an empirically derived stage model based upon an analysis of nine prominent open systems stage models of organizational change and effectiveness. They identified four stages of organizational growth and development: an entrepreneurial stage, a collectivity stage, a formalization and control stage, and a structure elaboration and adaptation stage. The Katz and Kahn (1978) model excludes the first stage. In contrast to the other eight models, the Adizes (1979) model is recognized by Quinn and Cameron as the "only one that accounts for both maturing and declining stages. Simply put, the model suggests that organizations develop through distinctive stages—from infancy to maturity—and that they decline in distinctive stages—from maturity to death—depending on the emphasis placed on the four different activities" (p. 39). Because of its comprehensiveness as a theoretical model and its applicability to a wide range of organizations, an adaptation of the Adizes model is detailed here. Although, as described, a number of organizational life cycle models are useful for examining an organization longitudinally, we highlight the Adizes stage model in this chapter because of the recognition of its completeness by organizational scholars relative to other models such as the respected Katz and Kahn model (Quinn & Cameron, 1983).

Organizational Stages of Development

Based on the work of Adizes (1979, 1988, 1999) and Greiner (1972), six stages of organizational development and decline are described here (Sperry, 1993, 2002). They are new venture, expansion, professionalization, consolidation, early bureaucratization, and late bureaucratization. These stages of organizational development are important in understanding the development of mobbing. Organizations have periods in their growth and development when, during times of expansion, transition, and decline related to increasing external threats, the organization is more likely to create conditions that give rise to the emergence of mobbing.

STAGE 1: NEW VENTURE

Stage I of an organization's development involves the conception of a new venture. The critical tasks at this stage include defining a target group (e.g., pet lovers, students, computer users) and developing a product or service that targets such a group. Accomplishing these tasks requires the ability to extend or create a market need; the willingness to make a risky investment of time, energy, and money to create an organization that satisfies the unmet need; and the ability to create an embryonic organizational structure that can provide that service to the target group (Adizes, 1979; Gupta & Chin, 1994). These abilities are characteristic of the entrepreneurial leader, and the entrepreneurial leadership style is most compatible with this stage (Lorange & Nelson, 1987; Scott, 1971).

STAGE II: EXPANSION

Stage II is the stage of rapid growth (Gupta & Chin, 1994). Stage II commences very quickly or after the organization has been in Stage I for a number of years. The major problems that occur in Stage II involve growth rather than survival. Organizational resources are stretched to their limits as a new wave of members joins the organization, as demands for services increase, and as the organization's original, often primitive, day-to-day operating system becomes overwhelmed. Organizational "growing pains" are painfully present. Growing pains signal that changes are needed and cannot be ignored; they imply that the organization has not been fully successful in developing the internal system it needs for the given stage of growth (Flambolz & Randle, 2000).

STAGE III: PROFESSIONALIZATION

Stages I and II represent the entrepreneurial organization. Even though they may have lacked well-defined goals, policies, plans, or controls, these organizations prospered. However, as critical size is being achieved, the organization begins experiencing "growing pains" as its members outgrow its initial structure and operating systems (Flambolz & Randle, 2000). New structures and operating systems must be implemented (Katz & Kahn, 1978). Another wave of new members requires more formal planning, defined roles and responsibilities, performance standards, and control systems. Developing a strategic planning and management system then becomes the critical task at Stage III. This in turn requires organizational development efforts that provide the concurrent level of skills training needed to implement this management system.

STAGE IV: CONSOLIDATION

After transitioning to a professionally managed system, the organization can focus its efforts on consolidation (Katz & Kahn, 1978; Quinn & Cameron, 1983; Torbert, 1974). Consolidation means maintaining a reasonable increase in growth while developing the organizational culture. Culture becomes a critical concern in Stage IV since current members may no longer share the organization's original core values, vision, and mission of what the organization is or where it is going. At this stage, the knowledge base and skills of members are regularly upgraded. Leadership that combines entrepreneurship and integration is most compatible with Stage IV functioning. At Stage IV, individual members who are able to function interdependently with superiors, coworkers, and subordinates are most compatible with the organization's collaborative or participative styles.

STAGE V: EARLY BUREAUCRATIZATION

As the organization transitions to Stage V, a subtle but clear shift occurs from substance to form. Status seeking, "business as usual," and appearances characterize the behavior of members. Later in this stage, the focus shifts to internal turf wars. Backbiting, coalition building, and paranoia are common (Adizes, 1979; Pfeffer, 1981). Growing pains are particularly intense as members' dissatisfaction mounts (Adizes, 1979; Lorange & Nelson, 1987). In some organizations, negativity threatens to poison the organization's climate. Leadership at first was content to rest on the organization's laurels, but now shifts to a self-protective mode. Cliques become the usual mode of communication. The best and brightest start leaving the organization. The emphasis has clearly shifted from growth and maintenance to decline. The structures and the planning and development functions are much less responsive than in previous stages. Leadership is marked by administration and, in the later part of this stage, by inefficient administration. Decentralization and delegation become increasingly threatening to leadership, and efforts to recentralize power are frequent during this stage. Counter-dependency behavior, including passive-aggressivity, becomes commonplace, reflecting demoralization among workers as well as among managers.

STAGE VI: LATE BUREAUCRATIZATION

Many of the subunits and subsystems of the organization become clearly dysfunctional during Stage VI. Miscommunication is commonplace, and two-way communication is limited or nonexistent. Coordination and follow-through are the exception rather than the rule: "My right hand is seldom aware that my left hand exists, much less knows what it is doing." New members are no longer informed of the mission statement and strategy, and, for all members, the organizational culture reflects a sense of helplessness and a lack of common direction. "Come late, leave early," "do as little as you have to," "don't try to change anything," "protect job security at all costs" are attitudes reflecting the organizational culture in Stage VI. The critical function at this stage is to forestall and avoid extinction, as the organization is figuratively in intensive care and is being maintained by external life-support systems. The corporate subsystems are conflictual and nonresponsive to the needs of both members and clientele. Little, if any, training and development occurs. Administrators struggle to buy time and prolong the organization's life. But inefficiency and ineffectiveness are to be expected (Adizes, 1979; Lorange & Nelson, 1987; Nystrom & Starbuck, 1984; Pfeffer, 1981). Clients find access to responsive subsystems the exception rather than the rule. Not surprisingly, the re-emergence of dependency among members complements the autocratic style of leaders. The eventual demise of the organization seems inevitable, and consultants report that the prognosis for organizations in Stage VI—even after heroic interventions—is poor (Adizes, 1999). Table 7.1 summarizes these stages.

COMMENTARY ON DEVELOPMENTAL STAGES

Organizations are particularly sensitive to mobbing and other forms of abusiveness during periods of transition between stages, particularly as an organization attempts to reorganize and restructure. Strandmark, Lillemor, and Hallberg (2007) found that periods of workplace reorganization or restructuring often gave rise to workplace abuse. In our experience, mobbing is also likely to occur in the expansion and bureaucratization stages.

Individual, Group, and Organizational Risk Factors for Mobbing

Because mobbing is such a complex social process involving individual, group, and organizational dynamics and their interaction, identifying risk factors for mobbing

Table 7. 1 **Stages of Organizational Growth and Decline***

Stage	Description
New Venture	Stage of launching a new organization, or unit of it, to meet an unmet need; tasks are to define a targeted market, to develop a product/service targeted to it, and to inspire worker effort and loyalty
Expansion	Stage of rapid growth; task is to develop a basic operating system and infrastructure that fosters efficiency and effectiveness, and to deal with "growing pains," including increased demands and high turnover
Professionalization	Stage of internal growth and stabilization; task is to implement a strategic management system and shift from entrepreneurial to professional leadership
Consolidation	Stage in which growth and worker and customer commitment is maintained; task is to develop a consistent, healthy corporate culture, emphasize product/service quality, and avoid risky expansion
Early Bureaucratization	Stage in which corporate vision blurs and erosion of commitment results in inefficiency, demoralization, passive aggressivity, and loss of talented personnel; task is to maintain operating systems
Late Bureaucratization	Stage of impaired communication and productivity with a culture marked by despair; task is to shore up the organization with downsizing, infusion of funds, and sell-offs of units, products, or service lines

*Based on Sperry (1993, 2002).

at each of the three levels is difficult. A beginning body of research exists that, we believe, needs to be augmented, especially in terms of research examining the interaction effects of these individual, group, and organizational dynamics. In terms of individual dynamics, personality factors of both victims and offenders were discussed in detail in Chapter 6.

Our view is that all the antecedents of mobbing, including individual dynamics, group dynamics, and organizational dynamics, are potential risk factors. Table 7.2 summarizes some of the risk factors or vulnerabilities associated with these individual, group, and organizational dynamics. This is not meant to be a definitive list, nor should these issues be considered "predictors" of mobbing. Rather, based on experience and some research, we suggest that they are factors associated with abusiveness.

Table 7.2 Individual, Group & Organizational Dynamics:
Risk Factors for Mobbing

Dynamics	Mobbing Risk Factors in Workplaces and Schools
Individual	***Victim/Target (workplace)***: "Career" or "calling" work orientation; conscientious; high achievers; limited evidence of low self-confidence, anxiety, and psychological problems ***Victim/Target (school)***: Likely to be perceived as weak or different; few friends; may be in transition to new school or school group ***Offender/Perpetrator (workplace)***: Narcissistic, including malignant narcissism ***Offender/Perpetrator(school)***: Lacking empathy; low awareness of how others perceive them; aggressiveness; anxiety; depression; low self-esteem; bully-victim status; conflicting evidence about level of social competence
Group	***(both)*** strong ingroup vs. outgroup sentiment; breakdown of legitimate group cohesion; conflicts over values
Strategy	***(both)*** large discrepancy between stated vs. actual core values
Structure	***(workplace)*** high job strain, work overload, low support among workers, low organizational cohesion, low job security ***(school)*** high job strain among teachers and school counselors ***(both)*** role ambiguity and role conflict
Culture	**(workplace)** high productivity, abusiveness-prone culture **(school)** high performative culture, jock or violence prone-culture
Leadership	***(both)*** narcissistic, self-aggrandizing, exploitation of others for personal gain, anti-subordinate behaviors, self-interested and focused on personal power and ambition, grandiose organizational visions, poor communications, lack of responsiveness to abusive workplace behavior
Members	***(workplace)*** unquestioned loyalty of workers to the organization, weak union and/or poor employee–management relations, low perceived job security ***(school)*** unquestioned allegiance of parents to administrators and school policy; weak or ineffectual teachers union ***(both)*** limited family support system, limited peer support system
Environment	***(workplace)*** highly competitive environment, shrinking market share ***(school)*** expectation for winning sports teams, high academic achievement, and external recognition of extracurricular groups like music, theatre, and debate.
Stage	***(both)*** reorganization and transition between stages; at or between early and late bureaucratic stages

Individual, Group, and Organizational Dynamics in Mobbing: Workplace Setting Illustration

The following example of workplace mobbing illustrates a common pattern in organizational mobbing: the dereliction of duty by leadership who act by taking no action to prevent obvious abuse and harm to a member—even when the member complains and requests help. The example also illustrates both the individual dynamics that made Gerry especially vulnerable to the negative acts of his coworkers and the protective effects of his job—rather than career or calling—orientation to work.

SURPRISED AT A NEW JOB LOCATION

Gerry Bennett had worked as a personal banker for the past 7 months at the university branch of TEC Bank. Before transferring there, he had been at another branch for 3 years while he completed his undergraduate degree and worked part-time as a teller. During that time, he had observed this family owned bank expand aggressively. Upon graduation, he was promoted to personal banker and transferred to the university branch, where he replaced the incumbent personal banker who had been "one of the team" at that branch for nearly 10 years. Gerry was about 12 years younger than other personnel at the branch, and the bank president had ordered the transfer in an effort to lure university students, faculty, and staff to the branch. Needless to say, the staff members at the branch were not particularly happy to welcome Gerry. Most of Gerry's coworkers were cordial but distant; however, three did not welcome him at all. They were upset over the manner in which the transfer came about, and they wanted their "old" personal banker back.

Mobbing by three employees began almost from the first day Gerry arrived at the branch. He soon sensed that two of the senior tellers wanted to have him transferred out or fired. Soon, three other employees joined that group. After 3 months, the situation had become intolerable. He found it almost impossible to do his job—achieve his targeted goals—in the face of all the sabotaging behaviors directed toward him. In addition, Gerry was not able to be very supportive to his wife, who was depressed about her recent miscarriage, the second in 2 years. He began taking antidepressants and participating in psychotherapy soon after the mobbing began. Gerry experienced severe headaches, irritable bowel syndrome, and insomnia.

His efforts to enlist the support of human resources (HR) personnel were fruitless. They were decidedly unhelpful, although they did finally launch a formal investigation in the fifth month of Gerry's employment at the branch. During the course of the investigation, Gerry was subjected to intensive and aggressive questioning by management, although only brief statements were taken from other branch staff. Working conditions had become unbearable and because there were no openings at other branches for personal bankers or similar positions, his only choice was to take a teller position at another branch—at a significant pay cut—or leave the bank entirely.

An assessment of the bank's group and organizational dynamics suggested why and how mobbing and other abusive behaviors were fostered within the organizational context in which the bank and its personnel functioned. Here is a summary of that assessment, beginning with a description of how Gerry's individual dynamics interacted with the larger group and organizational dynamics.

INDIVIDUAL DYNAMICS

Given his hardworking pattern, seriousness, and desire to please, Gerry's personality style could be characterized as anxious and dependent. Because of his need to please others and be accepted, he was particularly sensitive to his coworkers' abusive remarks and behaviors. However, his work orientation at the bank seemed much more job-oriented than career-oriented. His real passion was playing golf. He was mentored by his golf-pro father from an early age, and Gerry's dream had been to play on the professional tour. He and his wife had agreed that if things didn't change for the better soon, he would leave the bank and, with his father's sponsorship, join the professional golf tour—at which he would make more money than he could at the bank, even if he finished last. As his father has repeatedly told him, "You can always use your business degree when you're not able to play competitively anymore. So, play now while you can."

In short, it appeared that while the influence of Gerry's personality dynamics of wanting to please and be accepted by others likely made him more vulnerable to his coworkers' abusiveness, that vulnerability was offset by his job orientation and his option of leaving the abusive work environment to pursue his life-long passion. The end result was that the impact of mobbing was considerably less than if he had had a career orientation in which his personal and professional identity were deeply invested.

GROUP DYNAMICS

The ingroup involved in the mobbing consisted of five of the eight tellers at the branch. Because the branch manager did not directly intervene to stop the abusive behaviors, she was colluding with it through her acts of omission. Such group dynamics, when unwittingly fostered by organizational dynamics, prove quite distressing and disabling for many victims, particularly for those whose individual dynamics provide additional vulnerability.

ORGANIZATIONAL DYNAMICS

Strategy
The stated mission and marketing slogan of the bank was: "Put your money with neighbors you can trust." Advertising emphasized that the bank was locally owned

and responsive to the community. The strategy was to expand aggressively and compete with regional banks on the basis of the lowest service charges and the best customer service in the area. Their stated core values were integrity, loyalty, caring, and putting customers and employees first.

Structure

The bank had nine branch offices and a main office in a large metropolitan area in the southeast. It had three organizational layers, with branches having two layers: tellers and the personal banker who were managed by a branch manager, with the main office having a third level of senior management, headed by the bank president. The bank had reasonably adequate policies and procedures for business transactions. Its employee code of conduct addressed discrimination based on ethnicity, religion, and age, in addition to an anti–sexual harassment policy and a broad policy covering other forms of harassment, presumably mobbing and bullying. Gerry was surprised that training in prevention of harassment was not a part of new employee orientation, nor was there ongoing training for existing employees. Gerry also learned that the president believed that personnel matters had a way of "handling themselves" beyond the basics of hiring, payroll, and benefits, and so he downplayed HR's role. In contrast to other banks in the region, his HR department was headed by a director rather than a vice president (VP). Instead, his HR director reported to the VP of operations. The director had a staff of three direct reports.

Culture

The bank culture reflected the personality of the president who, like his father, the bank's founder, was an entrepreneur who believed that sheer effort of will and a "whatever it takes" attitude was sufficient to "beat the big boys," the regional and national banks in the area. The bank's actual values were hard work, loyalty, and pragmatism. When in doubt, personnel were expected to "make things happen." (Remember that their stated core values were integrity, loyalty, caring, and putting customers and employees first.)

Leadership

The founding president was an entrepreneur with a heart. He had wanted employees to feel like family. When the bank was small, with just two branches and a central office, the president knew all employees. However, as rapid expansion occurred, his ability to know all his employees changed considerably. A common predicament among entrepreneurial leaders is that their strategy is focused on market expansion rather than on professionalizing the organization. Accordingly, the bank's structure reflected this strategy, particularly regarding HR, which was considered by the founder as having limited importance and value. He believed that HR's role was to hire, pay, and manage benefits rather than to encompass the broader role of enhancing employee health and well-being.

Members

Most of the older bank personnel had been hired by the founding president and felt cared for. Their loyalty to him and to the bank was high. Many older employees remained because they were vested in the pension program and were close to retirement. Loyalty among newer personnel was considerably lower, and they were more likely to embody the new president's pragmatic, "whatever it takes" view.

External Environment

The bank had holdings of $11.2 billion but a net profit–loss of $428 million. As a result, its Composite Star rating of 1 was indicative of a financial institution that was significantly below average financial condition. In short, the bank was in trouble due to its costly branch expansion initiative and many questionable mortgages and car loans. Its strategy of offering free checking and the lowest service charges only amplified its problems. As a result, top management's concerns were focused primarily on corporate survival, with little time or energy left to focus on employee health and well-being

Developmental Stage

At the time of the mobbing, TEC Bank was in transition from the expansion stage to the professionalization stage. Nine branches had been opened in the space of 5 years, and the number of employees had increased exponentially during that time. TEC needed to implement a strategic management system, which would require an upgrading and integration of its operating systems. Among others things, its HR function would have to be greatly expanded.

COMMENTARY ABOUT "SURPRISED AT A NEW JOB LOCATION"

A search of the local newspaper's backfiles and court records revealed two pending lawsuits and one Equal Employment Opportunity Commission (EEOC) investigation initiated by personnel against the bank for wrongful termination within the previous 5 years. In one suit, the court had ruled for the terminated staff, and the EEOC found that the bank had failed to provide due process in a sexual harassment claim. The EEOC required that the bank revise its code of conduct, particularly that a due process clause be added to its nonharassment policy.

In short, an assessment of the bank's organizational dynamics revealed an organization that focused on aggressive expansion. This expansion outgrew some of its operating systems, particularly HR. This was unfortunate because, although the founder was deeply concerned about employee well-being in the beginning, concern for employee well-being appeared to have been eclipsed by rapid branch expansion. Consequently, forces that fostered abusiveness were allowed to develop unchecked and were even unwittingly reinforced.

Individual, Group, and Organizational Dynamics in Mobbing: School Setting Illustration

The following example describes a case of mobbing at a private school in which a male middle-school student was assaulted. We outline the group and organizational dynamics involved and explain why this case represents a case of mobbing and not a case of bullying.

ABUSE AT A MIDWEST PRIVATE SCHOOL

A private school in the Midwest is being sued for negligence, assault, battery, breach of duty, and invasion of privacy on allegations that a middle-school student there was assaulted by a fellow student in a locker room after football practice. The attacker allegedly pulled the boy's genitals so forcefully that the boy had to be hospitalized for bruising, abrasions, and blood in his urine. Sheriff's deputies investigated the assault, but closed the case after the boy's family declined to prosecute saying, "They did not wish to see their son revictimized during criminal court proceedings." The family, however, after much reflection and discussion with friends and professionals, did decide to file a civil lawsuit against the school. "Why sue the school?" one might ask. The abuse was perpetrated by a fellow student and not by a school official or employee. How is this an example of mobbing and not simply bullying? That individual, group, and organizational dynamics were clearly involved makes this a case of mobbing and not bullying. The explanation and analysis follow.

INDIVIDUAL DYNAMICS

Reportedly, the attacker, another middle school student, had "a penchant for violence" and previously engaged in violent behavior at the school. He subsequently left the school or was expelled prior to the suit being filed. Problems with impulse control, a past history of aggressive, acting out behavior, and developmental problems in the area of expressive language were all features of the perpetrator's personal history.

GROUP DYNAMICS

While the attack took place, other middle school students were in the locker room and observed it. One of these students stood by laughing after stealing the boy's clothes. Another videotaped the assault and distributed the video to other students.

ORGANIZATIONAL DYNAMICS

Both of the victim's parents had worked at the school for more than a decade and sent their other children to the same school as well. One of the perpetrator's parents had also worked at the school for a period of time. Cultural and leadership dynamics seemed to have fostered the mobbing behavior itself, and the subsequent effort to downplay the attack.

Culture

The suit contended that the private school fostered a culture of recklessness among football players. The attorney representing the parents contended that "the attitude at the school has been that such physical contact was a normal display of youthful aggression and was just a case of boys being boys." The lawsuit stated that the school was protecting itself and downplayed the attack because the attacker's grandfather had served on the school's board and the attacker's parent had worked at the school. Reportedly, the school failed to discipline the attacker. The school's core values and culture may explain why the victim's parents initially declined to prosecute. The parents said that they feared their son would be revictimized in criminal court proceedings. In actuality, they may have declined out of fear of reprisal from those supporting the school, including powerful alumni.

Leadership

Reportedly, neither the school's president nor the coach made efforts to rectify the situation. They did not launch an immediate investigation of the incident and circumstances leading to it, nor did they discipline the other boys who were involved in the distribution of the video, even though, reportedly, both the school president and coach had been made aware of the existence of the video. In fact, the junior varsity football coach was also named in the suit for negligence and breach of fiduciary duty because of his alleged failure to supervise the students and to halt distribution of the video. It is noteworthy that the school's president has apparently made no public or private apology or announced a plan to prevent such behavior from occurring in the future.

Members

It appears that members of the school community—namely, students, teachers, and parents—were highly protective of the school and concerned about preserving its reputation in the larger community, even at the expense of students who had been harmed by the culture of recklessness in the football program. Despite the nonsportsman-like behavior of the attacker and onlookers, members sought to protect their school and what it said it stood for rather than disclose a serious harm done to another of its members. Ingroup and outgroup dynamics appear to have been powerful in maintaining the silence of the members to outsiders, such as the media. In this case, members cooperated with each other and demonstrated strong group cohesion through the creation of insiders and outsiders, an ingroup and an outgroup. The ingroup stood together in grotesquely minimizing a serious harm perpetrated on a member who had now been designated as an outsider through the operation of group dynamics.

External Environment
While the school had once enjoyed a unique status in the larger community, in recent years it found itself competing with similar private schools for students and for financial support from the community at large. News reports and court records indicated that the school was experiencing financial troubles and that it had a few pending lawsuits.

Developmental Stage
The school appeared to be in transition between consolidation and early bureaucratization. In such a transition stage, the school was vulnerable to both internal and external threats to its financial viability. Accordingly, personnel matters—including mobbing or other forms of abusiveness—were often underplayed in the hopes that they would "go away by themselves," or the complainant was targeted as the "real problem."

COMMENTARY ABOUT ABUSE AT A MIDWEST PRIVATE SCHOOL

The fact that the victim's parents, as well as the perpetrator's parent, had all worked at the small private school at one time or another suggests that the school community was close-knit. It may account for why the victim's parents initially declined to prosecute the case—ostensibly because they did not want their son to be revictimized in court proceedings, but more likely out of fear of reprisal from those supporting the school. Furthermore, a case could be made that the school's culture of recklessness appeared to have fostered and activated individual and group dynamics of abusiveness that ultimately took the form of mobbing one of its own members. A key indicator of the organization's involvement was leadership's failure to sanction the attacker. Had this case been a case of bullying, the perpetrator would have acted abusively, but school personnel would not have been a party to the abuse—either directly or indirectly.

Conclusion

In cases of mobbing, be they at workplaces, at schools, or in other kinds of organizational settings, the tendency to look at the individual(s) involved and to ignore the organizational context is a powerful one known as the *fundamental attribution error* (Jones, 1979, 1990; Jones & Harris, 1967) that we described in Chapter 1. Understanding mobbing requires examining the organizational context and recognizing that some tools are available both for helping to understand how and why mobbing develops and for identifying organizational risks for its development. In the previous chapter, we looked at organizations cross-sectionally and examined their subsystems in order to identify systemic vulnerabilities most likely to give rise to mobbing. In this chapter, we took a longitudinal perspective and examined the stages of growth, development, and decline within organizations in order to provide tools for mapping where an organization might be in its development and what risk factors for the emergence of mobbing are associated with that particular organizational life cycle stage.

Combined together, cross-sectional and longitudinal organizational analyses provide an empirically derived means for gaining a retrospective understanding of the organizational context in mobbing cases that have already occurred and for a prospective mapping of organizational risk factors that may potentially give rise to mobbing cases in the future. Given the relative lack of attention to organizational context in the development of mobbing, such tools for organizational analyses can only be of help in understanding what happened when a mobbing has occurred in the past and in working to prevent mobbing from happening in the future.

As we discussed in this chapter, the organization is a human system that is developing and changing and that is both influencing and influenced by its internal and external environment, as well as by the individual and group dynamics of its members and other stakeholders. A useful understanding of the influences and specific "risk factors" for abusive behavior in school and workplace settings can be established by attending to the interaction of individual dynamics, group dynamics, and organizational dynamics. We again note that the propensity for attributing the cause of mobbing to the pathology of the perpetrator(s) is very limiting both in preventing and in correcting its ill effects. We emphasize that both group and organizational dynamics have enormous influence on the behavior of individuals. Our primary focus in this chapter and in this set of chapters on the organization has been to emphasize the central role of the organization in the development of mobbing—a point that continues to be overlooked in the mischaracterization of so many cases of mobbing as bullying. Our analysis of organizational dynamics both cross-sectionally and longitudinally provides a basis for understanding high leverage points for organizational intervention that we will discuss in Part 4, as part of our discussion of recovery and prevention strategies.

Part Three

CONSEQUENCES OF MOBBING

8

Health and Well-Being

Trauma is a psychophysical experience, even when the
traumatic event causes no direct bodily harm.
—Babette Rothschild (2000, p. 5)

This section of the book focuses on examining the consequences of mobbing across a number of basic life domains. These basic life domains include individual and family health and well-being, family and social relationships, and career and work performance. We place considerable importance on investigating the consequences or effects of mobbing on victims and their families. As we described in Chapter 3, our definitions of mobbing, both in the workplace and in schools and other settings, include a clear statement of its negative consequences. As we mentioned in that chapter, many definitions do not. In their study of negative workplace behaviors in the United Kingdom's National Health Service (NHS), Burnes and Pope (2007) concluded that "our findings suggest that it is not necessarily the frequency with which a negative behavior occurs which matters, but the effect on those concerned" (p. 301), and they recommended reconsidering definitions to include an effect or impact component—a position with which we obviously agree and to which we devote this section of the book.

In this chapter, we examine the extensive and growing body of research linking negative health outcomes to exposure to mobbing and other abusive workplace behaviors. Table. 8.1 presents a comprehensive overview of research within the last decade, and, in particular, within the last 5 years, that demonstrates strong associations between negative physical and psychological health consequences and victimization through mobbing or bullying. We have made every effort to report new research since the publication of what has rightfully become regarded as the major summary of existing international research about abusive workplace behaviors and their consequences (Einarsen, Hoel, Zapf, & Cooper, 2003a). By necessity, the research summary includes research that uses "bullying" as the name of the social process studied in relation to health consequences. Using our definitions and standpoint, we would maintain that many of those studies in fact examined the phenomenon of mobbing. Nonetheless, to provide a comprehensive overview of the research, both bullying and mobbing research is included. We also included studies that addressed the health consequences of bullying and mobbing for children and adolescents.

It would be impossible for us to review and discuss every health problem associated with mobbing and bullying. That is why we regard Table 8.1 as so important—it can provide direction to readers to multiple studies demonstrating specific negative health outcomes. The relevance of negative health consequences from mobbing and bullying will also be incorporated into the discussion in Chapter 9 about the impact of mobbing on family and career and in Chapter 11 about the development of personalized recovery plans.

Mobbing Is a Public Health Issue

Health consequences are a central area of concern when considering mobbing and its effects. Behaviors, even negative behaviors that do not lead to negative outcomes, are usually not given much special attention. Mobbing has a long history of association with negative outcomes for its victims, yet the negative health outcomes of mobbing are only beginning to garner the attention needed for action at a public health level. These negative health outcomes have potentially devastating effects on the victim, on the victim's family, and on the victim's social functioning. They provide a justification for classifying mobbing as an identifiable risk factor for physical and psychological health problems, making it a public health problem. The research about negative health outcomes related to mobbing also points to the presence of disparities in physical and mental health status and care between the population of those who have been mobbed and those who haven't, again supporting the public health nature of the problem.

Reviewing the negative health consequences of mobbing and bullying in relation to their pervasiveness leads to the inevitable conclusion that mobbing and bullying are public health problems requiring the attention of communities, employers, schools, families, and individuals. A problem requiring public health action is one that (a) occurs frequently and widely, (b) causes serious disability, injury, or suffering, (c) is amenable to effective intervention, and (d) for which acceptable interventions exist. The body of research from around the world about the negative health consequences of mobbing and bullying supports the contention that mobbing should be treated as a public health issue, with associated public health actions designed to reduce its frequency and societal health burden.

In addition to the public health issues related to mobbing, there are additional reasons for considering its health consequences. As anti-mobbing organizational policies and healthy workplace legislative initiatives gain momentum, health consequences will be an important factor for organizations to understand in evaluating the seriousness of the problem and in evaluating their exposure to liability,

Table 8.1 **Evidence-based Health Consequences of School and Workplace Mobbing and Bullying**

Authors	Research Study/Sample	Country	Health Consequences
Arseneault, Walsh, Trzesniewski, Newcombe, Caspi, and Moffit (2006)	Subsample of children aged 5–7 exposed to bullying selected from the Environmental Risk Longitudinal Twin Study, a nationally representative sample, consisting of 2,232 children; initial assessment at age 5 with follow-up at age 7 and comparison with nonbullied controls	United Kingdom	Physical harm: Bruises, cuts, and burns Psychological harm: Bad dreams, tummy aches, school avoidance Pure victims demonstrated: Internalizing problems Unhappiness at school Girls who were pure victims also demonstrated: Externalizing problems
Cassitto and Gilioli (2003)	Investigation of burnout, mobbing-related adjustment disorder, and post-traumatic stress disorder (PTSD) in patient cohort at a workplace health clinic	Italy	Depression Phobic syndromes Anxiety syndromes Hypertension Heart disease Eating disorders Drug addiction.

(Continued)

Table 8.1 **Evidence-based Health Consequences of School and Workplace Mobbing and Bullying** *(Continued)*

Authors	Research Study/Sample	Country	Health Consequences
Chen, Hwu, Kung, Chiu, and Wang (2008)	Cross-sectional survey of 231 nurses, nurses' aides, and clerks at a psychiatric hospital; 25% reported being a victim of a form of workplace harassment or violence in the past year, over 50% reported witnessing workplace harassment or violence in the past year, and over 60% had personally experienced some form of workplace harassment or violence during their employment	Taiwan	High anxiety levels about physical violence Moderate anxiety levels about verbal abuse PTSD symptoms
Corney (2008)	Heideggerian hermeneutic phenomenology; intensive interviews with two nurses who had experienced workplace bullying	United Kingdom	Sleeplessness Nausea Anxiety Tachycardia Excessive crying Reduced self-esteem Self-blame Feelings of paranoia Intense panic

Study	Description	Country	Findings
De Vogli, Ferrie, Chandola, Kivimäki, and Marmot (2007).	Prospective cohort study of 8,298 civil service workers in London	United Kingdom	Coronary heart disease Poor physical and mental functioning
Forero, McLellan, Rissell, and Bauman (1999)	Cross-sectional survey of 3,918 schoolchildren between 11 and 16 years, 12.7% of whom reported being bullied in the last school term and 21.5% of whom reported both being bullied and bullying	New South Wales, Australia	(Results for the "bullied" category only) Loneliness Rejected by other students at school Disliked school Skipped school more frequently
Gruber and Fineran (2008)	Survey of 522 middle and high school students, comparing the impact of bullying and sexual harassment victimization	United States	Lower self-esteem Poorer mental health Poorer physical health More trauma symptoms Greater substance abuse (Health outcomes across all dimensions worse when bullying contained a sexual harassment component)

(Continued)

Authors	Research Study/Sample	Country	Health Consequences
Hoel, Faragher, and Cooper (2004)	Correlational study between (a) self-reported bullying and health outcomes, (b) exposure to negative behavior and health outcomes, (c) level of experience of bullying and health outcomes among various groups, and (d) individual negative acts and effects on mental health; sample consisted of 5,288 male and female participants across 70 organizations in Great Britain, including the public, private, and voluntary sectors	United Kingdom	(a) Physical and mental health problems, with high mean score suggesting onset of PTSD symptoms for some victims (b) Significant correlation between experience of negative workplace behaviors and physical and mental health problems (c) Significant correlation between respondents who were currently being bullied and respondents who had been bullied within the last 5 years and physical and mental health problems (d) For 26 out of the 29 negative behaviors, significant negative effects on mental health

Author (year)	Description	Country	Outcomes
Kivimaki, Virtanen, Vartia, Elovainio, Vahtera, and Keltikangas-Järvinen (2003)	Two surveys of cohort of 5,432 hospital employees using prospective data of newly diagnosed depression and coronary heart disease in participants disease-free at baseline	Finland	Depression Coronary heart disease
Lewis (2004)	Qualitative case studies of 15 university lecturers who had experienced bullying	Wales	Powerlessness Humiliation Inferiority Withdrawal Embarrassment Shame Anger Despair Sadness Exhaustion Isolation Emotional distance from partners.
Lutgen-Sandvik (2008)	Qualitative analysis of 20 workers exposed to workplace abuse	Global	Intense negative emotional experiences consisting of stigmatization, traumatization, loss, and assault on personal and professional identity

(Continued)

Table 8.1 **Evidence-based Health Consequences of School and Workplace Mobbing and Bullying** (*Continued*)

Authors	Research Study/Sample	Country	Health Consequences
Matthiesen and Einarsen (2004)	Anonymous survey of 180 victims of prior or ongoing exposure to workplace bullying who were members of support groups for bullied workers	Norway	Psychiatric distress Cumulative (type 2) trauma PTSD
Mitchell, Ybarra, and Finkelhor (2007)	Telephone survey of national sample of 1,501 youth Internet users aged between 10 and 17 years about experiences of offline interpersonal victimization (i.e., bullying and sexual abuse) and online interpersonal victimization (i.e., sexual solicitation and harassment)	United States	All forms of interpersonal victimization related independently to: Depressive symptoms Delinquent behavior Substance use
Niedhammer, David, Degioanni and 143 occupational physicians (2006)	Cross-sectional survey of general working population in southeast France; sample consisted of 3,132 men and 4,562 women; 8.8% of the men and 10.7% of the women reported exposure to bullying (using Leymann's definition of mobbing) in the previous 12 months	France	Depression Depression lasting beyond the exposure to bullying
Nansel, Overpeck, Pilla, Ruan, Simons-Morton, and Scheidt (2001)	Representative sample of 15,686 students in grades 6 through 10	United States	Poor social and emotional adjustment Greater difficulty making friends Poorer relationships with classmates Loneliness

Nolfe, Petrella, Blasi, Zontini, and Nolfe (2008)	Diagnostic clinical trial of 733 participants referred to a work psychopathology medical center after experiencing workplace mobbing	Italy	Major depression PTSD
Pompili, Lester, Innamorati, De Pisa, Puccinno, Nastro, Tatarelli, and Girardi (2008)	Examined suicide risk in subjects exposed to mobbing; sample included 102 people, both men and women	Italy	52% found to have some risk of suicide, with 20.6% identified as medium to high risk of suicide
Gini and Pozzoli (2009)	Conducted a meta-analysis of quantitative and qualitative studies about the relationships between bullying and psychosomatic complaints in children and adolescents aged 7–16. Three random effects meta-analyses were conducted for three groups of children (a) victims, (b) bullies, and (c) bully-victims	Included studies were from around the world	Victims, bullies, and bully-victims all had higher risks for psychosomatic problems than did noninvolved peers
Punzi, Cassito, Castellini, Costa, and Gilioli (2007)	Examined 226 clinical records, from 1997 to 2003, of patients reporting a mobbing situation	Italy	Exhaustion Sleep disorders Mood disorders Sexual disorders
Quine (2003)	Anonymous survey of 1,000 junior hospital physicians, equally divided between men and women; 37% reported having been bullied in the previous 12 months, whereas 69% reported having witnessed the bullying of others	United Kingdom	Increased psychological distress Decreased job satisfaction.

(Continued)

Table 8.1 Evidence-based Health Consequences of School and Workplace Mobbing and Bullying (*Continued*)

Authors	Research Study/Sample	Country	Health Consequences
Sourander, Ronning, Brunstein-Klomek, Gyllenberg, Kumpulainen, Niemelä, Helenius, Sillanmäki, Ristkari, Tamminen, Moilanen, Piha, and Almqvist (2009)	National birth cohort study from ages 8 to 24; participants were 5,038 children born in 1981, with histories of bullying and victimization obtained at age 8 from parents, teachers, and self-reports; purpose was to assess relationship between childhood bullying and victimization and later psychiatric hospitalizations	Finland	Girls who were frequently victimized were at higher risk for long-term psychiatric involvement irrespective of their psychiatric status at baseline Boys who were both bullies and victims of bullying were found to be at the highest risk for long term psychiatric morbidity
Tehrani (2004)	Survey of 165 care professionals—40% of whom had been bullied in the previous 2 years and 68% of whom had witnessed bullying	United Kingdom	PTSD with symptom clusters different from those experiencing acute trauma High levels of re-experiencing and arousal forming a single cluster and avoidance a separate cluster

Tomei, Cinti, Sancini, Cerratti, Pimpinella, Ciarrocca, Tomei, and Fioravanti (2007)	Systematic literature review and meta-analysis of existing studies on health effects of mobbing	Italy	Psychosomatic symptoms Stress Anxiety Negative perception of environment.
Tracy, Lutgen-Sandvik, and Alberts (2006)	Qualitative research study of 27 victims of workplace abuse	United States	Intense negative emotional experiences; metaphors of nightmares, water torture, being beaten, and being character assassinated are examples of the expression of intense negative emotional experiencing subsequent to mobbing
Van der Wal, De Wit, and Hirasing (2003)	Correlational study of bullying (both direct and indirect) and psychosocial health of 4,811 children between the ages of 9 and 13 years	The Netherlands	Increased depression and suicidal ideation for both boys and girls

(Continued)

Table 8.1 **Evidence-based Health Consequences of School and Workplace Mobbing and Bullying** *(Continued)*

Authors	*Research Study/Sample*	*Country*	*Health Consequences*
Westhues (1998, 2004, 2005a, 2005b)	Series of qualitative case study analyses of mobbed professors	Canada and the United States	Insomnia
			Nightmares
			Obsessive thinking
			Stomach aches
			Nausea
			Weight gain/loss
			Diarrhea
			High blood pressure
			Blurred vision
			Respiratory infections
			Hives
			Heart palpitations
			Chest pains
			Panic attacks
			Sudden death
			Depression
			Joint suicide
			Homicidal rage

Source	Description	Country	Consequences
Workplace Bullying Institute-Zogby International (2007)	Representative survey of 7,740 US adults	United States	Psychological or physical stress-related negative health consequences
Yildirim and Yildirim (2007)	Cross-sectional and descriptive study; sample included 505 nurses, 86.5% of whom reported exposure to workplace mobbing in the previous 12 months	Turkey	10% considered committing suicide Feeling tired and stressed Headaches Excessive eating or loss of appetite Gastrointestinal problems Extreme sadness and crying Life away from work was negatively impacted

should anti-mobbing policies or legislation be enacted. For example, in most cases of workplace injury, the more serious the injury, the greater the liability of the organization. In terms of public health actions to mitigate negative health outcomes, schools and workplaces are primary sites of potential intervention.

Health Consequences of Mobbing: Injury Not Illness

Davenport, Schwartz, and Elliott (1999), the authors of the first book about mobbing in the United States, maintain that psychological problems suffered as an outcome of having been mobbed at work constitute workplace injuries and not illnesses. The distinction is a critical one, especially since so many of the negative health outcomes associated with mobbing are psychological in nature. It's much easier to ignore, minimize, or blame the victim for a work-related negative psychological health outcome than it is to do the same for a work-related physical injury.

When a forklift truck drops its palate on a worker stocking shelves and the worker breaks his leg, there is no dispute that the worker has sustained a workplace injury. When a worker's personal and professional reputation is systematically assaulted by coworkers and managers, and the worker suffers major depression and becomes suicidal, it is not nearly as clear that the worker has sustained a workplace injury according to our current understandings. Where psychological and psychosocial disorders are concerned, organizations and other workplaces have been less ready to see these injuries as related to workplace conditions. Instead, they have reverted to traditional cultural understandings of mental and psychosocial disorders as arising from within the individual and as unrelated to events or social conditions in the workplace. The difference between a psychological injury sustained in the workplace and a psychological disorder attributed to individual psychological functioning is an essential one for understanding the effects of mobbing. The research reflected in this chapter makes the case for understanding psychological harm subsequent to mobbing in organizations and institutions as injuries, not as individual psychopathology.

The issue of psychological injury is also important because one of the more common ways to mob a victim is to use either direct labeling or innuendo to characterize the target as mentally unstable or mentally impaired in the first place, thereby blaming the victim for his or her own predicament in the workplace (Davenport, Schwartz, & Elliott, 1999; Duffy & Sperry, 2007; Leymann & Gustafsson, 1996; Namie & Namie, 2000, 2009a). This "blame the victim" mentality in workplace mobbing is no different than that once associated with sexual harassment, sexual assault, and rape cases, in which the victim was the one "put on trial" and required to establish innocence, not the perpetrator.

The use of psychological labeling to discredit individuals, as often occurs in mobbing, is one of the worst forms of abuse of psychiatric and psychological knowledge. It is associated with totalitarian regimes and the suppression of political and ideological dissent, as in China and the former Soviet Union (Birley, 2002). When psychological labeling of complainants is used or abused by employers and the legal system to defend against tort claims resulting from workplace abuse, it contributes to the perpetuation of the stigma that has handicapped people with mental health problems as much as or more than the problems themselves (Jensvold, 1993).

Work and Protection of Physical Health and Safety

Going to work is supposed to be a relatively safe activity. Those who work in high-risk environments generally know the level of risk to which they may be exposed. For example, aid workers in conflicted areas of the world sign informed consents before being allowed to travel to the designated conflict area to do their job. They know what the general conditions on the ground are, and they know how easy or difficult it will be to leave the area and what kind of delays they might expect to encounter if the situation on the ground deteriorates or if they wish to leave for other reasons. Those working with dangerous machinery—for example, in meat processing plants—know the risks of forgetting to turn the machinery off before attempting maintenance. Workers have been dragged into these machines with deadly consequences. There is a reason that medical personnel working with magnetic resonance imaging (MRI) machines get very agitated if nonauthorized personnel or patients walk into the MRI rooms. The magnets in the MRIs are so powerful that metal objects like scissors can fly out of someone's pocket across the room. Technicians working with biological materials requiring containment are extensively trained to prevent contamination and, depending upon the level of biological containment involved, may be subject to routine decontamination procedures at the end of each work day.

Industry, the public, and occupational safety specialists take it for granted that these kinds of working environments are made as physically safe as possible, are continuously monitored, and that all personnel are extensively and specifically trained to understand how to maintain optimally safe working conditions and to protect themselves and others from harm. It is not just high-risk work environments in which physical safety is a concern. If they wish to avoid significant liability, grocery stores can't have broken shelving at the end of an aisle that could stick someone in the eye. From small offices to large office buildings, when floors are being washed or polished, cones are used to reroute traffic or signs are posted to indicate that the floor is wet or slippery. It is second nature for supervisors and managers in office settings to be on the lookout for the curled up edge of a nonslip mat that could trip someone and cause them to fall. Awareness of safety issues in the workplace is at a high enough level that responsible employees not charged with workplace safety duties will address or report what they consider to be hazards on their own initiative. Although it is certainly not a perfect world, issues of physical safety in the workplace are addressed at many levels, both formal and informal, within organizations and by outside regulatory bodies. The same cannot be said for emotional and psychological safety in the workplace.

The United Stated Department of Labor, Bureau of Labor Statistics for 2007, the most recent data available, reports nonfatal occupational injuries and illnesses requiring days away from work according to four categories; namely, the nature of the illness or injury, the part of the body involved, the event or exposure leading to the illness or injury, and the source of the illness or injury. The website of the Bureau of Labor Statistics (2007) provides an example (¶3) in which a nurse's aide sprains (nature of injury or illness) her back (body part involved) as a result of overexertion in lifting (event or exposure leading to the illness) a patient (identified as the source). In the 2007 statistics, the body parts involved in injuries included the head, eye, trunk, and extremities—arms and legs, and hands and feet. Additional categories of "body systems" and "multiple parts" were also included. The nature of the injuries and illnesses named reflected the focus on the musculoskeletal system with sprains, fractures, amputations, carpal tunnel syndrome, and tendonitis being among the most common. The skin was another body system highly represented, with injuries like cuts, burns, and lacerations identified frequently.

The Occupational Safety and Health Administration (OSHA) defines a work-related injury or illness in this way: "An injury or illness is considered by the Occupational Safety and Health Administration to be *work-related* [emphasis theirs] if an event or exposure in the work environment either caused or contributed to the resulting condition or significantly aggravated a preexisting condition" (Bureau of Labor Statistics, n.d., ¶ 1). The Bureau of Labor 2007 statistics did not list any illnesses or injuries ordinarily associated with mental, psychosocial, or emotional health. Under their heading "Events or exposure leading to the illness or injury," the only heading that could potentially involve coworkers is "assaults and violent acts by person." The source of injury list does not include psychological abuse by others.

It is fairly clear that the physical safety of workers has been a priority of OSHA and that implementation of safety standards within workplaces has led to substantially safer physical environments. We hope that regulatory standards for maintaining healthy workplaces will catch up with the extensive body of research noted in this chapter indicating negative health outcomes from workplace mobbing and bullying resulting from complex group and organizational dynamics. As we have reviewed, systems for reporting workplace physical injuries and maintaining safe physical work environments are in place and have yielded large-scale positive health benefits. Public health actions to address the negative consequences of workplace mobbing are equally needed to ensure both the psychological as well as the physical safety and well-being of workers.

Work and Protection of Psychological and Emotional Health

Improvements in workplace physical safety have led to an increase in focus on overall employee well-being, with many companies offering wellness programs, employee assistance programs for help with personal and family problems, on-site gyms or off-site gym memberships, smoking cessation programs, and a host of other wellness-based programs. These kinds of programs fit nicely with Spurgeon's (2003) suggestion that overall well-being, including both physical and psychological health, should be a focus of workplace health. Many workers take advantage of these kinds of programs when possible.

What these programs don't address, however, is the reality of workplace mobbing and its potential toll on both the physical and psychological health of the worker and the worker's family. Psychological and emotional workplace safety has largely been ignored in the United States and, until it is addressed, we cannot say that overall well-being in the workplace has been a focus of attention, with the exception, in recent years, of a relatively small number of researchers, mental health practitioners, and advocates who have taken the issue of workplace mobbing seriously and worked to bring it to public attention.

Notwithstanding, there is a body of research describing the construct of employee well-being and its relationship to organizational life. This research addresses what Spurgeon (2003) has identified as the shift in occupational health away from a primary focus on physical health and safety toward a much wider focus on overall well-being that includes psychological well-being as a core component. Spurgeon states that "improvements in physical conditions at work, as well as in society as a whole, have meant that health expectations have risen beyond those which consist simply of an absence of disease. Instead, there is now more frequent expression of the need for a more general sense of 'well-being,' a concept which recognizes both the psychological and physical components of health" (p. 327). In the brief review of employee well-being and organizational health research that follows, it is increasingly clear that the organizational structure, its leadership, and their strategies have the most influence on employee well-being or lack of it. There is no getting away from the ethical implications that, with such influence, comes accountability and responsibility.

Employee Well-Being and Organizational Health

Hart and Cooper (2001) have proposed a strongly evidence-based organizational health framework for understanding occupational stress and well-being. The uniqueness of their model is that it replaces the individually based stresses-and-strains approach to examining workplace health and well-being with a systemic framework that requires examining individual employee health and well-being in relation to organizational performance and outcomes. Since our focus on negative health outcomes from mobbing includes organizational accountability, it makes sense that we would endorse a model of occupational health and well-being that also includes organizational responsibility as an important dimension when things go well and both the employee and organization are functioning within an optimal range of health and well-being. In Hart and Cooper's model, employee well-being consists of the cognitive component of job satisfaction and the emotional components of morale and distress, with morale representing positive job affect and distress representing negative job affect. However, employee well-being is only a part of the picture, one systemically connected to individual and organizational factors and to organizational performance outcomes.

The organizational performance outcomes that Hart and Cooper's (2001) model link to employee well-being include discretionary job performance (i.e., taking the initiative, work enhancement activities, etc.), customer satisfaction, absences and sick leave, medical expenses, workers' compensation claims, and job turnover. When employee and organizational well-being are high, employees perform more discretionary job-related activities, customer satisfaction is higher, and job turnover is lower. When employee and organizational well-being are low, the opposite is the case. Mobbing would clearly be an indicator of poor overall organizational health, with associated low levels of employee well-being and high levels of negative job performance indicators.

Cotton and Hart (2003) report that "quite different occupational groups (e.g., teachers and police) are more similar than different in that generic organisational factors exert the strongest influence on levels of well-being" (p. 122).This, in spite of the conventional wisdom that police officers would be more stressed by the operational factors of risk and danger in their work environment than teachers coping with difficult students. The practical application of the Hart and Cooper (2001) organizational health model, which includes employee well-being as a central component, is that the most effective and enduring interventions for improving both employee well-being and organizational performance are those made at the organizational leadership and organizational development levels, not at the individual employee level. Our conceptual model of the salience of organizational structure, strategies, culture, and leadership as key determinants of mobbing parallels the organizational health framework for understanding how employee well-being is either promoted or obstructed.

A focus on organizational caring and employee well-being already takes place in organizations that Nonaka and Nishiguchi (2001) would identify as "high care." In these organizations, management pays attention to employee social relationships and fosters the sharing of knowledge through internal social networks. Employees are not left alone, in isolation in high-care work environments. The result is the creation of shared knowledge throughout the organization and the development of sustainable capacity building. In high-care organizations, attention to the quality of social relationships is built into the organization's structure, leading to the development of strong social networks that become the conduits for knowledge sharing. High-care organizations are probably not immune from mobbing, but the importance of caring for people and encouraging the sharing of knowledge is clearly at odds with the American cultural values of competitiveness and "every man for himself." Work environments that are high on competition and low on caring are incubators for the development of workplace mobbing.

In Table 8.1, both the physical and psychological threats to well-being experienced by those who have been exposed to mobbing and bullying are described. The findings leave no doubt that mobbing and bullying are significant public health issues requiring public health actions and effective organizational interventions. These interventions, as well as preventions strategies, will be discussed later in Part IV of this book.

As is apparent from Table 8.1, research studies from around the world indicate the presence of both physical and psychological health problems in the aftermath of exposure to mobbing and bullying. The research studies cited offer an overview of both the depth and the breadth of the negative health consequences since they include both qualitative and quantitative research findings. The qualitative studies provide a window into how workers who have been mobbed experience this devastating social process and how it has affected their views of themselves, the workplace, and the world. The quantitative studies provide a snapshot of the range of negative health consequences, both physical and psychological, that workers who have been mobbed experience during and after the mobbing. The studies are from around the world and include recent research samples from countries as diverse as Australia, the United Kingdom, Taiwan, Canada, Turkey, the United States, and continental European countries. A glance at the "Health Consequences" column suggests that, if these health effects were identified in workplaces and related to physical hazards, an army of occupational and health specialists would be sent in to remediate the situation because the seriousness and pervasiveness of the health outcomes begins to look epidemic. Table 8.1 reveals that, for many workers around the world, the concept of employee well-being is nothing but a shattered dream with psychological and emotional well-being particularly splintered. Workers don't function in isolation, and the degree of injury associated with workplace mobbing has direct effects on marital and intimate relationships and on marital and family functioning, as well as on the workplace and its level of functioning. The family, relationship, and career consequences of mobbing will be addressed in Chapters 9 and 10.

Mobbing and Post-Traumatic Stress Disorder (PTSD)

In the majority of research studies cited, symptoms of anxiety and post-traumatic stress syndrome (PTSD) are listed as negative health outcomes. Leymann (1992), the German psychiatrist working in Sweden who originally identified "mobbing" as a highly destructive workplace phenomenon, believed that PTSD was the correct diagnosis for the majority of patients whom he saw in his workplace mobbing clinic in Sweden. Whether anxiety symptoms resulting from workplace mobbing meet the criteria for a diagnosis of PTSD has been a subject of debate (Einarsen & Mikkelsen, 2003). The reason for the debate revolves largely around the first item of Criterion A1 in the American Psychiatric Association's *Diagnostic and Statistical Manual of Mental Disorders* (DSM-IV-TR), which describes the nature of the stressor to which a person must have been subjected in order to be diagnosable as having PTSD. Currently, the stressor is described as the experiencing or witnessing of traumatic event(s) that threatens the physical safety and integrity of oneself or others and to which the person experiencing or witnessing the event(s) responds with intense fear, or helplessness, or horror (American Psychiatric Association, 2000).

The workgroups meeting to create the DSM V, which is due out in May 2013, are examining the criteria for making a diagnosis of PTSD, including the particularly contentious Criterion A1, and are evaluating research findings and clinical perspectives relevant to it. In their research, Boals and Schuettler (2009) concluded: "Based on our results, we agree . . . that a variety of events, not only those that currently meet A1 criterion, can result in significant levels of PTSD symptoms" (p. 461). In relation to Criterion A1, the findings of Boals and Schuettler (2009) are in agreement with the earlier findings of Gold, Marx, Soler-Baillo, and Sloan (2005), who concluded that events less extreme than those suggested by Criterion A1 can also lead to PTSD. These conclusions are also supported by the research of Bodkin, Pope, Detke, and Hudson (2007) at McLean Hospital in Massachusetts, who found that about 80% of the participants in their traumatized group (i.e., meeting Criterion A1), their equivocally traumatized group (i.e., subthreshold traumatic events that would include events like workplace mobbing), and their nontraumatized group met the criteria for PTSD, thus raising significant questions about whether major trauma is required to cause PTSD.

In 2005, the authors of a large cohort study in the Netherlands similarly concluded that "our study adds to the evidence that PTSD is perhaps not specific to A1 criterion traumatic events, but that it can also arise after life events" (Mol et al., 2005, p. 499). Their research supported their hypothesis that less severe stressors like chronic illness or work-related problems that change one's view of who one is in the world can also lead to PTSD. Ten years ago, Bremner (1999) said that "there is a natural tendency to resist stress-related diagnoses, given their potentially explosive impact on societal approaches to responsibility and accountability" (p. 351). Our goal is to encourage the continuation of the dialogue about social responsibility and accountability in light of the evidence generated about the health impact of school and workplace mobbing and abuse since Bremner made his well-know statement. The findings about the health impact of school and workplace mobbing and abuse presented in this chapter also lend strong credence to the development of PTSD symptomatology in the aftermath of mobbing, which would currently be categorized as a subthreshold stressor.

In cases of mobbing, threats to one's physical integrity are less frequently present, but are noted nonetheless in the literature (Westhues, 2005a). Many victims of mobbing meet the criteria of PTSD if we take the position that assaults to one's personal and professional identity and emotional and psychological stability do in fact threaten one's physical integrity and represent serious threats to the self. Character assassination, belittling, attempts to turn others against the mobbing victim, attacks on one's professional identity and competence, and many other negative acts associated with mobbing strike at the very heart of a person's sense of self-identity and wholeness. Mobbing victims often describe feeling invisible or like a nonperson (Duffy & Sperry, 2007). They have been ostracized and segregated from the work community and accompanying web of social relationships. They are no longer whole and have become "other."

Such threats to one's sense of personal integrity and reputation during workplace mobbing do result in threats to one's physical integrity. One only needs to review the negative health outcomes in Table 8.1 that cite coronary heart disease, suicide, and sudden death as possible negative health consequences. The recent work of Pompili, Lester, Innamorati, De Pisa, Puccinno, Nastro, Tatarelli, and Girardi (2008) demonstrates the results of their efforts to assess the suicide risk of mobbing victims. In their study, 52% of those exposed to mobbing were assessed as posing some suicide risk, and over 20% were assessed as posing a medium to high suicide risk. Leymann (1987), as part of his pioneering research, found that about 15% of suicides in Sweden could be attributed to having experienced workplace mobbing. Death is, of course, the ultimate threat to one's physical integrity but the potential severity of the psychological and emotional symptoms suffered by mobbing victims also threaten physical integrity.

Another way of looking at trauma as a threat to one's physical integrity, even if the trauma is primarily psychological, is through the emerging field of traumatology. Robert Scaer (2005), a neurologist and leader in the traumatology field, argues persuasively that trauma has a cumulative effect and alters the brain and body. He states clearly that "in the brain of the trauma victim, the synapses, neurons, and neurochemicals have been substantially and indefinitely altered by the effects of a unique life experience" (p. 58). He adds that "almost any social setting where control is lost and relative helplessness is part of the environment can easily progress to a traumatic experience. Perhaps the most obvious and pervasive source of this insidious societal trauma is in the workplace" (p. 132). Scaer's meaning is clear. Trauma cannot easily be separated out between physical and psychological effects because all trauma affects both the brain and the body. The effects of trauma accumulate over time, and this may provide a conceptual framework for understanding why some mobbing victims suffer more severely than others. Those who have had fewer life traumas have had less negative brain alteration over time and may be able to bounce back more easily than others whose life trajectory has included multiple traumas. No one escapes trauma in life, be it the accumulation of the smaller traumas of everyday life, or the larger traumas that inscribe themselves in the brains of their victims and fundamentally alter the way the brain functions.

The other clusters in the criteria for diagnosis of PTSD involve (a) intrusive recollections or reexperiencing of the traumatic events; (b) avoidance, withdrawal, and numbing; and (c) hyperarousal and hypervigilance. Individuals meeting the criteria for less than 3 months are classified as having acute PTSD. Those meeting the criteria for 3 months or longer are classified as having chronic PTSD. Post-traumatic stress disorder or its symptoms are listed as negative health outcomes in the majority of research cited in Table 8.1. In commenting on the symptoms of PTSD, Scaer (2005) stated that "the broad spectrum of expression of these symptoms reflect a basically cyclical, bipolar dysfunction involving the brain and most of the regulatory systems of the body—autonomic, endocrine, and immune" (p. 42). The high frequency of PTSD as a health consequence in victims of workplace mobbing and other workplace abuse suggests that victims of workplace mobbing are vulnerable to the same range of psychological and physical problems as are victims of torture, victims of war, victims of natural disaster, refugees, combat soldiers, first responders to emergencies and disasters, and others who have dealt with extreme stressors that tax all of one's biopsychosocial systems. Because of impaired immune function, mobbing victims are also vulnerable to the flare-up of preexisting medical conditions and the development of new ones.

The following brief case example provides a glimpse of what the phenomenology or lived experience of enduring a mobbing is like from the perspective of coping with symptoms of PTSD. An analysis of the case is included in the example, which draws further implications for the health of Ingrid, the subject of the case. The "Analysis" section includes considerations for treatment and care of Ingrid and others experiencing PTSD or its symptoms. Key points may be applied to the broader understanding of other mobbing victims with similar health profiles as Ingrid's and include important considerations for involvement of partners and spouses who are also likely to be impacted by a partner's workplace mobbing.

A Case of Post-Traumatic Stress Disorder in the Airline Industry

Ingrid was a victim of sustained workplace mobbing involving both management and a group of coworkers. The mobbing lasted for over 2 years and continued even after she quit her job, through ongoing attacks on her professional reputation. Ingrid had been a fast-rising pilot in a small but growing regional airline company. She was a first officer (copilot), and was on track to be promoted to captain. Her flight simulator performance and technical skills were rated as superior, and most pilots in the company wanted her as their first officer because of her dependability.

There were exceptions, however, and the Chief Pilot was one of them. He saw Ingrid as a potential threat to his status and ordered the flight staff routers to assign Ingrid only to short flights that would preclude her from getting experience and certification on larger aircraft. Such certification was tied to promotion and higher pay.

The Chief Pilot also told the vice-president (VP) for flight operations that Ingrid was "uncooperative and difficult to work with." The VP simply accepted the information without any follow-up or fuller investigation of such a career-busting negative personal characterization. The flight staff routers were also ordered to assign Ingrid as first officer to a pilot who was generally known to be cantankerous and authoritarian in the cockpit. The flight staff routers quickly got the message that Ingrid was to be handled differently than the other pilots and began to gossip about her and treat her with disdain themselves. Ingrid questioned her routings and the fact that she was not being given the opportunity to become certified on larger aircraft. Her questions were never directly answered and, over the course of 18 months, Ingrid began to hear rumors about what the Chief Pilot and flight staff routers had been doing. The flight staff routers had become so negative toward Ingrid that they refused to take her phone calls and took weeks to get back to her. Additionally, they took the initiative upon themselves to schedule her for the worst flight assignments with the least potential for development and upgraded certification and presented their "draft" schedules to the Chief Pilot for his approval. With smugness, a chuckle, and a "we'll show her" comment, the Chief Pilot consistently gave his approval to the schedule developed by the flight staff routers. Had Ingrid not been the professional that she was, flight safety could have been jeopardized as a result of the insidious personal and professional undermining to which she had been subjected. She was so worn down that she simply quit—exactly what the Chief Pilot had been hoping she would do. When she tried to get references, other airlines were told things like "her record speaks for itself— she flew small aircraft on short routes." As a result, Ingrid found reemployment very difficult.

Ingrid had nightmares in which the faces of the people involved in the mobbing appeared like monsters. The nightmares began at some point during the mobbing and lasted for about 8 months after she quit her job. In her mind, she replayed situations and interactions that happened during the mobbing and was in disbelief that people she thought she could trust had acted the way they had toward her. She couldn't bring to conscious memory some of the critical events in the mobbing, in spite of her attempts to do so, thus indicating the involvement of parts of the brain in the storing, processing, and retrieval of the traumatic memories and images. Ingrid's sense of her future was vague and uncertain. Sometimes she didn't see herself as having much of a future. She cried a lot, and spent a lot of time in bed. At the same time, Ingrid became hyperaware of her environment and was especially sensitive to interpersonal cues and to the body language of others. She had lost confidence in herself and in her abilities, was awkward around new people, and was going to have to relearn how to be comfortable with herself and with others if she ever was going to be able to work again.

ANALYSIS AND KEY POINTS

Ingrid's symptoms meet the diagnostic criteria for PTSD if we use the expanded understanding of trauma described above. Her ability to trust her relational network has been severely impacted. She continues to be at risk of generalizing her traumatic work experiences to a much broader range of relationships in her life, which may include her husband and family. She is at risk of activating any preexisting medical conditions as a result of impaired immune function subsequent to her workplace mobbing. She is also at risk of developing new medical problems. In terms of the need for appropriate therapeutic and supportive intervention, Ingrid's situation is urgent. The key points that follow highlight Ingrid's health status resulting from being mobbed and basic treatment considerations.

- Therapeutic interventions for Ingrid and others who experience workplace mobbing should only be provided by psychotherapists who understand the nature and health outcomes of workplace mobbing. Ingrid risks further mistreatment, albeit unintended, from psychotherapists who would interpret her symptoms in terms of individual psychopathology. Trauma specialists may be helpful as long as they also understand mobbing in terms of the systemic organizational and group dynamics involved.
- Symptoms may persist beyond the duration of the mobbing itself.
- Medical monitoring of Ingrid's general health and any preexisting conditions is important. A program of immune strengthening through nutrition, exercise, rest, and positive social support should be initiated.
- Marital therapy is indicated to help Ingrid and her spouse understand the impact of mobbing on their relationship and to develop strategies for improved communication, warmth, and mutual support and responsiveness, especially in the early post-mobbing phase.

This brief case example of Ingrid and her development of PTSD subsequent to workplace mobbing illustrates the insidiousness of mobbing, the development of adverse health symptoms, their related time frames, and basic treatment considerations. The case also provides key points in terms of understanding basic elements required for appropriate psychological care for mobbing victims, the importance of attending to their overall health and immune functioning, and the importance of attending to the systemic effects of the mobbing and its health consequences on marriages and other intimate relationships.

The next case example, "A Case of Mobbing in the Operating Room," describes the case of multiple victims of mobbing as a result of abusive workplace supervision and the role and involvement of the larger organization in the form of the hospital administration. The case provides ample detail that illustrates both the abusive supervision (Tepper, 2000) and the victims' collective attempts to stop it. The physical and psychological health consequences of the mobbing victims are also described. The detailed analysis includes discussion of the specific negative acts to which the mobbing victims were subjected and their individual and group responses to them. The key points in this illustration focus on group and organizational dynamics and on the differential responses by the group and the organization that resulted in some mitigation of the potential negative effects from the mobbing.

A Case of Mobbing in the Operating Room

Anesthesiologists are medical doctors (MDs) who administer anesthesia to those who are about to undergo surgical or medical procedures. Nurse anesthetists are registered nurses with advanced training and certification who are also credentialed to administer anesthesia. Patients today usually receive anesthesia from a care team that often includes anesthesiologists and certified registered nurse anesthetists (CRNAs) working together.

In a medium-sized community hospital in a rural area, an anesthesiologist was hired to take over an anesthesia department that was composed primarily of CRNAs with many years of experience. Historically, a physician had been the anesthesia department head so the new hire did not represent administrative change. But things did start to change and change dramatically. The new department head required that the group of four CRNAs take a recent year's anesthesiology exam for physicians wishing to become board certified in anesthesiology—an exam required only for physicians and not for nurse anesthetists. The department head wanted to assess the knowledge base of the CRNAs now under his direct supervision, and he had them sit the exam at the hospital on their own time. The CRNAs were privately furious because they had all been required to pass their own CRNA exam and to maintain their licenses by taking continuing CRNA education courses. The anesthesiology exam was for physicians and included a pain management section that did not fall under the scope of practice for nurse anesthetists. They protested to the hospital administrator, who told them not to worry about it, to just go along with it and take the exam, and that it wouldn't make any difference whether they passed the exam or not because they all had their own licenses to practice.

One of the nurse anesthetists became so anxiety-ridden at the thought of having to take an unnecessary exam and fearful that he would be humiliated if he failed it that he refused to take it. The other three wanted to do the same but felt pressured into taking the exam. Two of the CRNAs passed the exam, and one failed it by a few questions. The new department head made no attempt to hide his surprise that two of the CRNAs passed the physicians' exam and that the third almost passed it. However, he wasn't finished "testing" the CRNAs. Next, he went live with his "skills assessment" process. The anesthesiologist department head began entering the operating room when the patients were already asleep and quizzing the CRNAs about the patient, the patient's status, and the rationale for the type of anesthesia the CRNA had selected. The quizzes were done publicly, in front of the operating room nurses, attendants, and surgeon. Needless to say, the nurse anesthetists did not like the new department head but were so focused on their patients that initially they just automatically answered the department head's questions when in the operating room. At some point, they began to share their quiz stories with one another and again went to the hospital administration with more or less the same outcome as before—they were told that the anesthesiologist is new and feeling his oats—just ignore him. The anesthesiologist department head still wasn't finished testing his CRNA team members. This time, he went into the operating rooms of the CRNAs—focusing on two of them—and fiddled with the valves on the gas machines to see if they would notice. The department head's behavior in these instances was both exasperating and distracting to the nurse anesthetists involved, causing them to have to pay attention both to their patient and to what their department head was doing with their machines. They looked to their operating room colleagues for the support that they were sure would be there. It wasn't.

The now toxic atmosphere of the nurse anesthetists' working environment—which was primarily the hospital suite of operating rooms and environs—became even more toxic as a result of the reactions of the operating room nursing staff and several surgeons. Their operating room colleagues had all heard about and many had witnessed the anesthesiologist department head actively demeaning the CRNAs as they worked and were responsible for patient care. None of them spoke out against the practices of the new department head. Instead, they responded by distancing themselves from the nurse anesthetists and stopped including them in their usual operating room jokes and banter. All four of the CRNAs began to feel shut out, isolated, and further demeaned as a result. The surgeons, who were not hospital employees, did not want to be seen to go against their anesthesiologist colleague and the operating room nurses were uncertain what was happening and did not want to get involved. Their "not wanting to get involved" stance took the form of distancing and avoiding their nurse anesthetist colleagues. The rhythm of the operating room, the pattern of personal interaction among the operating room team, and the pattern of banter and jokes that served as a tension diffuser all changed. The abusive supervision of a bully department head had morphed into mobbing.

By this time, 6 months had passed and the CRNAs had decided as a group that either their testing and evaluation by the new department head was finished or they were finished at that hospital. Within a few weeks of their third trip to the hospital administration, the new department head resigned citing a new position at a larger hospital in an urban area. The CRNAs could not have been happier, but the health problems that they had been experiencing to varying degrees persisted for some of them long after the departure of their malignant, narcissistic department head. Collectively, the nurse anesthetists had experienced the following negative health outcomes during their mobbing: anger, suspiciousness, anxiety and worry about patient safety and their own job security; fear; preoccupation and diminished ability to concentrate; intrusive angry thoughts and reliving some of their humiliating experiences; insomnia and nightmares; hypervigilance, especially when doing their jobs of administering anesthesia; and self-imposed isolation. Not all of the CRNAs experienced all of the negative health outcomes, and the intensity of the symptoms varied individually from person to person. A couple of them also experienced chronic severe headaches and gastrointestinal problems.

ANALYSIS AND KEY POINTS

The mobbing lasted for approximately 6 months (the minimum period Leymann [1990, 1996] used to distinguish mobbing from other negative workplace behaviors). All of the nurse anesthetists were exposed to the mobbing for the same length of time and worked in the same department under the same department head and administration. Although one refused to take the physicians' board exam because of intense anxiety and fear of humiliation, the others did not distance themselves from him or leave him out of future discussions about how they should handle the situation. For the most part, the nurse anesthetists, who were both male and female, aged between 30 and 60 years, and who had very different home lives and living situations, hung in together and remained socially cohesive and communicative with each other.

Such cohesion does not always happen in mobbing situations, given both the pressures on workers to keep their jobs and the power of the mobbing social process to segregate, demonize, and cut victims off from others, including from other victims. Being a member of a club of workers who have been mobbed is not desirable, nor is it a ticket to success within an organization. Workers will do many thing to avoid joining that club, including distancing themselves from mobbed workers, denying or minimizing the abuse they have experienced at the workplace, and effectively joining the mobbing by turning against a mobbed coworker or remaining silent and not going to that person's aid or defense (Duffy & Sperry, 2007; Einarsen, Hoel, Zapf, & Cooper, 2003b).

In this mobbing situation, although all of the nurse anesthetists experienced negative health outcomes, primarily psychological symptoms, they did not all experience the same symptoms or, in the case of shared symptoms, they did not all experience them to the same degree. An important difference in the treatment of the mobbing victims by the department head was the number and intensity of negative acts to which they were exposed. Two of the nurse anesthetists who worked mostly day shifts and who handled most of the scheduled surgeries were exposed to more negative acts than were the other two nurse anesthetists who worked evening and night shifts covering labor and delivery and emergencies. Some of the recent research on mobbing and negative health outcomes is looking at the relationship between the number and type of negative acts and negative health outcomes and finding a strong direct relationship between them (Hoel, Faragher, & Cooper, 2004; Punzi, Cassito, Castellini, Costa, & Gilioli, 2007).

It also might be useful here to tease out the negative acts to which these nurse anesthetists were subjected, not in terms of number, but in terms of the nature of the act. Overshadowing this whole mobbing process was the power and status differential between physicians and nurses. Even though the nurses had advanced training, they were nurses, not physicians, and the power and status differences were significant. Most of the negative acts to which the nurse anesthetists were directly subjected could be classified under the heading of abusive supervision, a set of negative behaviors that can be associated with mobbing. The anesthetists were intimidated by being coerced into taking an exam not designed to evaluate their training but designed instead to evaluate the training of a physician whose status was higher and whose professional knowledge base was different. The department head further demonstrated hostility to the nurse anesthetists by not responding to their complaints and by persisting in his requirement to have them take the physicians' Anesthesiology Board Exam. He expressed further hostility by requiring them to take the exam at the hospital on their own time. The nurse anesthetists were publicly humiliated by being quizzed on a number of occasions in the operating room, in front of other nurses, aides, and physicians. These were not medical students. The hospital was not a teaching hospital, and neither the nurse anesthetists nor surgeons had requested consultations from the anesthesiologist department head. The department head interfered with the ability of the nurse anesthetists to perform their jobs by entering the operating room and fiddling with the valves on the anesthesia gas machines, causing the nurse anesthetists to become distracted and to shift focus from their patients to also monitor what their department head was doing.

Although not actively or directly aligning with their department head, the administration was complicit in the mobbing by not addressing the serious concerns raised by the nurse anesthetists in their initial complaints and when they complained a second time, thus leaving the CRNAs to cope with a difficult workplace situation for 6 months. Subjecting licensed health care providers to supervision that includes being forced to take a licensing exam for a different health care profession than the one for which they were trained represents egregious abuse that should have been immediately stopped by the administration. When the nurse anesthetists complained to the administration about the practices of their supervising department head, it should have been clear to the administration that the members of a critical care department were at risk because of abusive supervision by the anesthesiologist department head. This lack of action on the part of the administration is an example of mobbing by an act of omission—failure to do something that was required to stop the mobbing from continuing or escalating. To the hospital administrators, the anesthesiologist was a scarcer resource in their rural area than were the nurse anesthetists, so their tolerance levels for problematic behavior on the part of the anesthesiologist was initially higher than it should have been. The mobbing was serious, negatively affecting the health of four nurse anesthetists and putting patient safety at risk. In the end, the administration acted to preserve the department by demanding the resignation of the anesthesiologist department head. Whether the administration acted under threat of a mass resignation of the anesthetists or because it was the most ethical choice to make under the circumstances is difficult to know.

Another possible explanation for the administration's action was the growing risk to patient safety. In this situation, patient safety was an obvious critical issue, but the administration's delay in action does raise the question of whether the psychological and emotional safety of the employees was ever a real concern. To the administration's credit, however, was the fact that they did not escalate the mobbing by questioning the credibility and stability of the nurse anesthetists who brought in the complaints. In the classic Leymann (1990) and Leymann and Gustafsson (1996) five-phase mobbing model, administrative involvement usually leads to questioning of the professional and even personal status of the victims by labeling them as not credible, over-reactive, or even unstable and mentally ill. Another group in this mobbing was the witnesses to the abusive supervision of the anesthetists; that group consisted of the surgeons, nurses, and aides in the operating rooms where the quizzing and other forms of "testing" of the nurse anesthetists took place. No one from this group spoke up, even though they spoke among themselves. This is another example of the significance of acts of omission in mobbing cases. Doing nothing is doing something, and in mobbings, the inaction of witnesses leads to further isolation and segregation of mobbing victims, increasing the potential for negative health effects. The following list summarizes the key points from the case.

- This case illustrates the significance of acts of omission in fueling mobbing— the initial failure to act on the part of the administration and the failure to speak out against the abusive supervisor on the part of the surgeons and operating room staff.
- The victims of this mobbing hung in with each other and provided mutual support. This was a critical dimension of this case and in all likelihood mitigated some of the negative health effects.
- A conceptual and research area that needs to be addressed is why, in many mobbings, witnesses avoid providing active support to the victims whom they know are being abused and mistreated, and why victims so often become ostracized and avoided by others in the workplace who previously were amicable and friendly to them.

- This mobbing took place in an organization dedicated to the improvement of health. Organizational health and wellness programs fall far short of the mark when they focus on issues like nutrition and exercise and even stress management without paying serious and timely attention to active complaints about abusive behavior within their own organization.
- Instances of mobbing vary in their intensity and toxicity. The administration was able in this case to avoid further damage to the employees by refraining from questioning their credibility and/or stability when they lodged complaints. This step alone prevented the mobbing from progressing to a more toxic form. Although the organization initially played down the seriousness of the abusive supervision, which then evolved into mobbing, the administration did eventually take appropriate action, thereby limiting damage to the victims and organization itself. Nonetheless, in addition to the adverse health consequences for the victims, workgroup relationships, especially with respect to trust and cohesion, had been damaged.

Workplace Mobbing Results in Both Short- and Long-Term Health Effects

As destructive as mobbing is on the health of victims, it would not be illogical to think that once the mobbing ended or once the victim was removed from the workplace setting in which the mobbing took place, negative health consequences would also taper off. Niedhammer, David, Degioanni, and 143 occupational physicians (2006) conducted a large survey of the general population in southern France. They found that depressive symptoms were associated with workplace mobbing and persisted long after the mobbing ended. They also found that being a witness to bullying increased the risk of depressive symptoms for that witness. What their research suggests is that workplace mobbing represents a severe stressor, with health consequences that may persist over time.

An important issue in understanding the physical and psychological effects of mobbing is the difference between the immediate and short-term health effects and the long-term ones. More research has been done on the long-term effects of mobbing than on the short-term effects and for a very good reason. The immediate psychological effects of mobbing on a victim are often disbelief and denial. A person who has been a conscientious and committed worker within an organization may be among the last to know that they are being mobbed. When awareness of what is occurring finally dawns, it dawns in bits and pieces, not as a fully formed narrative. It may take quite a long time, if ever, for the full plot line of the people, motivations, and events that have made up the mobbing to be known by the victim. Outrage and anger may quickly or slowly follow the disbelief and denial, but follow they will. The real emotional pain and hurt and physical and psychological sequelae follow when the victim becomes aware that she or he is also powerless to effect necessary change to end the mobbing. Since mobbing is a systemic process involving organizational and group dynamics, there is little hope of turning the negative events around in one's favor by oneself. As the process of the mobbing intensifies, a sense of powerlessness and ultimately helplessness may also follow. The events of the mobbing and the victim's reaction to them occur in chronological order, as do the psychological and physical health consequences. We can hypothesize that physical and psychological heath consequences from workplace mobbing will be related to many mediating variables, one of which will be the degree of the victim's awareness of the events of the mobbing and the degree of their acknowledgment that, however horrible and devastating, these adverse events have indeed occurred. In other words, as awareness and acknowledgment of the negative acts associated with mobbing increase over time, so do the associated psychological and physical sequelae.

Conclusion

It has only been 20 years since Heinz Leymann did his foundational research in mobbing and laid out the health consequences for those unfortunate enough to have been victim of it. All research cited in this chapter on health consequences of workplace abuse has been published since 2003, with the exception of the Australian study of schoolchildren. The physical disorders identified as occurring in relation to exposure to mobbing include coronary heart disease, hypertension, gastrointestinal problems, headaches, overall reduction in physical health and functioning, and sudden death. The psychosomatic symptoms include sleep disorders, eating disorders, addiction problems, and the experience of generalized stress, fatigue, and exhaustion. The psychosocial symptoms identified include negative perceptions of one's environment, loneliness, rejection by other students at school, dislike of school, skipping school, decreased job satisfaction, emotional distancing from life partners, and generalized negative impact on life away from work. In mobbing, psychological symptoms such as anxiety, depression, dissociation, paranoia, and suicidal ideation and behaviors can be severe. In fact, certain clusters of these symptoms are characteristics of psychiatric disorders such as PTSD, other anxiety disorders, and mood disorders, to name the more common. The identity symptoms include feelings of stigmatization, powerlessness, inferiority, shame, and humiliation, and assault on one's personal and professional sense of self. Overall, the evidence strongly suggests that being mobbed is a risk factor for physical and/or psychological health problems, making mobbing a public health issue that cannot be ignored. We remind readers of the important distinction drawn by Davenport, Schwartz, and Elliott (1999) about the negative health consequences related to mobbing—that these are injuries not illnesses.

A large body of pre-2003 research on the health consequences of workplace abuse and mobbing is based on work conducted largely in Europe (e.g., Brodsky, 1976; Einarsen, Matthiesen, & Skogstad, 1998; Matthiesen, Raknes, & Røkkum, 1989; O'Moore, Seigne, McGuire, & Smith, 1998b; Vartia, 1996, 2001; Zapf, Knorz, & Kulla, 1996). This research on health outcomes mirrors the later research described in this chapter and includes many of the same psychological issues of trauma, anxiety, and depression. In a relatively short span of three decades, we have accumulated empirical evidence of serious to severe damage to one's physical, psychosocial, and psychological health, as well as profound damage to one's sense of personal identity from mobbing. In 1991, Wilson stated that workplace abuse was more injurious than all other sources of workplace stress combined. In 2005, Lapierre, Spector, and Leck found through their meta-analysis that job satisfaction was significantly lower for those who experienced nonviolent workplace aggression than for those who experienced workplace nonviolent sexual aggression. In 2008, Hershcovis and Barling conducted a meta-analysis of studies of outcomes of both workplace abuse and sexual harassment and found that workplace abuse was associated with worse outcomes than sexual harassment. The research studies cited in this chapter and other research referred to in this discussion section make the unequivocal case that workplace abuse and mobbing may lead to serious health problems for exposed workers. The evidence has come in from many parts of the world over a 30-year period and has repeatedly produced the same set of findings; namely, that workplace mobbing and abuse results in serious physical and mental health problems for victims.

Not every worker subjected to workplace abuse and mobbing will experience the same health consequences or the same intensity of health consequences. Why this is the case is speculative at this point and is related to the theoretical frameworks used to understand individual differences in health outcomes of mobbing victims. Scaer's (2005) trauma framework presented earlier suggests that the effects of trauma are cumulative over the course of a life, and that the impact of trauma on brain structures reflects the cumulative magnitude of all trauma exposure. Those with histories of more prior trauma are likely to be more globally impacted in terms of physical and psychological health consequences. Further conceptual refinement and empirical research is required to understand more clearly the factors that mediate the often long-term negative health consequences of workplace mobbing. It is our hope that additional research and conceptual refinement will be able to help us identify more specific protective and vulnerability factors that in turn will enable us to offer more effective, individually tailored help to mobbing victims.

9

Family and Relationships

For in grief nothing "stays put." One keeps on emerging from
a phase, but it always recurs. Round and round. Everything
repeats. Am I going in circles, or dare I hope I am on a spiral?
—C. S. Lewis (1976, p. 67)

In this chapter, we focus on two basic life domains impacted by the experiences of mobbing and bullying, whether those experiences are school- or workplace-based. The life domains that are the focus of this chapter are family and social relationships. An additive effect occurs between health consequences suffered as a result of mobbing and their impact on family life and social relationships—the more severe the health consequences, the greater the impact on family life and on social relationships. In this chapter, we examine the range of possible individual responses to mobbing episodes, including individual neurophysiological responses, and look at how those individual responses interact within family and social relationships. We also provide vignettes and examples that illustrate the impact of mobbing on family life and social relationships at both work and school.

The Effects of Mobbing and Bullying on Family Relationships

The impact of mobbing and bullying on family life is an area about which little research exists. To develop intervention and prevention programs that will effectively address the human suffering caused by mobbing and bullying, more research on the impact of school and workplace mobbing on family life is critically needed. The research that does exist comes largely from anecdotal reports and a small cohort of qualitative studies (Jennifer, Cowie, & Anaiadou, 2003; Lewis, 2004; Lewis & Orford, 2005; Tracy, Lutgen-Sandvik, & Alberts, 2006; Westhues, 2005c). Duffy and Sperry (2007) provide an overview of the impact of mobbing on families:

Family members of mobbing victims, of course, are significantly affected. Changes in communication patterns, changes in affect, increased irritability, and negativity are inevitably going to strain even the best of relations. The victim's preoccupation with the mobbing experience is likely to result in both obsessive preoccupation and general lack of communication or in a need to constantly talk about the mobbing as if it were the only aspect of the victim's life. The mobbing experience, left untreated, can take over the identity of the victim and rob the victim of a sense of self and rob the family of the multidimensional person they knew and cared for. (p. 401)

Klein (2005), in reflecting on how he survived his experience of being mobbed as a professor in the School of School Work at Memorial University in Canada, cited the support of his partner as indispensable. However, he also noted that, at first, it was hard for her to believe that things at work were as bad as he described. Klein said that "with time, she realized that it wasn't only as bad as described—it was worse. Sadly, her idealistic views and any respect she might have for my colleagues eroded away long ago" (p. 70).

An internationally renowned foreign-born surgeon who was mobbed by the medical community in the Canadian city to which he had recently moved provided an anonymous account of his mobbing (Westhues, 2005c). The surgeon had his privileges to practice medicine suspended subsequent to written accusations of patient mistreatment that had been sent to him with the names of the patients, the situations, and the complainants erased. The surgeon and his wife, also a physician, ultimately left Canada for good. An independent investigator, who received the patient files of the surgeon in blinded form, found nothing wrong with the treatment he had provided to his patients. In summing up the effects of the mobbing he endured, the surgeon stated that "they did enormous damage to me and my wife. They ruined our possibility of immigrating in Canada and making a much needed contribution to the underserved health system" (p. 194). The surgeon concludes his account with the reflection that, had he not left Canada, he would most likely have died, given that his main coronary artery was found to be 95% obstructed soon after his return to his home country. De Vogli, Ferrie, Chandola, Kivimäki, and Marmot (2007), in their prospective study of over 8,000 civil service workers in the United Kingdom, found that those reporting higher rates of unfairness at work were more likely to experience a coronary event. The study found that workplace unfairness was an independent predictor of coronary heart disease and overall poorer health functioning. This physician experienced the whole mobbing episode as unfair, unjust, and lacking in due process, making him highly vulnerable to the coronary event that he avoided through rapid intervention after leaving Canada.

In their study of how women experienced social relationships after workplace bullying, Lewis and Orford (2005) found a significant negative ripple effect on family relationships. The increased need for support and reassurance that accompanied workplace bullying strained even the strongest relationships. Some of the relationship stress was linked to an increasing focus by the bullied worker on issues in the workplace rather than on issues at home or in the relationship. Lewis and Orford summarized the ripple effect on family relationships: "Personal relationships were perceived as at best surviving, and even relationships which participants had experienced as strong and supportive were unable to work well as bullying continued" (p. 37). Hecker (2007), in encouraging a discussion of workplace mobbing among professional librarians, noted the high price paid by family and friends who were relied upon to provide emotional support to victims. He stated that "this reliance burden may cause alienation and exhaustion in family and friends and can damage and destroy the mobbing target's personal life" (p. 444). Since a cardinal feature of mobbing is psychological and sometimes physical isolation within an organization, the mobbing victim only has the support of family and friends at a time of intensely high need. At any given time, family and friends, because of their own circumstances, may not have an adequate supply of time and emotional support to meet the high demand for these resources from their mobbed family member or friend.

Typologies of Responses to Mobbing/Bullying: How They Impact Individual and Family Functioning

The experience of being mobbed can be an encompassing or totalizing experience for the victim. Olafsson and Johansdottir (2004) identified a taxonomy of victim reactions to workplace abuse: seeking help, avoidance, assertiveness, and doing nothing. It must be remembered that these categories of responses occur after a victim has been subjected to bullying or mobbing for a protracted period of time and has already endured a variety of forms of workplace abuse and humiliation. The act of responding to the abuse takes its toll, and each of the categories in Olafsson and Johansdottir's taxonomy of victim responses can also be understood as a manifestation of one of the primary ways in which an organism responds to a life threat; namely, fight, flight, or freeze. The way in which victims respond to school and workplace mobbing will have particular effects on their physiology and on the kinds of emotional and behavioral responses that they and their families must face. The negative ripple effect (Lewis & Orford, 2005) on family relationships emanates, in part, from the unique neurophysiological responses exhibited by the mobbing victim. In this book we have looked at the network of systemic interactions and influences that converge in the development of mobbing episodes; namely, the interplay of individual, group, and organizational dynamics. How individuals respond to the intensity and destructiveness of mobbing episodes is also a function of their individual neurophysiology—a critical but often overlooked part of the systemic elements involved in the response to mobbing. For example, mobbing victims who are highly reactive and those who are nonreactive as a result of shock and numbing are both going to impact other family members differently than is a mobbing victim who more openly talks and grieves about the events.

In Olafsson and Johansdottir's (2004) typology of responses to workplace abuse, "seeking help" and "assertiveness" can be understood as "fight" responses. Avoidance can be understood as a "flight" response and doing nothing can be understood as a "freeze" response. The "freeze" response occurs when fight or flight are either not feasible or have been tried and failed. In the "freeze" response, the organism "is in a precarious state of abnormally dysregulated and fluctuating autonomic nervous activity" (Scaer, 2005, p. 45). Numbing, emotional shock, cognitive effects like loss of concentration and inability to focus are all indicative of a "freeze" response. There is an experience of unreality, of "this can't really be happening." A common reaction of many mobbing victims, even long after the abusive events have ended, is bewilderment and shock that the events ever happened, indicative of "stuckness" in the freeze state.

Djurkovic, McCormack, and Casimir (2005), in their study of victim reactions to workplace violence, found that doing nothing—what they described as an avoidance response, but what we describe as a freeze response—was the most common victim reaction to workplace abuse. The freeze response of doing nothing makes sense in work environments in which victims of mobbing have little faith or trust that their supervisors and organization will do something to help them and when victims' perceived options for mobility are low. Mobbing victims who freeze are most likely to be employees with few perceived options for moving on. These freeze responders believe they cannot rock the boat by doing anything because they fear losing their jobs and the ensuing financial and career fallout. For mobbing victims who do nothing or freeze, the interaction among their neurophysiological and behavioral responses to the inherent threat in workplace abuse, the group dynamics of those involved in the abuse, and the organizational response or lack of it is a classic illustration of mobbing.

The Freeze Response Goes Home: What Happens to Victims and Families

Of course, these neurophysiological and behavioral responses to the experience of mobbing don't stay at work. They go home with the victim. Lewis (2004), in his qualitative case studies of university lecturers who had experienced workplace abuse, found powerlessness and emotional distance from partners to be among a relatively long list of health consequences. Powerlessness and emotional distancing from one's partner can be associated with the shutting down and physiological preservation common in the freeze response. Distancing, lack of emotional or intellectual involvement with one's partner, and feelings of powerlessness are indicative of a freeze response. A partner or spouse who has experienced the trauma of workplace mobbing and who has reacted by shutting down in a classic freeze response is unlikely to meet the expectations of a partner for intimacy, mutuality, and responsiveness. Punzi, Cassito, Castellini, Costa, and Gilioli (2007), in their study of clinical records of mobbing victims, found exhaustion and sexual problems, among other health problems, in those who had been exposed to mobbing. Prolonged exhaustion can be another example of a freeze response triggered by the experience of helplessness in workplace mobbing. Spending evenings and weekends lying on the couch or in bed are indicative of the neurovegetative state associated with the freeze response to trauma. For both mobbing victims and their family members, understanding the freeze or do-nothing response is important because it is likely to be the most common form of response (Djurkovic et al., 2005).

These self-protective efforts to conserve energy are evolutionary adaptations to helplessness in the face of life threats. Active engagement in emotional and sexual intimacy and in family life requires stores of energy and focused attention that may well be unavailable to victims of severe mobbing. It is no surprise that Josipović-Jelić, Stoini, and Celić-Bunikić (2005) identify family problems and divorce as common outcomes in workplace mobbing. Unresolved freeze responses resulting from traumatization, as in workplace mobbing, are dangerous. Scaer (2005) stated that "traumatization . . . may result in sustained exposure to abnormal levels of cortisol, resulting in real physical damage to the brain in the form of loss of neurons and synapses in the hippocampus" (p. 75). Scaer's findings mirror the earlier findings of O'Brien (1997), in which prolonged stress was identified as a potential cause of permanent brain damage as a result of the same glucocorticoid cascade. Unresolved freeze responses capture the traumatized victim in endless loops of emotional and psychological playback. These repetitive loops inscribe themselves in brain circuitry and, unless resolved, will change both the structure and function of the brain. Resolution of the freeze response ordinarily involves taking some action. In animals, the discharge of the freeze response involves some form of movement, often while the animal is still immobile. In humans, resolution of the freeze response requires the restoration of personal agency and the initiation of actions that begin to move one out of the past and into a present and a future. In Chapter 11, we will discuss what mobbing victims need to do to develop effective recovery plans.

The Flight Response Goes Home: What Happens to Victims and Families

In addition to the freeze response, "fight" and "flight" are other possible responses to workplace mobbing that carry their own risks and benefits. In following Olafsson and Johansdottir's (2004) taxonomy of victim responses to workplace abuse, and associating those responses, as we have, with the fight, flight, or freeze responses to threats and trauma, we are left with seeking help and assertiveness as forms of the fight response and avoidance as a form of the flight response. In responding to school and workplace mobbing, there is no guaranteed safe or effective category of response. Risks abound no matter what the response, and actions have consequences both for the victim and for the victim's family. Moving on and releasing oneself from trauma after school or workplace mobbing requires a successful adaptation of one of the fight, flight, or freeze responses or a successful sequential combination of them. It is important to understand that, when discussing responses to mobbing as fight, flight, or freeze, we are making no moral associations with the choice of behaviors; for example, we are not seeing the fight response as an expression of hostility (although it could be) or the flight response as an instance of cowardice. We understand all of these responses as evolutionary adaptations to life threats and, in so doing, we view mobbing as a life threat.

We are equating Olafsson and Johansdottir's (2004) classification of avoidance as a category of victim response to mobbing and bullying with flight in the fight, flight, or freeze taxonomy. Mobbing victims engage in avoidance or flight behaviors as solution attempts when they take sick leave, deliberately keep a low profile in their work setting, have as little involvement as possible with those involved in the mobbing, seek transfers to different departments, voluntarily leave employment, and, in extreme situations, commit suicide. At home with family members, a typical avoidance or flight response to mobbing is to not want to talk about it. Family members may become frustrated if they want to be of active support but are denied the opportunity because their loved one is locked in avoidant silence about what is happening in school or at work.

The surgeon whose case we discussed at the beginning of this chapter (Westhues, 2005c) initially was assertive in fighting back against the charges of patient mistreatment leveled against him. Having had his privileges to practice medicine suspended, he ultimately left the country so that he would be able to continue to practice his profession and escape the mobbing. It was his editor who advised him to write his account anonymously to ensure that the mobbing would not follow him. The surgeon, however, made it clear that he would continue to fight back, but from the hopefully safe distance of his homeland. In this surgeon's case, we can infer that his most effective action in escaping the mobbing and trauma was leaving the country—an avoidance or flight response. However, he made it clear that he would continue the fight response that he had initiated before making the decision to leave in a continuing effort to set the record straight. Megan Meier, the student whose case we discussed in Chapter 4, committed suicide, the ultimate flight response, in an effort to escape the horrendous personal attacks to which she had been subjected. Megan, too, had initially fought back by responding to the cyber attacks against her by using angry language in her own postings back to her attackers. Both the surgeon and Megan Meier, although in very different ways, responded in a sequence of fight and then flight behaviors to escape from their mobbings. Both escaped, but for vulnerable young Megan, at the cost of her life. The effects on both their families will be life-long and will percolate down to future generations through the sharing of emotionally charged family stories and narratives about the life-altering events surrounding the mobbings. In a study of over 100 people who had been exposed to mobbing, 52% were found to have some risk of suicide, with 20.6% identified as having a medium to high suicide risk (Pompili, Lester, Innamorati, De Pisa, Puccinno, Nastro, Tatarelli, & Girardi, 2008). Most family members of mobbing victims are not aware of the suicide risks and, if their family member who has been mobbed attempts or completes suicide, they may carry burdens of guilt that traumatize them for the rest of their lives.

The Fight Response Goes Home: What Happens to Victims and Families

Olafsson and Johansdottir's (2004) categories of "assertiveness" and "seeking help" are associated with the fight response in the fight, flight, or freeze taxonomy. In their study, Djurkovic, McCormack, and Casimir (2005) found that help-seeking behaviors were the least likely responses by victims of any of the categories and were only correlated with workplace abuse that included violence. Help-seeking behaviors include filing internal grievances and making formal reports to supervisors, human resources, or to union representatives. One of the sober reminders from Leymann's (1990) work is that when management gets involved in the mobbing process, the situation is more likely to worsen for the victim than it is to improve. Rayner (1998, 1999), not surprisingly, found that the help-seeking response to workplace abuse yielded little support; in particular, over 50% of those who sought help from their supervisors received none, and around 25% of those who complained about bullying were threatened with dismissal. These statistics provide more evidence of the "blame the victim" response to workplace mobbing and bullying.

Assertiveness is another fight response, and is associated with directly confronting those involved in the mobbing and requesting that they cease and desist. Rayner (1998, 1999) found that standing up to a bully was not all that effective and even backfired. In her studies, 41% of victims who confronted the bullies responsible for abusing them found that it had no effect. To make matters worse, just as many who had confronted the bullies were tagged as troublemakers. Assertiveness behaviors also include filing lawsuits and complaints with regulatory bodies. The effectiveness of filing such lawsuits and complaints as a category of the fight response is unknown. Victims who respond to life threats by standing up for themselves and fighting back are more likely to experience anger and irritability, which will also spill over into family relationships.

If the victim chooses to fight back by filing a lawsuit, becoming a plaintiff is usually a lengthy and stressful experience itself and impacts the family as well as the victim. It involves having to relive the mobbing episodes through the process of finding and organizing documentary evidence (if any exists), developing a coherent timeline and summary of the events to prepare for trial, retelling the experience in trial, and responding to the predictable "blame the victim" strategy of the defense—all of which is potentially retraumatizing. If, at any point during the mobbing, the victim has responded to the trauma by freezing, then some events may be difficult or impossible to recall as a result of the effect of trauma on memory. The financial costs of legal action put stress on the entire family, not just on the victim. Asking perpetrators to cease and desist from their mobbing and filing lawsuits and complaints with regulatory bodies are not the only examples of the fight response. Revenge and the desire to get back at the people perceived to be the cause of the victim's distress and occupational, school, and personal undoing is also a possibility.

Homicidal rage is the ultimate fight response. "Going postal" is a slang term that means someone becomes suddenly and uncontrollably angry, even to the point of violence. The term originated from a series of shootings involving current or former United States Postal Service (USPS) workers who shot and killed managers, coworkers, police, and the general public. Between 1986 and 2006, more than 47 people were killed by such workers. Patrick Henry Sherrill was one individual who "went postal" and whose case illustrates the enormity of the pressures he was under at work. On August 19, 1986, two supervisors at an Edmond, Oklahoma, postal facility verbally castigated Sherrill in an effort to further increase his productivity. Sherrill, who had excellent annual performance reviews, was then threatened with termination if his productivity did not increase appreciably. He left the office a visibly shaken man and called union headquarters in hopes of transferring to a maintenance job. After learning that such a transfer was doubtful, he went home, got a gun, and returned and responded to his supervisors' demands with fatal gun fire (Dungan, 2002).

When a victim stands up to the group of mobbers or to the organization in which the mobbing took place and fights back, family members may become secondary mobbing victims. In a mobbing at a small-town educational institution, the spouse of the victim who worked in the organization had a long-standing and financially rewarding business relationship with the organization that had begun before the spouse went to work for the institution. After the victim filed a complaint with an external regulatory agency, the spouse was confronted by members of the finance and legal departments and told that they were concerned about the continuation of the business relationship as they feared that funds generated by the business relationship might be used to finance actions against the institution. The business relationship was subsequently terminated by the institution. Parents who stand up for their children who are mobbed at school also risk being scapegoated by the school and by other parents. They may be told that they are "babying" their child or that their child "must learn to fight his or her own battles" or that "they are putting the reputation of the institution at risk."

How Social Relationships at Work and School Are Impacted by Mobbing

In optimal situations, the workplace functions as a source of satisfaction for employees at many levels: there is the nature of the work itself and the satisfaction that most people derive from "a job well done." There is the sense of supporting one's family and contributing to the community in which workers take pride. There is the experience of sociability and teamwork that workers and colleagues enjoy on the job, in spite of the occasional conflict or difference of opinion. For many workers, because of the amount of time they spend at work, work-related friendships become key sources of support and companionability. Hochschild (1997), a sociologist who researches work–home balance, has suggested that, for many couples faced with the guilt of spending so much time away from home and with the heavy demands of running a household and caring for children, work has become the escape and sanctuary that home once was. If work is the new sanctuary, then the relationships with coworkers that are formed there become even more important. But what happens to those important relationships when someone in the workplace becomes a victim of mobbing?

Witnessing Mobbing and Refusing to Get Involved

Rayner (1999) reported that, not infrequently, workplace observers were too afraid to report workplace abuse. One explanation for coworkers assuming an "I don't want to get involved" stance is fear of becoming the next victim. Another possible explanation is that other workers observing the abuse may take the position that it is management's or administration's responsibility to work out such problems. In his research on nurse bullying, Lewis (2006) stated that "witnesses to such acts [workplace abuse] face a difficult dilemma. Support from colleagues is often nonexistent, as many fear also becoming a target, or are concerned for their own position and career advancement, i.e., they do not want to be seen as trouble makers. Targets in such situations face an uphill struggle for redress" (p. 55).

When You Don't Get a Little Help from Your Friends

Without collegial or coworker support, the mobbed worker is left in a very isolating situation, experiencing further betrayal and shame. The mobbed worker is likely to have counted on the emotional if not actual support of colleagues whom he or she considered as friends. If this support is not forthcoming, or if it is withdrawn at some point during the mobbing episode, the mobbed worker is likely to experience a sense of double betrayal, first by the organization as a whole and then by coworkers or colleagues whom the mobbed worker had regarded as supportive. This sense of betrayal engenders mistrust that is generalized to other social situations and relationships. The betrayal can also be turned against the self and experienced by the mobbed worker as profound self-doubt or self-hatred.

Studies have also found that, among schoolchildren who are being abused by other children, many bystander students observed the abuse but did nothing to intervene (O'Connell, Pepler, & Craig, 1999). Jeffrey (2004) provides a range of possible explanations for why peer bystanders to school bullying often don't do anything to help; namely, fear, guilt, distress, anger, lack of sympathy, embarrassment, fear of retaliation, or dislike of the child being bullied. The frightening lesson for bullied children from such deliberate noninvolvement by peers may be that, when in need, they can't count on anyone, even their friends, for help.

Salmivalli (2010), in her careful review of the research about bullying and peer groups, pointed to the complexity of the relationship between a bullied child and peers. The longer a child has been victimized, the greater the likelihood that the child will continue to be set apart and victimized and the greater the generalized dislike of the child by the peer group (Ladd & Troop-Gordon, 2003; Schuster, 2001). On the other hand, Salmivalli also pointed out that the research suggests what at first glance might seem paradoxical; namely, that when more children in a class are victimized, the harm tends to be less severe in terms of intra- and interpersonal maladjustment than when just one or two children are victimized. Membership in a group, even in a group of victimized peers, seems to confer protective benefits, whereas victimization that is relatively singular results in even greater isolation of the child and significantly greater harm. Salmivalli also notes that, in spite of the research suggesting that children's attitudes are generally strongly anti-bullying (Rigby & Johnson, 2006), their actual behavior when faced with bullying situations rarely leads them to go to the defense of a victimized child (Salmivalli, Lappalainen, & Lagerspetz, 1998). For both children and adults, a significant gap frequently exists between espoused attitudes and subsequent behaviors when confronted with an actual situation. About children, Salmivalli stated that "there seems to be a disconnect—something prevents children from defending their bullied peers even if they think that it would be the right thing to do and have intentions of doing so" (p. 115).

It should come as no surprise that students who have been bullied at school experience higher rates of loneliness and feelings of rejection (Forero, McLellan, Rissell, & Bauman, 1999). In addition, bullied students have been found to have greater difficulty making friends than their nonbullied counterparts and have overall poorer relationships with their classmates (Nansel, Overpeck, Pilla, Ruan, Simons-Morton, & Scheidt, 2001). We recognize the child sitting alone in the cafeteria, the teenager walking alone to the next class, the young child hanging out alone on the playground as deviations from the expected group and social interactions critical to healthy child and adolescent development. Yet, these are precisely the types of behavioral manifestations associated with the loneliness and rejection experienced by victims of school mobbing.

In Chapter 8, we dealt with the health consequences of mobbing and bullying. So far in this chapter, we have reviewed the effects of mobbing and bullying on family relationships and its impact on the social relationships of victims in school and workplace settings. In Chapter 10, we will examine how mobbing impacts career, work performance, and professional identities. If we were to select one word to describe the effects of mobbing and bullying on all of these domains of life, that word would be "loss." Figure 9.1 provides an overview of the losses experienced by those who are victimized by mobbing both at school and work. The white circles refer to workplace losses, and the gray circles refer to both school and workplace losses. In this chapter, we focused on family and relationship losses; in Chapter 10, we discuss losses relating to job and work performance.

Conclusion

A number of double-binds are implicit in the discussion of the family and social relationship consequences of mobbing. For the child or adolescent who is mobbed in school, changing schools is usually not a viable option. If a student is assigned to a school by resident district, or if parents choose a school based on its reputation and proximity to either their home or work, making such a change is disruptive to the entire family, even if it is possible. In the case of students at school, it is much more likely that they will remain in the same school where the abusive behavior occurred. A temporary escape for such students is skipping school and developing a generalized dislike of it (Forero et al., 1999). On the other hand, if the child has even a small network of social support at the school where victimization has taken place and the parents decide to remove the child from the school, the child suffers the loss of that small but critical support.

A particularly poignant double-bind to which both mobbing victims and their families are subjected is the mobbing victim's need for support. Family members may question the severity of the abuse reported by their spouse, child, or other relative, and they may begin to wonder if the family member is causing the abuse in some way. At the same time, they may be angry that such abuse is occurring and want to do something about it. Meanwhile, the family member who is the mobbing victim is in need of support and care. Because of the protracted nature of mobbing, family members' resources for providing support and reassurance may be stretched to the limit, potentially adding guilt to the turmoil already being experienced by the mobbed family member.

The role of friends and coworkers can be a source of significant disappointment and bewilderment for children, adolescents, and adults who are being mobbed.

Legend: White circles = Workplace only; Grey circles = School and workplace

Figure 9.1 Mobbing-related Losses.

It is natural to expect support from those with whom one has had friendly, supportive, or cordial relationships prior to the mobbing. When support is not forthcoming, or is withdrawn, the person who has been mobbed is thrust into distressing self-reflection about the nature of the relationships prior to the mobbing and can begin to question and doubt his or her own judgment.

How people respond to the abusive behavior of mobbing can be generally categorized into one or more of the fight, flight, or freeze responses. As we described above, many mobbing victims do nothing, hoping it will all go away, numbing themselves to the pain of daily living at school or work. Of the fight, flight, or freeze responses, the freeze response is the most worrisome in terms of its long-term effects on a person and will be the subject of further discussion in Chapter 11.

Loss is the theme that runs through the discussion in this chapter about the effects of mobbing on career, family, and friendships. Nonetheless, there are lessons to be learned from the acknowledgment of multiple losses and the experience of double-binds during school and workplace mobbing. We have listed some that we think are the most important and hopefully useful.

- Family support is important for mobbing victims, yet victims' understandable demands for reassurance and comfort can be taxing for family members.
- The mobbing of a family member creates a negative ripple effect on other members of the family.
- There is a risk of secondary victimization as a result of standing up for a family member who has been mobbed.
- Because of the multiple losses typically experienced by mobbing victims, mobbing constitutes a traumatic life threat.
- The ways in which mobbing victims respond to the abuse they have experienced can be understood in terms of the fight, flight, or freeze taxonomy.
- Lack of support by peers (schoolmates and coworkers) during bullying and mobbing creates a sense of mistrust that can be generalized to other relationships.
- The experience of mobbing threatens personal and professional identities in ways that are profound and enduring.

We might add that acceptance of the kinds of losses and contradictions described in this chapter takes time for both the victims of mobbing and their family members. Making sense of them takes even longer.

10

Career and Work Performance

It is puzzling that we have never found a single case where the employer, as the other party, could find himself at fault and give the employee some redress for wrongs suffered.
—Heinz Leymann (1990, p. 124)

In the wake of workplace mobbing, losses related to career and professional identity accelerate. The mobbing victim is vulnerable to loss of confidence, loss of a primary source of identity in the world (that of occupation and career), associated financial losses, and real threats to reemployability. In this chapter, we discuss the misleading notion that people who are mobbed or who otherwise suffer workplace abuse can solve it by changing jobs. Mobbing creates employment double-binds for its victims that do not necessarily end by leaving or changing jobs, as necessary as that may be at times. We examine how mobbing can result in voluntary or involuntary loss of employment and related losses of health and retirement benefits. We review the compelling research about job disengagement in the wake of workplace mobbing, and look at how mobbing impacts one's beliefs in a just world and profoundly alters one's sense of personal and professional identity. We conclude this chapter by returning to the case of Lee, whom we introduced in Chapter 1, and examining the impact of his termination on his future career trajectory.

So, If You Don't Like It Here, Leave: The Illusion of Choice

In societies, like the United States, that place a high value on individualism, a common-sense response to misery at work is the suggestion that a person is free to leave. This may be the case in job sectors for which there is high demand and a shortage of skilled workers. In times of recession and contracting economic growth, however, very few job categories allow workers the option to change jobs at will. And, even within those rare categories of employment in which workers are theoretically highly mobile, workers are still constrained by other responsibilities and commitments, such as the location of extended family members, some of whom may need their attention and care; the job opportunities of a spouse or partner that also must be taken into consideration; the schools available for children and especially for special-needs children; the preference for particular geographic locations within which to live; access to medical care for self or family members; and, last but by no means least, the involvement in meaningful informal and/or formal social networks of friends, church communities, and civic and cultural activities. Ironside and Seifert (2003) put to rest the myth that a person is "free" to leave a destructive job situation:

> The difficulty with this argument is that when there is unemployment amongst a given category of worker then quitting is not realistic. You are only free to quit in the same sense as you are free to leave a room when a person with a gun says that you are free to leave but that if you do they will shoot you. The misuse of "free" should not disguise the material choices available. (p. 385)

It would be difficult to make the point more clearly than Ironside and Seifert do. In spite of our cultural mythology about our freedom to pick and choose jobs, the hard reality is quite different.

Loss of Income and Health and Retirement Benefits

Workplace mobbing, by definition, is designed to eliminate targeted individuals from the workplace by discrediting them through a variety of abusive behaviors and by rendering them suspect should they be audacious enough to want to remain in the organization. Scaer (2005) states that "the abused employee is often helpless to change the circumstances of his or her employment, and when deliberate abuse occurs, it constitutes a life threat associated with the loss of income and health and retirement benefits" (p. 132). The immediate impact of mobbing on a victim is either the real or threatened loss of a job. In the United States, with almost all health insurance tied to employment, loss of a job also brings with it loss of health insurance and loss of retirement benefits, and, in some cases, loss of life insurance. If the mobbing victim is the primary insured person within a household, then not only are his or her individual health insurance benefits terminated upon job loss, but so are the health benefits of the rest of the person's family. In a family in which either the mobbing victim or a family member has serious or chronic medical problems, loss of health insurance can be catastrophic.

If the family is sufficiently affluent to afford private health insurance, the premiums are usually exorbitant, and preexisting condition clauses may exclude the very conditions most in need of being covered by the health insurance. In the

United States, the situation is bleakest for those in their 50s, who are more likely to have developed some medical problems but are still a number of years away from eligibility for Medicare coverage. This age group also has a more difficult time gaining reemployment. For example, a mobbing victim in her 50s who voluntarily left her job had been diagnosed many years earlier with a benign neoplasm. A private health insurance underwriter told her that she was now uninsurable by the private health insurance sector. She was also the primary insured for her family members, and they too became uninsured. In cases like hers, the loss of health insurance benefits and the loss of income become a literal life threat. Mobbing victims like this woman are exquisitely double-bound. Had she remained in her job, she was also at risk for serious medical problems (cf., Chapter 8). The case of the surgeon (Westhues, 2005c) described in Chapter 7, who was mobbed in Canada and who ultimately made the decision to leave Canada for his homeland, is again illustrative. Had he not left the community within which he was mobbed, he believes he would have died from a heart attack.

Involuntary or Voluntary Job Loss

In the United States, the Workplace Bullying Institute/Zogby International's (2007) large study of workplace abuse found that the victim of workplace abuse was either fired or driven out—otherwise known as *constructive discharge*—in 24% of the cases. In 40% of the cases, the victim voluntarily left employment due to workplace abuse. In 13% of the cases, the victim transferred within the organization and remained, but in a different unit. In a staggering 64% of cases, victims of workplace abuse lost their jobs either voluntarily or involuntarily. Lutgen-Sandvik (2006), in an effort to develop more U.S.-based data about workers who suffered abuse, conducted a qualitative study in which she analyzed the narratives of 30 workers who were either victims or witnesses of workplace abuse. She concluded that, for many abused workers, leaving, threatening to leave, or thinking about leaving was an act of defiance or resistance in the face of workplace abuse. Lutgen-Sandvik stated that among the 30 narratives were stories of 224 workers who quit as result of workplace abuse. She said that "workers reported talking to each other about quitting, encouraging each other to leave, spreading information about job opportunities, championing those who had 'escaped,' and helping colleagues find jobs" (p. 415). Although Lutgen-Sandvik's findings underscore the emphasis that workers who have been exposed to workplace abuse place on exiting the organization, they also are suggestive of collegial support and standing by one another. Such narratives are at odds with other accounts of witnesses and bystanders providing no help and no support and distancing themselves from the victims (López-Cabarcos & Vázquez-Rodríguez, 2006). At the executive level, only 35% of CEOs returned to active executive leadership positions within 2 years of being fired for a number of reasons, including "unjust conspiratorial overthrow"

(p. 77). Forty-three percent of the fired CEOs basically ended their careers (Sonnenfeld & Ward, 2007).

In other countries, even where there are much greater employment protections than in the United States, studies also indicate that mobbing victims gave serious consideration to leaving their jobs. In mobbing sector studies of university professors and researchers in Turkey and Spain (López-Cabarcos & Vázquez-Rodríguez, 2006; Tigrel & Kokalan, 2009), a desire to leave one's job was a common reaction to having been mobbed. In the Turkish university study, Tigrel and Kokalan concluded that "at the end of the interviews all participants shared that the mobbing behaviors they had been exposed to were successful and that they wanted to change their jobs when possible" (p. 98). In the United Kingdom, Rayner (2002) found that approximately 25% of those who experienced workplace abuse left their employment and that about 20% of witnesses of workplace abuse also left. Burnes and Pope (2007), in their study of negative behaviors among employees of the National Health Service in the United Kingdom, found that approximately 70% of those exposed to negative behaviors considered changing their jobs within their organization or by leaving it, and about 20% actually did.

The research is clear that workers who experience abuse, and even those exposed to it but not direct victims of it, are impacted in multiple ways, a primary way being consideration of whether to remain in the organization or work unit or to leave. For most victims of mobbing, leaving the job unit or organization is a serious consideration, albeit one typically fraught with fear. Adults do not leave jobs lightly. That they would give serious consideration to such an extreme measure as a way of solving the problem of workplace abuse reflects how devastating an experience it is to be a victim of mobbing.

Job Disengagement and Withholding Work

Lutgen-Sandvik's (2006) analysis of resistance to workplace abuse identifies response strategies used by those exposed to abuse. The strategies include anger, defiance, and other forms of resistance. She identified labor withdrawal and working-to-rule as other forms of resistance in which workers, as a result of anger, exhaustion, hopelessness, or reduced commitment simply cannot or do not produce the volume of work or the quality of work that they had produced prior to workplace abuse. Pearson, Andersson, and Porath (2000) spent 5 years systematically studying what they refer to as "workplace incivility." They defined these incidents of workplace incivility as mildly abusive episodes of rudeness and discourteousness. In isolation, these acts could seem somewhat mild, but cumulatively, they are the stuff of which mobbing is made.

In their study, Pearson, Andersson, and Porath (2000) interviewed and conducted workshops with over 700 workers, managers, and professionals in a wide variety of fields. Additionally, they received responses to their questionnaires about workplace mistreatment from 775 other employee respondents, again representing a purposefully wide sample of organizations across the United States. What they found is striking in terms of the depth of impact on work performance subsequent to workplace incivility or mistreatment, even in its relatively mild manifestations. Here are some of their key findings:

- More than 50% of the respondents said they were distracted from their work as a result of workplace incivility or mistreatment and were further distracted by worrying about whether such episodes would recur.
- More than 30% of the respondents deliberately reduced their commitment to the organization as a result of becoming a victim of workplace incivility or mistreatment. These respondents did not work beyond what was outlined in their job descriptions, and they withdrew their previously characteristic extra efforts. They also reduced their contributions to the organization as a whole by making decisions such as withdrawing from committee membership and activity and by reducing their contributions to new ideas and organizational innovation.
- About 25% intentionally decreased their work efforts directed at meeting their own work responsibilities. This group discontinued putting forward their best efforts at work.

In their study in Spain, López-Cabarcos and Vázquez-Rodríguez (2006) likewise found that 12% of those in their sample reduced their involvement at work after experiences of psychological harassment.

Work withdrawal and reduced job engagement are important on a number of levels. Engaged workers are those who are enthusiastic and excited about their work. They are involved in their job and tend to be high achievers and high producers (Roberts & Davenport, 2002). In a rational world, high achievers and high producers are the kinds of workers that most organizations want, yet it is these high achievers who are often targeted and become victims of mobbing (Bultena & Whatcott, 2008). The studies cited here about work withdrawal and job disengagement suggest that the individual employee or worker who has been the victim of negative workplace acts experiences significantly reduced overall job satisfaction and is likely to respond to that dissatisfaction through work withdrawal and job disengagement. In what may be a surprising finding, Lapierre, Spector, and Leck (2005) concluded from their research that women found nonsexual aggression at work to be more associated with overall reduced job satisfaction than sexual aggression. At the personal, individual level, job satisfaction and personal life satisfaction are fairly highly correlated (Judge & Watanbe, 1993; Spector, 1997). Job dissatisfaction as a result of workplace mobbing leads to reduced overall life satisfaction. At the organizational level, job dissatisfaction, job disengagement, and organizational performance are interrelated. The Gallup Organization has conducted proprietary studies of organizational engagement for over

30 years. Harter, Schmidt, and Keyes (2003) conducted a meta-analysis of the relationship between employee engagement and business outcomes using the Gallup studies. Their findings are best summarized in this statement:

> Work is a pervasive and influential part of the individual and the community's well-being. It affects the quality of an individual's life and his or her mental health, and thereby can affect the productivity of entire communities. The ability to promote well-being rather than engender strains and mental illness is of considerable benefit not only to employees in the community but also to the employer's bottom line. The emotional well-being of employees and their satisfaction with their work and workplace affect citizenship at work, turnover rates, and performance ratings. (p. 207)

The evidence is compelling. Those who are victims of workplace mobbing leave their jobs at higher rates and become disengaged from their work at higher rates. Such job turnover and job disengagement, at the personal level, is life-altering, causing loss of enjoyment of life and loss of well-being. Moreover, at the organizational level, and even the community level, turnover and job disengagement are associated with lower levels of productivity and more negative business outcomes.

Reemployability

In the United States, 64% of those who experienced workplace abuse either were fired or left voluntarily (Workplace Bullying Institute/Zogby International, 2007). One implication of this statistic is that a significant number of individuals are displaced and out of work as a result of mobbing. This group faces specific practical issues in obtaining reemployment, irrespective of the nature of the economy at any given point in time. Some of those who have experienced mobbing may find other employment while considering leaving their abusive workplace, but before either voluntary or involuntary termination. Reemployability after mobbing is an unresearched area, so it is difficult to know how successful or unsuccessful employees are who seek to find another job after experiencing workplace abuse but before termination. Those who are successful are certainly more fortunate than their unsuccessful counterparts who find themselves out of work through either voluntary or involuntary termination, even though they may have been looking for another job. Let's look at the obstacles this group faces.

Most employment applications require a detailed listing of former jobs, especially covering the previous 5 years. They usually require identifying one's supervisor and giving permission for the hiring company to contact the employee's former company and/or supervisor. Workers seeking new employment who were mobbed at their previous employment are double-bound in this situation. They can't realistically decline permission to contact their former employer and seriously believe that they stand a chance of consideration for a position in the new company. On the other hand, they are left in a state of dread and uncertainty about what the former employee might say about them. Former employers of mobbed workers have power beyond what is reasonable to influence the career trajectory of an employee who left due to workplace abuse. They may indeed have the power to influence whether the mobbed worker ever works again.

One action that mobbed former employees can take to find out what their employers will say about them to a prospective employer is to hire a company that specializes in employment verification and reference checking. For a fee, these companies will call former employers, supervisors, and coworkers and compile a written report of the responses given to them about the former employee in question. Ethical employment verification companies do not lie about who they are but present themselves as working on behalf of multiple employers and clients. Organizations that are mobbing-prone and have had problems with mobbing and workplace abuse in the past are the very ones most likely to have had previous contact with these employment verification companies and to be on guard. The best that employment verification companies can do is determine what a former supervisor or coworker might say when the company is being asked formally for a reference through official channels. It is the informal, unofficial channels that are more troubling and the source of much defamatory information about workers who have experienced mobbing and workplace abuse. For example, a mid-level manager who threatened to leave the organization because of being subjected to a series of workplace abuses was told by a high-level executive of that company that "I will see to it that you never work again."

The reality is that mobbing doesn't end just because a person no longer works for the organization in which the mobbing occurred. Active mobbing can continue post-termination, and the uncertainty and fear associated with reemployability and what the former employer may say about the person to a prospective employer may continue for extended periods of time. Employment uncertainty for both employed and unemployed persons has been demonstrated to have substantial detrimental effects (Dekker & Schaufeli, 1995; De Witte, 1999; Mantler, Matejicek, Matheson, & Anisman, 2005).

Loss of Belief in a Just World

Belief in a *just world* refers to constructs about whether people believe that the world is generally a just and a fair place and whether they believe that what happens to them in their personal lives is fair and just. Whether people believe that what happens to them personally is fair seems more important in predicting mental health and positive adjustment than whether they believe generally that the world is just and fair (Sutton & Douglas, 2005). The research on just world beliefs, according to Dalbert (2001), has identified three profound implications for thinking and acting; namely, belief in a just world allows people to trust that others are treating them fairly, belief in a just world supports personal assimilation of injustices, and belief in a just world necessitates that people act fairly and justly toward others.

Mobbing and workplace abuse are unfair and unjust. Research conducted by Adoric and Kvartuc (2007) found that victims of mobbing experienced the world as basically unjust, and the more severe the negative acts involved in the mobbing, the more unfair and unjust they saw the world. In their study, they also concluded that mobbing victims began to distance themselves from the belief that their personal worlds were fair and just. In essence, mobbing victims began to reject the notion of both a globally fair and just world and a personally fair and just world. The implications of these findings are important because they suggest that basic belief systems through which people tend to make sense of their experience gave way for mobbing victims, leaving them vulnerable to increased feelings of isolations, suspicion, and mistrust. Adoric and Kvartuc stated that "more than simply reducing trust, perceived victimization by mobbing seems to deprive the individual of an important basis for his or her expectations regarding the restoration of justice. In that regard, social support to mobbing victims both in coping with mobbing and in the reparation and compensation of injustice might be particularly important" (p. 270). Such shattered beliefs that the world is reasonably fair may offer some explanation as to why mobbing victims reduce their engagement and withdraw from work. More research is needed to determine how enduring and generalizable these feelings of mistrust and suspicion are to other areas of their lives.

Loss of Professional and Personal Identity

A professional in the same community as a woman who had been mobbed sent a request through LinkedIn, a professional social networking site, asking to connect with her. She wrote back to him saying that she would connect with him but that she had not posted a profile because she didn't know who she was anymore. He made the LinkedIn connection and kindly wrote back to her saying that he knew who she was. Especially in Western cultures, personal identity is closely tied to professional and job identity. Most conversations in the United States between people who have just met include a question from one or both conversational partners about what kind of work the other does. The answers to the question are used to locate the person in terms of education and socioeconomic status. The nature of one's work, especially in the United States, is a major signifier of accomplishment and social influence.

Voluntary or involuntary loss of a job as a result of mobbing cuts to the very heart of a person's professional and, often, personal identity. Lutgen-Sandvik (2008) conducted a fascinating study of the threats to identity from workplace abuse and the remedial steps abused workers took to rebuild and restore their identities. She called this process of rebuilding and restoring "identity work" and found that the challenges to identity faced by workers who had been abused were different at each stage of the abuse process. In the first stage, as the abuse was commencing, Lutgen-Sandvik determined that threats to identity had to do with loss of a sense of personal safety and questioning of one's perceptions of what was happening in the workplace. Such threats to one's understanding and acceptance of one's own experiences are not trivial. People navigate through the world based on how they make sense of it. If they cannot trust their own processes of meaning-making and begin to continuously question their own conclusions, psychological stability is quickly jeopardized. For example, conscientious workers who previously felt secure in their jobs and who subsequently learn that others are making accusations of incompetence and dereliction of duty about them are understandably going to question their prior perceptions of their whole work environment. They are also going to question the legitimacy of their earlier feelings of comfort and security at work. Once this phase of the mobbing process has begun, nothing will ever be the same again. The world has changed for the mobbed worker. In many ways, the onset of workplace mobbing is its most pernicious phase because the victim must rapidly process all kinds of new and disquieting information that is being circulated about him or her and try to make sense of it. In a study of Turkish academics who had been mobbed, all of the mobbing victims reported being initially unaware that they were being mobbed and consequently initially blamed themselves (Tigrel & Kokolan, 2009).

Lutgen-Sandvik (2008) described the identity threats her research revealed during the active phase of workplace abuse, when victims were no longer in any doubt that they were the targets of multiple hostile, aggressive acts by others in their workplaces. She points out, extending the work of Leymann (1990) and Leymann and Gustaffson (1996), that the threats to identity emerge in the active phase of mobbing as a result of the experience of being disbelieved, blamed for being the victim, and negatively labeled. It is at this stage during a mobbing that attacks on the victim's personal and professional reputations are most likely and most injurious. Duffy and Sperry (2007) state:

> Being mobbed can result in a profound sense of shame and powerlessness on the part of the victim who may not know the language of mobbing and therefore does not know how to name what has happened. Instead of understanding mobbing as a reversion to a more primitive aggressive state common to all animals, the person who has been mobbed most often has received little support, has been isolated, and has constructed the meaning of the experience as that of shameful personal failure. (pp. 398–399)

Blaming the victim during workplace mobbing and bullying has also been identified by a number of scholars as a common organizational response (Bernardi, 2001; LaVan & Martin, 2008). Victim-blaming results in further traumatization, beyond the trauma of being the target of aggressive workplace acts and deepens the identity crisis into which the worker has already been thrust. Ironically, committed and conscientious workers are more likely to take to heart the accusations that they are at fault and question their own intentions and behaviors. The lack of congruence between their commitment to their jobs, their positive work ethics, and their repudiation and devaluation during a mobbing results in the shattering of long-held beliefs such as, "If you do a good job you will be rewarded," and initiates a cascade of self-doubt and loss of confidence.

In what Lutgen-Sandvik (2008) referred to as the "post-bullying" phase, her research indicated that identity threats to victims consist of loss of the sense of being a valued worker or professional, loss of career and associated professional identity, and profound loss of belief in the world as fair and just. Cumulatively, mobbed workers experience a crushing set of threats to their personal and professional identities, to their beliefs and values about fairness and justice in the world (Adoric & Kvartuc, 2007; Lutgen-Sandvik, 2008), to their trust in their own perceptions and interpretations of what is happening around them, to their confidence in themselves, and to their beliefs about whether they will be able to recover and have a decent future.

Day-to-day life requires that we trust our experiences of the world and that we use those experiences iteratively to help us make sense of things. Our experiences of life also serve as navigational tools for moving forward in the world. The ultimate loss endured in mobbing is the inability to trust in the reliability of one's own perceptions and interpretations of experience. It is a crippling loss, requiring mobbing victims to relearn the territory of their own lives. A professional who had been mobbed and who later left her employment described her experience of being at a staff meeting in a new job, a position she thought she would never have again. She said that, in the middle of expressing her viewpoint in the meeting, she would stop cold and question herself about whether she was talking too loudly or coming on too strong and try to figure out how the others were reacting to her so that she could adjust what she was saying or how she was saying it. In short, she had internalized the stigma from her previous mobbing and carried it with her as the invisible handicap it was.

Loss of Professional and Personal Identity: What Happened after Lee Was Fired?

Lee never appealed his termination from his control room job in the nuclear power plant and, when he was escorted out of the nuclear power plant where he had worked for a number of years, he walked away ashamed, not knowing how he was going to get another job. There were only 104 commercial reactors in the United States at 65 nuclear power plant sites, so the community of on-site power plant quality assurance (QA) supervisors and managers was a relatively small one. And, like most technical and professional groups, they got together annually at meetings and conferences. Working in the nuclear power plant industry was all that Lee knew, but more importantly, it was a job for which he was eminently suited both by temperament and training. Lee had the mental focus and discipline to watch the control room screen for hours, studying it for deviations that could signal trouble. He felt at home in the control room and was committed to the maintenance of safety within the nuclear power plant environment. In a rational world, Lee was the kind of employee that nuclear power plants across the country would compete to hire. It had been over a year since Lee was terminated, and he had applied without success for every opening for which he was qualified.

In the beginning, Lee was numb and in shock about being fired. He obsessed over the events that led to his firing and, in his meticulous way, went over every piece of information that came out in the subsequent investigation of the equipment failures and operational shutdowns. He hadn't realized that his coworkers and supervisors regarded him as a "pain in the ass," as overly perfectionistic, and as a threat to their end-of-year bonuses. After the investigation, he at least knew that much. What he still didn't know—but was beginning to suspect—was that his work was actively sabotaged and that he was fired based on a conspiracy of lies and silence between the technician in the field who triggered the shutdowns, his manager, and the QA supervisor. As Lee increasingly put things together in his own mind, he began to feel wronged and unjustly treated. He tried not to get caught up in feelings of anger, suspicion, and mistrust because he needed all of his energy to get another job, and he wasn't having much luck. He had nightmares in which he was flipping hamburgers or handing out towels to people in cabanas on the beach. Lee wanted to be back in the control room.

When he filled out applications for jobs at other power plants, Lee had to list the job from which he was fired and his supervisor's name. He also had to give permission for the prospective employer to contact his former employer. Over the course of the year, Lee had applied for nine jobs at various power plants. Even though he loved where he was living, he was willing to relocate—he knew he had to be willing to move to ever have a chance of working in the nuclear power plant industry again. His training and credentials exceeded the minimum required, and his experience was substantial.

Lee wasn't sure whether his former employer could tell prospective employers that he had been fired. To make his application look better and to help deal with having to manage the fact of being fired, Lee thought that it would be a good strategy to send the last few performance evaluations he had received along with his job application. Because the evaluations were focused primarily on skills, competence, and performance, Lee's evaluations had been reasonably good. Although his former manager had wanted to "get his licks in" on Lee's evaluation, the structure of the evaluations had precluded him from being able to do so. As it turned out, Lee never received so much as a phone interview. He was certain that the news of his firing had travelled through the QA community informally, and he had no idea what to do about it. So, when another job opened up, Lee applied again and, this time, he got the job. He was fortunate insofar as his training and experience were relatively scarce commodities and that the industry had begun to expand again and needed more skilled technicians like Lee.

Even though he had to move hundreds of miles, Lee was happy. He wanted to get married, and he viewed his new job and opportunity to work in the nuclear power plant environment as the fresh start he had been dreaming about. He even started to think of moving in a positive way, as part of his fresh start in life. When he went to work on his first full day, after many days of plant orientation and safety drills, Lee's QA supervisor pulled him aside and said that he expected him to be a team player. Lee was confused because he had always viewed himself as a team player, following the rules and working to ensure plant safety. It began to dawn on Lee that the supervisors at his new job knew what had happened to him but hired him anyway because of a shortage of skilled technicians in his area. Above all, Lee did not want a repetition of what had happened at his last job.

As Lee began to acclimate to the environment of his new job, he found himself second-guessing himself. This was a new and disconcerting experience for Lee. When Lee studied the wall-size computer display that tracked the internal and external environments at the nuclear power plant facility, he never missed spotting those out-of-range indicators referred to as deviations. He knew what the protocol was—log the time, place, and nature of every deviation. Lee didn't question his abilities, but he did question how he would be perceived by his coworkers. He didn't want the reputation of being a perfectionistic troublemaker. Lee wanted to stay "under the radar" at this job. So, he started making subjective assessments about which deviations were important and which weren't and only logged those that he thought were important. Lee knew it was a dangerous practice because sometimes what appeared to be a relatively small deviation could be the result of a more significant deviation offset by other factors.

In making subjective assessments about which deviations to log, Lee was violating protocol. He was also violating his own values. Lee knew that what he was doing in the control room could, in fact, compromise safety. He felt and acted like a trapped animal. He was scared about the risks he was taking at work. He was scared about the possibility of being fired again. He was angry that he felt forced to take those risks as a result of what had happened in his previous job—the specific details of which were still largely unknown to him. Lee felt everything had turned out wrong and wondered how he could be in such a predicament when all he had done was follow protocol. What was supposed to be a fresh start for Lee was souring quickly.

Analysis

Lee's mobbing and subsequent firing resulted in the expectable loss of income and health and retirement benefits. The process of obtaining a new job was predictably complicated and drawn out with anxiety and uncertainty about its outcome. Mobbing affected some basic pragmatics of Lee's life; namely, postponing marriage until he was able to get another job and having to move to another location hundreds of miles away from where he had been settled.

The more unexpected effects on Lee's career and work performance were what happened after he became reemployed. Lee lost confidence in his ability to do his job accurately and according to protocol without becoming subject to pejorative characterizations of perfectionism. He had attributed his difficulties and firing in his former job to these characterizations, but was at a loss to know how to be someone he wasn't.

Being in the position of having to hide and manage his past work problems kept him from feeling free to discuss specific job expectations and any potential impact of logging deviations on other workers. Rather than being an experience that Lee was able to use in his professional development to understand and talk about systemic issues, the effects of having been mobbed at his previous job pushed him into increased isolation and fear. He didn't trust his supervisors or coworkers, and he didn't trust himself. He concocted a horrible solution that relied on making subjective assessments about the significance of deviations that left him feeling wretched and that also potentially compromised safety. Without fairly quick intervention, the outlook for Lee's career performance and advancement could not have been worse.

Conclusion

The first and most obvious decision for those experiencing workplace abuse is whether to remain in a job where one is being mobbed or to leave. If the victim chooses to remain in the job, he or she is likely to be subjected to continuing abusive behavior, and further, is likely to be blamed for it. If the victim chooses to leave the job, he or she is subject to the vicissitudes of loss of income, loss of health and retirement benefits, inability to obtain a decent reference that is likely to affect reemployability, and damage to professional reputation. Mobbing victims find themselves exquisitely double-bound when considering leaving or staying.

In addition, mobbing victims are subject to the enduring effects of having been mobbed that show up in their impact on self-confidence and in loss of trust and pleasure in the work environment. Second-guessing oneself, looking over one's shoulder, wondering who is supportive and who is antagonistic can preoccupy workers who have been mobbed and who are fortunate enough to obtain reemployment. Mobbing can be an assault on a worker's core identity, one that has enduring effects on work performance and identity and from which it is not easy to recover.

Part Four

RECOVERY, SOLUTION, AND PREVENTION

11

Recommending a Personal Therapeutic Plan

Remembering and telling the truth about terrible events are prerequisites both for the restoration of the social order and for the healing of individual victims.
—Judith Herman (1997, p. 1)

In the previous sections of the book, we focused on describing and understanding mobbing as a social process involving individual, group, and organizational dynamics. We then examined how mobbing occurs and looked closely at its consequences across a number of life domains. In this section, we focus on recovery, solutions, and prevention of mobbing.

This chapter is about the process of recovery and healing from school or workplace mobbing. Table 8.1 illustrated the range of evidence-based health consequences from mobbing and bullying for schoolchildren and for adult workers. Even the most cursory review of those health consequences reveals their severe and even life-threatening nature. This chapter is focused on the individual victims of mobbing and the recovery plans that they need to develop in order to heal. We provide therapists and other health care professionals with specific suggestions and guidelines for effective treatment of the trauma of school and workplace mobbing, and the evidence and rationale upon which those recommendations are based. That evidence and rationale is based on how the brain and body typically react under situations of extreme stress, as occurs frequently in school and workplace mobbings. Therapists and other health care providers can only help victims and their families make informed choices about best treatment when they understand the complexity of the impact of mobbing on a victim's body, brain, and mind. In this chapter, we provide such information, so that health care professionals can work more effectively with victims and their family members to help them understand what has happened to them and to help them make treatment choices based on that understanding.

We recognize, of course, that the mitigation and prevention of mobbing involves raising widespread awareness about mobbing and its threat to health, career, and family and social relationships. Preventing mobbing will also need to include commitment to the development of anti-mobbing policies by schools and organizations, and the corresponding development of humane and effective strategies for conflict resolution. These issues will be addressed in the remaining chapters of the book. In spite of the pervasiveness of mobbing and bullying, many individual victims exist for whom there is little in the way of a template for recovery. For example, a highly educated adult victim of workplace mobbing expressed her frustration that she could not find anything in the professional literature addressing strategies for recovering from mobbing and bullying—a literature for which she hungered to help her through her own ordeal, which had gone on for several years. The goal of this chapter is to provide professionals with a framework for such a recovery template and to help them give mobbing victims and their families the tools with which to construct a personalized plan for recovery. As we previously indicated, we choose to use the term "victims" throughout this book to indicate that mobbing results in injuries, just as natural disasters and automobile accidents do. We do not suggest that victims of mobbing are weak—quite the contrary. What we do suggest is that victimization is the outcome of mobbing and must be acknowledged as such.

We hold the position that there is no "one size fits all" formula for recovering from mobbing. Individuals vary in their responses to mobbing and in the degree to which their neurophysiology becomes involved and activated. Some mobbing victims will seem particularly vulnerable and manifest multiple and severe symptoms, whereas others who experience similar degrees and durations of hostile behaviors directed toward them will seem more resilient and able to move on with life more quickly. Research on stress and post-traumatic stress disorder (PTSD) indicates that social support will moderate the individual response to a current trauma, but that exposure to previous trauma and the magnitude of the current trauma will exacerbate the response (Kulka, Schlenger, Fairbank, Hough, Jordan, & Marmar, 1990).

Mobbing, Trauma, and the Body

The early work of Leymann (1990) outlined a number of health outcomes among mobbed workers, in particular, psychosomatic symptoms. Somatic symptoms are a common indicator of trauma (Scaer, 2005). Leymann and Gustaffson (1996) identified PTSD as a frequent outcome of workplace mobbing. Many of the health consequences listed in Table 8.1 include symptoms from one of the clusters of the *Diagnostic and Statistical Manual of Mental Disorders* (DSM-IV-TR) (American Psychiatric Association, 2000) diagnostic criteria for PTSD or for PTSD itself. A number of the symptoms in Table 8.1 represent more severe symptoms than those required to make the diagnosis of PTSD. We consider school or workplace mobbing to represent a serious trauma or life threat. School or workplace mobbing is not an acute trauma, like witnessing a shooting or being involved in a serious car accident. It is chronic trauma, consisting of aggressive acts directed toward the victim over time and one that often includes personal attacks.

The student in school or the worker in an organization is trapped in contexts from which they cannot easily leave but within which they are the targets of ongoing abusive acts. Most mobbing victims in school and in the workplace are stuck—they cannot easily leave without risking even more adverse life consequences, even though remaining in the abusive environment almost guarantees further abuse. People who are stuck in such approach–avoidance conflicts pay the price in neurophysiologic health, which may become permanently damaged (O'Brien, 1997, Scaer, 2005, van der Kolk, 2006). Scaer (2005) emphasized that "limiting the definition of trauma to extreme stress is like defining the iceberg by its tip. Trauma rather must be defined by the specific physiologic changes that occur in the body and brain related to any negative life experience and to the perpetuation of those changes over time" (p. 287). What Scaer is saying is that trauma ultimately comes to be located in the neurophysiology of the victim, not in the situation or event, hence the variety of responses to it.

Therefore, in developing a personalized plan for recovery from mobbing, the place to start is by identifying the kinds of primary autonomic nervous system responses and their intensity that the mobbing victim has manifested. Neurophysiological responses form an important part of the systemic network of elements involved in how individual victims respond to mobbing. The other components of the systemic network influencing victims' responses to mobbing include other individual characteristics, the dynamics of the group involved in the mobbing, and the response to the mobbing by the organization. As initially introduced in Chapter 9, in relation to typologies of responses to mobbing, neurophysiologically primed responses to threat are fight, flight, or freeze. In a school or workplace mobbing, the victim, once aware of the threat, will be primed to fight, flee, or freeze, depending upon the circumstances.

The traumatic reactions induced by being mobbed at work or school, unless treated, can doom a mobbing victim to an emotional replaying and physiological reexperiencing of the events of the mobbing, as if they were occurring in the present rather than being understood as part of one's past (Scaer, 2005, van der Kolk, 2006). Trauma reactions remain alive and active in neuronal networks and can be activated by stimuli suggestive of the original trauma, even many years later. The trauma of mobbing, even if there was no physical aggression, lingers in the body in the form of exaggerated startle responses, heightened skin conductance, increased heart rate, and emotional imagery associated with autonomic nervous system responses (Lang, 1979; Scaer, 2005; van der Kolk & van der Hart, 1991). Hence, the meaning-laden phrase coined by van der Kolk (1994) captures the neurophysiology of the trauma experience: "the body keeps the score."

Successful and Unsuccessful Neurophysiological Responses to Mobbing

"Trauma can be conceptualized as stemming from a failure of the natural physiological activation and hormonal secretions to organize an effective response to threat" (van der Kolk, 2006, p. 282). The autonomic nervous system is composed of two branches, the sympathetic nervous system and the parasympathetic nervous system (Pliszka, 2003). The sympathetic nervous system prepares the organism to move in response to threat. That movement would usually involves fight or flight, both of which take considerable energy and body resources, which a regulated sympathetic nervous system puts at the disposal of its owner. When a person senses a threat, the sympathetic nervous system enters a state of heightened arousal in which heart rate increases, blood flows to the skeletal muscles and brain, glucose is released to provide energy to the body, and adrenaline floods the system, thus increasing the supply of oxygen to the brain and muscles, keeping the person alert and focused (Pliszka, 2003).

The parasympathetic nervous system, on the other hand, slows the heart rate and enhances the digestive process and is associated with the downshifting of the organism into a state of rest (Pliszka, 2003). The freeze response or "playing possum" is associated with the activation of the parasympathetic nervous system (Scaer, 2005). The freeze response is indicated by physical collapse and immobility. Freezing is only a successful response to threat if the person or animal escapes as a result. In the animal world, a predator may leave an intended victim alone if the victim appears already dead. In mass shootings, victims have reported feigning death to avoid actually being targeted by the shooter. Freeze is extraordinarily unsuccessful as a response to life threats if it results in failure to take needed action (Leach, 2004) or if it results in the extreme freeze response: sudden death, caused by autonomic dysregulation leading to such a slowing of the heart rate that the brain is deprived of sufficient oxygen to sustain life (Scaer, 2005).

In the case of mobbing, if a victim decides to fight back by complaining about abusive behavior to supervisors, and they respond by respectfully listening to the victim's story and taking appropriate action to protect the victim and resolve the bullying or mobbing, the fight response will have been completed successfully. In addition, the mobbing will have been resolved satisfactorily, and the parties will move on untraumatized. If a mobbing victim or victim's parents assesses the school or workplace situation as untenable, and the victim decides to leave despite the likelihood of subsequent losses, but feels fortunate to be out of the situation and confident enough about the future, the flight response will have been completed successfully. In these examples, which unfortunately are the least likely, mobbing victims will not be traumatized because they responded to a threat with a successful fight or flight. Failure of the fight-or-flight response to resolve a life threat is an unsuccessful neurophysiological solution attempt that can lead to a dangerous and dysregulated freeze response.

Approach–Avoidance Dilemmas and Double-Binds in Mobbing

However, if the fight or flight has not been successful and a mobbing victim fights back by complaining to supervisors who then respond by labeling him as a trouble-maker or as unstable and his situation deteriorates, the fight response will have been unsuccessful and the victim's pent-up energy will not have been released. Likewise, if a victim voluntarily leaves school or the workplace and then faces unmanageable losses and perhaps continued mobbing after leaving, the flight response, which also took considerable stores of energy, will have been interrupted and that pent-up energy will remain undischarged. These latter scenarios form the basis of the freeze response, which is defined either as an interrupted fight-or-flight response or more simply as helplessness (Levine, 1997; Scaer, 2005).

Fight and flight use considerable stores of energy from the body and, when successful escape from threat through fight or flight has been accomplished, the body gradually returns to equilibrium and discharges excess stores of energy in the process. What happens when fight or flight is unsuccessful and the person has not been able to escape a life threat, despite their best efforts at fighting back or fleeing? People who have been caught in failed flight-or-fight responses frequently move to a freeze response, with the energy stores used in the fight or flight attempts unreleased. Consider this example: A woman is out alone at night walking her dog on a quiet street by a river. A man whom she did not recognize from her neighborhood was walking across the street from her next to the river. Because he was unfamiliar in the area, the woman was keeping him under discreet surveillance. Suddenly, he charges at her running at high speed from across the street. There is no one around to help her, so she doesn't scream; she knows in an instant that she can't outrun him even though she's a runner, she doesn't know if he has a weapon, and she knows he would be much stronger than she even if he didn't have a weapon. She feels trapped—all options are dangerous. Her knees feel jelly-like and begin to wobble. She collapses to the ground in a classic freeze response. The man, suddenly and inexplicably, runs away from her in the opposite direction. The woman gets up off the ground and runs frantically toward home, thus discharging the pent-up energy left over from her freeze state. The freeze response causes problems only when there is no opportunity to discharge an interrupted fight or flight response and the stored energy remains "alive" within the body (Levine, 1997; Scaer, 2005).

Mobbing and the Freeze Response

Scaer (2005) stated that "the healthy animal freezes only when it enters a state of helplessness" (p. 49). In this state, the animal or person is caught in an approach–avoidance conflict in which the apparent action alternatives are all fraught with danger. For mobbing and bullying victims, complaining about mistreatment and fighting back can be dangerous choices, as can leaving a school or workplace with the attendant changes and inevitable losses that follow such an action. When neither seeking help nor trying to ignore the problem is effective, and further harm is the result of both courses of action, a mobbing victim is helpless, and becomes vulnerable to a physiological freeze response. Consider the following instance of an academic and cleric who was mobbed at a Canadian university.

Herbert Richardson, the former theology professor at the University of St. Michael's College in Toronto, who is the focus of Westhues' (2005b) book, *The Pope Versus the Professor,* wrote a foreword to the 2005 edition of that book. In his foreword, Richardson mentions another professor at St. Michael's, Father John Kelly, who also was the school's former president. Richardson describes how Kelly was fired for insisting that professors be allowed to maintain their academic freedom. Richardson writes of Kelly that "for his views, he was abruptly banished from the campus. Disheartened, just a few weeks later, John Kelly died" (Westhues, 2005b, p. xii).

Scaer (2005) stated that "a number of studies on sudden, unexplained death clearly reflect the dangers of excessive activation of the freeze response . . . in humans" (p. 47). Scaer described "the true freeze response" (p. 46) as being dangerous because it precipitates a chain of cardiovascular events that, unresolved, can lead to death. Whether John Kelly's death was a result of the freeze response, we do not know. What we do know from Richardson's account (Westhues, 2005b), however, is that Kelly's death was associated very closely in time with his removal from his university position and his banishment from the campus. We also know that Kelly's life and identity had revolved around his work at the university. One of the many evils associated with banishment, social isolation, and shunning is that a person can't escape them by fleeing, and fighting back, even if successful, will not remove the stain of the stigma already imposed on one by the original banishment and isolation. Banishment and social isolation, common in mobbings, are exquisitely cruel forms of interpersonal abuse, leaving victims vulnerable to dangerous freeze responses.

The Embodiment of Trauma

For both children and adults, exposure to prolonged interpersonal abuse (as is the case in school and workplace mobbing) results in the most severe forms of traumatic symptomatology (van der Kolk, Roth, Pelcovitz, Sunday, & Spinazzola, 2005). Trauma remains present in the body, through its inscription in associational networks of neurons in the brain (van der Kolk, 2006). When individuals are reminded of a particular trauma, it causes activation of parts of the cortex and limbic system of the right hemisphere of the brain and relative deactivation of parts of the cortex of the left hemisphere of the brain, particularly the cortical regions of the left brain that are associated with expressive speech. Thus, a particular trauma (such as school or workplace mobbing) and future reminders and memories of that mobbing promote the simultaneous activation of intense emotion and the relative suppression of abilities to reflect on its significance and to talk about it. Emotion is intensified while the capacity to think and talk about it is reduced.

Trauma is also embodied in procedural memory related to efforts to escape or survive the index threat (Scaer, 2005). *Procedural memory* is the memory of how to do things and, by definition, includes sensory-motor memories. In trauma, sensory-motor memories consist of emotionally charged memories of attempts to deal with and escape from threats to safety, security, and life. Even after the particular trauma is long past, cues and reminders of it can alter activity in the cortex and limbic system of the brain and initiate emotionally charged sensory-motor memories, resulting in individual reactions that appear as if the trauma is happening in the present (Levine, 1997; Scaer, 2005; van der Kolk, 1994, 2006; van der Kolk & van der Hart, 1991). Like all trauma victims, the victims of school and workplace mobbing are subject to these same body memories and reactivations when faced with cues or reminders of the mobbings. Therefore, the cardinal rule of effective treatment for mobbing victims is to remember the body and include it in treatment.

Assessment of Victims and Family Members

In this section, we shift from considering the neurophysiological basis of trauma treatment to its application in the treatment of mobbing victims. We identify assessment considerations and review treatment goals and strategies for accomplishing these goals. We also discuss the special needs of child victims of school mobbings. An important part of this treatment application section is our flexible template for designing a personalized plan for recovery from mobbing that can be utilized by health care professionals, victims, and their families.

Information from each of the following assessment areas will provide the therapist and other health care providers with an understanding of the clinical presentation of the mobbing victim from the perspectives of individual (including neurophysiological) and social functioning. Understanding the unique imprint of mobbing on a victim's personal and interpersonal functioning will allow for the development of an optimal treatment plan for the victim. Because of the absence of clinical literature on assessment of victimization from mobbing, we provide examples of interview questions that can be used to create a scaffolding to assess mobbing severity.

VICTIM'S ABILITY TO RECALL AND NARRATE THE EVENTS OF THE MOBBING

An important indicator of the degree of traumatization of a victim of school or workplace mobbing is the degree to which the victim is able to both recall the events and details of the mobbing and the degree to which he or she is able to articulate a coherent narrative about them. The more coherent a victim's recall and narrative account, the less severe the cognitive impact on the victim (Siegel, 2003). This area is assessed by asking the victim to tell the story of the mobbing in as much detail as possible.

VICTIMS' AND FAMILY MEMBERS' PERCEPTIONS OF THE SCHOOL OR WORKPLACE MOBBING

This information is best obtained from both the victim and a close family member, so that the fullest description can be provided. It is important to obtain the victim's account of the mobbing and the victims' perceptions of how he or she was harmed and/or continues to be harmed. In what areas of life has the victim experienced the greatest hurt and harm? How has the victim's identity as a human being, student, workforce member, and/or professional been impacted? How does the victim incorporate the story of the mobbing into his or her personal autobiography? How do the victim and victim's family members make sense of the mobbing? Do they hold anyone accountable? What impact has the mobbing had on the personal and professional identities of family members? Have they stood up for the victim or blamed the victim? What has been the response to either of those courses of action? How have perceptions of the mobbing changed over time?

FAMILY AND SOCIAL SUPPORT

Obtaining information in response to the following questions will help provide a window into the dynamics of the victim's family and the availability of other social support networks. By assessing this domain, the therapist will be able to identify what education the victim and family need to understand the process of mobbing, especially group and organizational involvement in it. Victims of mobbing and their family members who are provided with education about the group and organizational dynamics involved in mobbing are much less likely to assume a "blame the victim" attitude. The following are examples of the kinds of questions that will help a health care provider assess the family's current role and future potential in a healing alliance.

What is the level and quality of family and social support available to the victim? What family members have the most information about the group and organizational dynamics involved in the school or workplace mobbing and the nature of the victim's reactions over time? What have they done that has been both helpful and unhelpful in their efforts to support the victim? Are they any friends who maintain regular contact with the victim and who know the history of events surrounding the school or workplace mobbing? To whom is the victim most likely to turn for support and reassurance? How are individual family members impacted by the school or workplace mobbing, and what have their responses to it been? What help do family members need to understand the dynamics in school and workplace mobbing, so that they too will feel supported?

NEUROPHYSIOLOGICAL ASSESSMENT AND SYMPTOMS

This is a key area of assessment because it involves understanding the degree to which brain and body systems have incorporated active or unresolved memories of the abusive events of the school or workplace mobbing. These questions can help assess the degree of traumatic shock experienced by the victim and what the victim's solution attempts were in terms of fight, flight, and freeze responses.

When the victim became aware that he was the subject of interpersonal abuse at school or work, how did he respond? Was he in disbelief? Did he deny the events were happening—try to keep a low profile? Did he want to quit his job or change schools? Did he stand up for himself and try to enlist the support of peers or coworkers? Did he tell teachers or supervisors about what was going on? Did he confront the people involved in the mobbing and try to get them to stop? Did the victim become angry? Is the victim still angry now? Did he spend a lot of time in bed, or out of school or work on sick leave? Did he seem to "give in" to the abuse, or become resigned to it and just "take it?" Did the victim engage in a combination of the above behaviors? What primary autonomic responses did the victim display in terms of fight, flight, or freeze responses? Did he display a combination of responses?

Now also is the time to assess for PTSD or traumatic stress symptoms. Does the victim have intrusive thoughts, nightmares, and/or flashbacks of instances of the abuse? To what degree does the victim replay the events of the mobbing? Does the victim avoid talking about what happened or have difficulty in doing so? Is the victim easily aroused or agitated? What cues trigger heightened arousal? Does the victim startle easily?

PSYCHOLOGICAL AND BEHAVIORAL ASSESSMENT

Child, adolescent, and adult victims should be assessed for depression and suicide. Child and adolescent victims should also be assessed for substance misuse, self-injury, school avoidance and truancy, and delinquent acts.

PHYSICAL ASSESSMENT

All school and workplace mobbing victims should be medically evaluated. Gastrointestinal disturbances and sleep problems should be assessed for in child, adolescent, and adult victims. For adults, a primary focus area should also include cardiovascular assessment.

Development of Therapeutic Goals and Strategies

Therapeutic goals should be based on the individual and family assessments and be individually tailored. Victims and their families risk ineffective treatment, at best, and harmful treatment, at worst, if their treatment provider is unfamiliar with both mobbing and trauma. Any discussion of therapeutic interventions to assist in the resolution of mobbing-related trauma must include the dimension of time. The Personalized Plan for Recovery from Mobbing, presented at the end of this section, will help therapists identify specific therapeutic tasks and challenges related to particular phases of a mobbing episode. For clients who are in the midst of a mobbing episode and who remain at work or at school, the therapeutic challenges and considerations are different than for clients who have left a school or workplace where they were victimized by mobbing.

The following are general treatment goals that are based on the evidence from health outcomes for bullying and mobbing victims and best practices in treating victims of trauma.

- *Create a supportive therapeutic relationship* that is perceived by the victim and family members as nonjudgmental, responsive, and warm. It is only within the context of this kind of empathic relationship that trust and interpersonal attunement can be restored (Cohen & Mannarino, 2004; Fosha, 2003).
- *Encourage development of a coherent narrative account* of the effects on the victim and his or her family of the school or workplace mobbing. This account should fit temporally and meaningfully into the victim's broader autobiography and include recognition of the hurt and harm suffered as a result of the mobbing. Ideally, the narrative would also include elements of lessons learned from the mobbing experience about protecting oneself emotionally and acknowledgment of the risk and uncertainty present in life and the limits of personal control. Coherent narrative accounts are suggestive of the integration of cognitive and affective aspects of experience (Breire & Scott, 2006; Cohen & Mannarino, 2004; Lawson, 2009; Siegel, 2003).
- *Gradually expose the victim through dialogue* to the abusive events of the mobbing and their harmful effects.
- *Inquire about the bodily sensations that the victim perceives* when recalling the mobbing. This dialogue must only be done within the context of a safe, secure, and trusting therapeutic relationship. Focusing on body sensations during dialogue about the mobbing can help the victim to integrate the sensory-motor aspects of procedural memories related to the mobbing experience (Fosha, 2003). Van der Kolk (2003) stated that "to help traumatized individuals process their traumatic memories, it is critical that they gain enough distance from their sensory imprints and trauma-related emotions so they can observe and analyze their sensations and emotions without becoming hyperaroused or engaging in avoidance maneuvers" (p. 187). Levine (1997) and Scaer (2005) address the importance of recollecting and reexperiencing traumatic content from a safe distance, while also including attention to body sensations, as central to the discharge of unreleased energy from a truncated freeze response.
- *Promote acknowledging and grieving the losses* incurred as a result of the school or workplace mobbing. Lutgen-Sandvik (2008), in her study of bullied workers

and trauma, identified grieving as a specific task of healing. Grieving is neuro-biologically important because it is a way forward for traumatized individuals to begin to incorporate the story of their suffering into their own larger auto-biography, thereby promoting brain integration and greater emotional regulation.

- *Encourage the mobbing victim to initiate action* in pursuit of collaboratively developed goals. Mobbing victims, like most trauma victims, have difficulty initiating effective action (van der Kolk, 2006). The therapist can be very helpful in supporting the mobbing victim in the identification of even small goals and in taking incremental steps to achieve these goals. Taking action involves the combination of cognition and movement, a basic combination that promotes brain integration and traumatic resolution (Levine, 1997).
- *Utilize psychoeducation.* Mobbing victims and their families can be helped in the process of healing by understanding that mobbing is a devastating systemic social process that involves not just the victim and perpetrators, but also the school or organization itself. Understanding that most mobbing victims and their family members have been blind-sided by the events of the mobbing can help a compassionate therapist to normalize the bewilderment and shame that frequently accompanies mobbing. Adults, adolescents, and children are best served when they recognize that mobbing is a systemic social problem, not an individual problem. Giving mobbing its name (Hillard, 2009) can be powerfully therapeutic for victims and their family members, who may never have heard of it before it happened to them.
- *Encourage involvement in recreational and leisure activities enjoyed by the victim,* particularly those that include movement and control of the body. Examples of such activities are walking, running, bicycling, swimming, other sports including team sports, dancing, yoga, breathing exercises, and martial arts. Creative activities like music, painting, journaling, gardening, and cooking, based on the victim's preferences, should also be encouraged (Lawson, 2009). Engagement in enjoyable recreation and leisure activities promotes movement, body and breath control, social interaction, goal accomplishment, and affect regulation—all of which are important in the integration of traumatic events in brain circuitry and in helping to locate the trauma in the past, where it belongs (van der Kolk, 2006).

The therapeutic goals for mobbing victims just outlined are not linked to specific models of therapy. However, some therapeutic models place a greater emphasis on the role of the brain and the body in trauma and may, therefore, be more helpful for mobbing victims. No outcome studies examine the effectiveness of particular models of therapy for mobbing victims. Hopefully, such research will be conducted in the future. In the meantime, we briefly review a sample of models of therapy that have demonstrated usefulness in helping victims of other forms of trauma.

Helping Mobbing Victims Reclaim Themselves and Reconnect with Others

We take the position that mobbing victims who exhibit any symptoms of a stress or trauma reaction, either immediate or delayed, should seek appropriate treatment. We take this position in light of the repeated research suggesting that PTSD remains unchanged without treatment (Taylor, Thordarson, Maxfield, Federoff, Lovell, & Ogrodniczuk, 2003). The following therapeutic models are the most likely to incorporate techniques shown either clinically or through research to enhance the integration of traumatic residue in the brain and body.

- *Exposure therapy*. Exposure therapy utilizes in vivo or imagined recall of traumatic stimuli or events within the context of a safe and affirming therapeutic environment. Exposure therapy emphasizes the reduction of avoidance (Taylor, Thordarson, Maxfield, Federoff, Lovell, & Ogrodniczuk, 2003).
- *Eye movement desensitization and reprocessing (EMDR)*. Eye movement desensitization and reprocessing is a treatment modality that incorporates recalled traumatic material in combination with stimulated oscillatory movement (e.g., tracking the therapist's finger from side to side) that involves bilateral brain hemispheric activity (Shapiro, 1995, 1999).
- *Relaxation training*. Relaxation training involves educating clients in a range of relaxation strategies and in recognizing internal sensations and body cues that signify the need to utilize one or more of the learned relaxation strategies (Taylor et al., 2003).
- *Sensorimotor psychotherapy*. Ogden and Minton (2000) define sensorimotor psychotherapy as "a method for facilitating the processing of unassimilated sensorimotor reactions to trauma and for resolving the destructive effects of these reactions on cognitive and emotional experience" (p. 149). This approach to psychotherapy is specifically indicated for victims of trauma and focuses on the ways in which trauma experiences become embodied in victims. It utilizes specific techniques for healthy reintegration of the body, brain, and mind (Minton, Ogden, & Pain, 2006).
- *Somatic experiencing*. Somatic experiencing uses what Levine (1997) refers to as the wisdom of the body to track physical sensations, and, through a series of focused exercises, release energy trapped in the nervous system subsequent to traumatic life events. This process results in the extinguishing of internal somatic sensations and stereotypical movements developed in response to the trauma (Scaer, 2005).
- *Narrative therapy*. Narrative therapy focuses on helping clients articulate stories and autobiographies of the events and meanings that have given the shape to their lives. In trauma work, narrative therapy includes a primary focus on not only the meaning of the trauma but also on how a person has responded to that trauma and what skills, knowledge, and values they have discovered

through their suffering. Narrative work helps clients to weave and integrate their trauma experiences into a coherent self-story or autobiography (Denborough, 2006; White, 2007a).

- *Neurofeedback.* Neurofeedback or neurotherapy is a form of biofeedback that provides clients with information about the real-time state of their brain wave frequencies and amplitudes. Neurofeedback encourages self-regulation by rewarding brain wave activity that falls within the desired range and inhibiting brain wave activity that fall outside of the desired range. Over time, the desired regulation of brain wave activity becomes more stable. Neurofeedback can be used to increase alertness, to deepen relaxation, or a combination of both. This treatment has demonstrated effectiveness in a clinical trial of patients with PTSD (Hammond, 2005).

This set of treatment modalities does not exhaust the set of those that may be of help to victims of trauma, especially mobbing victims. However, these modalities have demonstrated clinical and/or research effectiveness with clients who have experienced a range of traumas. They also incorporate brain and body integration, which is critical to long-term healing after trauma exposure. As van der Kolk (2006) has stated, "In the field of trauma treatment a consensus is emerging that, in order to keep old trauma from intruding into current experience, patients need to deal with the internal residues of the past" (p. 287). The Personalized Plan for Recovery from Mobbing that follows provides a flexible template that can be used by health care professionals, victims, and family members to promote lasting recovery (Table 11.1).

Special Considerations for Protecting Child and Adolescent Mobbing Victims

In school mobbing, the sense of safety and security necessary for optimal growth and development has been taken away. For adolescents, the developmental tasks of establishing personal identity and forging successful relationships with peers have been thwarted by the experiences of interpersonal abuse. For adolescent victims of school mobbing, the ground on which they stood to make sense of their world is no longer stable. For younger children, the experience of mobbing threatens the security needed to explore the world more independently. Child and adolescent victims of school mobbing need a strong adult ally who will stand beside them and create a perimeter of safety while clearly acknowledging the moral wrong that has been perpetrated against the child or adolescent. Ideally, this ally will be a parent. Helping the child or adolescent to manage the complex reactions that are age-related and inevitable following a school mobbing requires that the parent or caregiver do the following consistently: believe in and affirm the child or adolescent's experiences, remain calm when the child or adolescent becomes upset

Table 11.1 **Designing a Personalized Plan for Recovery from Mobbing**

Early Mobbing Phase
Employees or students are becoming aware of the aggressive acts associated with the mobbing: Establish Physical and Interpersonal Safe Zones

- In the workplace:
    - o   Identify spaces in which you can be physically and emotionally safe. If there are no such places, consider sick leave or other leave of absence.
- At school:
    - o   In collaboration with school personnel, parents and student must identify physical spaces where student feels safe and secure. If no such spaces exist, appeal to school or district administration for help in identifying such safety zones or consider change of school.

Recall, describe, and document critical events in the mobbing:
Build Coherent Narratives

- For employees:
    - o   Tell the story of the events of the mobbing, at your own pace, to a trusted family member or friend.
    - o   Collect e-mails, memos, reprimands, disciplinary actions, evaluations, and any other documentary materials relating to the mobbing.
    - o   Log, journal, or document as much detail about the events as you can. This record will help you to fill in the gaps later, should you have difficulty in recall. It will also help in therapies, such as exposure therapy, that have demonstrated effectiveness in trauma recovery work.
    - o   The documentary materials and log or journal will also be helpful should you decide to pursue grievances, regulatory complaints, or lawsuits.
    - o   Give copies of all materials to a trusted family member or friend for safekeeping. This is important because you might find yourself wanting to throw out all signs and symbols of the mobbing to feel free of it.
- For students and parents:
    - o   Parents need to listen nonjudgmentally and help their child to tell the story of the events of the mobbing. Parents should make detailed notes later about what their child described and keep these and all documentary materials for safekeeping and possible future use.
    - o   If electronic or written communications are part of the mobbing, parents need to help their child gather those materials.
    - o   Parents should encourage their child to write about the events of the mobbing or to draw pictures of it in intervals tolerable to the child or adolescent.
    - o   Parents need to take charge of the situation in as supportive, nonjudgmental, and calm a way as possible. A child or adolescent mobbing victim needs to be reassured that their parent or caregiver is their ally.
    - o   Contact school personnel and seek immediate intervention.

Table 11.1 **Designing a Personalized Plan for Recovery from Mobbing (*Continued*)**

Peak Mobbing Phase
Employees or students are victims of ongoing abusive acts, both overt and covert, and are experiencing some combination of isolation, humiliation, shame, hurt, and fear. Continue strategies from Early Mobbing Phase: Assess Physical, Emotional, and Behavioral Responses to the Mobbing

- For employees:
  o Obtain a medical examination and include a cardiology checkup in the exam. Tell your health care provider what is happening at work. Bring this book, chart, or other literature about mobbing with you, so that your health care provider will have resource information about mobbing. This resource information will help health care providers avoid harmful misdiagnoses.
  o Pay attention to the feelings, sensations, and experiences that you are having in your body. Notice how your body feels when you are tense and stressed. Notice how your body feels when you are relaxed, and what is different in your body between states of tension and states of relaxation. Encourage relaxation.
  o Reflect on your own emotional and behavioral responses to the mobbing. Try to identify how you are responding and what you are doing both at work and at home. Ask a trusted family member or friend to help you in this process. Go at your own pace.
  o Evaluate whether any of your responses have made a difference in improving the situation at work. If any have, continue those actions that have been helpful.
  o Identify any strong or overwhelming feelings of sadness, anger, despair, or desire to lash back at the perpetrators. Share these feelings with a trusted family member or friend. Seek immediate professional help.
- For students and parents:
  o Obtain medical examination for the child and adolescent. Focus on any special problems like regressed behavior, psychosomatic symptoms, self-injury, etc. As above, bring resource information about mobbing to health care provider.
  o Help the child or adolescent pay attention to the feelings and sensations in his or her body and to notice how the feelings and sensations associated with tension and stress and those associated with relaxation differ. Encourage relaxation.
  o In a nonjudgmental way, help the child or adolescent reflect on how he or she is feeling and responding to the hurtful events in the mobbing.
  o As appropriate, help the child or adolescent to identify any responses that have helped him or her to feel better and to continue those that have been helpful.
  o Monitor the child or adolescent for signs of anxiety, depression, suicidal thoughts, or rage. Seek immediate professional help and support of caring family and friends. Mobbing can be life-threatening.

(Continued)

Table 11.1 **Designing a Personalized Plan for Recovery from Mobbing**
(*Continued*)

Obtain Knowledgeable Professional Help as Needed

- For employees:
  - o Mental health professional with knowledge of both trauma and mobbing (Needed)
  - o Couples or family therapist
  - o Career counselor or career coach
  - o Attorney specializing in employment law for employees
- For students and parents:
  - o Mental health professional with knowledge of both trauma and mobbing (Needed)
  - o Family therapist
  - o Attorney specializing in educational law

Make Self-Care a Priority

- For employees, students, and family members:
  - o Rest and relaxation
  - o Nutrition
  - o Exercise
  - o Spiritual practices, meditation, breathing

Review Options for Staying or Exiting the Organization or School

- For employees:
  - o Remain and seek redress
  - o Remain and not seek redress
  - o Exit and seek redress
  - o Exit and not seek redress
- For students and parents (parents **must** ensure the physical safety and emotional security of child or adolescent):
  - o Notify school personnel and request intervention
  - o If intervention is effective, continue monitoring
  - o If intervention is ineffective, make school change and seek redress
  - o If intervention is ineffective, make school change and do not seek redress

Mobbing Resolution Phase
This may be a protracted period of time (from months to years) in which employees or students acknowledge and grieve the losses from mobbing and begin the process of reclaiming and restoring their lives. Continue strategies from Early and Peak Mobbing Phases:

Accept and Grieve Losses from Mobbing

- For employees, students, and parents:
  - o Acknowledge losses and associated feelings
  - o Express feelings about losses to trusted family member or friend

(*Continued*)

Table 11.1 **Designing a Personalized Plan for Recovery from Mobbing (*Continued*)**

Reaffirm Values by Which You Wish to Live

- For employees, students, and parents (parents to help and support children and adolescents in this process in age-appropriate way):
  - o Identify beliefs and values that have provided strength and hope throughout the mobbing
  - o Foster self-compassion
  - o Foster empathy and compassion for others
  - o Acknowledge life's uncertainties and unfairness
  - o Reclaim belief in self
  - o Appreciate the presence of those who have stood by you and supported you throughout the mobbing

Engage in Meaningful Life Activities

- For employees, students, and parents (parents to help and support children and adolescents in this process in age-appropriate way):
  - o Develop new interests and reengage with old interests
  - o Develop new skills and brush up on old ones
  - o Care and nourish trusting relationships
  - o Do something creative
  - o Experience laughter, fun, and pleasure
  - o Set realistic goals and begin to work toward attaining them
  - o Project yourself into a positive and satisfying future

Support for Family Members of Employees and Students (during all phases of mobbing)

- o Obtain accurate information about mobbing and its effects on victims
- o Obtain accurate information about legal and educational rights
- o Know that recovery for mobbing victims is attainable with support
- o Practice self-care

or distressed, and regulate their own emotional responses to witnessing the suffering of their child or adolescent (cf., Cook et al., 2005). The parent or caregiver will also be the model for the child or adolescent in initiating appropriate action to end the mobbing. Effective parental action to stop mobbing will provide a route back into engagement with the world for the child or adolescent.

Trauma and the Past in the Present

Time alone is unlikely to heal the wounds inflicted by mobbing. As we have seen, trauma is timeless, and victims can respond to triggers of past traumatic events as if the trauma were happening in the here and now (van der Kolk, 2006). Unresolved trauma denies victims both a present and a future by the relentless demands of past injuries that are reexperienced as if in a continuous present. Levine (1997) and Scaer (2005) locate trauma in the body and in neurobiological responses triggered by overwhelming events. When that neurobiology implodes inward on the victim and causes further personal injury, such as agitation, hyperarousal, dissociation, and other forms of extreme stress (van der Kolk et al., 2005), we are much more likely to be discerning and compassionate than when that same neurobiology explodes outward and contributes to the injury and deaths of others. Consider Levine's (1997) reflections on women emerging from the numbness of a freeze response after experiencing the trauma of sexual violence:

> When women who have been raped begin to come out of shock (frequently, months or even years later), they often have the impulse to kill their assailants. In some instances, they may have the opportunity to carry this through. Some of these women have been tried and sentenced for "premeditated" murder because the time lapse was viewed as premeditation. Some injustices may have occurred due to the misunderstanding of the biological drama that was perhaps being played out. It is possible that a number of these women may have been acting upon the profound (and delayed) self-protective responses of rage and counterattack that they experienced coming out of agitated immobility. These reprisals may be biologically motivated, and not necessarily by premeditated revenge. Some of these killings could have been prevented by effective treatment of post-traumatic shock. (p. 102)

As we have discussed, mobbing is a form of interpersonal abuse and results in victimization. Interpersonal victimization that is prolonged in nature results in the most severe forms of traumatic injury (van der Kolk et al., 2005). Since mobbing meets the criteria of prolonged interpersonal victimization, it is not illogical to expect that vulnerable mobbing victims will from time to time feature as media headliners after committing single or multiple homicides. Such homicidal rage is the organizational equivalent of the perfect storm—the convergence of individual vulnerability and traumatized neurobiology with abusive group behavior in the context of organizational complicity or indifference.

Conclusion

Trauma, shock, and all other symptoms that emerge subsequent to school and workplace mobbing cannot be ignored. To do so further harms individuals who already have been harmed too much. Mobbing victims in general have a difficult time reestablishing trust, regaining self-confidence, reentering the workplace if they have left it, and returning to school. Effective treatments for the range of symptoms that mobbing victims may present is available. However, because of the widespread lack of understanding of the mobbing phenomenon and its health consequences by both the lay and professional communities, mobbing victims must exercise caution in selecting health care providers. The last thing that mobbing victims and their families need is to be relabeled and blamed. Although the focus in this chapter was on addressing the unique needs of individual victims of mobbing and helping to build a scaffolding for their recovery, we believe that best practices for mobbing victims also include involvement in couples and family therapy. Although the individual burden from mobbing is great, so too, is the family burden.

Because mobbing is the insidious and undermining process that it is, and because it represents chronic trauma and an ongoing life threat, it affects the victim's neurobiology, physiology, and mental state in complex ways. As a result, developing an effective personalized treatment plan for recovery is contingent upon adequate knowledge of how the experience of mobbing is likely to affect body, brain, and mind. In this chapter, we presented information that is essential in understanding why mobbing victims respond the way they do and what options for treatment are available and reflective of current best practices. Based on this information, health care providers, mobbing victims, and family members are in a much better position to select a treatment package that makes the most sense in their particular circumstances.

12

Understanding Organizational Support Systems

I realized that my office, like most offices in America, was
programmed to accept and encourage gossip.
—Sam Chapman (2009, p. 10)

The reality of mobbing conflicts with the expectation of most victims and their families that employers and school administrators should provide safe and protective work and school environments. Although some employers and school administrators are conscientious about protecting employees and students from abusiveness, others are not as conscientious. In this chapter, we look through the lens of organizational dynamics at how organizations view and respond to their members. We do this by looking at the continuum of organizational responses from those that are purely self-protective at the expense of employees and members to those that include individual employee and member well-being as central to overall organizational well-being. We begin with a discussion of how organizations tend to view the concerns and expectations of their employees or students. We then address the reality that safety is not assured because an organization has an anti-mobbing or anti-bullying policy. Detailed illustrations from workplace and school settings are used to develop these themes and to provide the basis for understanding available organizational supports systems, so that victims and their families will know what kinds of responses they can realistically expect from their organizations.

How Human Resources and Management Typically Respond to Mobbing

How do human resources (HR) personnel and management typically respond to complaints of mobbing? The recent Zogby International Survey, the U.S. Workplace Bullying Survey (Workplace Bullying Institute, 2007) provides an answer to that question. It is the largest national survey of mobbing and bullying, involving

7,740 interviews of a sample representative of workers in the United States. As well as providing critical baseline data about prevalence, the U.S. Workplace Bullying Survey provides a sobering picture of the attitudes and actions of HR and top management with regard to mobbing and bullying. The main finding was that HR either did nothing (in 44% of cases) when they were approached by a mobbing or bullying victim for help or actually made the situation worse for the victim, in 18% of cases. This finding lends support to the belief of many that HR supports and protects managers and the organization more than its workers.

In a subsequent survey of 400 respondents, Namie (2008) found that, in 53% of the cases in which workers reported workplace abuse, the managers basically did nothing to stop it. Instead, in 71% of the cases in which workers reported abuse, managers were said to have retaliated against the worker who made the complaint. When management did respond, 40% of the respondents considered the manager's investigation to be inadequate or unfair, with less than 2% of investigations described as fair and safe for the victim. It is chilling to learn that, in 24% of cases, when a victim filed a complaint, it led to retaliation by managers and resultant job loss for the victim. In contrast, respondents reported that negative consequences for the offenders arose in only about 8% of the cases.

Furthermore, it has been noted that anti-mobbing programs are unlikely to succeed if they are initiated solely by HR. Without the support of top management, HR efforts to implement organizational change will not occur at all, or if they do will not be long lasting (Namie & Namie, 2009b). In other words, expecting HR to correct and prevent mobbing is unrealistic. Top management must make the decision to faithfully address mobbing in their organizations if anti-mobbing efforts are to be successful. Only top management can adequately fund the policy writing, training, and education necessary for a successful program, and they must consistently support the anti-mobbing program if there is ever to be a healthy and respectful organization. From a general organizational perspective, Pfeffer (2007) stated that "workplaces in America and elsewhere show pervasive job dissatisfaction, distrust, and disengagement, with the evidence suggesting that these problems are getting worse and have a number of negative consequences for employers as well as employees" (p. 115).

The challenge to have mobbing concerns addressed within a deteriorating organizational milieu is not an easy one. King (2004) reported on the results of studies from leading global consulting firms for human resources in which one finding was that 44% of employees believe that senior management lacks honesty and integrity, and another finding that 20% of employees believe their companies lie to them.

Who Needs Protection: Organizations or Members?

When employees have a personal concern, they are likely to look to HR for assistance. Unfortunately, HR departments are not always what most of us have come to believe about them. Believing that HR is a friend or employee advocate leads many an employee to disclose things to HR, such as the details of personal challenges or how he or she really feels about the organization or his or her bosses. This might be momentarily cathartic, but it could endanger the person's job in the long run since HR's function is different from what most believe. In fact, HR's "primary function is *not* to help employees, it is to protect the company *from* its employees. And that edict will override every other responsibility" (Shapiro, 2005, p. 25).

UNDER THREAT: EXCESSIVE ORGANIZATIONAL PROTECTIONISM

These rather startling words are those of Cynthia Shapiro (2005), a former vice president of HR, who now consults, speaks, and writes about workplace issues. Shapiro contends that HR personnel are only as good as their ability to protect an organization from unwanted or unforeseen difficulties. She maintains that organizations are zealous about protecting themselves from legal issues and lawsuits since the "downtime, cost, threat to profits, and potential threat to the very survival of the organization can be staggering. If you're seen as a legal threat you could be out as fast as they can get rid of you without opening themselves to liability" (Shapiro, 2005, p. 26).

Similarly, she counsels employees to seriously consider the likely consequences associated with filing a workers' compensation claim. Noting that although workers who file such claims are protected by law from retaliatory job loss, they are not protected from reorganizations, layoffs, or downsizing, Shapiro (2005) says that corporations will often remove such an employee through one of these means as quickly as possible. They will take such action not only because of the injury and health risks involved, but also because the claim is viewed as a sign of "disloyalty" to the organization, particularly if the individual has health insurance that would cover the claim.

Why is loyalty so important to organizations? The reason is that "protection" is a core value and motivation of many organizations. In a litigious society, protection is the primary concern of many organizations. By putting one's own needs ahead of the organization's need to protect itself from liability and inconvenience, that individual is perceived to be disloyal. Consequently, that individual is tagged as someone who is neither a team player nor trustworthy, and is therefore expendable. "Threatening a company's sense of *protection* is the number one cause of job loss today" (Shapiro, 2005, p. 14, italics added).

Does research support Shapiro's (2005) observations? Recent research suggests that HR is not a likely resource for help with abusiveness. One study found that HR resists involvement in mobbing or bullying because it considers them to be managerial issues. Accordingly, HR only becomes involved with mobbing or bullying after a formal complaint is made (Rayner & McIvor, 2006). Thus, HR personnel are likely to turn a deaf ear to those asking for help in informal ways and only become responsive when a formal complaint is filed. Furthermore, it was found that HR often dealt with each complaint separately and failed to examine the bigger picture. Another researcher found that HR professionals were reluctant to label case scenarios as mobbing or bullying, even when the presented scenarios contained all the behaviors defined as mobbing or bullying in the professional literature (Harrington, 2007). Instead, they labeled mobbing or bullying behavior as "management style" differences. Because the research and practice evidence suggests that HR's role has shifted from protecting workers to protecting management, HR personnel appear to feel powerless and lacking in credibility in dealing with workplace abusiveness (Ferris, 2009). The result is that workers should not generally expect HR to be their advocate in situations involving mobbing and other workplace abusiveness.

Given U.S. employees' general attitude towards their workplaces, it seems likely that many American employees would already be somewhat wary of finding support within their organizations and HR departments. A 2005 Conference Board survey conducted among 5,000 U.S. households found that 67% of employees either did not identify with or feel motivated to promote their organization's business goals, 50% said they felt disengaged or disconnected from their employers, and 25% of employees said they just showed up at work to collect paychecks.

In light of these rather sobering research findings, how seriously should Shapiro's (2005) warnings be taken? Depending on the dynamics of a particular organization, the advice should be taken very seriously. What about the organization's responsibility to afford protection to its members? This also depends on the dynamics of a particular organization. Organizations differ greatly with regard to the health of their organizational dynamics and can be graded across a continuum in terms of overall health. Figure 12.1 (adapted from Sperry, 2009b) portrays such a continuum, in which one end represents very healthy organizations and the other represents very abusive organizations.

Organizations nearer to the abusive end of the continuum are more likely to be the kind of organizations that Shapiro (2005) is describing, wherein an organization's needs for protection and loyalty take priority over a member's needs and expectations. Organizations on this end of the continuum tend to be preoccupied with self-protection against outside threats to their existence. They may be able to afford protection to those members who are perceived as loyal, but it is unlikely

*Based on Sperry, 2009b

Figure 12.1 Continuum of Organizational Health and Abusiveness.*

this protection will be afforded to those considered "disloyal" members or members of the "loyal opposition"; namely, hard-working members of the organization who are not afraid to express their opinion or challenge practices or procedures that they consider not to be in the best interest of the organization, its members, or its mission.

In contrast, organizations nearer to the healthy end of the continuum are likely to be less focused on self-protection and thus more able to be responsive to members' needs and expectations. Such organizations also have a much higher tolerance for the expression of dissent and divergent points of view. Organizations that are rated as the "best places to work" tend to be such healthy organizations. Such organizations make it a priority to afford protection to their members and are not threatened by the expression of divergent points of view within their ranks.

OPEN TO DIFFERENCE: WORKING FOR THE BEST COMPANIES

Every year, *Fortune* magazine publishes the results of the most extensive survey of employees in American corporations. The survey results are entitled: "The 100 Best Companies to Work For." For its 2009 survey, *Fortune* sent questionnaires to a minimum of 400 randomly selected employees from 353 companies. It also conducts a "cultural audit" of each company. This audit included questions about corporate demographics, pay, and benefits, and open-ended questions about the company's values and philosophy, its quality of communications, turnover and absenteeism rates, and so on. It is noteworthy that only one educational institution, Vanderbilt University, has ever been included in the top 100 organizations, and that was in 2009.

Workers at these best companies feel they are well-compensated, have high job satisfaction, and are committed to their organization. Presumably, these employees also feel safe on the job and are not as likely to experience mobbing in comparison with those who work at other companies. These best companies, and other similar organizations, tend to be healthy organizations.

Best companies utilize HR management practices that are referred to collectively as "high-commitment" practices. According to Pfeffer (2007), these high-commitment HR practices include organizational commitment to training in order to develop employee skills and knowledge; employment security arising from mutual commitment to expectations for a long-term employment relationship; reward structures based on group or team performance, as well as on individual performance; decentralized decision-making, in which workgroups have meaningful influence on decisions and outcomes within their purview; and transparent information sharing, so that communication loops are accessible to all. Nonaka and Nishiguchi (2001) refer to these kinds of work environments as "high-care," in which a premium is placed on the quality of social relationships between managers and employees and among employees themselves, and in which the structure of the organization is designed to facilitate the sharing of knowledge and the enhancement of interpersonal relationships.

Organizations that embrace high-commitment HR practices have much less need for organizational protectionism and are therefore much safer environments for victims of mobbing or other workplace abuse to obtain help and support. The reality is, however, that the proportion of firms that have adopted a full complement of high-commitment HR practices is relatively low (Pfeffer, 2007), making it more likely that Shapiro's (2005) warnings about HR departments should be taken seriously when considering looking for organizational support in cases of mobbing.

How an Effective Human Resources Department Deals with Mobbing

Shapiro (2005) made it clear that many HR departments view their primary role as protection of the organization, rather than its employees. So, how would these HR departments handle complaints of mobbing? Shapiro did not address bullying or mobbing but, based on her discussion of how these corporations view sexual discrimination complaints, we can infer that HR departments would not be very supportive. From an employee's perspective, such HR departments are neither helpful nor effective. But, how would an effective HR department function?

With regard to mobbing, an effective HR department would likely function in the following manner. First, it would develop and communicate a precise definition of workplace mobbing. Second, it would develop and implement an effective anti-mobbing policy. Third, it would increase awareness of the signs and effects of mobbing by way of training programs that involve all employees and managers in the organization. Fourth, it would develop a confidential reporting structure, including a policy and procedures for investigating complaints of mobbing. Fifth, it would develop a policy and procedures for dealing with both victims (i.e., treatment, counseling, coaching, job reassignment if indicated, etc.) and offenders (i.e., sanctions, such as corrective counseling, coaching, suspension, termination, etc.). Sixth, it would be vigilant about incidents of mobbing or other abusive behavior, and monitor organizational dynamics and specific indicators such as turnover rates, slips in performance, increases in absenteeism, and short-term disability (Young, 2008).

In a few workplaces, largely outside of the United States, there is growing recognition of the inherent double-binds in designating HR personnel as contact persons for victims of mobbing or other forms of workplace harassment. For example, in Canada, Marje Burdine, an organizational consultant who has helped companies craft respectful workplace policies, has also entered into relationships with several of them in which she serves as an external resource to company employees under the title of "respectful workplace advisor." Burdine states that "there needs to be a safe place in an organization for an individual to go and seek help. It has to be someone who reports to no one else" (Hood, 2004, p. 89).

In Finland, companies are legally mandated to provide occupational health services for employees. These occupational health services workers, who represent a range of health and mental health professions, are independent of both management and employees and are not an extension of management. Their neutrality allows them to be of help to both victimized employees and to the organizations in problem-solving and improving organizational conditions. They assume a systemic stance in analyzing workplace bullying and mobbing issues by including the organization or workgroup as the unit of analysis and not the individual (Vartia, Korppoo, Fallenius, & Mattila, 2003). Having an independent contact person or ombudsman who is outside of the chain of reporting relationships in a company, but who is clearly identified as a contact or resource person in the event of workplace mobbing, is an idea worthy of serious consideration and reflection.

Utilizing an independent external contact is one strategy that holds some promise for managements serious about turning the tide on mobbing. Another strategy that seems to be gaining some momentum is the development of "no-gossip" policies as an HR tool. Gossip, negative characterizations of an employee's personality, personal life, or job performance, and the spreading of malicious rumors are behaviors common in mobbing and in mobbing-prone organizations. McKnight (2009) described her meeting with the HR director during her job interview at PrintingForLess.com, an online printing company in Montana that has adopted high-commitment HR practices and a no-gossip policy. McKnight said that the HR director told her that "there's no back-stabbing here, and no office politics. Gossiping and talking behind someone's back are not tolerated" (p. 9). She accepted employment at PrintingForLess.com and signed their "agreement to values" form, indicating that she would abide by the no-gossip policy. For McKnight, the policy at PrintingForLess.com resulted in an organizational climate that was significantly better than that at her previous employment, and she sees the policy as fostering greater teamwork.

Proponents of no-gossip policies (Chapman, 2009) see them as ways of increasing organizational productivity, improving organizational culture, and reducing organizational liability. However, such policies are not without their critics. In an ethnographic study of workplace politics conducted at an elementary school, Hallett, Harger, and Eder (2009) found that gossip provides a map of the informal organization and can also be a source of positive information and cohesiveness. Our view is that no-gossip policies work best in combination with a set of high-commitment HR practices and are potentially useful as a core anti-mobbing strategy. Such policies signal HR's and management's intention to hold themselves accountable for fostering a positive workplace culture and hold members of the organization accountable for upholding it.

Workplace Organizations and Situations

The attitudes and responses of workplace organizations to mobbing and other abusive behaviors differ considerably. Although there is a growing literature on workplace mobbing, there is little if any research on organizational types with regard to mobbing. Our consulting experience largely matches a typology proposed by Ferris (2004). Ferris' typology represents the results of practice-based evidence across a large cohort of individuals and organizations and reflects a comprehensive set of possible organizational responses to mobbing or bullying. The following is our rendering of three types of organizations in terms of such organizational dynamics as strategy, structure, culture, and leadership. Note the stance of each with regard to anti-mobbing policies, policy enforcement, anti-mobbing training, and handling of mobbing complaints.

TYPE I ORGANIZATION

The first type of organization is typically characterized by an emphasis on productivity and profits. Their accountability is primarily toward shareholders, not employees. As a result, employees experience high levels of work stress, absenteeism, and worker's compensation claims. Such organizations are characterized by high job strain, meaning that employees are faced with high demands for job performance, including pressure to achieve and meet tight deadlines. They also perceive themselves as having little control over the manner in which they perform their job. The result is that turnover is high, morale tends to be low, and benefit use for medical and behavioral health services is high. Leadership in such organizations, including HR, tends to be defensive about mobbing. Their attitude appears to be that such abusive behavior is acceptable. They typically attribute the cause of mobbing to "weakness" on the part of the victimized employee. Accordingly, they are likely to be dismissive of mobbing complaints. If a manager in such an organization intervenes, it would be to advise the victimized employee to toughen up and stop being a victim.

TYPE II ORGANIZATION

The second type of organization is usually characterized by a bureaucratic or rule-oriented structure. Often, these are governmental or educational institutions. A large percentage of their employees may serve in professional job classifications, and job expectations and reporting relationships are usually clearly specified. These organizations have an employee code of conduct that usually includes anti-mobbing or anti-bullying and/or anti-harassment policies. It is not surprising, then, that employees expect that their organization will implement such policies and codes, and are surprised or shocked when they are not enforced. Leadership in such organizations is hierarchical, and accountability is primarily directed toward meeting annual indices as well as statutory or accreditation standards, while concern for the well-being of employees is secondary. This organization is likely to attribute the cause of mobbing to "personality conflict" between two employees, and will hold both parties responsible for the conflict. Nevertheless, the organization is more likely to blame the victim for having the type of personality that aggravated the offenders. If a manager in such an organization intervenes, it would usually involve telling the parties to solve the problem themselves. Mediation may be available in this type of organization but is unlikely to result in a change of strategy, structure, culture, and leadership.

TYPE III ORGANIZATION

The third type of organization is typically characterized as a reasonably successful for-profit organization or even a successful nonprofit organization. Previously, it may have been a Type II organization that had dealt with complaints of mobbing or bullying and mismanaged them. But, because of a court directive or a top management decision, this organizational type may have taken action to effect changes in the organization's strategy, structure, culture, and leadership, which for all practical purposes eliminated mobbing. Their strategy and culture are likely to reflect respect and support and protection for all stakeholders, including employees and customers. Such organizations have revised their nonharassment policy to include mobbing, they require nonharassment training for managers, and they provide coaching and counseling to mobbed employees, while investigating and resolving the issue. Because of the organization's principles and practices, when mobbing does occur, employees typically respond well to the organization's response. The organization's responses to a mobbing victim typically include medical care, if needed, coaching, counseling or therapy, and restoration of the victim to wholeness within the workplace. Victimized employees are likely to feel cared for and validated by the organization's response and therefore likely to remain in that organization. Finally, in comparison with the other two organizational types, mobbing rarely occurs in this type of organization.

Table 12.1 summarizes this discussion of the organizational types. It highlights specific organizational dynamics, such as strategy, structure, culture, and leadership, that are realistic markers of whether and how these policies will be enforced in a particular organization.

Homicide—The Ultimate Fight Response

A series of homicides between 1985 and 2006 involved employees of the United States Postal Service (USPS). One well-publicized incident occurred in Royal Oak, Michigan. There, a recently fired postal worker, Thomas McIlvane, killed four

Table 12.1 **Workplace Organizational Types and Organizational Dynamics**

Organizational Dynamic	Type I	Type II	Type III
Strategy: Actual Core Values	Self-protection	Self-protection	Respect and protection of all stakeholders
Structure: Anti-Mobbing Policy	No	Yes	Yes
Culture:	Unhealthy and abuse-prone	Somewhat abuse-prone	Healthy and respectful; zero tolerance for harassment and discrimination
Structure: Policy Enforcement	No	No	Yes
Leadership: Attitude and Response to Mobbing	Human resources (HR) is defensive and dismissive of mobbing complaints	Only partially responsive and helpful to mobbing victim	HR and others are responsive and helpful to mobbing victim

managers and wounded six others who had been involved in his termination and then killed himself. By examining the combination of individual, group, and organizational dynamics, a case can be made that what sparked this infamous murder spree was the mobbing of McIlvane by some managers at that postal center and his tragic response of shooting and killing them.

INDIVIDUAL DYNAMICS

McIlvane, as well as other postal workers involved in shootings, was under severe job-related stress and had lost his job (Denenberg & Braverman, 1999). McIlvane, a former U.S. Marine and a champion kick boxer with a black belt in karate, had been fired a year before the shooting for cursing at his supervisor as well as threatening other clerks and fighting with customers. On several occasions, he had threatened violence if he was not reinstated. He appealed the dismissal through a union grievance procedure, but lost an arbitration hearing prior to the shootings.

GROUP DYNAMICS

The operative group dynamics involved at the Royal Oak postal center was ingroup versus outgroup. Extreme negativity and longstanding tension characterized the relationships between managers and workers. Workers felt they were being treated inhumanely by their supervisors. Resentment toward management was so intense that, after the shootings, it was reported that postal workers had defaced the names of two dead managers on the memorial that was erected outside the building (Denenberg & Braverman, 1999).

ORGANIZATIONAL DYNAMICS

Strategy

The motto attributed to the USPS is: "Neither snow nor rain nor heat nor gloom of night stays these couriers from the swift completion of their appointed rounds." Core values of loyalty, caring, reliability, and fast service are reflected in this motto. It is ironic that loyalty and caring seemed absent in management–worker relations, although management's demand for fast service from workers appears to have been unrelenting. As a government agency, the Postal Service had adopted anti-discrimination and anti-sexual harassment policies, and if it were also required, would have adopted an anti-mobbing and harassment policy.

Structure

In many ways, the USPS resembled a paramilitary organization, with a disciplined, hierarchical, and bureaucratic structure. High-speed sorting machines had previously replaced many workers at the Royal Oak center, but instead of layoffs, management found various other ways of reducing the workforce through harsh discipline and measures that fostered high job strain. Managers amplified minor worker infractions into major issues to justify firing a particular worker. The result was increased verbal altercations and violent assaults on managers by postal employees (Denenberg & Braverman, 1999).

Culture

This strategy and structure may explain the toxic climate, filled with tension, distrust, and animosity among managers and workers. As in other high job strain organizations with high negativity toward managers, an abuse-prone culture is inevitable.

Leadership

The dominant management style in the USPS has been described as authoritarian and militaristic (Denenberg & Braverman, 1999). A large-scale study by a third party of the entire postal service confirmed this leadership style (National Center on Addiction and Substance Abuse, 2000).

Members

Postal workers experienced high levels of job strain and animosity toward their managers. The result was that these workers externalized their frustration and acted out in fighting, as in the case of McIlvane, or internalized it through the development of medical and psychiatric disabilities.

External Environment

Economic conditions in the 1980s and technological advances profoundly influenced the work environment in the postal service. Mail-sorting machines and laser barcodes on envelopes meant that thousands of postal jobs were becoming obsolete. The pressure to compete with private delivery services like FedEx, UPS, and Purolator drove the USPS to replace paid workers with machines. Instead of mass layoffs, post offices began cutting hours and finding ways to fire employees to cut back the work force. Job insecurity therefore was extremely high in the postal service, both during and after mail-sorting and barcode-reading technology was introduced (Denenberg & Braverman, 1999).

COMMENTARY

As in similar murder sprees precipitated by mobbing of the shooters, it seems that at the Royal Oaks postal center the constant pressure exerted by managers had a decidedly negative impact on most if not all workers. However, for Thomas McIlvane, who was already predisposed to react in a violent and deadly fashion, and who then became the target of ongoing abuse by at least four of the Royal Oaks managers, his murderous actions seem sadly predictable.

In the wake of the Royal Oaks and other postal service shootings, the federal government commissioned an extensive study of the entire postal service. The Report of the United States Postal Service Commission on a Safe and Secure Workplace (National Center on Addiction and Substance Abuse, 2000) is a sober reflection of the structure, culture, and leadership of this violence-prone federal agency. The study reports on an extensive questionnaire completed by postal employees throughout the nation. Postal workers were found to have more negative attitudes than employees in the rest of the national workforce about work, coworkers, and management. Postal workers believed that supervisors were the primary cause of their fear for their own safety at work. They also believed that their employer did not take action to protect them against violence, and that many managers and supervisors tried to provoke employees to violence.

Subsequent to the survey, the postal service has attempted to change the way managers related to workers. Since 1996, a number of changes in the organization have occurred. Investigators in 2000 devoted more than 100,000 hours to investigating incidents and threats, double the time spent in 1992. As part of their training, all managers are required to take courses on spotting and handling dangerous situations. Postal officials have also established an annual opinion survey that allows employees to rate their bosses, much like college students assess professors; the responses figure in supervisors' promotions and raises. These changes appear to be working, as witnessed by a drop in reported assaults at post office facilities from 424 in 1990 to 214 in 2000 (Toufexis, 2001).

Although training personnel to identify individuals who may be at high risk for acting out violently may be useful, we take the position that the more important and more effective strategy for improving overall workplace culture and relationships and reducing mobbing is the implementation of the full complement of high-commitment HR practices. The following illustration, although not resulting in anything like the homicidal fight response of the previous case, shows a set of HR practices that sadly ignored the management of intangible human capital assets like innovation and employee knowledge and skill. These human capital assets have been identified as the essence of a company's value (Becker, Huselid, & Ulrich, 2001).

HUMAN RESOURCE'S RESTRICTED SCOPE OF PRACTICE

The case of Gerry Bennett was previously introduced in Chapter 7. His experience of being mobbed began soon after he was transferred to another branch of TEC Bank. Within 3 months, the number of offenders involved in the mobbing increased from two to five. With a potent mix of gossip and sabotaging behaviors, Gerry found it almost impossible to achieve his targeted goals. His health and that of his wife, who was already depressed about a recent miscarriage, suffered. At that time, he filed a complaint with HR.

So, what provisions did TEC Bank have for dealing with his complaint of mobbing? In reviewing the bank's employee code of conduct, Gerry found that TEC Bank had the expected anti-discrimination and anti-sexual harassment policies. Gerry also discovered a broad policy covering forms of harassment such as bullying or mobbing, but saw that there was no training for any employees about preventing harassment. Not surprisingly, Gerry's efforts to enlist the support of HR personnel were fruitless. They were decidedly unhelpful, but after a lengthy delay, they launched a formal investigation. The investigation was biased against Gerry as he was referred to as the "problem" from the very beginning of it. The final report bore that out in its conclusion: "There appears to be a poor 'fit' with Mr. Bennett and his peers. Our recommendation for resolving the situation is for him to be transferred to another branch."

One reason that HR was not particularly helpful was that it had a limited number of personnel, and its primary functions were restricted to hiring, payroll, and benefits. Unlike other banks with a vice president (VP) of HR and several HR specialists, TEC Bank had only an HR director who reported to the VP of operations. Besides its director, the HR department consisted of three personnel, one of whom was a secretary-receptionist.

COMMENTARY

The fact that TEC Bank had an anti-harassment policy, which presumably covered mobbing, is commendable. The fact that it did not offer employees training regarding the policy, and then did not enforce the policy following Gerry's formal employee complaint suggests that the strategy of TEC Bank was more focused on protecting itself than on protecting its employees and other stakeholders from harassment and abusiveness. The structure of the bank with regard to HR is consistent with that strategy, as witnessed by the limiting of HR functions to hiring, payroll, and benefits. This, along with what appears to be an abuse-prone culture, indicates that TEC Bank had little regard for either protecting its employees from abusiveness or supporting those who were victims of it.

It is ironic that the bank's marketing slogan is, "Put your money with neighbors you can really trust." If these are how trusting neighbors act, don't move into that neighborhood! Working for such an organization is plainly and simply hazardous to one's health. *Caveat emptor* is appropriately applied to such organizations.

It is unfortunate, but organizations like TEC Bank are unlikely to adopt anti-mobbing policies until they are forced by court order or state or federal legislation. Many corporations are not yet convinced that they need such policies, and until they are mandated, many will not voluntarily adopt them, even though research consistently points out that having and enforcing anti-mobbing and other anti-harassment policies saves money, reduces turnover (especially of top employees), and reduces absenteeism and medical and psychiatric costs (Namie & Namie, 2009b).

School Organizations and Situations

We have looked at workplace organizations that either do not have anti-mobbing policies or have them but do not enforce them, and we have examined the complexities of organizational supports, such as HR, when evaluating whether the workplace can be a source of support for mobbing victims. This section focuses on school organizations and addresses what should be a basic concern of parents; namely, how they can know if a particular school will protect their children from mobbing and other abusive behaviors. Four possible school situations are addressed in this section: schools that do not have anti-mobbing policies; schools that have them, but do not enforce them; schools that have such policies, but only partially enforce them; and schools that have policies and effectively enforce them. School policies addressing mobbing need to include cyber-mobbing to encompass mobbing involving the Internet that continues after school and off campus. In the following section, we provide a series of examples illustrating each of the possible ways listed above in which schools could react to the issue of ensuring safety from mobbing. We also include a discussion of parental responsibility in protecting children from victimization by mobbing.

A SCHOOL FAILS TO TAKE MOBBING SERIOUSLY

This example illustrates the first possible situation: schools that do not have anti-mobbing policies and are unlikely to effectively deal with mobbing and other harassment. Chapter 7 described an incident of mobbing of a middle-school male student in a locker room at a private school. The boy was savagely assaulted by a fellow football player in a locker room after football practice while other students jeered and one took a video, which was subsequently viewed by others not directly involved. The lawsuit contended that the school fostered a culture of recklessness among football players and that neither the school's president nor the junior varsity football coach made efforts to stop or correct the situation. The junior varsity football coach was also named in the suit because of his alleged failure to supervise the students and to halt the distribution of the video. In this situation, rather than protecting the targeted student, the school appeared to be protecting itself from bad publicity and legal liability. The lawsuit alleged that the school downplayed the attack and failed to discipline the attacker, presumably because the attacker's grandfather had served on the school's board and the attacker's parents had worked at the school.

Commentary
In this example, the school's primary motivation was self-protection, as in certain workplace organizations described above. This kind of school culture is particularly dangerous for its members. A "blame the victim" mentality prevails, and students who are mobbed and their parents cannot count on the school organization to intervene on their behalf. In such environments, any interventions that occur are self-protective and aimed at organizational damage control. Interventions to address damage done to students through mobbing occur only if they make the school look better or if the school is legally forced to take reparative or restorative action. Such schools are dangerous places.

CAMPUSES THAT DON'T ENFORCE MOBBING/HAZING POLICIES

This discussion illustrates the second possible situation: schools have anti-mobbing policies, but do not enforce them or only selectively enforce them. *Hazing* is a form of mobbing, albeit a ritualistic form that is centuries old. Even though nearly all colleges and universities have anti-hazing policies, these policies are not always enforced. The National Study of Student Hazing is an extensive study of the experience of hazing among college students. It surveyed 11,482 undergraduate students enrolled at 53 colleges and universities and included more than 300 interviews with students and campus personnel at 18 of those institutions. Hazing was defined as "any activity expected of someone joining or participating in a group that humiliates, degrades, abuses, or endangers them regardless of a person's willingness to participate" (p. 2). Alcohol consumption, humiliation, isolation, sleep-deprivation, and sex acts were hazing practices common across different types of student groups. Overall, some 55% of all college students involved in clubs, teams, and student organizations experience hazing. The highest rate of hazing (74%) occurred among students who were members of varsity sports teams, fraternities, or sororities (Allan & Madden, 2008).

Particularly notable was the finding that 25% of coaches or organization advisors were aware of the group's hazing behaviors, but did nothing to stop them. Since coaches and advisors have leadership functions in the organizational structures of colleges and universities, such leaders are complicit in hazing when they are aware it is occurring and do nothing to stop it. In cases where leadership is aware that hazing is occurring and do nothing, hazing meets the criteria for mobbing rather than bullying.

Commentary

In the school context, hazing is not limited to colleges and other institutions of higher education but is on the rise in high schools (Edelman, 2005). By its nature, hazing, a unique form of mobbing that involves subservience and obedience, requires a conspiracy of silence to carry out. That conspiracy, as noted in the preceding discussion, often involves school personnel. Edelman recommends that federal and state legislatures enact laws requiring affirmative action on the part of school administration and other personnel to both prevent and report hazing, with criminal penalties attaching for failure to do so. He maintains that anti-hazing policies, by themselves, will be inadequate. We believe that failure to report known incidents of hazing among minors violates the existing child abuse reporting requirements to which all school personnel are already bound.

PARENTS FAIL TO TAKE MOBBING SERIOUSLY

This case illustrates the third possible situation: schools that have anti-mobbing policies, but only partially enforce them. A teenage girl and her parents sued an all-girls' private middle and high school, claiming it allowed mobbing to spread from the classroom to online social networks. Reportedly, the victim was verbally and physically taunted at school by classmates, and the harassment eventually moved online to Facebook, where she was targeted with a "hate page." The lawsuit claimed that, although the offenders were suspended for their actions, the harassment continued and included threats of harm in retaliation for reporting the behavior. The girl eventually dropped out of the school. In its defense of the claim that it did nothing to stop the continued mobbing online, the school contended that mobbing could not have occurred on school grounds since students are required to leave their cell phones in lockers and that the school did not have Internet access. A spokesperson for the school said the school had no control over what occurred off campus. She added: "This is not our role. At some point, the parents must take responsibility. It is neither feasible nor reasonable for a school to be expected to police students when they are off school property."

This case highlights the limitations of adopting and enforcing a school anti-mobbing policy. Here, the school had such a policy and presumably enforced it—it suspended the offenders for breaching the policy. However, even though the mobbing ceased within the school itself, it continued online after school and off campus. As the school spokesperson indicated, it is at this point that parents must assume responsibility for online after-school and off-campus behaviors, and it appears that these parent did not exercise adequate responsibility over their daughters.

Commentary
In a qualitative research study, Espelage and Asidao (2001) asked 89 middle school students in the 6th to 8th grades a series of questions about school bullying, including a question about what suggestions they might have for reducing it. The authors claimed that the students were serious and creative in considering their responses to the question about what should be done. The following finding from the study stands out:

> Consistently, kids felt that it was crucial to have confidentiality when it came to telling a teacher or principal about a bullying incident. These kids felt that the reason why children did not report bullying behavior more often was because those kids who were victimized were afraid of someone finding out that they told. Therefore, their suggestion was to make reporting a confidential matter. (p. 57)

The students' thoughtful answers in this particular study strongly emphasized the need for assurances of confidentiality before a young adolescent would feel safe in reporting the psychological abuse of another student. School counselors and school social workers work in contexts in which confidentiality is part and parcel of their relationships with students, parents, and faculty. These school personnel are an existing resource that could be used more by students to report the mobbing and bullying of other students, but only if students felt safe enough to do so. The challenge for school organizations is not just the implementation of a confidential reporting system—many schools already have that—but establishing its credibility and trustworthiness among the student body.

With a credible confidential reporting system in place, the chances would have been higher that some students would have reported the "hate page" described in the above case to school personnel, thus allowing them to work with the victim's parents and the offenders. This case also illustrates the increasing blurring of boundaries between what constitutes school-related and non–school-related behaviors and activities.

MANDATING INTERVENTION AND POLICY DEVELOPMENT

In 2007, Florida enacted an anti-bullying law requiring every school district in the state to have a strict bullying and harassment policy. The new law is called the Jeffrey Johnston Stand Up for All Students Act. It was named after a teenager, Jeffrey Johnston, who hanged himself in his bedroom closet after repeatedly being bullied in middle school. Jeffrey's mother, a teacher herself, worked tirelessly for nearly 3 years to persuade Florida schools and the state legislature to enact the law. The expectation is that the required policies will change the culture of schools that are abuse-prone to student-healthy cultures.

Districts had until December of 2008 to implement this law. The policy in each district is required to spell out a process for students to report bullying, to allow

Table 12.2 **School Settings and Organizational Dynamics Regarding Mobbing**

Organizational Dynamic	School Setting I	School Setting II	School Setting III
Strategy-Structure: Anti-Mobbing Policy	No policy	Policy is adopted but *not* enforced; often no training occurs	Policy is adopted *and* enforced; training is completed
Culture: Regarding Abusiveness and Health	Abuse-prone culture	Abuse-prone culture	Student-healthy culture; no tolerance for harassment and discrimination
Leadership: Attitude/Response to Mobbing Complaints	Ignore; nonresponsive	Only partially responsive and helpful to victims;	Responsive
Environment: Role/Attitude of Parents toward Mobbing	Parents are passive; blindly follow school leadership; most are unwilling to correct offenders	Parents are minimally involved; nominal support for anti-mobbing policy; more willing to correct offenders	Parents supportive of anti-mobbing policy; demand healthy school culture; most willing to correct offenders

anonymous complaints, to require school officials to investigate immediately and report quickly, and to provide counseling to victims and offenders. The policy must also cover cyber-bullying, and the law gives schools broad authority to deal with students who use computers to harass others (Weber, 2008). What is also interesting about this law is that it includes all employees of the school, as well as students.

Like workplace organizations, schools reflect a range of organizational supports—from the very weak to the strong—that victims of mobbing and their parents can call on to obtain help. The strength of the supports is tied to the organizational health of the institution. Table 12.2 summarizes this discussion of organizational types. It highlights specific organizational dynamics, such as strategy, structure, culture, leadership, and environment, that are realistic markers of whether and how anti-mobbing policies will be enforced in a particular organization.

Conclusion

Not all organizations are the same when it comes to protecting their members from mobbing. Some organizations effectively assume this responsibility while others do not. Since less healthy organizations typically view self-protection as their core value and basic motivation, these organizations are less likely to view the protection of their members as their highest priority when compared to healthier and more vital organizations. As we have pointed out, even though an organization has adopted an anti-mobbing and anti-harassment policy, this does not mean that the policy is enforced or is enforceable. This contrasts with organizations that have adopted such a policy, undertaken organization-wide training for all leaders and members, and assiduously enforced the policy along with implementation of a full complement of high-commitment HR practices. Such organizations are likely to espouse and live out core values that include respecting and protecting their members, rather than being fixated on their own self-protection.

13

Developing Systemic Recovery Skills

Lack of systemic wisdom is always punished.
—Gregory Bateson (2000, p. 440)

The preceding chapter addressed the capabilities and limitations of organizational support systems in responding to mobbing. Chapter 11 focused on individual and family recovery from mobbing and identified a number of specific strategies and recommendations for therapists and other professional health care providers offering help to mobbing victims and their families. In this chapter, we build on the previous two and examine the systemic intervention skills that professionals and organizations need to develop to provide platforms for sustained individual and organizational recovery from mobbing.

Since mobbing affects the organizations in which it occurs and to which mobbing victims may be returning, organizationally based interventions aimed at changing a mobbing-prone culture are also crucial. Organizations, whether workplaces or schools, can help themselves and mobbing victims by using organizationally based interventions such as mediation, executive coaching, and other affirmative anti-mobbing strategies that we describe in this chapter. Organizational professionals may also endeavor to modify organizational dynamics to reduce the consequences or effects of mobbing, as well as its antecedents.

In Chapter 11 , evidence-based psychotherapeutic interventions were presented that focused on body–mind integration from trauma and the restorying of personal autobiography to encompass the trauma. This chapter addresses the knowledge base of group and organizational dynamics involved in mobbing that mental health professionals and organizational consultants need to know, in order to promote both individual and organizational recovery. We include a discussion of integrative individual–organizational psychotherapeutic considerations, and of specific organizational strategies and interventions designed to provide systemic recovery.

Psychotherapy Strategies and Interventions: What Professionals Need to Know

In this section, we outline the differences between conventional psychotherapeutic strategies and psychotherapeutic strategies integrative of understanding of group and organizational dynamics. Therapists' professional obligation to understand the nature of mobbing and its organizational components also is discussed.

CONVENTIONAL THERAPEUTIC APPROACHES

Victims of mobbing seek out or are referred for psychotherapy or counseling in the hopes of relieving their psychological distress and of coming to terms with their jobs and careers. Therapists and counselors who lack knowledge and experience in working with such clients are likely to employ a conventional counseling strategy of providing the client-victim with support and symptomatic relief. However, such a strategy may not be sufficient to achieve symptomatic relief nor to provide sufficient resolution to the job concerns of victims. Furthermore, conventional therapy is unlikely to prevent the reoccurrence of mobbing or to change the organization's dynamics. Victims who remain in or return to organizations where their mobbing occurred, and where no organizational change has occurred, are likely to be revictimized since the conditions that gave rise to the mobbing have not changed. Unfortunately, too many therapists may even believe that the mobbing was an aberration and is unlikely to recur.

In short, mobbing victims present a particular challenge to therapists and counselors for a number of reasons. To meet these challenges effectively, therapists need to have a working knowledge of the dynamics of mobbing, the typical effects of mobbing on victims, and an understanding of the group and organizational dynamics involved in mobbing. Clinical case conceptualization and treatment planning must include formulations that encompass the constellation of how the particular individual responded to being mobbed and the group and organizational dynamics involved in the particular episode. Because most therapists have little training and experience with mobbing, it should not be surprising that client mobbing victims are not responsive to conventional therapeutic approaches that do not address the antecedents and consequences of mobbing.

THERAPIST PREREQUISITES FOR EFFECTIVELY WORKING WITH CLIENT MOBBING VICTIMS

Accordingly, there are some prerequisites for psychotherapists who hope to work effectively with client mobbing victims. It is essential that psychotherapists and other counselors working with mobbing victims have a working knowledge of the professional literature on mobbing and bullying. Without sufficient knowledge and awareness of the phenomenon of mobbing, therapists too often misinterpret the consequences of mobbing as well as underestimate its injurious effect on victims.

Knowledge of the dynamics surrounding mobbing is also necessary. It is not unusual for therapists who are unaware of its unique psychodynamics, and its concomitant group and organizational dynamics, to misdiagnose victims as manifesting a personality disorder, often borderline personality disorder (Namie & Namie, 2004). Although post-traumatic stress disorder (PTSD) and depression are among the most common diagnoses associated with mobbing, too many therapists and other clinicians fail to make the diagnosis of PTSD in these cases (cf. Chapter 8). This is most unfortunate, since mobbing targets are, in fact, trauma victims with high rates of PTSD. As a result, such victims are not likely to be offered trauma-focused therapy. Based on extensive experience referring victims to therapists, Namie and Namie (2004) have concluded that, generally speaking, the most effective therapists for working with mobbing victims are those who are experienced in the treatment of domestic violence or trauma.

Therapists unfamiliar with mobbing and employee assistance program (EAP) counselors may refuse to hear details about the workplace mistreatment that the emotionally damaged client needs to verbalize. Instead, they may insist that something in the victim must have triggered the uninvited assault. This is harmful and compounds an already difficult situation. Counselors and therapists need to be mindful of how their pro-employer or pro-payor biases can be hurtful to these clients (Namie & Namie, 2004). On the other hand, therapists and EAP counselors who have a systemic perspective—or at least some understanding of group and organizational dynamics—can better appreciate how group and organizational dynamics interact with the client's individual dynamics and result in mobbing-related trauma. Accordingly, such therapists and counselors can more accurately and effectively formulate and plan interventions.

Having such an expanded perspective virtually ensures that the therapist or counselor will not commit the *fundamental attribution error* (Jones, 1979, 1990; Jones & Harris, 1967) and blame the victim for being mobbed. It is all too easy to misattribute mobbing injury to the victim rather than to the offenders and the organizational context within which the workplace abuse occurred (Namie & Namie, 2004). Table 13.1 provides a summary of these points.

Because mobbing targets are trauma victims, the therapeutic focus, in large part, should be directed at the trauma. As we discussed in Chapter 11, extrapolating from the broader trauma literature suggests that targets of workplace mobbing will benefit from interventions designed to decrease helplessness and increase a sense of personal agency and purpose. The goal in all trauma work is the restoration of a sense of personal agency (White, 2007b).

Personal agency can only be restored through the initiation of action. Scaer (2005) states that "because helplessness is the core state that defines

Table 13.1 **Psychotherapy Strategies: Prerequisites, Basic Caution, and Goal**

Therapist Prerequisites for Working Effectively with Mobbing Client-Victims:

1. Knowledge and awareness of mobbing in terms of its antecedents, processes, and physical, psychological, and relational consequences
2. A basic understanding and awareness of group dynamics and organization dynamics, particularly as they influence the client-victim
3. Knowledge of the client-victim's organization's attitude and response to current and previous claims of mobbing and related abusive behaviors
4. Some experience working successfully with clients with a trauma history
5. A willingness to assume an advocacy role when dealing with the target's organization, including supervisor and human resources personnel, as indicated

Basic Caution: The client (victim) can recover from his or her psychological wounds and return to a work environment that has not changed, thereby becoming exposed to further harm.

Therapeutic Goal: To assist the client-victim in reducing symptoms, reviewing personal career goals, deciding on the most realistic course of action, and supporting the pursuit of the decided upon course of action

traumatization, healing must be associated with empowerment and the perception of control. . . . Listening to stories of healing and redemption from those with similar life experiences expands victims' perceived options for healing" (p. 278). Similar life stories of mobbing can only hold healing potential for other victims if the stories are told. Untold stories cannot help anyone, including the victim. Westhues (2004) states that "by telling mobbing stories valuable knowledge will be shared so that we can all collectively learn how to reduce its incidence" (p. 19).

Developing a sense of personal agency implies taking actions, and therapists who work with mobbing victims can help them by exploring the range of available actions, from naming their experiences and telling their personal stories, to making decisions about remaining or leaving in the current workplace, to making further decisions about filing grievances and taking legal action. To promote the client-victim's autonomy and to begin to assist the client in the reclamation of personal agency, it is the therapist's task to help the mobbing victim assess the range of viable actions that will be most personally meaningful and helpful. Counseling strategies include assessment and intervention at the individual, family, and organizational levels.

AN INTEGRATIVE INDIVIDUAL-ORGANIZATIONAL THERAPEUTIC STRATEGY

An alternative to the conventional therapeutic strategy of providing support and symptomatic relief to the individual mobbing victim is an integrative therapeutic strategy wherein both trauma issues and group and organizational dynamics are addressed. This therapeutic strategy assumes that organizational dynamics exert considerable influence on employees and that such dynamics foster, support, and reinforce mobbing in particular organizations. Therefore, an integrative therapeutic strategy requires that the therapist be sufficiently aware of the particular organization's dynamics and attitudes toward mobbing and other abusive behavior. It also requires that the therapist become aware of the organization's previous responses toward any form of workplace abuse, such as racial discrimination and sexual harassment. In short, such an integrative therapeutic strategy presupposes that the therapist understands the organization's dynamics and its attitudes and response to mobbing and other abusive behaviors. Based on this understanding, the therapist can assist clients to carefully consider their options and then to work collaboratively in implementing the most viable one.

Generally speaking, organizational responses to mobbing and related forms of harassment and abuse fall into one of four categories (based on Sperry & Duffy, 2009). Table 13.2 summarizes these responses, which reflect the basic dynamics of an organization. The reader will note that these responses span a continuum from very negative to very positive.

Victims have a number of possible courses of actions they may or should pursue. Should they stay or leave the organization? Should they initiate a lawsuit or complaint to a federal agency, such as the Equal Employment Opportunity

Table 13.2 **Organizational Responses to Mobbing***

1. Very negative response to mobbing concerns; previous complaints were essentially ignored and there have been few if any legal consequences to the organization. An anti-mobbing policy is considered unnecessary; if one exists, it has not been implemented nor is it supported by management.

2. Somewhat negative or an inadequate response to mobbing concerns; corrective actions taken only because of court or administrative order; an anti-mobbing policy may have been adopted but has not been implemented through training of managers and employees, nor is there a commitment to it or to a respectful workplace by all levels of management.

3. Reasonably positive response to mobbing concerns; actions taken in response to previous or pending mobbing complaints; some organizational changes in structure, culture, and leadership, and an anti-mobbing policy is implemented, but some managers still tolerate subtle forms of mobbing.

4. Very positive response to mobbing concerns; organization changes in structure, culture, and leadership, including implementing anti-mobbing policies with a commitment by all levels of management.

*Based on Sperry and Duffy (2009).

Commission (EEOC)? Should they continue in therapy, and if so, should it include work with a specialist in PTSD? Knowledge of the organization's responses to the current mobbing and to past episodes and its particular organizational dynamics should guide decisions about interventions. Even apparently straightforward interventions, such as encouraging a client to file a complaint in a harassment-prone organization can be fraught with danger (i.e., such action may result in even greater harm to the employee). Furthermore, it should be clear by now that it is professionally untenable, and probably malpractice, for a therapist to auto-matically suggest that the target return to his or her abusive work (or school) situation without first carefully analyzing and discussing various factors—including individual, group, and organizational dynamics—and other possible options with the client.

What are these possible options? At least four options are possible (based on Sperry & Duffy, 2009), and Table 13.3 characterizes them. In addition to assessing organizational type, assessment of the organization's past levels of respon-siveness to harassment and mobbing situations can provide useful information in considering which of the four options is most viable and realistic for a particular client. An online public records search can often help a therapist to learn some information about an organization's history of harassment and discrimination complaints and its responses to them. An online search of the local newspapers can also be useful.

The following two cases illustrate how a therapist or counselor can focus treat-ment. The reader will note that the organization's dynamics, as well as the nature of its responses to mobbing, provides a useful basis for helping a client consider various options.

Following-Up on Ingrid

You might recall the case of Ingrid, which was introduced in an earlier chapter. Briefly, she was a copilot and the target of sustained workplace mobbing involving both management and a group of coworkers. Besides the torment she endured, her career goal of becoming qualified as a pilot certified to fly large aircraft was

Table 13.3 **Mobbing Victim Options***

1. Remain in the workplace, continue therapy, and seek redress
2. Remain in the workplace, continue therapy, but not seek redress
3. Leave the workplace, continue therapy, and seek redress
4. Leave the workplace and continue therapy, without seeking redress

*Based on Sperry and Duffy (2009).

effectively thwarted by the mobbing. After some 18 months of abuse, she quit her job only to find herself effectively blackballed by other carriers. She experienced nightmares, hyperawareness, and hypersensitivity to interpersonal cues. She had lost confidence in herself and in her abilities and was at increased risk for the development or exacerbation of health conditions. Her sense of the future and the prospects of ever working again, particularly as a pilot, appeared bleak. As noted in the analysis of the case, individual and couples therapy seemed essential in helping Ingrid and her spouse understand the impact of mobbing on their relationship, as well as the ordeal involving her job, her health, and her career.

Ingrid and her husband consulted with a therapist who was unfamiliar with mobbing. As a result of input from the therapist, Ingrid chose Option #4 (leave and continue counseling without seeking redress). Had she consulted a therapist knowledgeable about mobbing and organizational dynamics, it is likely she would have chosen Option #3 (leave the workplace, continue therapy, and seek redress). Possibly, she might even have chosen Option #1 (remain in the workplace, continue therapy, and seek redress) had she consulted an informed therapist before quitting her job. Other options may have been chosen in light of a review of the airline's previous response to harassment. The airline had been sued three times in the previous 7 years for harassment and/or wrongful termination. In two of the suits, the court had ruled for the terminated employee. The third suit was still pending. As a result of the suits, the board of directors demanded that the "cowboy" culture of the airline had to change and that a nonharassment policy be added to its code of conduct. Unfortunately, the policy was not in place when Ingrid filed a complaint with the airline's human resources (HR) director.

In terms of organizational responses to mobbing, the airline seemed to have been a type I organization (see Chapter 12) before the lawsuits were filed, but now was a type II and possibly was moving toward becoming a type III organization. Thus, as a result of recent lawsuits and the board of directors' demand that the culture be changed, there was increasing likelihood that top management and HR would have less tolerance for mobbing and would at least impose sanctions or even terminate perpetrators.

Ingrid's example is illustrative in that her case represents a typical outcome of psychotherapy with a therapist not knowledgeable about mobbing and its associated organizational dynamics. The therapy helped Ingrid to remove herself from an abusive workplace environment, but it fell short of helping her to obtain redress or justice, and it also fell far short of addressing Ingrid's now even more complicated career prospects. In Gerry's case, which follows, Gerry was mobbed at a branch bank to which he had been purposefully transferred to provide particular services. Without consulting a therapist, Gerry made the same decision as Ingrid—he left the organization entirely, not seeing any alternative. He made a self-protective decision that was based on inadequate information about how mobbing occurs and what other options might have been available to him in his particular set of circumstances.

Following-Up on Gerry

Gerry's case was also introduced and discussed in earlier chapters. You may recall that Gerry had worked as a personal banker at a regional bank in the northeast that had expanded aggressively in the past decade. He had been with the bank about 4 years and at its university branch for only 9 months. Gerry had been transferred there in an effort to lure more business from the local university. Since the bank employees had no input on Gerry's transfer and were angry at the loss of their previous personal banker, Gerry's coworkers were unhappy and bent on revenge. Mobbing began almost from his first day. Gerry experienced severe headaches, irritable bowel syndrome, depression, insomnia, and intermittent chest pains. His efforts to enlist the support of HR personnel had been fruitless, and their investigation of his complaints biased, at best. Since there were no openings at other branches for personal bankers or similar positions, his only choice was to take a teller position at another branch, at reduced pay, or leave the bank entirely.

Had someone in a situation like Gerry's consulted a therapist knowledgeable about mobbing and organizational dynamics, an assessment of the bank's organizational dynamics might have resulted in the same decision Gerry made, Option #4 (leave and continue counseling without seeking redress). However, careful consideration of other alternatives might have resulted in different short- and long-term outcomes, given the bank's history of regulatory complaints against it. In terms of its organizational response to mobbing, the bank was closer to a type II than a type I organization because it was required by the federal government to revise its nonharassment policy. This means that the bank was vulnerable to subsequent legal action and that if someone like Gerry had decided on Option # 3 (leave, continue counseling, and seek redress), it might have been possible for the courts or a federal agency, such as the EEOC, to require that he be given a similar position at another branch without prejudice. It also could have meant that, had the bank's responsiveness to mobbing moved closer to that of a type III organization, or that if Gerry had felt more empowered and supported in a decision to stay and seek redress, then Option #1 would have been another viable alternative for him.

COMMENTARY

These two cases realistically reflect some of the essential concerns that arise in working with victims of mobbing and related abusiveness. The therapist's role is to work mutually with the victim to consider such concerns, related organizational dynamics, available options, and responses to mobbing at the individual and organizational levels, and then support the victim's decision about work continuation and implementation of the decision. In both Ingrid's and Gerry's cases, working with a therapist unfamiliar with mobbing and organizational dynamics could have considerably exacerbated the effects of mobbing.

Psychotherapy with Victims: Additional Considerations

A therapist who agrees to work with a victim of mobbing or related abusiveness is expected to function in a competent manner. Even though minimum requirements for competent practice can be specified (see Chapter 9), therapists who endeavor to work successfully with these client-victims, must be more than minimally trained and experienced. The challenge of working with mobbing victims may be as or more challenging than working with any other client who presents with a complex history and symptom presentation. Because of the interplay of group and organizational dynamic with the client's own individual dynamics, the therapist can be expected to face a number of unique professional challenges.

It should be increasingly clear that first-order, common-sense solutions, such as encouraging the victim "to try harder" or to just "move forward and forget about it," or "to just ignore those people" will not work and will likely exacerbate the injury. Similarly, organizations that are abuse-prone do not change by themselves, and when they are ordered to change by a court or federal agency, the process of change is difficult. Organizational dynamics, particularly in an abuse-prone culture, can persist for generations unless and until the commitment and resources are provided by top management so that change is even possible. Victims who remain in or return to abuse-prone organizations can be expected to face similar or even greater harm. For example, Campbell (2004), in her longitudinal study of the culture of a single university over a 6-year period during which the occupants of almost all of the top leadership positions changed, found that the organization's cultural value of "silence and passive obedience" remained remarkably unchanged, as did a number of other values. The salience of actual organizational values as they are manifest in organizational culture, although difficult to assess, cannot be overlooked by therapists when working with client mobbing victims.

In short, working with mobbing victims can be overwhelming for many therapists. Furthermore, working with such clients will challenge the basic view that most therapists have of the practice of psychotherapy. The need to exercise the advocacy function during psychotherapy, a part of the ethics codes for psychologists and counselors, seldom presents itself with most clients. However, in working with victims of mobbing, the advocacy function should be routinely exercised. For example, when a mutually agreed upon treatment plan includes the victim returning or attempting to return to the offending organization, the therapist may find it necessary to leave the comfort of his or her therapy office to meet with workplace or school personnel to arrange for the victim's return and the conditions necessary for that return. This may include some accommodation, such as the transfer of the victim or the offender(s) out of the work unit or classroom. Because the victim is likely to be considered disabled under the Americans with Disabilities Act (ADA), it is quite likely that the workplace will be required to make "reasonable accommodations," and it is the therapist's role to advocate for such accommodations. Because legal redress can be another aspect of the treatment plan, the therapist should expect involvement with attorneys and the legal system. This is another common venue in which the exercise of advocacy can arise.

Peer Counseling in the School Setting

This is the first opportunity in this chapter to address intervention strategies specific to the school setting. Peer support and peer counseling have long been effective interventions in school settings. When school counselors advocate for and implement a peer support system in a school, or they develop a peer counseling program, they are engaging in a consultative function. Similarly, when school counselors arrange for a victim to work with a peer counselor, they function in a consultative role, while the peer counselor functions in a therapeutic role.

In recent years, many schools have developed peer support systems to counteract bullying and other interpersonal difficulties in school settings. Peer support systems take a number of forms, including mentoring, befriending, conflict resolution, advocacy and advice-giving, and peer counseling. Research has found these approaches to be effective in reducing the negative effects of bullying for victims (Naylor & Cowie, 1999).

When it comes to mobbing and bullying, peer counseling has largely been utilized to provide support for the victim. However, in addition to developing skills in supportiveness, peer counselors can also be taught the basic skills of active listening, empathy, problem-solving, and role-playing. Accordingly, they can talk to victims either individually or in small groups and engage in awareness-raising, awakening of feelings of responsibility, and in encouraging students to take action against bullying with suggestions on how to do so (Salmivalli, 1999).

ILLUSTRATING PEER COUNSELING

Jocinta is a 10-year-old first-generation Jamaican American girl who recently transferred from a neighborhood public school to St. James Academy, an Episcopal K-12 school, when an opening occurred in mid year. She is physically smaller than the other girls in her class and is also considered "different" because of her olive complexion and slight accent. Soon after her arrival, some girls in her class started to tease her and call her names on the playground at recess and at lunchtime. Jocinta typically responded by tearing up and running from the group of girls. The Academy, like others in the Episcopal diocesan school system, had adopted an anti-mobbing policy 2 years ago, even though there was "little need for it" according to the principal, who stated that there were no previously reported complaints. Nevertheless, after a few days of increasing teasing and name calling, the mobbing moved to Facebook, with threats against Jocinta in the form of a hex. A number of teachers were aware of what was happening to Jocinta, her isolation from her peers, and also aware of the Facebook hex. Their failure to intervene or to notify the administration was inexplicable. It wasn't long before Jocinta began hyperventilating, having difficulty sleeping, and was refusing to go to school.

When Jocinta's mother learned of the abusive behavior and threats on Facebook postings, she went immediately to the principal and demanded that this abusive behavior against her daughter be stopped. Since the school was primarily white, with only 10% minorities, the principal, who valued cultural sensitivity and awareness, was sensitive to any complaint of racism. Consequently, the principal met with the identified group of girls, reviewed the anti-mobbing policy, and told them to stop their abusive behavior. For all practical purposes the abusive behavior stopped immediately, but Jocinta was still symptomatic and was reluctant to return to school. The school had an established peer counseling program that the two school counselors had developed 3 years previously. The program included a focus on cultural awareness and sensitivity and had been helpful for a number of students, particularly minorities. The senior school counselor arranged for a 15-year-old Hispanic female, whose mother had emigrated from Jamaica, to meet with Jocinta for peer support and peer counseling. The two girls related comfortably with each other from the beginning. The peer counseling consisted mostly of support, active listening, and encouragement, with oversight provided by the senior school counselor.

COMMENTARY

In this case, peer counseling provided Jocinta the opportunity to relate to someone close to her age who was very familiar with her cultural roots, particularly her fears about the hex. If the situation had not improved dramatically, the senior school counselor was ready to refer Jocinta to a bicultural Jamaican American therapist in the community.

Consultation Strategies and Interventions

With regard to mobbing, the goal of organizational consultation is to foster a culture and climate of respect, the opposite of abusiveness, and to modify organizational dynamics that previously supported and reinforced abusiveness. Achieving this overall goal is predicated on attaining several related objectives. These objectives are listed in Table 13.4.

This section describes some consultation strategies and interventions helpful in dealing with organizational dynamics influencing mobbing. These include

Table 13.4 **Organizational Consultation Strategies: Goal and Objectives**

Goal: To foster a culture and climate of respect, the opposite of abusiveness, and to modify organizational dynamics that have supported and reinforced abusiveness; achieving this overall goal is predicated on attaining the following objectives:

- Develop a respectful organizational or institutional policy, which includes an anti-abuse, anti-mobbing policy
- Train all members of the organization in the policy. Includes description of mobbing factors and consequences
- Train all supervisory personnel on early recognition, response, and conflict resolution and related strategies
- Modify the performance appraisal process, so that respectful behaviors are expected, evaluated, and rewarded
- Implement a procedure (specified in the anti-mobbing policy) for receiving and handling mobbing complaints for investigation, and for taking corrective action with the offender(s), and responding to needs of the victim

conflict resolution, managerial interventions, executive coaching, organizational consultation, and consultation with aggressive bullies in school settings.

CONFLICT RESOLUTION

Conflict management and alternative dispute resolution can be a cost-effective and fair method of resolving a variety of types of workplace disputes. Although there is considerable research on the effectiveness of conflict management and alternative dispute resolution in the resolution of race-based and sexual harassment workplace disputes (Costello, 1992), there is less research on their use in the prevention and resolution of workplace abuse or mobbing claims. Alternative dispute resolution involves three related dispute resolution processes: direct negotiations, arbitration and adjudication, and mediation (Hoffman, 2006). In direct negotiation, both parties attempt to reach an agreement that meets their common needs. It is typically private, with little or no third-party involvement, and the parties determine the outcome rather than a judge or other outside decision-maker. In arbitration, both parties present their case to an impartial third party, who then makes a decision—usually binding—that resolves the conflict. In adjudication, each party present proofs and arguments to a neutral third party—typically a court or administrative agency—who has the power to deliver a binding decision. Mediation, also called *assisted negotiation*, is a voluntary and informal process in which the disputing parties select a neutral third party to assist them in reaching a negotiated settlement. The mediator is a trained dispute facilitator who has no power to impose a solution on the parties (Lipsky, Seeber, & Fincher, 2000).

MEDIATION

Ferris (2009) noted that mediation is considered an appropriate potential intervention for mobbing and pointed out that, in Quebec, legislation has made mediation a mandatory part of the resolution process. However, she stated that, in her
experience, mediation in mobbing cases can fail and even further harm the alleged
victim. In her clinical experience, mediation is more likely to fail when the mediator is unfamiliar with the nuances of mobbing; in addition, when a power differential exists between the alleged victim and perpetrator, the party with less power
may be at a disadvantage.

If mediation is utilized, Ferris (2009) advises that each party be interviewed
separately to determine their agreement and willingness to engage in the process,
their understanding of the mediation process and any fears they may have about
the process, and their psychological fitness to participate in the mediation process. Mediation may not be a feasible resolution process if the alleged victim is too
vulnerable psychologically to effectively participate, and/or the alleged perpetrator is too angry to effectively participate.

INTERVENTIONS WITH ABUSIVE MANAGERS

Research rather consistently shows that those who engage in workplace mobbing
and abusive behavior are likely to be supervisors and managers (Zapf, Einarsen,
Hoel, & Vartia, 2003). A recent national survey found that 72% of bullies are bosses
(Workplace Bullying Institute/Zogby Survey, 2007). A legitimate question to raise
is: Can abusive managers be stopped from acting in an abusive fashion? Laura
Crawshaw (2007) is a management consultant and executive coach who specializes
in working with abusive managers, whom she refers to as "abrasive bosses." She is
convinced that many of these problematic bosses, if properly coached and mentored,
can be rehabilitated rather than fired or simply left to continue engaging in abusive
behavior. She also works with the managers of these problematic individuals and
provides them with ways of understanding abusiveness and strategies for addressing
it. To avoid confusion, Crawshaw designates these abusive supervisors as "bosses."

Typically, that boss's employees will let the manager know directly or indirectly
that they are experiencing abuse at the hands of a particular boss. She suggests the
following six-point game plan for dealing with the abrasive boss. First, gather the
perceptions of abusiveness from those who report to that boss. Second, present the
wounded feelings of those employees as facts to the boss. Third, disarm the boss's
expected defensiveness. Fourth, make the business case for caring for employees to
the boss. Fifth, threaten the boss with definitive consequences, including termination, for continued abusiveness. And, sixth, offer help to the boss. Usually, this help
involves executive coaching. Furthermore, early detection of abuse by the manager
of the abusive boss allows for early intervention, including help for the abused
employees and help for the abusive boss (Crawshaw, 2007).

COACHING MANAGERS

Because of their inherent formal power, managers can easily attack the job performance or even the personal life of subordinates. On the other hand, managers also have the power to positively influence a culture of respect in their workplace unit both through their modeling and the enforcement of respectful behavior among subordinates. Some believe that such managerial influences represent the single greatest point of leverage in eliminating mobbing from an organization (Ferris, 2009). Holding managers accountable for their behavior and providing them with the skills and abilities to manage their behavior can be achieved through executive coaching. Because of their psychological training and experience, mental health professionals with organizational and consulting backgrounds who do executive coaching have a distinct advantage in working with abusive managers that coaches with other training and backgrounds may not have. Such executive coaching necessarily focuses on helping managers examine their abusive behaviors, its triggers, and consequences. Also, paying attention to managers' own attitudes toward employees and their understanding of the concept of mobbing should be an essential part of the coaching process.

ILLUSTRATING EXECUTIVE COACHING

A senior manager with a long history of hostility toward his staff was referred for executive coaching. He had been observed on several occasions glaring at a particular employee, storming out of his area, withholding praise, being rude, making negative comments about the employee's competence, calling names, providing excessively harsh criticism, and reprimanding that employee in front of others. He had also given the particular employee a performance review that was innuendo-ridden and unsubstantiated. The company president personally called for coaching after a key employee quit and workplace abuse was clearly identified as the cause of the turnover. The executive coach began by meeting with the senior vice president (VP) of marketing to whom this abusive manager reported. It was recommended that the VP do a performance review interview with this manager, during which the manager would be told that if he wanted to continue in his job, his behavior would have to improve.

The manager was also recommended but not required to undergo an assessment and coaching by a mental health consultant arranged for by the company. Workplace psychological evaluations are subject to abuse because of power differentials and misuse and misinterpretation of findings, even when the intent is to help an abusive manager. However, in this case, the manager agreed and underwent a psychological assessment by a consulting psychologist. This assessment suggested that the manager was aware of his behavior and its impact on others. The manager, though, understandably was worried about the process of assessment. He was less worried and became more engaged in the process when the consulting psychologist clearly described during the informed consent process how the assessment would be conducted, how the findings would be reported, and who would have access to them. The consulting psychologist provided this information, in writing, to the manager along with a copy of a document signed by management agreeing that recommendations for remediation only and no actual psychological test findings would be presented to them. Testing revealed a pattern of mistrust and suspiciousness, social isolation, and negativity. A checklist of mobbing behaviors was also administered. This checklist formed the basis for the subsequent coaching.

The consultant then met with the manager and discussed mobbing in terms of the business risk to the employer, including turnover, lowered productivity, and lawsuits. Next, he reiterated the VP of marketing's expectation that the manager risked loss of employment if his abusive behavior did not stop. He arranged to meet with the manager twice a week for executive coaching. The coaching extended for 16 sessions, during which the marketing VP and other senior managers provided ongoing feedback to the coach about the manager's progress. Significant improvement in the manager's behavior was achieved and maintained over the next business quarter. At the time of the next annual performance management review, some 6 months after coaching was completed, the manager maintained adequate respectful behavior and his performance review reflected this progress.

ORGANIZATIONAL CONSULTATION

In addition to these one-on-one forms of consultations, the consultant can be involved with other interventions that can directly impact organizational dynamics. These include assisting an organization in reviewing and revising their code of conduct and developing an anti-mobbing policy, as well as in providing training to all employees and managers of the organization in the implementation of the policy (these interventions are described in detail in Chapters 14 and 15).

Various types of executive consultation can be provided to managers. A common type is the training of managers in both recognizing and dealing with mobbing behavior. This may include empathy training, conflict resolution strategies, and anger management. Consultation can also be provided to the whole organization with regard to modifying corporate structures, culture, and leadership behavior. A useful place to begin is to conduct surveys and interviews to determine the extent to which the organization's actual core values match its stated values. Typically, the discrepancy is striking, particularly in those organizations in which complaints of mobbing or other abusiveness have been lodged. When top management faces a striking discrepancy between its espoused and actual core values, it is more likely to be motivated and willing to support a change in corporate culture.

CONSULTING WITH AGGRESSIVE BULLIES IN SCHOOL SETTINGS

School counselors typically find it easier and safer to work with mobbing and bullying victims rather than perpetrators. Nevertheless, counselors are expected to meet with alleged perpetrators to collect information or prepare a disposition, such as a treatment referral. In this consultation role, school counselors may face perpetrators whom they find difficult, challenging, or even threatening. Accordingly, they might find the distinction made in the professional literature between youthful proactive and reactive aggression helpful (McAdams & Schmidt, 2007; Price & Dodge, 1989; Raine et al. 2006). Reactive aggression is characterized as a "hot-blooded," automatic, defensive response to immediate and often misperceived threat. Once the presenting threat is relieved, reactive aggressors are likely to be remorseful. They are often referred to as having "a short fuse" because they tend to be intolerant of frustration, easily threatened, impulsive and over-reactive in response to any source of stress or fear, and unpredictable in their tantrums and outbursts.

By contrast, those with proactive aggression display an organized, purposeful, and often premeditated form of abusive behavior. Their aggression serves as a tool for personal gain, status, self-gratification, and almost always for emotional control. Their strategies for emotional control include pressing sensitive buttons to elicit desired affective responses from others and displaying false emotions themselves (e.g., crying or remorse) to deceive others of their aggressive intentions. These individuals initiate aggressive acts without provocation and against those whom they see as the most vulnerable and least threatening targets for exploitation. They are not remorseful and are seldom willing to take responsibility for their action, preferring instead to blame others. It is these aggressors whom peers, teachers and parents commonly refer to as bullies. Their aggressive behavior is likely to continue unabated until they develop genuine empathy for others, their aggressive behavior ceases to satisfy their appetitive needs, or they have access to more satisfying, prosocial ways to maintain positive self-esteem. Again, we introduce the caution that the term "bully" can and has been used purposefully as part of the mobbing of a worker or student. Notwithstanding that, the distinction between reactive and proactive aggression is useful.

The optimal goal of interventions is for aggressive students to develop a level of empathy for others that effectively restricts their willingness to hurt others for personal gain. Consultation interventions to arrest this proactive aggression involve convincing the students that the personal benefit of their aggression is outweighed by both its negative consequences and the tangible benefits of prosocial behavior. To achieve this objective, schools must have a structured system of behavioral expectations that explicitly defines responsible student behavior, effectively exposes students' failures to fulfill those responsibilities, and specifies consequences for irresponsibility. The consequences of aggressive behavior must be significant enough to eliminate its utilitarian appeal, and there should be no loopholes through which the proactive aggressor can talk his or her way out of responsibility. There also must be appropriate consequences for bullying behavior.

The following recommendations are offered by McAdams and Schmidt (2007) for dealing with youth identified as proactive aggressors:

- Provide clear behavioral expectations that are free from loopholes or ambiguity.
- Avoid debates and arguments.
- Avoid repetitious or standardized responses.
- Reinforce positive achievements, but cautiously.
- Don't drop your guard.
- Focus on feelings rather than facts.
- Don't stop at consequences; teach prosocial behaviors.

Conclusion

When the victims of mobbing are unable to restore some sense of normalcy in their lives, they may be receptive to seeking or taking a referral for psychotherapeutic help. We began this chapter by outlining the somewhat unique challenges that psychotherapists face when they agree to work with mobbing victim clients. We also describe a number of prerequisites for effectively working with mobbing victims. These include a knowledge and awareness of the psychodynamics of mobbing and its deleterious personal, financial, family, relational, and career consequences, as well as the antecedent individual, group, and organizational dynamics. Prerequisites also include a knowledge of the offending organization's attitudes and response to current and previous mobbing or other workplace abuse claims. We suggested that not all therapists are suited for working with mobbing victims.

Similarly, the demands are equally great for organizational and executive consultants who are contracted by organizations to help their managers deal with abusive bosses, engage in executive coaching, and perform other organizational interventions. Nevertheless, counter-weighing these demands is the personal and professional satisfaction of dealing with very difficult situations and circumstances and being successful in making a difference in the lives of clients and organizations affected by mobbing and related workplace abuse. Included in the discussions in this chapter is the importance of due process for all parties in mobbings and an awareness that, increasingly, labeling someone in the workplace or school as a "bully" can initiate mobbing of the person so labeled.

14

Mobbing Prevention Strategies

In situations where evil is being practiced, there are perpetrators,
victims, and survivors. However, there are often observers of the
ongoing activities or people who know what is going on and do not
intervene to help or to challenge the evil and thereby enable evil to
persist by their inaction.
—Philip Zimbardo (2008, p. 317)

Chapter 13 addressed the need for developing systemic skills to foster individual and organizational recovery from mobbing. These skills included understanding professional responsibilities in working with mobbing victims, developing integrative individual–organizational psychotherapeutic interventions, and utilizing organizational strategies and interventions designed to provide systemic individual and organizational recovery. However, besides fostering recovery, it is critically important that organizations endeavor to prevent mobbing from happening in the first place. Organizations—whether workplaces or schools—can take concrete and effective measures to prevent mobbing. Typically, these measures involve policy development, training, and other activities to foster a healthier and more respectful climate and culture within organizations. Here, we examine various professional strategies that organizations can and must take to prevent mobbing and reduce its associated morbidity.

Workplace Mobbing Prevention Strategies

There are many ways in which workplace organizations can safeguard workers and foster cultures of respect and integrity, the opposites of mobbing and other forms of abusiveness.

These efforts can be approached in a piecemeal and unintentional fashion, or in a strategic and intentional fashion. We favor strategically focused initiatives. Recently, some best practices have been proposed for workplace organizations, although they might easily be adapted to school organizations as well. Table 14.1 provides such a list. Note that change begins and is directed by senior management.

Table 14.1 **Best Practices for Preventing Mobbing and Fostering a Respectful Workplace***

Senior management will:

1. Acknowledge mobbing as an organizational issue
2. Own the problem as an organizational problem
3. Develop a strategic plan to identify and monitor progress in creating and maintaining a respectful workplace
4. Invest in anti-mobbing policy development and training for all: managers, human resources (HR) personnel, and employees
5. Provide resources regarding mobbing to managers and employees and to support personnel including coaches, employee assistance programs, mediators, legal advice, and other support lines
6. Maintain healthy networks with professionals and take time to meet with and discuss issues with these professionals
7. Ensure that all demonstrate no tolerance of abusive workplace behaviors
8. Select applicants for employment—including all levels of management—based on integrity, respectfulness, and support for diversity
9. Assess integrity, respectfulness, and support for diversity as a performance standard in performance appraisal reviews and reward them
10. Implement processes for informal and formal complaint resolution

*Based on Rayner and McIvor (2006).

The rest of this section amplifies many of these best practices. They include raising awareness, assessing for the presence of mobbing, policy development, training, coaching human resources (HR) personnel, school-based mobbing prevention programs, and selection, performance management, and reward systems.

RAISING AWARENESS ABOUT MOBBING AND FOSTERING A CULTURE OF RESPECT AND TOLERANCE

Raising awareness of mobbing and engaging an organization in understanding the issues may be sufficient for those organizations that have a strong commitment to respectful workplaces. Other organizations may require a greater understanding of the abusive experiences of personnel in their workplaces. Although the prevalence of workplace mobbing/bullying is ubiquitous, many organizations in North America have ignored the phenomena because, in most states and provinces, no legislation requires organizations to manage this type of harmful workplace behavior. It often takes a civil lawsuit or extreme turnover to underscore the importance of addressing mobbing and bullying in a workplace.

Consultants can serve organizations well by bringing the issue of mobbing and related abusiveness to the attention of senior management. Presenting the business case for dealing quickly with mobbing is a very effective way of introducing the need for policy development and training for the prevention of it. Consultants can introduce the topic of mobbing in several ways. First, the business case can be presented by asking whether the senior manager is aware of the phenomenon of mobbing and whether the manager would be interested in understanding it in greater depth. Second, a company's experience with mobbing can be elicited by asking whether the organization has dealt with mobbing or mobbing-like complaints in the past. Third, the consultant can ask if the organization regularly conducts worker or staff satisfaction or stress surveys. If mobbing is operative within an organization, it is likely to manifest as a negative work climate, hostile relationships with peers or managers, high rates of sickness and leaves of absence, high rates of employee turnover, and high rates of worker compensation claims. These performance indicators are a key part of the organizational health model (Cotton & Hart, 2003; Hart & Cooper, 2001) introduced in Chapter 8. Fourth, the consultant can indicate that the direct and indirect costs of mobbing in the workplace are increasingly expensive to the organization, and that many organizations have developed policies and procedures to address mobbing as part of their respectful workplace policies. Such a conversation can increase management's awareness of mobbing and set the stage for other consultation interventions.

ASSESSING THE PRESENCE OF MOBBING

If an organization contact indicates that surveys, interviews, or employee discussions suggest that mobbing has occurred, or if he or she is interested in understanding the nature and extent of this behavior in the workplace, two approaches are effective. The first approach involves conducting an anonymous survey about mobbing/bullying behaviors in the workplace. Rayner, Hoel, and Cooper (2002) provide a useful overview of such a survey, including examples of survey questions. Consultants with specialized training and experience in assessment and survey development are particularly well positioned to use or develop survey techniques in the workplace, school, or other institutional setting. Surveys are useful for taking a snapshot of organizational climate and related issues because they can be conducted and analyzed quickly. An effective strategy is to conduct the survey and disseminate survey results in an expeditious manner. Providing feedback about the survey results relating to organizational climate and mobbing in small groups of members of the organization usually activates considerable interest in addressing the problem. It shouldn't be too surprising that workers and staff may be become further engaged in developing more comprehensive and meaningful actions than are managers (Ferris, 2009).

Interview data can be even more useful than survey data. Although more costly, interviews can provide greater depth of insight into mobbing considerations.

Kvale (2007) points out that, historically, interviews have been powerful methods for producing knowledge about human situations and for ultimately changing the way particular human situations are understood and managed. As such, interviews conducted by neutral outside consultants can provide rich data about organizational climate and mobbing that have potential for laying the foundations for positive organizational change. A semi-structured individual interview format, followed by a team interview format and follow-up discussion can be most effective. A formal report to the organization is an essential component of the change process since it identifies the problem, provides recommendations, and sets the expectation that the organization will address the problem. Needless to say, useful reports are those that are straightforward and provide specific recommendations.

DEVELOPING AN ANTI-MOBBING POLICY

Workplace abuse appears to be more prevalent in organizations without anti-mobbing or anti-bullying policies (Einarsen & Skogstad, 1996; Rayner, Hoel, & Cooper, 2002). Accordingly, consultants can and should encourage all organizations to develop a policy and train HR personnel and all managers across the organization in the identification and management of mobbing. Training should also be extended to all workers or staff. There are several models for developing such policies. Richards and Daley (2003) provide the details of policy development, implementation, and monitoring, and Chapter 15 of this book provides a detailed description of the strategy of policy development. Offering policy development assistance in the form of a half-day workshop for organizational leaders and other key members is often useful. This allows for multiple stakeholder engagement in the process and tailoring of anti-mobbing policy to each organization. Such workshops provide participants with a description and definition of mobbing, exposure to organizational resources available for recognizing and reporting abusiveness, and information about help for victims and offenders. Needless to say, unless the formulated policy is subsequently disseminated to the organization, monitored, and enforced, it is unlikely to make an impact.

TRAINING

Policy development and training are inseparable. Optimally, training begins with senior managers, followed by HR personnel, and then should include all workers and staff. Typically, training with senior staff and HR involves 1 1/2 to 2 days, whereas training with workers and staff can be accomplished in a half-day workshop. This kind of timetable is congruent with the research findings of Cotton and Hart (2003), which strongly indicate that focusing on leadership training and improving people management skills among organizational leadership is one of the most powerful interventions available for improving overall organizational climate and organizational health, of which employee well-being is a key constituent part.

The contents of a general training workshop usually begin with a discussion of major concepts, such as the business and ethical case for preventing mobbing, followed by a description and definition of mobbing. It is critical to differentiate mobbing from sexual harassment and workplace violence, and to emphasize the importance of maintaining a safe and respectful work environment for all. Next, the training shifts to options for addressing mobbing behaviors. These include identification of behaviors experienced as negative and harmful, how to talk to someone about behavior that is offensive, and how to report or make a complaint about such behavior.

For senior managers and HR personnel, training needs to be more detailed and to emphasize distinct responsibilities for both managers and HR. At a minimum, this training should include the content of the half-day workshop, as well as additional content. The problems stemming from mobbing should be addressed at individual, group, and organizational levels. A discussion of organizational dynamics that may unwittingly be activating and reinforcing abusive behavior is essential. The importance of this discussion about organizational dynamics, organizational climate, and leadership behaviors cannot be overstated. Since managers and HR personnel have responsibilities for dealing with mobbing above and beyond those of workers and staff, sufficient time needs to be directed at the skills and methods needed to help managers and HR acquire these skills. This skill set includes active listening, respect for diversity of people and perspectives, conflict resolution, and even performance management.

The procedure as well as the process of investigating allegations of mobbing must be thoroughly discussed. Readers will find a useful and comprehensive overview of the investigative process in Merchant and Hoel (2003). Their review of the investigative process includes particularly useful sections on caring for the investigator, who, by definition, is in a highly demanding role, and on the importance of resisting undue pressure from either managers or staff. A discussion of the implications of not addressing complaints in a supportive manner is an essential part of the training. The importance of establishing a respectful workplace and a climate of civility needs to be continuously reinforced. Finally, the workshop should include some additional skills required by senior managers in dealing with allegations of mobbing. These include the ability to maintain records and keep confidentiality, timely investigation and reporting, report writing skills, listening skills, keeping the alleged victim safe throughout the investigation findings period and afterward, and the ability to make decisions that reflect justice (Ferris, 2009; Merchant & Hoel, 2003). It goes without saying that training materials and the design of the workshops be cogent, engaging, of the highest professional quality, and tailored to the unique needs of the participants.

SELECTION, PERFORMANCE MANAGEMENT, AND REWARD SYSTEMS

The adage "an ounce of prevention is worth a pound of cure" is particularly applicable to management functions of selection, reward and sanctions, and appraisal and management of worker performance. Even though research on the individual antecedents of mobbing is limited, a modest correlation between tests of integrity and counterproductive workplace behaviors has been noted (Sackett & DeVore, 2002). Accordingly, consultants can assist an organization in reviewing its selection and interview process in assessing the integrity and respectfulness of prospective employees, while also recognizing the diversity of ways in which people express themselves.

This matter of the divergent ways in which people express themselves is an important one for dealing with issues of mobbing. Friedenberg (2008) has put forward the intriguing proposition that the socio-linguistic practices and interactional styles of members of the working class, immigrants, and first-generation immigrants are more likely to lead them to become mobbing victims. The sense of obligation to perform and succeed, and the direct verbal styles associated with a number of immigrant groups are more likely to result in their being mobbed, according to Friedenberg, a linguistics expert. If Friedenberg is right, and research is surely needed to explore her intriguing possibility, class, immigrant status, or other differences may put certain persons just enough outside of the dominant cultural group within an organization that they miss the linguistic and paralinguistic nuances of the dominant culture and, because of such differences, are therefore placed at higher risk of being mobbed. Also in relation to different ways of self-expression, Cotton and Hart (2003), based on their extensive organizational health research, stated that "there is no justification for organisations utilizing selection and recruitment processes to screen out individuals who have higher levels of emotionality" (p. 125). Emotionality is a universal human attribute that is both neurobiologically and culturally mediated. Within a wide range of normal variance, screening out for emotionality would be individually and culturally discriminatory.

In addition to selection, the consultant can also assist organizations in reviewing their performance management system in light of anti-mobbing and healthy, respectful workplace and school policies. The expectation that workers and managers will relate in a respectful manner that is tolerant of differing and divergent opinions can be established as a formal, regularly reviewed performance standard. Consultants can also assist organizations in reviewing organizational reward and sanction systems, so that workplace respectfulness and support for diversity is formally supported. Lawler (2003) studied the performance management practices of 55 *Fortune 500* companies and concluded the following about the results of his study:

> They [results] strongly support the view that performance appraisal systems are more effective when there is a connection between the

results of the performance management system and the reward system of the organization. This finding, hopefully, will end the debate about whether an appraisal system is damaged by using it to determine the amount of someone's pay increase, the size of their bonus, or the stock options that they receive. It argues strongly that organizations make a mistake when they separate appraising performance from determining pay changes. (p. 402)

Rewarding integrity and tolerance for diversity is a novel but logical next step in developing practical measures for improving organizational climate and preventing mobbing. The challenge, of course, is in operationalizing workplace values like integrity and respect for diverse opinions but it is a challenge worth taking up, given the pervasiveness of mobbing and bullying and the health burden these behaviors impose both individually and societally. Finally, all three of these management functions; namely, selection, performance management, and rewards, along with a leadership style that balances productivity with respectfulness, can positively and significantly influence the culture of the organization.

CONSULTING WITH HUMAN RESOURCES PERSONNEL

Human resources plays a critical role in the prevention, detection, and correction of mobbing in workplace and school organizations. Human resources can exert significant leverage in organizations. Consultants have greatly assisted HR personnel in defining their various roles in dealing with management, workers, and staff about mobbing. Beginning with policy development and training, HR has an unparalleled opportunity to collaborate with organizational members at all levels to make the workplace or school psychologically safe for all. Such proactive efforts to prevent mobbing and improve overall organizational health can do much to reverse the sentiment of many workers and staff that HR has relinquished its advocacy role for worker and staff well-being and instead has been overly focused on protecting the organization. Consultants can do much to facilitate this collaboration by helping organizational leaders and HR avoid simplistic frameworks for understanding and preventing mobbing.

Furthermore, consultants can provide or arrange for training on investigation skills, supportive actions, active listening, problem solving, and appropriate referrals for both victims and offenders. Helping the HR professional to distinguish mobbing from other forms of harassment and to develop the necessary skill sets to provide initial aid and support to victims is of critical importance.

TEC BANK FOLLOW-UP

TEC Bank was introduced in Chapters 7 and 12 as the bank where Gerry Bennett had worked as a personal banker and where he had become the target of mobbing by his coworkers. At the time of the mobbing, the bank was in transition from expansion stage to the professionalization stage of its development as an organization. You may recall that several new branches were opened in the space of 5 years. The bank's entrepreneurial founder and president had a very limited view of HR's function in the organization, and so the department was quite small. The main task of an organization in the professionalization stage is to implement a strategic management system that would require, among others things, a much larger HR department with greatly expanded HR functions.

On the advice of both an executive consultant and the bank's legal counsel, the president agreed that HR needed to expand its function and take a more proactive stance in ensuring the safety of employees and customers. Accordingly, three new HR personnel were added, and the HR director was promoted to the rank of vice president of HR. Additionally, the bank contracted for five more security officers.

At the same time, another complaint of mobbing had been filed with HR. A systems consultant agreed to consult on the case but also proposed a policy development, training, and reporting-monitoring program to the president. The president agreed and authorized the VP of HR to implement a healthy workplace policy with specific anti-mobbing provisions. This policy would include a training program for all employees, as well as a compliance reporting and monitoring system. At the first meeting of the policy development team, the president gave his strong support for the initiative. The team consisted of 12 members, representing a cross-section of the organization's stakeholders. It secured input from all bank employees and the board of directors. A 2-day training session was focused on recognizing and responding to mobbing and was implemented for all managers, including the president, management team, and all branch managers. Afterward, all other bank employees participated in a half-day program on the healthy workplace policy, with special emphasis on the specific procedures for dealing with mobbing and other abusive behaviors.

The consultant also engaged in coaching the VP of HR on several matters relating to her expanded role as a vice president. This included coaching on developing her staff, as well as dealing effectively with mobbing and harassment issues. She and four of her HR professionals were sent for training on investigating mobbing and other harassment claims. A program for monitoring complaints, as well as an annual climate assessment of the bank's new healthy workplace policy was initiated. The annual performance appraisal system was changed to a performance management system in which all employees would now also be evaluated on the bank's core values, which included respectfulness and support for divergent perspectives. Incentives were tied to high performance in practicing respectfulness and in supporting divergent perspectives and ways of expressing those perspectives.

School-Based Mobbing Prevention Strategies

The good news is that, every year, more school systems are adopting bullying prevention programs. The bad news is that the efficacy of these various programs has yet to be established. Recently, the Blueprints for Violence Prevention, launched by the Center for the Study and Prevention of Violence at the University of Colorado began a review of existing prevention programs. Using stringent standards of scientific efficacy, the center reviewed over 600 such programs. It identified 11 programs that met all of these standards, and 18 other programs were identified as meeting most of the standards. The identified programs addressed at-risk youth behaviors, including substance abuse, poor academic performance, behavioral/emotional problems, and bullying. Among the various programs, the Olweus Bullying Prevention Program was one of the few identified as an evidence-based program (Blueprint for Violence Prevention, 2002–2004). Because this is the most well-known and most widely adopted prevention program in school districts, it is briefly described here.

OLWEUS BULLYING PREVENTION PROGRAM

The Olweus Bullying Prevention Program (Olweus, Limber, & Mihalic, 1999) is a whole-school, multilevel approach for the reduction and prevention of bullying. To stop bullying, it must be addressed at every level of a student's experience. For that reason, prevention programs typically target four systemic or organizational levels: the individual level, the classroom level, the school level, and the community level. The underlying assumption of a whole-school approach is that bullying and peer victimization are systemic problems, and intervention programs must be directed at the entire school, rather than at individual bullies or victims. Advantages of whole-school programs are that the entire school community becomes sensitized to the problem of recognizing and responding to bullying and that stigmatization of bullies and victims is avoided (Smith, Schneider, Smith, & Ananiadou, 2004).

More specifically, the Olweus Bullying Prevention Program (Olweus et al., 1999) is designed to improve peer relations and make schools safer, more positive places for students to learn and develop. Backed by more than 30 years of research and successful, worldwide implementation, it is a long-term, system-wide program for change. The main goals of the Olweus Program are to reduce existing bullying problems among students; prevent new bullying problems; achieve better peer relations at school; and create safer, more effective learning environments.

The core components of the Olweus Program are implemented at the individual, classroom, school, and community levels. These include intervention with victims and perpetrators of bullying, regular classroom meetings with students to increase knowledge and empathy, school-wide rules against bullying, school staff meetings concerning the program, formation of the Bullying Prevention

Coordination Committee, training for school staff and committee, and parents' involvement through discussion and information sessions.

Training is essential for successful program implementation and continuity in subsequent years. This training includes school administrators, as well as every adult involved in overseeing, planning, and implementing the program, including teachers, counselors, support staff, bus drivers, custodial staff, and parents.

Program Effectiveness

Whole-school approaches, particularly the Olweus Bullying Prevention Program, have been found to be effective in middle- and upper-school environments for reducing the incidence of bullying and improving attitudes toward school and academic achievement (Smith et al., 2004), but the effectiveness of the program has not been tested in low-income schools. It has been noted that higher rates of behavioral problems and socioeconomic and cultural differences pose a major challenge to implementing effective anti-bullying interventions in schools located in impoverished communities (Hong, 2009). In a recent study evaluating the effectiveness of the Olweus Bullying Prevention Program, students from ten public middle schools participated. The schools included seven intervention schools and three controls. Relational victimization decreased by 28%. Physical victimization decreased by 37% among white students, but no program effect was noted for minority students. Students in the intervention schools were more likely to perceive that other students more actively intervened in instances of bullying than did the students in the control schools (Bauer, Lozano, & Rivara, 2007).

ORGANIZATIONAL DYNAMICS AND SCHOOL PREVENTION PROGRAMS

Even though a whole-school prevention program, such as the Olweus Bullying Prevention Program (Olweus et al., 1999), is effective in a particular school, this does not necessarily mean it will be successful in another. Every school has unique organizational dynamics. As a result, some schools will be able to integrate the Olweus model into their organization's strategy, structure, and culture much more easily than others. Accordingly, a review of a school's organizational dynamics should be undertaken when choosing members of the coordination committee, necessary resources, the timing of initiation of the program, and most importantly, the likely barriers that might impede program implementation.

HAYWORTH JUNIOR HIGH SCHOOL

Hayworth (a pseudonym for an actual school in the case study by Coyle, 2008) is a large junior high school with 1,050 7th- and 8th-grade students, as well as 65 faculty members, four guidance counselors, a principal and an assistant principal, plus support staff. The student body is of predominantly middle and lower socio-economic status with little racial and ethnic diversity. This school utilizes individualized student scheduling rather than teaming. Following a serious school violence event 3 years previously, the school added a full-time school resource officer to its other security measures, which included locked doors and video cameras throughout the school.

Hayworth had unsuccessfully attempted to implement the Olweus model program 7 years earlier in the aftermath of a school shooting incident. Subsequently, the decision was made to implement the Olweus Bullying Prevention Program. The anti-bullying program was experiencing success in its second year of implementation. Coyle (2008) developed the case study of Hayworth Junior High to better understand the process of program implementation, the complex nature of the context in which it occurred, and the meaning of the process to those involved in the implementation. In-depth interviews were conducted with nine informants. These included faculty from both 7th and 8th grades, the principal, a guidance counselor who was also a parent of a student in the school, and the school resource officer. Seven of the participants were members of the Olweus Bullying Prevention Core Team, including the core team coordinator. Four of these seven member participants were on the original core team when implementation was tried and failed 7 years previously. Additional data were collected by the researcher. These included observation of the signs and symbols posted throughout the building; talking informally with randomly selected groups of students seated in the cafeteria; field notes; and school documents, including the district's mission statement, harassment policies, and bullying policies.

An analysis of the data offered some keen insights into how organizational dynamics influenced the implementation of the prevention program. Coyle (2008) identified several of what she calls "barriers" and "bridges" to implementation.

- *Barriers impeding implementation.* The school staff identified a number of barriers they faced in their effort to integrate and implement the Olweus model in their school. Chief among these was the school's size. The large enrollment impeded efforts to create ongoing connections with students, a factor critical to the success of implementing any program. An even bigger barrier recognized by the staff was the local community's lack of openness to change and diversity.
- *Bridges supporting implementation.* By contrast, a number of factors emerged that supported the implementation of the prevention program. Chief among these was the school's strategy, wherein the primary mission of the school was a commitment to learning. This was supported by structural factors such as an established policy of zero tolerance for bullying, realistic expectations for implementation and success, and educational practices and structures that supported learning and integration of the prevention program. The school's organizational culture of warmth, caring, and collaboration further supported implementation of the anti-bullying program. School cultural characteristics

that also supported implementation included a sense of family, warmth, and collaboration. Manager–member dynamics included strong connections among staff and between staff and students (Coyle, 2008).

Conclusion

Several strategies have been described that organizations can utilize to safeguard and prevent mobbing and its consequences. This chapter has emphasized preventive strategies and interventions aimed at mob-proofing an organization. It is noteworthy that schools have done considerably more than workplace organizations to make their organizations more secure and respectful. One possible reason is that many workplace organizations still do not have anti-mobbing policies. It may well be that federal legislation is needed for mobbing to be significantly reduced in the workplace, just as federal legislation largely reduced sexual harassment. Chapter 15 addresses both policy development and legislative efforts with regard to mobbing.

15

Policy and Legislation

A policy makes a clear statement about what an organization thinks, its relationship with staff, and how it expects people to work within its culture.
—Jon Richards and Hope Daley (2003, p. 247)

In this chapter, we review policy strategies for preventing mobbing. In the area of policy development, anti-bullying policies are relatively recent, and anti-mobbing policies are almost nonexistent. The critical difference between them is the degree to which the policy includes the organization as a key player etiologically in the development of mobbing and, therefore, as a key player in its resolution and elimination. For both mobbing and bullying, policy strategies are important because, when properly drafted, they directly connect mobbing and bullying to the clear public health threats that they are. We identify the essential components of a school anti-mobbing policy, placing emphasis on the organizational responsibilities of school leadership. We also take a school- and community-wide perspective and examine the responsibilities of major stakeholder groups in the development and implementation of school anti-mobbing policies. In regard to workplace mobbing, we review a sample organizational anti-mobbing policy and discuss its key elements.

We also provide a brief overview of existing U.S. legislation prohibiting school bullying and a report on legislative efforts to introduce healthy workplace bills offering legal protection and remedies for non–status based harassment in the United States. There is an important difference between non–status based and status-based legal protections against workplace abuses. Status-based legal protections cover individuals who experience discrimination or harassment based on race, color, religion, sex, national origin, disability, and age. Non–status based legal protections cover all individuals who experience workplace mobbing and other forms of abuse, irrespective of whether they are members of a protected class. In our overview, we also include a report about what other countries have done with regard to the introduction of anti-mobbing legislation in acknowledgment of the worldwide efforts to address mobbing and bullying.

Although school bullying has already been declared a public health threat in the United States for children and adolescents (Eisenberg & Aalsma, 2005; Srabstein, Berkman, & Pyntikova, 2008), our work extends the importance of the public health implications of bullying to include the more severe forms of school and workplace mobbing. School and workplace mobbings are public health threats equal to or greater than school bullying. Consequently, schools and organizations have an obligation to respond to these public health threats by developing policies that clearly define mobbing, expressly prohibit it, include sanctions for participating in it, and explicitly link mobbing to physical and/or psychological victimization.

Developing School Anti-Mobbing Policies

Schools are unique organizational contexts in that they are continuously interfacing with multiple stakeholder groups and are accountable to multiple stakeholders. To develop comprehensive and effective anti-mobbing policies, all of these stakeholder groups must be involved in meaningful ways. The school organization consists of teachers and staff, coaches, principals, other administrators, and, depending upon whether the school is a public or private entity, a range of possible community advisory boards or boards of directors. Students, parents, and the community at large represent the other stakeholder groups within the school community. In efforts to prevent mobbing and reduce harm to students served by schools, all of these stakeholder groups have responsibilities in the development and implementation of anti-mobbing policies. The perspective and input of each stakeholder group is needed to develop anti-mobbing policies that will work in their school communities and to ensure that anti-mobbing policies, once developed, are fully implemented and not just paid lip service. Figure 15.1 lists the major responsibilities of each stakeholder group in the development and implementation of effective anti-mobbing policies.

The stakeholder responsibilities identified in Figure 15.1 reflect the importance of recognizing the school as a wider community, including school personnel, students, parents, and the community itself within which the school is located. An anti-mobbing policy is likely to rise or fall based on the commitment to the policy of these primary stakeholder groups. The more inclusive the policy is of the multiple stakeholder groups, the greater the likelihood of its success in preventing mobbing and reducing harm to children and adolescents.

A number of policy development components that need to be articulated in a school anti-mobbing policy are, however, the primary responsibility of the school and school governing body. These components are the organizational responsibilities of the school and school governing body and should be incorporated into every school anti-mobbing policy. We list here those key organizational responsibilities of the school that should be articulated in an anti-mobbing policy:

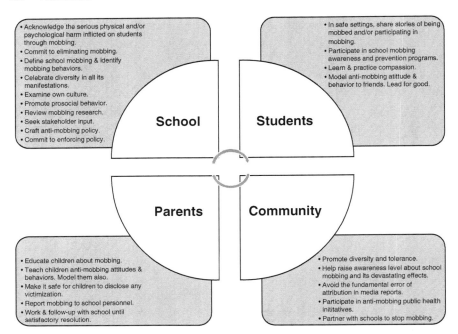

Figure 15.1 Stakeholders' Responsibilities in School Anti-Mobbing Policy
Development & Implementation.

- The school's unequivocal commitment to eliminating mobbing.
- An acknowledgment of the serious and sometimes fatal health consequences
  of mobbing (see Chapter 8).
- A statement of the affirmative values of the school community upon which the
  anti-mobbing policy is based (for an example, see the sample organizational
  anti-mobbing policy later in this chapter). For children and adolescents, this
  statement of organizational values should also specifically recognize minors as
  a vulnerable population requiring proactive measures to keep them safe from
  physical and psychological harm.
- A workable definition of school mobbing, with examples of specific mobbing
  behaviors common to children and adolescents (see Chapters 3 and 4).
- A statement of the responsibilities of the school leadership to develop school-
  wide anti-mobbing training programs for all school personnel and prevention
  programs that include all of the major stakeholder groups.
- A statement of the responsibilities of the school leadership to model integrity
  and respectfulness to all members of the school community.
- Acknowledgment that trained school personnel will intervene immediately
  when school mobbing occurs or is suspected of having occurred, and a
  description of procedures for how interventions will be conducted.

- A description of a range of evidence-based resolution strategies that emphasize resolution with dignity; such strategies may include mediation, peer counseling and support, and use of a variety of restorative justice frameworks. School settings are ripe for the use of alternative dispute resolution processes like justice circles (Boyes-Watson, 2008), restorative justice practices (Crawford & Newburn, 2003), and mediation.
- A description of safe and confidential procedures that students who have claims of mobbing may use to lodge their complaints and seek resolution and safety.
- The inclusion of adult school personnel as being bound by the provisions of the anti-mobbing policy both in relation to students and in relation to other school personnel.
- A commitment to working cooperatively with parents and other community members to resolve instances of mobbing.
- Sanctions for student, parent, or school personnel abuse of the anti-mobbing policy by filing false or malicious claims of mobbing.
- Means for the periodic review and evaluation of the anti-mobbing policy.

The detailed articulation of these important provisions of a school anti-mobbing policy and the partnering with the major stakeholder groups to eliminate mobbing from the wider school community will go a long way toward increasing awareness of the destructiveness of school mobbing and reducing its prevalence. Everyone in the school community has responsibilities to participate in ending school mobbing and its potentially life-altering affects on students and their families.

Workplace Anti-Mobbing Policy Development

There are two primary reasons why organizations should take seriously the issue of creation of anti-mobbing and anti-bullying policies. The first reason is enlightened self-interest. It is extraordinarily costly in terms of absenteeism, sick leave, staff turnover and retraining costs, litigation, and damage to a company's reputation to remain exposed to the negative consequences of workplace mobbing and bullying, even in the current absence of U.S. legislative requirements to address the problem. In the United Kingdom, Pinkerfield (2006) reported that the cost to British industry of workplace bullying was in the region of £2 billion, and 19 million lost work days annually. In the United States, where Lutgen-Sandvik, Tracy, and Alberts (2007) identified prevalence figures of lifetime exposure to workplace abuse in the range of 35%–50%, the costs of workplace mobbing and bullying are substantial. In the largest survey of its kind in the United States, the Workplace Bullying Institute/Zogby International conducted the U.S. Workplace Bullying Survey (2007) and found that 37% of U.S. workers had been bullied. The costs of workplace bullying to employers and insurers is estimated at $250 billion annually in the United States. This includes the costs of litigation, employee health care costs, accidents attributed to job stress–induced fatigue, and employee turnover and retraining (Workplace Bullying Institute, "How employers pay," n.d.).

The second reason for paying attention to the development of workplace mobbing policies is the central role that employers and workplaces play in the public health care system of the United States. The Institute of Medicine (2002), in its analysis of the future of public health in the 21st century, noted that employment and workplaces provide health-protective effects through income, job stability, and social ties but can also harm health through poor working conditions and job-related stress. By taking steps to prevent workplace mobbing and foster positive working environments, employers are actively promoting the nation's public health. This may be a good citizen or "do the right thing" reason, but economic advantages also accrue to businesses and organizations that make policy decisions to safeguard their workers' health. The Institute of Medicine (2002) stated that "employers should be concerned about the health and well-being of their employees for a number of reasons. Healthy employees consume fewer benefits in the form of benefit payments for medical care, short- and long-term disability, and workers' compensation. Furthermore, healthy employees are more productive than their nonhealthy counterparts because they are absent less often and are more focused on their tasks while at work" (p. 275).

The following sample organizational anti-mobbing policy provides an example of an anti-mobbing policy that is based on four key principles: the importance of reducing and eliminating a public health threat, the centrality of the organization in reducing and eliminating mobbing, the active valuing of diversity among employees, and tolerance for divergent points of view and respect for dissent. Our sample policy reflects essential components of an effective anti-mobbing policy. The goal of this sample policy is the elimination of mobbing. Effective anti-mobbing policies are aimed at abusive behaviors that cause harm to other workers. They should never be formulated or interpreted as attempts to reduce free speech or restrict the infinite and interesting varieties of human expression. This policy, like other effective anti-mobbing policies, is also not directed at policing differences of opinion or occasional conflict.

Sample Organizational Anti-Mobbing Policy

1. Purpose of the Policy

The purpose of this policy is to reaffirm our commitment to preventing workplace mobbing and all other forms of workplace abuse, and to intervene rapidly to end such abuses when they occur. Our organizational core values are integrity, dignity for all, transparency, and the active valuing of all our employees and clients/customers. In our commitment to tolerance and increasing organizational diversity, we include our commitment to respecting diverse and divergent points of view. We acknowledge the diversity of people and thought as a source of organizational vitality. We understand that well-meaning people may see and do things differently from one another. The principle upon which this policy rests is that conflict resolution is best achieved through conversation and dialogue.

2. Definition of Mobbing

We regard workplace mobbing and other forms of workplace abuse as a public health issue, potentially resulting in physical and/or psychological harm and injury to victims. We define workplace mobbing in the following way (see Chapter 3):

Workplace mobbing is nonsexual harassment of a coworker by a group of members of an organization for the purpose of removing the targeted individual(s) from the organization or at least a particular unit of the organization. Mobbing involves individual, group, and organizational dynamics. It predictably results in the humiliation, devaluation, discrediting, and degradation, loss of professional reputation and, often, removal of the target from the organization through termination, extended medical leave, or quitting. The results of this typically protracted traumatizing experience are significant financial, career, health, and psychosocial losses or other negative consequences. Mobbing has different levels of severity. In contrast to mobbing, bullying is abusive and harmful behavior directed at a specific target or targets by a single offender. The bully may be a peer or supervisor, but other members of the workgroup are not involved, although others may have observed the abuse. Unlike mobbing, there is little or no direct organizational involvement in the abusive behavior. In short, workplace mobbing and bullying can be conceptualized along a continuum of health and abusiveness, on which bullying is a less severe and encompassing form of abusiveness than mobbing.

3. Examples of Mobbing Behaviors

The following is a list of examples of mobbing behaviors with which workers at all levels in the organization should be aware. This list is provided to help all members of the organization participate in the maintenance of a positive workplace environment by refraining from participation in these types of behaviors:

a. Spreading false information about a worker
b. Failing to correct information known to be false about a worker
c. Spreading malicious gossip and rumors
d. Discrediting a person's workplace commitment and contribution
e. Making personal characterological attacks and invoking a person's private life in order to discredit the person
f. Belittling
g. Name-calling, in particular, using psychiatric or psychological labels to discredit and therefore isolate a worker from others

h. Attempting to turn other people against another worker by "whispering campaigns," organizing coalitions against another worker, and coordinating or participating in any other forms of covert attack on another member of the organization

i. Minimizing job-related competencies and exaggerating job-related limitations

j. Isolating a worker physically by separating him or her from coworkers or isolating a worker occupationally by not including him or her in communication loops required to do his or her job

k. Assigning unfair and unreasonable workloads and deadlines

l. Preventing a worker from obtaining necessary resources for the satisfactory completion of his or her duties

m. Sabotaging a worker's work product or ability to complete his or her work

n. Vandalizing the personal property of another worker, for example, defacing his or her photographs or breaking his or her mementos or decorations

o. Using abusive supervision, which includes making unsubstantiated negative comments about supervisees verbally to others and/or in writing in personnel evaluations

p. Making false claims of mobbing or abuse against another worker, for example, filing false workplace violence or harassment reports or using the tenets of this policy in bad faith to victimize another worker

4. Responsibilities for Insuring that Mobbing Does Not Occur

a. Individual employee responsibilities:

i. Understanding what mobbing is and the potential physical and psychological harm and injury that can result from it

ii. Attending required education programs about preventing mobbing

iii. Modeling respectful behavior to all other employees and demonstrating tolerance for the diversity of people and opinions within the organization

iv. Adhering to the guidelines of this policy

b. Management responsibilities:
All levels of management:

i. Acknowledging mobbing and other forms of abusive behavior as an organizational problem that will be handled effectively and decisively

ii. Modeling integrity and respectful behavior to all employees

iii. Selecting job applicants based on integrity and tolerance for diversity of people and thought

iv. Establishing integrity and tolerance as a performance standard for all, and rewarding integrity and tolerance in performance appraisal reviews

v. Ensuring that legitimate concerns or criticisms about an employee's behavior or performance are handled in an appropriate and respectful manner

Senior management:

i. Incorporating the creation and maintenance of a respectful workplace in the corporate strategic plan and then monitoring progress toward that end

ii. Ensuring the implementation of an anti-mobbing policy and training for all organizational employees

iii. Ensuring that adequate resources are provided to managers, confidential complaint contact persons (CCCPs), and human resources (HR) personnel for thorough and timely investigation of mobbing complaints, and resources for correction, treatment, and prevention

5. Procedures for Initiating Mobbing Complaints

Complaints of mobbing will be taken seriously and investigated thoroughly, fairly, and as speedily as possible. Fair and speedy resolution of mobbing complaints is in the best interests of all individual parties involved and of the organization. Since we recognize that mobbing can occur across all organizational levels, we have identified CCCPs for every category of management and staff within our organization. These contact persons have received education about mobbing and are also trained in informal conflict resolution procedures. They receive updated training annually, reflecting the commitment of our organization to remedy and prevent mobbing. Initial complaints should be directed to the appropriate contact person for your unit. They are listed in the personnel handbook. The contact persons are bound by confidentiality agreements.

6. Procedures for Resolving Mobbing Complaints

a. **Informal resolution option.** If agreeable to all involved parties, an informal resolution option for mobbing complaints is available. This option involves facilitated dialogue designed to address and resolve complaints of mobbing and to maintain the dignity of all parties.

b. **Alternative dispute resolution option.** Again, if all parties are agreeable, alternative dispute resolution options will be provided. These options include mediation with an outcome of a written negotiated agreement signed off on by all parties; restorative justice models, within which the victim will be restored to wholeness within the organization and those who participated in mobbing will be provided with strategies for change, such as contributing in specific ways to the fostering of positive workplace relationships; or use of other agreed-upon alternative dispute resolution models.

c. **Formal charge or grievance.** Descriptions of specific procedures for investigating formal charges of workplace mobbing are published in the personnel handbook. As an organization with a core value of transparency, how an investigation will be conducted, who will conduct it, and how evidence will be evaluated is described. By their nature, workplace investigations are stressful, and it is important that both the charging and charged parties have full access to information about the procedures involved in the conduct of a formal investigation from the outset.

7. Due Process and Confidentiality

Due process will be provided to all parties to a mobbing complaint, and the confidentiality of parties will be protected.

8. Time Frame

The organization, recognizing the erosive effects of mobbing on a victim, will conduct a thorough and fair investigation of charges of mobbing, but will do so in as short a period of time as is consistent with thoroughness and fairness.

9. Reporting of Findings

The findings of the investigation will be delivered to the charging and charged parties separately. They will be presented orally in the first instance, with each party given the opportunity to be accompanied and to have any questions that they may have answered. A written statement of findings will follow.

10. Accountability and Sanctions

A finding of workplace mobbing will result in the following: (a) an internal evaluation of the organizational context aimed at identifying and changing factors in the workplace that contributed to the mobbing episode, and (b) those found to be perpetrators of mobbing will be subject to either formal or informal sanctions.

11. Appeals Process

A process for appeal of the findings of a formal investigation is available to both the charging and charged parties. Appeal procedures are described in the personnel handbook. (Based on Duffy, 2009.)

Although we believe that all of the elements of the above policy are necessary, a few elements warrant further comment. The purpose statement expresses the organization's unequivocal commitment to eliminating mobbing. It also clearly affirms the organization's commitment to fostering diversity among employees and to respecting diverse and divergent points of view. This commitment to respecting diverse opinions is important because, in mobbing-prone organizations, dissent is not well tolerated. Anti-mobbing policies should expand an organization's understanding of diversity to include diverse ways of thinking and problem-solving. Mobbing-prone organizations are those most likely to silence dissent and to target dissenters. Anti-mobbing policies need to be written in such a way that they cannot be misused to target those who hold strong or minority views.

It is likely that as legislative efforts to enact healthy workplace laws proceed, more organizations will develop anti-mobbing and anti-bullying policies. Courts increasingly interpret organizational policies as part of the contract between the organization and employee (Yamada, 2007). Consequently, organizations may be held liable for harm done to victims of workplace mobbing. As awareness of the public health risk of workplace mobbing becomes more widespread, organizations are likely to be held liable for harm done to mobbing victims. Therefore, our sample organizational anti-mobbing policy includes a component addressing the responsibilities of all managers and the particular responsibilities of senior managers in ensuring that mobbing does not occur. Making management responsibilities explicit may at first glance seem to add a burden to managers and the organization. In fact, it does the opposite, by spelling out what actions managers will be held accountable for performing to prevent mobbing and foster a positive organizational climate. Proactive assumption by management of clearly defined responsibilities for preventing mobbing is much more likely to reduce both burden and liability.

Legislative Efforts to Prevent School and Workplace Mobbing and Bullying

School and workplace mobbing and bullying are recognized as public health problems in many countries around the world. In this section, we review the status of legislative efforts in the United States and around the world to prevent and eliminate mobbing and bullying. We look at legislative efforts to combat school mobbing and bullying and workplace mobbing and bullying separately.

U.S. School Bullying/Mobbing Legislation

At the federal level, H. R. 284 was proposed as an amendment to The Safe and Drug-Free Schools and Communities Act, which is part of the No Child Left Behind Act of 2001 (NCLB). The No Child Left Behind Act offers federal support for the promotion of school safety but does not specifically address school bullying and harassment. H. R. 284, as proposed, required states, school districts, and individual schools to develop anti-bullying and harassment prevention policies and programs as a condition of receiving federal funds. As of this writing, H. R. 284 has not become law.

In the United States, as of September 2008, 41 states had enacted legislation to prevent school bullying, harassment, and intimidation (National Conference of State Legislatures, Education Bill Tracking Database, Bullying, Harassment, and Intimidation, n.d.). As of 2008, 19 states have enacted cyber-bullying legislation as part of a larger anti-bullying law or as a separate cyber-bullying law. Cyber-bullying has provided some difficulties in use of language within the laws, and the terms "electronic communication," "electronic and Internet intimidation," and "cyber-bullying" have been settled on to designate a subcategory of bullying that is carried out over the Internet, through instant messaging, over the telephone, and through other electronic communications (National Conference of State Legislatures, Education Bill Tracking Database, Cyberbullying, n.d.).

Although these laws are intended to prohibit school bullying, there are large discrepancies in the ways in which "bullying" has been statutorily defined, the legislative principles underlying anti-bullying policy development, and the legislative mandates for prevention (Limber & Small, 2003; Srabstein, Berkman, & Pyntikova, 2008). In a study by Srabstein, Berkman, and Pyntikova (2008), of the 35 states that had school anti-bullying legislation at the time of their study, they found that only 16 of those states had enacted anti-bullying legislation that incorporated a systematic public health approach. They identified the following four components as necessary components of anti-bullying legislation from a public health perspective: "A clear definition of bullying, an explicit articulation of a bullying prohibition, implementation of prevention and treatment programs, and acknowledgment of the association between bullying and public health risks" (p. 15). We would like to see a day soon when "mobbing" is equally identified in legislative packages as the serious public health threat that it is.

Worldwide School Bullying/Mobbing Legislation

In 2002, Ananiadou and Smith (2002) surveyed the Ministries of Education or equivalent government bodies in all European Union member countries at the time and four associated countries to determine whether any legislation existed prohibiting school bullying. They were also interested in learning whether governments provided information to schools about bullying and bullying prevention programs. Many of the countries surveyed had national laws addressing and prohibiting school violence. A few countries had laws specifically addressing bullying.

The French community of Belgium (its own jurisdiction on educational matters), Germany, and Luxembourg had laws addressing school violence in a general way only. Finland, Malta, Sweden, and the United Kingdom had national educational laws prohibiting school bullying only. France and Ireland were the only countries of those studied that had national educational laws addressing both school violence in general and school bullying in particular. Austria, Denmark, Greece, Iceland, Italy, the Netherlands, Norway, Portugal, Spain, and Switzerland had no national educational laws addressing either school violence or school bullying.

Ananiadou and Smith's (2002) study is now several years old. Any legislative changes since that time adding the prohibition of school bullying to national educational laws would likely be a reflection of the increased body of knowledge about the consequences of school bullying and mobbing, greater media attention to the problem, and recognition of the negative health consequences suffered by victims of school bullying and mobbing that make the problem a national public health one.

Legislative Efforts in the United States to Prevent Workplace Bullying/Mobbing

Unlike in most countries of the European Union and Australia, there are currently no state or federal laws in the United States protecting workers from workplace bullying or mobbing. Ruth and Gary Namie of the Workplace Bullying Institute have worked with Suffolk University Law School professor David Yamada (2007) in crafting a bill known colloquially as The Healthy Workplace Bill. By 2009, some form of this bill had been written into legislation and introduced for legislative action in New York, Massachusetts, New Jersey, Vermont, Oklahoma, Utah, Illinois, Oregon, Connecticut, and Nevada. Since 2003, some form of the bill has been introduced, but not passed, in Washington State, Montana, Hawaii, California, Kansas, and Missouri (Workplace Bullying Institute, "Legal advocacy for workplace bullying laws," n.d.). This bill is the first in the United States to seek non–status based protections from psychological and physical harm for workplace victims of bullying and mobbing. Existing laws in the United States are status-based and protect workers from harassment and discrimination based on protected categories such as race, color, religion, sex, national origin, disability, and age.

Yamada's (2007) model bill is designed to protect workers from non–status based workplace harassment like bullying and mobbing, but is also crafted to discourage frivolous lawsuits. The core components of Yamada's model legislation include provision for compensation to those who can establish physical or psychological harm from workplace harassment, holding both individual employees and their employers liable for verified workplace harm to victims, encouraging employers to develop effective prevention policies and programs and to respond promptly and effectively to allegations of workplace bullying or mobbing, and providing incentives to employers for doing so.

Workplace Mobbing/Bullying Legislation Worldwide

In 2001, the European Parliament in its Resolution on Harassment at the Workplace 2001/2339 (INI; cited in Di Martino, Hoel, & Cooper, 2003) called on European Union member states to examine existing definitions and legislation involving workplace bullying and harassment, and encouraged its member states:

> To review and, if appropriate, to supplement their existing legislation and to review and standardise the definition of bullying; Urges the Commission to consider a clarification or extension of the scope of the framework directive on health and safety at work or, alternatively, the drafting of a new framework directive as a legal instrument to combat bullying and as a means of ensuring respect for the worker's human dignity, privacy, and integrity; emphasizes in this connection the importance of systematic work on health and safety and of preventive action. (p. 48)

Sixteen years ago, in 1993, Sweden was the first country to introduce anti-bullying and anti-mobbing legislation. The Swedish Work Environment Act affords protection to workers from physical and psychological harm in the workplace. In 1994, the Netherlands introduced the Working Conditions Act, which protects employees from physical and psychological workplace aggression. In 2002, France enacted legislation prohibiting sexual harassment and mobbing and introduced both civil and criminal penalties for violations. The French refer to mobbing as *moral harassment,* and their legislation against it places full responsibility on employers to protect employees from workplace mobbing. In Belgium, in 2002, legislation was enacted providing workers with protection from violence, moral harassment, and sexual harassment. The Belgian definition of moral harassment includes bullying and mobbing. Other European Union countries have collective bargaining agreements that include workplace harassment and psychological aggression in their provisions or have included injuries from workplace mobbing and workplace bullying under existing employment legislation (Di Martino et al., 2003).

The Quebec Labor Standards Law, enacted in Canada in 2004, was the first workplace law in North America against psychological harassment. In 2008, the federal Canadian Labour Code was revised to include workplace bullying as part of its provisions against workplace violence. In South Australia in 2005, the Occupational Health, Safety, and Welfare Act was revised to include provisions against workplace bullying and mobbing (Namie & Namie, 2009b).

The legislative movements in Europe, Canada, Australia, and more recently, the United States to prohibit workplace mobbing and bullying show an understanding of bullying and mobbing as public health issues and reflect efforts to improve overall working conditions for all workers. Recognizing the severe health consequences from workplace bullying and mobbing provides the link to acknowledging workplace mobbing and bullying as public health threats and occupational safety risks.

Legislation, whether for school or workplace, cannot by itself prevent mobbing. Legislation is not a panacea and must be part of a broad-based program to improve school and workplace culture, increase openness and transparency in organizational practices, and promote a sense of safety and security for all members of the school and organization. Legislation is also not without its own risks. According to Duffy (2009):

> The risk of introducing anti-mobbing or anti-bullying policies in low morale organizations marked by fear, mutual mistrust, and high levels of competitiveness is that the very policies instituted to prevent mobbing and bullying could be used to target high value employees perceived as threats by others. In addition, such organizations typically lack openness and transparency in the conduct of their internal procedures and operations and are therefore already more mobbing and bullying prone. (p. 250)

The positive side of anti-bullying, anti-mobbing legislation is that the health consequences are recognized as a public health threat and occupational safety risk. The down-side is that of unintended consequences and the risk of misuse of anti-bullying, anti-mobbing legislation to target high-value but idiosyncratic employees for elimination, and likewise to target challenging students for sanctions and/or expulsion. These risks are not trivial, and those charged with implementation of anti-mobbing, anti-bullying legislation at the local level should take them seriously.

Conclusion

In this chapter, we looked at how policy development and legislation can contribute to the prevention and reduction of school and workplace mobbing. We reviewed and analyzed two samples of anti-mobbing policies; namely, a school anti-mobbing policy and a workplace anti-mobbing policy. Anti-bullying policies do not address the group and organizational dynamics present in mobbing. Anti-bullying policies are therefore inadequate to address how organizational involvement in mobbing is manifested and the nature of the organization's responsibilities in stopping and preventing mobbing. Only anti-mobbing policies can tackle the complex interaction of individual, group, and organizational dynamics. How real-world anti-bullying and anti-mobbing policies will be implemented, tested, and evaluated remains an open question. Such policies are useful only to the extent that they are effective in preventing and reducing the overall frequency of mobbing and interrupting mobbing in progress. Policies will be most successful when they are paired with effective school- and organization-wide consciousness-raising, education, and training about the devastating processes of mobbing. We emphasize the need for policies to explicitly address the negative health consequences of mobbing and bullying, thus tying the problems to the public health issues that they are.

The status of legislative efforts to address bullying and mobbing varies from country to country and reflects the degree to which government is willing to hold individuals and organizations accountable for preventing bullying and mobbing. For example, in the United States, there is a much greater willingness to enact legislation aimed at preventing school bullying and mobbing than there is to enact workplace legislation, which is culturally regarded as placing unfair burdens on employers. However, advocacy efforts on behalf of healthy workplace bills have paid off, and they have been introduced in 16 states. In Europe, on the other hand, the situation is somewhat reversed. Workplace legislation that is either specific to mobbing or bullying or that includes anti-mobbing and anti-bullying provisions within existing legislation has been in place longer and is more fully developed than are educational laws proscribing bullying and violence within the schools.

When a child commits suicide after being mobbed or bullied, U.S. society appears much more willing to do something to prevent future mobbing or bullying in school settings than it does to prevent workplace mobbing after a series of workplace killings in which the killer has a history of being mobbed within an abusive workplace context. In the former, sentiment tends to center on blaming the bullies or mobbers; in the latter, sentiment overwhelmingly centers on blaming the "deranged lone killer." As we have discussed and illustrated throughout this book, both reactions fall short of the mark in terms of bringing about real change. Real change involves facing up to the role that organizations play in producing climates conducive to mobbing and bullying and in doing something about it.

16

Epilogue

Since narratives have temporality—a past, a present, and a future—it is important that remembering includes sharing visions of a changed future.
—Jaco J. Hamman (2005, p. 102)

Mobbing is an ubiquitous social process occurring in all of the major institutions and organizations of human life—school, work, religious organizations, the legal system, and even in communities where we live, like condominium and homeowners' associations. In the workplace, mobbing occurs during good times and bad, and we suspect that it is more likely to occur with impunity during bad times, when individuals and organizations are under the influence of multiple stressors and individuals feel relieved just to have a job. Mobbing can only be understood by analyzing the relationship between organizational elements, small group behavior, and individual reactions to stress and provocation. Looking only at individual behavior, or only at small group dynamics, or only at elements of organizational structure, function, and culture will lead inevitably to an incomplete and possibly misguided understanding of what is clearly a complex phenomenon. A systemic perspective is essential to avoid adding insult to injury by blaming victims for being mobbed.

The health impact of mobbing on adult workers and on children and adolescents in school is of an order of magnitude that cannot ethically be ignored. The literature about adverse health consequences from mobbing and bullying that we have gathered together provides a justification for a public health response to mobbing through the development of educational and interventional programs. Mobbing is a risk factor for poorer physical and mental health.

In mobbing episodes, the individual victim continues to bear the greatest burden and to suffer the most severe consequences. Prevention programs, the beginnings of anti-mobbing policy development, and alternative dispute resolution processes within high-care organizations committed to knowledge creation and the valuing of human capital show promise for preventing mobbing and effectively addressing it should it occur. Those without the good fortune to work or attend school in such high-care organizations are left to deal with the multiple negative consequences of mobbing on their own. Their therapists and health care providers have had few tools with which to organize effective interventions to help them recover. We sincerely hope that we have provided them with some of those tools in this book.

In Chapter 1, we introduced the case of Lee who worked in a nuclear power plant, and the case of Rachel Fannon whose story was documented by *ABC News*. Lee was mobbed at work, Rachel at school. The outcome for Lee was quite severe and prolonged in terms of shattering his self-confidence at work, tearing at his professional identity, and challenging his ethical principles and beliefs in a just world. We left Rachel Fannon's story where ABC did—after the revelation of 5 years of systematic physical and emotional abuse within more than one school, in which the teachers to whom she had turned for help reportedly did nothing other than offer her useless admonitions to be strong. We would like to end this book by returning to the stories of Lee and Rachel Fannon and imagining what might have happened and how they might have been treated differently if their organizations were aware of mobbing and had instituted anti-mobbing educational programs and policies.

In the case of Lee, his job structure and the organization's strategy for assessing safety outcomes were at odds. The metric in use was tabulating the number of deviations or errors identified and linking bonuses to reduction in those numbers. The metric was wrongly equated with safety. In fact, Lee's attention to detail in spotting deviations increased safety by allowing deviations to be assessed for their relative seriousness. Change in the organizational bonus system strategy would have removed pressure from both Lee and his coworkers, had the organization employed a more accurate indicator of safety than reduction in overall number of system deviations. Making this kind of a mistake in organizational strategy, by selecting an outcome metric that was not, in fact, a trustworthy indicator of safety, contributed to the mobbing of Lee and, ultimately, to a reduced safety environment. Change in the metric in use would undoubtedly have helped Lee, but the organizational culture also supported "ganging up" behaviors.

Organizational educational programs aimed at raising awareness of the nature of mobbing and its devastating health and occupational effects could have helped change the culture at the power plant, where ganging up on other workers was a common and thoughtless practice. In addition, an anti-mobbing policy that included a contact person or ombudsman to whom Lee could have shared his concerns would also have helped. Finally, after Lee found another job at a different power plant and started questioning his own judgments based on fear of a reprise of his previous mobbing experience, a therapist knowledgeable about mobbing and skilled in working with traumatized individuals would have been able to spot the unsuccessful flight behavior evident in Lee's new subjective decision-making that violated his own ethical principles. The therapist could have helped Lee to recognize and complete his unresolved flight response and to examine his options for improved functioning in his current job. With such organizational changes in place and his access to a skilled therapist, the outcome and future for Lee would have been much better.

Now let's return to Rachel Fannon. What needed to happen so that she would not have had to suffer for 5 years and end up with the emotional scars she described? Rachel said that she told teachers about the abuse she was experiencing at the hands of a group of other students. The teachers' responses, as reported, were decidedly unhelpful and placed the responsibility for changing the situation in Rachel's lap. Making victims responsible for changing the situation in which they are victimized is classic mobbing behavior on the part of organizational authorities, whether intended or not. It would have been next to impossible for Rachel to stop her mobbing. The teachers and administrators at Rachel's schools were responsible for stopping her mobbing—not Rachel by becoming "strong."

Teachers, as the first-responders in cases of mobbing, have huge responsibilities in conjunction with school administrators to protect children and adolescents from being mobbed. Teachers cannot be expected to exercise those responsibilities without proper training and skill building. We do not know whether Rachel's teachers went through systematic and recurrent training about recognizing and intervening in cases of mobbing. Effective and repeated training that emphasizes an organizational commitment to ending mobbing and bullying would have prepared teachers to do more than tell Rachel, as she reported, to be like an "Amazon woman."

Instead, as we imagine what might have been, the teachers and school administrators would have involved her parents, identified the group of other students involved in Rachel's mobbing, and insisted on the immediate cessation of all abusive behavior directed toward her, with clear penalties if the offending students failed to do so. They would also have provided Rachel with support and acknowledgment of the suffering she was experiencing. Rachel's schools apparently had anti-bullying policies in place. Those policies failed Rachel, as the school administrators involved reportedly acknowledged. Anti-mobbing and anti-bullying policies need to be reviewed and evaluated to ensure their full implementation and to assess effectiveness, with shortcomings identified and changed. We do not know whether this kind of policy review occurred in the schools Rachel attended.

In addition to teacher training and engagement, student engagement and buy-in to mobbing prevention programs must also be enlisted. Regular educational programs that describe mobbing and abusive behavior, that stake an unequivocal position against it, and that focus on the severe negative health and academic effects of mobbing are also necessary. None of these awareness and educational programs can be a one-time effort—these programs must be ongoing and reflect the absolute commitment of the school community to stop mobbing. We are aware of the multiple challenges and demands already placed on teachers who often work in less than ideal situations. It is the responsibility of the school community and school system to support teachers in becoming resensitized to the severity of school mobbing if we are genuinely interested in protecting our children.

It seems as if some of the formal elements were in place to protect Rachel Fannon from being mobbed, but they weren't enough. In reimagining what might have been different for Rachel, we imagine a menu of ongoing educational programs about mobbing involving the whole school community that would have created an environment in which both students and teachers would have stepped up to help her. We also imagine school counseling, in which Rachel would have revealed her situation to the counselor who would have immediately brought in her parents, contacted school administrators, and initiated a support and intervention process to end the abuse in its very early stages. That Rachel suffered for 5 years is both heartbreaking and unacceptable.

In the Preface to this book, we mentioned that the light in which we stand has been shed by the many researchers and scholars who have taken up the subjects of mobbing, bullying, and workplace abuse. It has been our intention to add to that light about mobbing, so that we can continue to work to understand it better and, most importantly, to stop it and help those affected by it. Where mobbing is concerned, as part of the professional community, we look toward a changed future with increased awareness of the process of mobbing and increased resources for its victims and those organizations and professionals interested in stopping it

References

Adams, A. (1992). *Bullying at work: How to confront and overcome it.* London: Virago Press.

Adizes, I. (1979). Organizational passages: Diagnosing and treating life cycle problems in organizations. *Organizational Dynamics, 9*(1), 3–24.

Adizes, I. (1988). *Managing corporate lifecycles.* Upper Saddle River, NJ: Prentice Hall.

Adizes, I. (1999). *Managing corporate lifecycles* (Rev. ed.). Upper Saddle River, NJ: Prentice Hall.

Adoric, V. C., & Kvartuc, T. (2007). Effects of mobbing on justice beliefs and adjustment. *European Psychologist, 12*(4), 261–271.

Albini, E., Benedetti, L., Giordano, S., Punzi, S., & Cassito, M. G. (2003). Dysfunctional workplace organization and mobbing: Four representative cases. *La Medicina del Lavoro [Workplace medicine], 96*, 432–439.

Allan, E., & Madden, M. (2008). *Hazing in view: College students at risk: Initial findings of the National Study of Student Hazing.* Retrieved from www.hazingstudy.org

Ananiadou, K., & Smith, P. K. (2002). Legal requirements and nationally circulated materials against school bullying in European countries. *Criminology and Criminal Justice, 2*(4), 471–491.

American Psychiatric Association. (2000). Diagnostic and statistical manual of mental disorders (4th ed., text revision). Washington, DC: Author.

Anderson, C. R., & Zeithaml, C. P. (1984). Stage of product life cycle, business strategy, and business performance. *Academy of Management Journal, 27*, 5–24.

Andersson, L. M., & Pearson, C. M. (1999). Tit for tat? The spiraling effect of incivility in the workplace. *Academy of Management Review, 24*, 452–471.

Ando, M., Asakura, T., & Simons-Morton, B. (2005). Psychosocial influences on physical, verbal, and indirect bullying among Japanese early adolescents. *Journal of Early Adolescence, 25*(3), 268–297.

Arseneault, L., Walsh, E., Trzesniewski, K., Newcombe, R., Caspi, A., & Moffit, T. E. (2006). Bullying victimization uniquely contributes to adjustment problems in young children: A nationally representative cohort study. *Pediatrics, 118*(1), 130–138.

Atlas, R. S., & Pepler, D. J. (1998). Observations of bullying in the classroom. *Journal of Educational Research, 92*(2), 86–99.

Arendt, H. (1963). *Eichmann in Jerusalem: A report on the banality of evil.* London: Faber & Faber.

Arendt, H. (1978). *The life of the mind: The groundbreaking investigation of how we think.* Orlando, FL: Harcourt.

Barnes, J., & Chong, J. (2009). Army sees sharp rise in suicide rate. *Los Angeles Times.* Retrieved from http://www.latimes.com/features/health/la-na-army-suicides30–2009jan30,0,6065061.story

Baron, R. A., & Neuman, J., H. (1996). Workplace violence and workplace aggression: Evidence on their relative frequency and potential causes. *Aggressive Behavior, 22*, 161–173.

Baron, R. A., & Neuman, J., H. (1998). Workplace aggression—the iceberg beneath the tip of workplace violence: Evidence on its forms, frequency, and targets. *Public Administration Quarterly, 21*, 446–464.

Bauer, N., Lozano, P., & Rivara, F. P. (2007). The effectiveness of the Olweus Bullying Prevention Program in public middle schools: A controlled trial. *Journal of Adolescent Health, 40,* 266–274.

Bateson, G. (2000). *Steps to an ecology of mind.* (Reissued ed.). Chicago: University of Chicago Press.

Batsche, G. M., & Knoff, H. M. (1994). Bullies and their victims: Understanding a pervasive problem in the schools. *School Psychology Review, 23,* 165–174.

Becker, B. E., Huselid, M. A., & Ulrich, D. (2001). The HR scorecard: Linking people, strategy, and performance. Boston: Harvard Business School Press.

Becvar, D. S., & Becvar, R. J. (2000). *Family therapy: A systemic integration* (4th ed.). Boston: Allyn & Bacon.

Bellah, R., Madsen, R., Sullivan, W., Swidler, L., & Tipton, S. (1985). *Habits of the heart: Individualism and commitment in American life.* New York: Harper & Row.

Bennis, W., & Nanus, B. (1986). *Leaders: Strategies for change* (2nd ed.). New York: Harper Business.

Beran, T., & Tutty, L. (2002). Children's reports of bullying and safety at school. *Canadian Journal of School Psychology, 17,* 1–14.

Bernardi, L. M. (2001). Management by bullying: The legal consequences. *Canadian Manager, 2(3),* 13–14.

Besag, V. (1989). *Bullies and victims in schools: A guide to understanding and management.* London: Open University Press.

Beverland, M., & Lockshin, L. S. (2001). Organizational life cycles in small New Zealand wineries. *Journal of Small Business Management, 39(4),* 354–362.

Birley, J. J. (2002). Political abuse of psychiatry in the Soviet Union and China: A rough guide for bystanders. *The Journal of the American Academy of Psychiatry and the Law, 30(1),* 145- 147.

Blueprint for Violence Prevention (2002–2004). *Blueprints model programs: Olweus bullying prevention program.* Retrieved from http://www.colorado.edu/cspv/blueprints/model/programs/BPP.html

Boals, A., & Schuettler, D. (2009). PTSD symptoms in response to traumatic and non-traumatic events: The role of respondent perception and A2 criterion. *Journal of Anxiety Disorders, 23,* 458–462.

Bodkin, J. A., Pope, H. G., Detke, M. J., & Hudson, J. I. (2007). Is PTSD caused by traumatic stress? *Journal of Anxiety Disorders, 21,* 176–182.

Bolt, J. (2005). Essays in response. In K. Westhues (Ed.), *The envy of excellence: Administrative mobbing of high-achieving professors* (pp. 100–119). Lewiston, NY: The Tribunal for Academic Justice/Edwin Mellen Press.

Bosacki, S. L., Marini, Z. A., & Dane, A. V. (2006). Voices from the classroom: Pictorial and narrative representations of children's bullying experiences. *Journal of Moral Education, 35(2),* 231–245.

Boyce, T., & Geller, E. (2001). Applied behavior analysis and organizational safety: The challenge of response maintenance. *Journal of Organizational Behavior Management, 21,* 31–60.

Boyer, P., & Nissenbaum, S. (1974). *Salem possessed: The social origins of witchcraft.* Cambridge, MA: Harvard University Press.

Boyes-Watson, C. (2008). *Peacemaking circles and urban youth.* St. Paul, MN: Living Justice Press.

Breire, J., & Scott, C. (2006). *Principles of trauma therapy: A guide to symptoms, evaluation, and treatment.* Thousand Oaks, CA: Sage.

Bremner, J. D. (1999). Acute and chronic responses to psychological trauma: Where do we go from here? *American Journal of Psychiatry, 156,* 349–351.

Brodsky, C. (1976). *The harassed worker.* Lexington, MA: Lexington Books.

Bueno de Mesquita, B. (2009). *The predictioneer's game.* New York: Random House.

Bultena, C. D., & Whatcott, R. B. (2008). Bushwhacked at work: A comparative analysis of mobbing and bullying at work. *Proceedings of the American Society of Business and Behavioral Sciences, 15(1),* 652–666.

Bureau of Labor Statistics, United States Department of Labor. (2007). *Nonfatal occupational injuries and illnesses requiring days away from work.* Retrieved from http://stats.bls.gov/iif/oshwc/osh/case/osnr0031.pdf

Bureau of Labor Statistics, United States Department of Labor. (n.d.). *Occupational safety and health definitions.* Retrieved from http://www.bls.gov/iif/oshdef.htm

Burnes, B., & Pope, R. (2007). Negative behaviors in the workplace: A study of two primary care trusts in the NHS. *International Journal of Public Sector Management, 20*(4), 285–303.

Campbell, C. R. (2004). A longitudinal study of one organization's culture: Do values endure? *Mid-American Journal of Business, 19*(2), 41–51.

Carney, A. G., & Merrell, K. W. (2001). Bullying in schools: Perspective on understanding and preventing an international problem. *School Psychology International, 22*(3), 364–382.

Cassitto, M. G., & Gilioli, R. (2003). Emerging aspects of occupational stress. *La Medicina del Lavoro [Workplace medicine], 94*(1), 108–113.

Ceci, S. J., & Bruck, M. (1995). *Jeopardy in the courtroom.* Washington, DC: American Psychological Association.

Chandler, A. D. (1962). *Strategy and structure.* Cambridge, MA: MIT Press.

Chapman, S. (2009). *The no gossip zone: A no-nonsense guide to a healthy, high-performing work environment.* Naperville, IL: Sourcebooks.

Chappell, D., & Di Martino, V. (2006). *Violence at work* (3rd ed.). Geneva: International Labor Office.

Chen, W. -C., Hwu, H. -G., Kung, S. -M., Chiu, H. -J., & Wang, J. -D. (2008). Prevalence and determinants of workplace violence of health care workers in a psychiatric hospital in Taiwan. *Journal of Occupational Health, 50*, 288–293.

Chung, C. (Reporter). (2001, November 28). *Bullies* [20/20]. New York: ABC News.

Churchill, N., & Lewis, V. (1983). The five stages of small business growth. *Harvard Business Review, 61*(3), 30–50.

Cleckley, H. (1976). *The mask of sanity* (5th ed.). St. Louis: Mosby.

Cohen, J., & Mannarino, A. (2004). Treatment of childhood traumatic grief. *Journal of Clinical Child and Adolescent Psychology, 33*, 819–831.

Collins, K., Mc Aleavy, G., & Adamson, G. (2002). *Bullying in schools: A Northern Ireland study. Research Report Series No. 30.* Bangor, Northern Ireland: Department of Education for Northern Ireland.

Collins, K., Mc Aleavy, G., & Adamson, G. (2004). Bullying in schools: A Northern Ireland study. *Educational Research, 46*, 55–71.

Conference Board. (2005, February 28). *U.S. job satisfaction keeps falling, the Conference Board reports today.* News Release. Retrieved from http://www.allbusiness.com/accounting/3487347–1.html

Conger, J., & Kanungo, R. (1998). *Charismatic leadership in organizations.* Thousand Oaks, CA: Sage.

Cook, A., Spinazzola, J., Ford, J., Lanktree, C., Blaustein, M., Cloitre, M., et al. (2005). Complex trauma in children and adolescents. *Psychiatric Annals, 35*(5), 390–398.

Corbin, J. M., & Strauss, A. L. (2008). *Basics of qualitative research: Techniques and procedures for developing grounded theory* (3rd ed.). Thousand Oaks, CA: Sage.

Corney, B. (2008). Aggression in the workplace: A study of horizontal violence utilising Heideggerian hermeneutic phenomenology. *Journal of Health Organization and Management, 22*(2), 164–177.

Cortina, L. M., Magley, V. J., Williams, J. H., & Langhout, R. D. (2001). Incivility in the workplace: Incidence and Impact. *Journal of Occupational Health Psychology, 6*, 64–80.

Costello, E. J. (1992). The mediation alternative in sex harassment cases. *Arbitration Journal, 47*, 16–23.

Cotton, P., & Hart, P. M. (2003). Occupational wellbeing and performance: A review of organisational health research. *Australian Psychologist, 38*(2), 118–127.

Coyle, H. (2008). School culture benchmarks: Bridges and barriers to successful bullying prevention program implementation. *Journal of School Violence, 7*(2), 105–122.

Crawshaw, L. (2007). *Taming the abrasive manager: How to end unnecessary roughness in the workplace.* San Francisco: Jossey-Bass.

Cropley, M., Derk-jan, D., & Stanley, N. (2006). Job strain, work rumination, and sleep in school teachers. *European Journal of Work and Organizational Psychology, 15*, 129–240.

Currier, J. (2008, July 1). Gov. Blunt signs law against cyber-bullying. *St. Louis Post-Dispatch*, p. D3.

Crawford, A., & Newburn, T. (2003). *Youth offending and restorative justice: Implementing reform in youth justice.* Cullompton, Devon, UK: Willan Publishing.

Dalbert, C. (2001). *The justice motive as a personal resource: Dealing with challenges and critical life events.* New York: Kluwer/Plenum.

Davenport, N. Z., Schwartz, R. D., & Elliott, G. P. (1999). *Mobbing: Emotional abuse in the American workplace.* Collins, IA: Civil Society Publishing.

Davidson, J., & Caddell, D. (1994). Religion and the meaning of work. *Journal for the Scientific Study of Religion, 33*, 135–147.

Deal, T. E., & Kennedy, A. A. (1982). *Corporate cultures: The rites and rituals of corporate life.* Reading, MA: Addison-Wesley.

Dekker, S., & Schaufeli, W. (1995). The effects of job insecurity on psychological health and withdrawal: A longitudinal study. *Australian Psychologist, 30*, 57–63.

De la Torre, V. (2009, January 27). Expelled teen withdraws motion in lawsuit vs. Miss Porter's School. *Hartford Courant*, p. A7.

Denenberg, R., & Braverman, M. (1999). *The violence prone workplace: A new approach to dealing with hostile, threatening and uncivil behavior.* Ithaca, NY: Cornell University Press.

Denborough, D. (Ed.). (2006). *Trauma narrative responses to traumatic experiences.* Adelaide, Australia: Dulwich Centre Publications.

De Vogli, R., Ferrie, J. E., Chandola, T., Kivimäki, M., & Marmot, M. G. (2007). Unfairness and health: Evidence from the Whitehall II Study. *Journal of Epidemiology and Community Health, 61*(3), 513–518.

De Witte, H. (1999). Job insecurity and psychological wellbeing: Review of the literature and exploration of some unresolved issues. *European Journal of Work and Organizational Psychology, 8*, 155–177.

Djurkovic, N., McCormack, D., & Casimir, G. (2005). The behavioral reactions of victims to different types of workplace bullying. *International Journal of Organization Theory and Behavior, 8*(4), 439–460.

Di Martino, V., Hoel, H., & Cooper, C. L. (2003). *Preventing violence and harassment in the workplace.* (European Foundation for the Improvement of Living and Working Conditions). Luxembourg: Office for Official Publications of the European Communities.

Dodge, H. J., Fullerton, S., & Robbins, J. E. (1994). Stage of the organizational life cycle and competition as mediators of problem perception for small businesses. *Strategic Management Journal, 15*, 121–134.

Dodge, H. J., & Robbins, J. E. (1992). An empirical investigation of the organizational life cycle model for small business development and survival. *Journal of Small Business Management, 30*(1), 27–37.

Duffy, M. (2009). Preventing workplace mobbing and bullying with effective organizational consultation, policies and legislation. *Consulting Psychology Journal: Practice and Research, 61*(3), 242–262.

Duffy, M., Giordano, V., Farrell, J., Paneque, O., & Crump. G. B. (2008). No child left behind: Values and research issues in high-stakes assessments. *Counseling and Value, 53*, 53–66.

Duffy, M., & Sperry, L. (2007). Workplace mobbing: Individual and family health consequences. *The Family Journal, 15*, 398–404.

Dungan, F. (2002). *Bushwhacked.* New York: Publish America.

Dussich, J. P. J., & Maekoya, C. (2007). Physical child harm and bullying-related behaviors: A comparative study in Japan, South Africa, and the United States. *International Journal of Offender Therapy and Comparative Criminology, 51*(5), 495–509.

Edelman, M. (2005). How to prevent high school hazing: A legal, ethical and social primer. *North Dakota Law Review.* 81 N. Dak. L. Rev. 309.

Einarsen, S. (1998). Bullying at work: The Norwegian lesson. In C. Rayner, M. Sheehan, & M. Barker (Eds.), *Bullying at work 1998 research update conference: Proceedings.* Stafford: Staffordshire University.

Einarsen, S. (1999). The nature and causes of bullying. *International Journal of Manpower, 20*, 16–27.

Einarsen, S., Aasland, M. S., & Skogstad, A. (2007). Destructive leadership behaviour: A definition and conceptual model. *The Leadership Quarterly, 18*, 207–216.

Einarsen, S., Hoel, H., Zapf, D., & Cooper, C. L. (Eds.). (2003a). *Bullying and emotional abuse in the workplace: International perspectives in research and practice.* London: Taylor & Francis.

Einarsen, S., Hoel, H., Zapf, D. & Cooper, C. (2003b). The concept of bullying at work. In S. Einarsen, H. Hoel, D. Zapf, & C. Cooper (Eds.), *Bullying and emotional abuse in the workplace: International perspectives in research and practice* (pp. 3–30). London: Taylor & Francis.

Einarsen, S., Matthiesen, S. B., & Skogstad, A. (1998). Bullying, burnout and well-being among assistant nurses. *The Journal of Occupational and Health Safety—Australia and New Zealand, 14*(6), 563–568.

Einarsen, S., & Mikkelsen, E. G. (2003). Individual effects of exposure to bullying at work. In S. Einarsen, H. Hoel, D. Zapf, & C. L. Cooper (Eds.), *Bullying and emotional abuse in the workplace: International perspectives in research and practice* (pp. 127–144). London: Taylor & Francis.

Einarsen, S., & Raknes, B., I. (1991). *Mobbing i arbeidslivet [Bullying at work].* Bergen, NO: Research Centre for Occupational Health and Safety, University of Bergen.

Einarsen, S., Raknes, B., I., & Matthiesen, S., B. (1994). Bullying and harassment at work and their relationships to work environment quality: An exploratory study. *The European Work and Organizational Psychologist, 4*, 381–401.

Einarsen, S., Raknes, B. I., Matthiesen, S. B., & Hellesoy, O. H. (1994). *Bullying and severe interpersonal conflict: Unhealthy interaction at work.* Soreidgrend, NO: Sigma Forlag.

Einarsen, S., & Skogstad, A. (1996). Prevalence and risk groups of bullying and harassment at work. *European Journal of Work and Organizational Psychology, 5*, 185–202.

Eisenberg, M. E., & Aalsma, M. C. (2005). Bullying and peer victimization: Position paper of the Society for Adolescent Medicine. *Journal of Adolescent Health, 36*, 88–91.

Eisenberg, M. E., Neumark-Sztainer, D., & Perry, C. (2003). Peer harassment, school connectedness and school success. *Journal of School Health, 73*, 311–316.

Elliott, G. P. (2003). *School mobbing and emotional abuse: See it—stop it—prevent it with dignity and respect.* New York: Brunner-Routledge.

Elkington, J., & Hartigan, P. (2008). *The power of unreasonable people: How social entrepreneurs create markets that change the world.* Boston: Harvard Business Press.

Espelage, D. L., & Asidao, C. S. (2001). Conversations with middle school students about bullying and victimization: Should we be concerned? *Journal of Emotional Abuse, 2*(2), 49–62.

Fanti, K. A., Frick, P. J., & Georgiou, S. (2009). Linking callous-unemotional traits to instrumental and non-instrumental forms of aggression. *Journal of Psychopathology and Behavioral Assessment, 31*, 285–298.

Farrington, D. P. (1993). Understanding and preventing bullying. In M. Tonry (Ed.), *Crime and justice.* Vol. 17 (pp. 381–458). Chicago: University of Chicago Press.

Fekkes, M., Pijpers, F. I. M., & Verloove-Vanhorick, S. P. (2005). Bullying: Who does what, when and where? Involvement of children, teachers and parents in bullying behavior. *Health Education Research: Theory and Practice, 20*(1), 81–91.

Ferris, P. (2004). A preliminary typology of organizational response to allegations of workplace bullying: See no evil, hear no evil, speak no evil. *British Journal of Guidance and Counselling, 32*, 389–395.

Ferris, P. (2009). The role of the consulting psychologist in the prevention, detection, and correction of bullying and mobbing in the workplace. *Consulting Psychology Journal: Practice and Research, 61*(3), 169–189.

Flambolz, E., & Randle, Y. (2000). *Growing pains: Transitioning from an entrepreneurial to a professional managed firm.* San Francisco: Jossey-Bass.

Follett, K. (2007). *World without end.* New York: Dutton.

Forero, R., McLellan, L., Rissell, C., & Bauman, A. (1999). Bullying behaviour and psychosocial health among school students in New South Wales, Australia: Cross sectional survey. *British Medical Journal, 319*, 344–348.

Fosha, D. (2003). Dyadic regulation and experiential work with emotion and relatedness in trauma and disorganized attachment. In M. F. Solomon, & D. J. Siegel (Eds.), *Healing trauma: Attachment, mind, body, and brain* (pp. 221–281). New York: Norton.

Fox, S., & Stallworth, L., E. (2009). Building a framework for two internal organizational approaches to resolving and preventing workplace bullying: Alternative dispute resolution and training. *Consulting Psychology Journal: Practice and Research, 61*(3), 220–241.

Friedenberg, J. E. (2008, April 11). *The anatomy of an academic mobbing.* The First Hector Hammerly Memorial Lecture on Academic Mobbing. The University of Waterloo, Ontario, Canada. Retrieved from http://arts.uwaterloo.ca/~kwesthue/frieden-hh.htm

Friedland, L., & Friedland, D. (1994). Workplace harassment: What mental health practitioners need to know. In L. Vandecreek, S. Knapp, & T. Jackson (Eds.), *Innovations in clinical practice: A sourcebook* (pp. 237–253). Sarasota, FL: Professional Resource Press.

Frick, P. J., & White, S. F. (2008). The importance of callous unemotional traits for the development of aggressive and antisocial behavior. *Journal of Child Psychology and Psychiatry, 49*, 359–375.

Garofalo, R., Wolf, R. C., Kessel, S., Palfrey, S. J., & DuRant, R. H. (1998). The association between health risk behaviors and sexual orientation among a school-based sample of adolescents. *Pediatrics, 101*, 895–902.

Garfinkel, H. (1956). Conditions of successful degradation ceremonies. *American Journal of Sociology, 61*, 420–424.

Garrett, A. G. (2003). *Bullying in American schools: Causes, preventions, interventions.* Jefferson, NC: McFarland & Co., Inc.

Garven, S., Wood, J. M., & Malpass, R. S. (2000). Allegations of wrongdoing: The effects of reinforcement on children's mundane and fantastic claims. *Journal of Applied Psychology, 85*(1), 38–49.

Gates, G. (2004, October). Bullying and mobbing (Part 2). *Labor Management,* p. 31.

Gini, G., & Pozzoli, T. (2009). Association between bullying and psychosomatic problems: A meta-analysis. *Pediatrics, 123*(3), 1059–1065.

Girardi, P., Monaco, E., Prestigiacomo, C., Talamo, A., Ruberto, A., & Tatarelli, R. (2007). Personality and psychopathological profiles in individuals exposed to mobbing. *Violence and Victims, 22*(2), 172–188.

Glad, B. (2002). When tyrants go too far: Malignant narcissism and absolute power. *Political Psychology, 23*(1), 1–37.

Gold, S. D., Marx, B. P., Soler-Baillo, J. M., & Sloan, D. M. (2005). Is life stress more traumatic than traumatic stress? *Journal of Anxiety Disorders, 19*, 687–698.

Golden, T. (2003). Foreword. In G. P. Elliott (Ed.), *School mobbing and emotional abuse: See it—stop it—prevent it with dignity and respect* (pp. xiii–xvi). New York: Brunner-Routledge.

Greiner, L. (1972). Evolution and revolution as organizations grow. *Harvard Business Review, 50*, 37–46.

Griffin, R. S., & Gross, A. M. (2004). Childhood bullying: Current empirical findings and future directions for research. *Aggression and Violent Behavior, 9*, 379–400.

Gruber, J. E., & Fineran, S. (2008). Comparing the impact of bullying and sexual harassment victimization on the mental and physical health of adolescents. *Sex Roles, 59*, 1–13.

Gupta, Y. P., & Chin, D. C. W. (1994). Organizational life cycle: A review and proposed directions for research. *The Mid-Atlantic Journal of Business, 30*(3), 269–294.

Hallett, T., Harger, B., & Eder, D. (2009). Gossip at work: Unsanctioned evaluative talk in formal school meetings. *Journal of Contemporary Ethnography, 38.5*, 584–618.

Hamman, J. J. (2005). *When steeples cry: Leading congregations through loss and change.* Cleveland: Pilgrim Press.

Hammond, D. C. (2005). Neurofeedback with affective and anxiety disorders. *Child and Adolescent Psychiatric Clinics of North America, 14*, 105–123.

Hanish, L. D., & Guerra, N. G. (2000). Children who get victimized at school: What is known? What can be done? *Professional School Counseling, 4*(2), 113–119.

Harrington, S. O. (2007). *Seeking understanding from inconsistency: An exploration of human resource management's response to bullying.* Paper presented at the 1st Portuguese Conference on Workplace Bullying: Increasing Awareness of Workplace Bullying: Concepts, research and solutions. Technical University of Lisbon, Portugal.

Harris, S. (2004). Bullying at school among older adolescents. *The Prevention Researcher, 11*(2), 12–14.

Hart, P. M., & Cooper, C. L. (2001). Occupational stress: Toward a more integrated framework. In N. Anderson, D. S. Ones, H. K. Sinangil, & C. Viswesvaran (Eds.), *Handbook of industrial, work and organisational psychology.* Vol. 2 (pp. 93–114). London: Sage.

Harter, J. K., Schmidt, F. L., & Keyes, C. L. (2003). Well-being in the workplace and its relationship to business outcomes: A review of the Gallup Studies. In C. L. Keyes, & J. Haidt (Eds.), *Flourishing: Positive psychology and the life well-lived* (pp. 205–224). Washington, DC: American Psychological Association.

Hartig, K., & Frosch, J. (2006, July). *Workplace mobbing syndrome: The "silent and unseen" occupational hazard.* Paper presented at Our Work . . . Our Lives: National Conference on Women and Industrial Relations, Brisbane, Australia.

Hecker, T. E. (2007). Workplace mobbing: A discussion for librarians. *The Journal of Academic Librarianship, 33*(4), 439–445.

Heinemann, P. -P. (1972). *Mobbning-Gruppvåld bland barn och vuxen [Mobbing: Group violence by children and adults].* Stockholm: Natur och Kultur.

Herman, J. (1997). *Trauma and recovery: The aftermath of violence—from domestic abuse to political terrorism.* New York: Basic Books.

Hershcovis, M. S., & Barling, J. (2008). *Comparing the outcomes of sexual harassment and workplace aggression: A meta-analysis.* Working paper, available from the authors at the University of Manitoba and Queen's University respectively.

Hillard, J. R. (2009). Workplace mobbing: Are they really out to get your patient? *Current Psychiatry, 8*(4), 45–51.

Hochschild, A. R. (1997). *The time bind: When work becomes home and home becomes work.* New York: Metropolitan Books.

Hodson, R. (2001). *Dignity at work.* New York: Cambridge University Press.

Hodson, R., Roscigno, V., & Lopez, S. (2006). Chaos and the abuse of power: Workplace bullying in organizational and interactional context. *Work and Occupations, 33*(4), 382–416.

Hoel, H., Faragher, B., & Cooper, C. L. (2004). Bullying is detrimental to health, but all bullying behaviors are not necessarily equally damaging. *British Journal of Guidance and Counselling, 32*(3), 367–387.

Hoel, H., & Salin, D. (2003). Organisational antecedents of workplace bullying. In S. Einarsen, H. Hoel, D. Zapf, & C. L. Cooper (Eds.), *Bullying and emotional abuse in the workplace: International perspectives in research and practice* (pp. 203–218). London: Taylor & Francis.

Hoffman, D. (2006). The future of ADR practice: Three hopes, three fears, and three predictions. *Negotiation Journal, 22,* 467–473.

Hofstede, G. (1991). *Cultures and organizations: Software of the mind.* New York: McGraw–Hill.

Hong, J. (2009). Feasibility of the Olweus Bullying Prevention Program in low-income schools. *Journal of School Violence, 8*(1), 81–97.

Hood, S. B. (2004). Workplace bullying. *Canadian Business, 77*(3), 87–89.

Hoover, J. H., Oliver, R., & Hazler, R., J. (1992). Bullying: Perceptions of adolescent victims in Midwestern USA. *School Psychology International, 13,* 5–16.

Hornstein, H. A. (1996). *Brutal bosses and their prey: How to identify and overcome abuse in the workplace.* New York: Riverhead Books.

Institute of Medicine, Board on Health Promotion and Disease Prevention. (2002). *The future of the public's health in the twenty-first century.* Washington, DC: The National Academies Press.

Ironside, M., & Seifert, R. (2003). Tackling bullying in the workplace. In S. Einarsen, H. Hoel, D. Zapf, & C. L. Cooper (Eds.), *Bullying and emotional abuse in the workplace: International perspectives in research and practice* (pp. 383–398). London: Taylor & Francis.

Janssen, I., Craig, W. M, Boyce, W. F., & Pickett, W. (2004). Associations between overweight and obesity with bullying behaviors in school-aged children. *Pediatrics, 113,* 1187–1194.

Jaques, E., & Clement, S. (1991). *Executive leadership: A practical guide to managing complexity.* Cambridge, MA: Blackwell Business.

Jawahar, I. M., & McLaughlin, G., L. (2001). Toward a descriptive stakeholder theory: An organizational life cycle approach. *The Academy of Management Review, 26*(3), 397–414.

Jeffrey, L. R. (2004). Bullying bystanders. *The Prevention Researcher, 11*(4), 7–8.

Jennifer, D., Cowie, H., & Anaiadou, K. (2003). Perceptions and experience of workplace bullying in five different working populations. *Aggressive Behavior, 29*, 489–496.

Jensvold, M. F. (1993). Workplace sexual harassment: The use, misuse, and abuse of psychiatry. *Psychiatric Annals, 23*, 438.

Jezebel. (2007, November 15). Are the parents who My-Space tormented Megan Meier into killing herself ready to atone? Retrieved from http://jezebel.com/gossip/drew-no-blood/are-the-parents-who-myspace+tormented-megan-meier-into-killing-herself-ready-to-atone-um-323254.php

Jones, E. E. (1979). The rocky road from acts to dispositions. *American Psychologist, 34*, 107–117.

Jones, E. E. (1990). *Interpersonal perception.* New York: Macmillan.

Jones, E. E., & Harris, V. A. (1967). The attribution of attitudes. *Journal of Experimental Social Psychology, 3*, 1–24.

Josipović-Jelić, Z., Stoini, E., & Celić-Bunikić, S. (2005). The effects of mobbing on medical staff performance. *Acta Clinica Croatica, 44*(4), 347–352.

Judge, T. A., & Watanabe, S. (1993). Another look at the job satisfaction-life satisfaction relationship. *Journal of Applied Psychology, 78*(6), 939–948.

Juvonen, J., & S. Graham. (Eds.). (2001). *Peer harassment in school: The plight of the vulnerable and victimized.* New York: Guilford Press.

Juvonen, J., & Graham, S. (2004). Research-based interventions on bullying. In C. E. Sanders, & G. D. Phye (Eds.), *Bullying: Implications for the classroom* (pp. 229–255). London: Elsevier Academic Press.

Juvonen, J., Nishina, A., & Graham, S. (2000). Peer harassment, psychological adjustment, and school functioning in early adolescence. *Journal of Educational Psychology, 92*, 349–359.

Juvonen, J., Nishina, A., & Graham, S. (2001). Self-views versus peer perceptions of victim status among early adolescents. In J. Juvonen, & S. Graham (Eds.), *Peer harassment in schools: The plight of the vulnerable and victimized* (pp.105–124). New York: The Guilford Press.

Kaiser Family Foundation and Children Now. (2001). *Talking with kids about tough issues: A national survey of parents and kids.* Menlo Park, CA: Kaiser Family Foundation.

Karasek, R., & Theorell, T. (1990). *Healthy work: Stress, productivity and the reconstruction of working life.* New York: Basic Books.

Karatzias, A., Power, K.G., & Swanson, V. (2002). Bullying and victimisation in Scottish secondary schools: Same or separate entities? *Aggressive Behavior, 28*, 45–61.

Katz, D., & Kahn, R. L. (1966). *The social psychology of organizations.* New York: John Wiley & Sons.

Katz, D., & Kahn, R. L. (1978). *The social psychology of organizations* (2nd ed.). New York: John Wiley & Sons.

Kazanjian, R. K. (1988). The relation of dominant problems to stage of growth in technology-based new ventures. *Academy of Management Journal, 31*, 257–279.

Keashley, L. (1998). Emotional abuse in the workplace: Conceptual and empirical issues. *Journal of Emotional Abuse, 1*, 85–117.

Keashley, L. (2001). Interpersonal and systemic aspects of emotional abuse at work: The target's perspective. *Violence and Victims, 16*(3), 233–268.

Keashley, L., Harvey, S., & Hunter, S. (1997). Emotional abuse and role state stressors: Relative impact on residence assistants' stress. *Work and Stress, 11*, 35–45.

Keashly, L., & Neuman, J. H. (2004). Bullying in the workplace: Its impact and management. *Employee Rights and Employment Policy Journal, 8*, 335–373.

Keashly, L., & Neuman, J. H. (2008). Aggression at the service delivery interface: Do you see what I see? *Journal of Management and Organization, 14*, 180–192.

Keashley, L., Trott, V., & MacLean, L. M. (1994). Abusive behavior in the workplace: A preliminary investigation. *Violence and Victims, 9*, 125–141.

Kets de Vries, M., & Miller, D. (1984). *The neurotic organization. Diagnosing and changing counterproductive styles of management.* San Francisco: Jossey-Bass.

Kimberly, J. R., & Miles, R. H. (1980). *The organizational life cycle.* San Francisco: Jossey-Bass.

King, R. (2004, February). The corporate antitrust problem. *Workforce Management*, p. 22.

Kivimaki, M., Virtanen, M., Vartia, M., Elovainio, M., Vahtera, J., & Keltikangas-Järvinen, L. (2003). Workplace bullying and the risk of cardiovascular disease and depression. *Occupational and Environmental Medicine, 60*(10), 779–783.

Klein, R. A. (2005). You can't turn someone down for promotion because you don't like him. In K. Westhues (Ed.), *Winning, losing, moving on: How professionals deal with workplace harassment and mobbing* (pp. 53–74). Lewiston, NY: The Edwin Mellen Press.

Kokkinos, C. M., & Panayiotou, G. (2004). Predicting bullying and victimization among early adolescents: Associations with disruptive behavior disorders. *Aggressive Behavior, 30*, 520–533.

Kulka, R. A., Schlenger, W. E., Fairbank, J. A., Hough, R. L., Jordan, B. K., & Marmar, C. R. (1990). *Trauma and the Vietnam war generation: Report of findings from the National Vietnam Veterans' Readjustment Study.* New York: Brunner Mazel.

Kvale, S. (2007). *Doing interviews.* Los Angeles: Sage.

Ladd, G., & Troop-Gordon, W. (2003). The role of chronic peer difficulties in the development of children's psychological adjustment problems. *Child Development, 74*, 1344–1367.

Lang, P. J. (1979). A bio-informational theory of emotional imagery. *Psychophysiology, 16*, 495–512.

Lapierre, L. M., Spector, P. E., & Leck, J. D. (2005). Sexual versus non-sexual workplace aggression and victims' overall job satisfaction. *Journal of Occupational Health Psychology, 10*(2), 155–169.

LaVan, H., & Martin, W. M. (2008). Bullying in the US workplace: Normative and process-oriented ethical approaches. *Journal of Business Ethics, 83*, 147–165.

Lawler, E. (2003). Reward practices and performance management system effectiveness. *Organizational Dynamics, 32*(4), 396–404.

Lawson, D. M. (2009). Understanding and treating children who experience interpersonal maltreatment: Empirical findings. *Journal of Counseling & Development, 87*(2), 204–215.

Leach, J. (2004). Why people "freeze" in an emergency: Temporal and cognitive constraints on survival responses. *Aviation, Space, and Environmental Medicine, 75*(6), 539–542.

Leavitt, H., & Bahrami, H. (1987). *Managerial psychology: Managing behavior in organizations* (5th ed.). Chicago: University of Chicago Press.

Leichtman, M. D., & Ceci, S. J. (1995). The effects of stereotypes and suggestions on preschoolers' reports. *Developmental Psychology, 31*(4), 568–578.

Lester, D. L., Parnell, J. A., & Carraher, S. (2003). Organizational life cycle: A five-stage empirical scale. *International Journal of Organizational Analysis, 11*(4), 339–354.

Levine, P. A. (1997). Walking the tiger: Healing trauma. Berkeley, CA: North Atlantic Books.

Lewis, C. S. (1976). *A grief observed.* New York: Bantam.

Lewis, D. (2004). Bullying at work: The impact of shame among university and college lecturers. *British Journal of Guidance and Counselling, 32*(3), 281–299.

Lewis, M. A. (2006). Nurse bullying: Organizational considerations in the maintenance and perpetration of health care bullying cultures. *Journal of Nursing Management, 14*, 52–58.

Lewis, S. E., & Orford, J. (2005). Women's experiences of workplace bullying: Changes in social relationships. *Journal of Community and Applied Social Psychology, 15*, 29–47.

Leymann, H. (1986). *Vuxenmobbning-psykiskt våld i arbetslivet [Mobbing-psychological violence in working life].* Lund, SE: Studentlitteratur.

Leymann, H. (1987). Sjalvmord til foljd av forhallanden i arbetsmiljøn [Suicide due to work conditions]. *Arbete, Menneska, Milj, 3*, 155–160.

Leymann, H. (1990). Mobbing and psychological terror at workplaces. *Violence and Victims, 5*, 119–126.

Leymann, H. (1992). Psykiatriska halsoproblem i samband med vuxenmobbning. En rikstackende undersøkningmed 2428 intervjuer [Psychiatric problems after mobbing: A study of 2428 individuals]. Report no. 3. Stockholm: Arbetarskyddsstyrelsen.

Leymann, H. (1993). *Mobbing: Psychoterror am arbeitsplatz und wie man sich dagegen wehren kann* [Mobbing: Psycho-terror in the workplace and how one can defend against it]. Hamburg, DR: Rowolht.

Leymann, H. (1996). The content and development of mobbing at work. In D. Zapf, & H. Leymann (Eds.), *Mobbing and victimization at work* (pp. 165–184). Hove, UK: Psychology Press.

Leymann, H., & Gustafsson, A. (1996). Mobbing at work and the development of post traumatic stress disorders. *European Journal of Work and Organizational Psychology, 5*, 251–275.

Leymann, H., & Gustafsson, A. (1998). *Suicides due to mobbing/bullying—About nurses' high risks in the labour market.* Geneva: World Health Organization (WHO) Internal Report.

Liefooghe, A. P. D., & Mackenzie Davey, K. (2001). Accounts of workplace bullying: The role of the organization. *European Journal of Work & Occupational psychology, 10*, 375–393.

Limber, S. P., & Small, M. A. (2003). State laws and policies to address bullying in schools. *School Psychology Review, 32*(3), 445–455.

Linder, D. (2003). *Famous trials: The McMartin preschool abuse trials.* Retrieved from http://www.law.umkc.edu/faculty/projects/ftrials/mcmartin/mcmartin.html

Lipsky, D., Seeber, R., & Fincher, R. (2000). *Emerging systems for managing workplace conflict.* San Francisco: Jossey-Bass.

López-Cabarcos, M. Á., & Vázquez-Rodríguez, P. (2006). Psychological harassment in the Spanish public university system. *Academy of Health Care Management Journal, 2*, 21–39.

Lorange, P., & Nelson, R. T. (1987). How to recognize and avoid organizational decline. *Sloan Management Review*, 41–48.

Lorenz, K. (1963). *Das sogennante boese [On aggression].* Wien: Dr. G. Borotha-Schoeler Verlag.

Lorenz, K. (1965). *Evolution and modification of behavior.* Chicago: University of Chicago Press.

Lorenz, K. (1968). *Aggression: Dess bakgrund och natur [Aggression: The background and nature].* Stockholm: Norstedt & Söner.

Luthans, F., Peterson, S. J., & Ibrayeva, E. (1998). The potential for the "dark side" of leadership in post-communist countries. *Journal of World Business, 33*, 185–201.

Lutgen-Sandvik, P. (2003). The communicative cycle of employee emotional abuse: Generation and regeneration of workplace mistreatment. *Management Communication Quarterly, 16*(4), 471–501.

Lutgen-Sandvik, P. (2006). Take this job. . .: Quitting and other forms of resistance to workplace bullying. *Communication Monographs, 73*(4), 406–433.

Lutgen-Sandvik, P. (2008). Intensive remedial identity work: Responses to workplace bullying trauma and stigmatization. *Organization, 15*(1), 97–119.

Lutgen-Sandvik, P., & McDermott, V. (2008). The constitution of employee-abusive organizations: A communication flows theory. *Communication Theory, 18*, 304–333.

Lutgen-Sandvik, P., Tracy, S. J., & Alberts, J. K. (2007). Burned by bullying in the American workplace: Prevalence, perception, degree, and impact. *Journal of Management Studies, 44*(6), 837–862.

McAdams, C., & Schmidt, C.(2007). How to help a bully: Recommendations for counseling the proactive aggressor. *Professional School Counseling, 11*(2), 120–128.

McCabe, B. C. (2005). The rules are different here: An institutional comparison of cities and homeowners associations. *Administration and Society, 37*(4), 404–425.

McCarthy, P., Sheehan, M. J., & Wilkie, W. (Eds.). (1996). *Bullying: From backyard to boardroom.* Alexandria, AU: Millenium Books.

McGuckin, C., & Lewis, C. A. (2006). Experiences of school bullying in Northern Ireland: Data from the Life and Times Survey. *Adolescence, 41*(162), 313–320.

McKnight, S. (2009, November 15). Workplace gossip? Keep it to yourself. *The New York Times*, p. BU9.

MacNeil, G. A., & Newell, J. M. (2004). School bullying: Who, why, and what to do. *The Prevention Researcher, 11*(3), 15–17.

Maccoby, M. (2000). Narcissistic leaders: The incredible pros, the inevitable cons. *Harvard Business Review, 78*, 68–77.

Mantell, M. (1994). *Ticking bombs: Defusing violence in the workplace.* Burr Ridge, IL: Irwin.

Mantler, J., Matejicek, A., Matheson, K., & Anisman, H. (2005). Coping with employment uncertainty: A comparison of employed and unemployed workers. *Journal of Occupational Health Psychology, 10*(3), 200–209.

Maslach, C., & Leiter, M. P. (1997). *The truth about burnout: How organizations cause personal stress and what to do about it.* San Francisco: Jossey-Bass.

Maturana, H. R., & Varela, F. J. (1998). *The tree of knowledge: The biological roots of human understanding* (rev. ed.). Boston: Shambhala.

Matthiesen, S. B., & Einarsen, S. (2001). MMPI-2 configurations among victims of bullying at work. *European Journal of Work and Organizational Psychology, 10*, 467–484.

Matthiesen, S. B, & Einarsen, S. (2004). Psychiatric distress and symptoms of PTSD among victims of bullying at work. *British Journal of Guidance and Counselling, 32*(3), 335–356.

Matthiesen, S. B., Raknes, B. I., & Røkkum, O. (1989). Mobbing på arbeidsplasses [Bullying at work]. *Tidskrift for Norsk Psykologforening, 26*, 761–774.

Merchant, V., & Hoel, H. (2003). Investigating complaints of bullying. In S. Einarsen, H. Hoel, D. Zapf, & C.L. Cooper (Eds.), *Bullying and emotional abuse in the workplace* (pp. 259–269). London: Taylor & Francis.

Meyer, M. (1994). Culture club. *Newsweek, 124*(2), 38–42.

Meynell, H. (2008, November). *How to destroy a don.* The Second Hector Hammerly Memorial Lecture, University of Waterloo, Canada.

Mikkelsen, G. E., & Einarsen, S. (2001). Bullying in Danish work-life: Prevalence and health correlates. *European Journal of Work and Organizational psychology, 10*, 393–413.

Milgram, S. (1974). *Obedience to authority: An experimental view.* New York: Harper & Row.

Miller, D., & Friesen, P. H. (1984). A longitudinal study of the corporate life cycle. *Management Science, 30*, 1161–1183.

Milliman, J., Von Glinow, M. A., & Nathan, M. (1991). Organizational life cycles and strategic international human resource management in multinational companies: Implications for congruency theory. *Academy of Management Review, 16*, 318–339.

Minton, K., Ogden, P., & Pain, C. (2006). *Trauma and the body: A sensorimotor approach to psychotherapy.* New York: Norton.

Mintzberg, H. (1984). Power and organization life cycles. *Academy of Management Review, 9*(2), 207–224.

Mishna, F. (2004). A qualitative study of bullying from multiple perspectives. *Children and Schools, 26*(4), 234–247.

Mitchell, K. J., Ybarra, M., & Finkelhor, D. (2007). The relative importance of online victimization in understanding depression, delinquency, and substance use. *Child maltreatment, 12*(4), 314–324.

Mol, S. S. L., Arntz, A., Metsemakers, J. F. M., Dinant, G. -J., Vilters Van-Montfort, P. A. P., & Knottnerus, J. A. (2005). Symptoms of post-traumatic stress disorder after non-traumatic events: Evidence from an open population study. *British Journal of Psychiatry, 186*, 494–499.

Mollen, S. E. (1999). Alternative dispute resolution of condominium and cooperative conflicts. *St. John's Law Review, 73*(1), 75–100.

Myers, D. W. (1996, July-August). The mythical world of workplace violence—or is it? *Business Horizons,* pp. 31–36.

Namie, G. (2003). Workplace bullying: Escalated incivility. *Ivey Business Journal: Improving the Practice of Management,* November/December, 1–6. (reprint No. 9B03TF09) 201.

Namie, G. (2008). *Employers' Response Study. Workplace Bullying Institute.* Retrieved from http://workplacebullying.org/res/2008WBIsurvey.pdf

Namie, G., & Namie, R. (2000). *The bully at work: What you can do to stop the hurt and reclaim your dignity on the job.* Naperville, IL: Sourcebooks, Inc.

Namie, G., & Namie, R. (2004). Workplace bullying: How to address America's silent epidemic. *Employee Rights and Employment Policy Journal, 8*, 315–333.

Namie, G., & Namie, R. (2009a). *The bully at work: What you can do to stop the hurt and reclaim your dignity on the job* (2nd ed.). Naperville, IL: Sourcebooks, Inc.

Namie, G., & Namie, R. (2009b). U.S. workplace bullying: Some basic considerations and consultation interventions. *Consulting Psychology Journal: Practice and Research, 61*(3), 202–219.

Nansel, T. R., Overpeck, M. D., Haynie, D. L., Ruan, W. J., & Scheidt, P. C. (2003). Relationships between bullying and violence among US youth. *Archives of Pediatrics & Adolescent Medicine, 157*, 348–353.

Nansel, T., Overpeck, M., Pilla, R., Ruan, W., Simons-Morton, B., & Scheidt, P. (2001). Bullying behaviors among US youth: Prevalence and association with psychosocial adjustment. *Journal of American Medical Association, 285*(16), 2094–2100.

Natelson, R. G. (1989). *Law of property owners associations.* Boston: Little Brown.

National Center on Addiction and Substance Abuse. (2000). *Report of the United States Postal Service Commission on a safe and secure workplace.* New York: Author.

National Center for Educational Statistics. (2007). Indicators of school crime and safety. *U.S. Department of Education, Institute of Education Sciences.* Retrieved from http://nces.ed.gov/programs/crimeindicators/crimeindicators2007/ind_11.asp

National Conference of State Legislatures, Education Bill Tracking Database. (n.d.). Public bill search topic areas: Bullying, harassment, and intimidation, all bill types. Retrieved from http://www.ncsl.org/programs/educ/educ_leg.cfm

National Conference of State Legislatures, Education Bill Tracking Database. (n.d.). Public bill search topic areas: Cyberbullying, all bill types. Retrieved from http://www.ncsl.org/programs/educ/cyberbullying.htm

Naylor, O., & Cowie, N. (1999). The effectiveness of peer support systems in challenging school bullying: The perspectives and experiences of teachers and pupils. *Journal of Adolescence, 22,* 467–479.

Neuman, J. H., & Baron, R. A. (1998). Workplace violence and workplace aggression: Evidence concerning specific forms, potential causes, and preferred targets. *Journal of Management, 24*(3), 391–419.

Niedhammer, I., Chastang, J., & David, S. (2008). Importance of psychosocial work factors on general health outcomes in the national French SUMER survey. *Occupational Medicine, 58*(1), 15–24.

Niedhammer, I., David, S., Degioanni, S., & 143 Occupational Physicians. (2006). Association between workplace bullying and depressive symptoms in the French working population. *Journal of Psychosomatic Research, 61*(2), 251–259.

No Child Left Behind Act of 2001 (Publication No.107–110, 20 U.S.C. 6301 et seq. 2002). Washington, DC: US Department of Education.

Nolfe, G., Petrella, C., Blasi, F., Zontini, G., & Nolfe, G. (2008). Psychopathological dimensions of harassment in the workplace (mobbing). *International Journal of Mental Health, 36*(4), 67–85.

Nonaka, I., & Nishiguchi, T. (Eds.). (2001). Knowledge emergence: Social, technical, and evolutionary dimensions of knowledge creation. New York: Oxford University Press.

Nystrom, P. C., & Starbuck, W. H. (1984). To avoid organizational crises, unlearn. *Organizational Dynamics,* 53–65.

O'Brien, J. T. (1997). The "glucocorticoid cascade" hypothesis in man. Prolonged stress may cause permanent brain damage. *British Journal of Psychiatry, 170,* 199–201.

O'Connell, P., Pepler, D., & Craig, W. (1999). Peer involvement in bullying: Insights and challenges for intervention. *Journal of Adolescence, 22,* 437–452.

Ogden, P., & Minton, K. (2000). Sensorimotor psychotherapy. *Traumatology, 6*(3), 149–173.

Olaffson, R., & Johansdottir, H. (2004). Coping with bullying in the workplace: The effect of gender, age, and type of bullying. *British Journal of Guidance and Counselling, 32*(3), 319–333.

Olweus, D. (1973). *Hackkycklingar och översittare. Forskning om skolmobbing [Hack chickens and bullies. Research on school mobbing].* Stockholm: Almqvist & Wicksell.

Olweus, D. (1977). Aggression and peer acceptance in adolescent boys: Two short term longitudinal studies of ratings. *Child Development, 48,* 1301–1313.

Olweus, D. (1978). *Aggression in the schools: Bullies and whipping boys.* Washington, DC: Hemisphere Press (Wiley).

Olweus, D. (1979). Stability of aggressive reaction patterns in males: A review. *Psychological Bulletin, 86,* 852–875.

Olweus, D. (1993a). *Bullying at school: What we know and what we can do.* Cambridge, MA: Blackwell.

Olweus, D. (1993b). Victimization by peers: Antecedents and long term outcomes. In K. H. Rubin, & J. B. Asendorf (Eds.), *Social withdrawal, inhibition, and shyness in childhood* (pp. 315–341). Hillsdale, NJ: Erlbaum.

Olweus, D. (2001). Peer harassment: A critical analysis and some important issues. In J. Juvonen, & S. Graham (Eds.), *Peer harassment in school* (pp. 3–20). New York: Guilford.

Olweus, D. (2003). Bully/victim problems in school: Basic facts and an effective intervention programme. In S. Einarsen, H. Hoel, D. Zapf, & C. Cooper (Eds.), *Bullying and emotional abuse in the workplace: International perspectives in research and practice* (pp. 62–78). London: Taylor & Francis.

Olweus, D., Limber, S. P., & Mihalic, S. (1999). *The bullying prevention program: Blueprints for violence prevention* Vol. 10. Boulder, Co: Center for the Study and Prevention of Violence.

O'Moore, M., & Lynch, J. (2007). Leadership, working environment, and workplace bullying. *International Journal of Organization Theory and Behavior, 10*(1), 95–117.

O'Moore, M., Seigne, E., McGuire, L., & Smith, M. (1998a). Victims of bullying at work in Ireland. In C. Rayner, M. Sheehan, & M. Barker (Eds.), *Bullying at work 1998 research update conference: Proceedings.* Stafford, UK: Staffordshire University.

O'Moore, M., Seigne, E., McGuire, L., & Smith, M. (1998b). Victims of bullying at work in Ireland. *The Journal of Occupational and Health Safety—Australia and New Zealand, 14*(6), 569–574.

Padilla, A., Hogan, R., & Kaiser, R. B. (2007). The toxic triangle: Destructive leaders, susceptible followers, and conducive environments. *The Leadership Quarterly, 18,* 176–194.

Patrick, R., & Currier, J. (2008, May 16). Relief and questions follow federal charges. Fraud statute typically used to go after hackers; some challenge its use. *St. Louis Post-Dispatch,* p. A1.

Pearson, C. M., Andersson, L. M., & Porath, C. L. (2000). Assessing and attacking workplace incivility. *Organizational Dynamics, 29*(2), 123–137.

Pellegrini, A. D. (1994). The rough play of adolescent boys of differing sociometric status. *International Journal of Behavioral Development, 17,* 525–540.

Perry, D. G., Kusel, S. J., & Perry, L. C. (1988). Victims of peer aggression. *Developmental Psychology, 24,* 807–814.

Peretz, E. (2009, July). The code of Miss Porter's. *Vanity Fair, 51,* p. 86.

Pfeffer, J. (1981). *Power in organizations.* Boston: Pitman Publishing.

Pfeffer, J. (2007). Human resources from an organizational behavior perspective: Some paradoxes explained. *Journal of Economic Perspectives, 21*(4), 115–134.

Pinkerfield, H. (2006, November). Beat the bullies. *Human Resources,* pp. 77–79.

Pliszka, S. R. (2003). *Neuroscience for the mental health clinician.* New York: Guilford.

Pokin, S. (2007, November 10). Pokin around: A real person, a real death. *St. Charles Journal.*

Pompili, M., Lester, D., Innamorati, M., De Pisa, E., Iliceto, P., Puccinno, M., et al. (2008). Suicide risk and exposure to mobbing. *Work, 31*(2), 237–243.

Price, J. M., & Dodge, K. A. (1989). Reactive and proactive aggression in childhood: Relations to peer status and social context dimension. *Journal of Abnormal Child Psychology, 17*(4), 455–471.

Prinstein, M. J., Boergers, J., & Vernberg, E. M. (2001). Overt and relational aggression in adolescents: Social-psychological adjustment of aggressors and *victims. Journal of Clinical Child Psychology, 30,* 479–491.

Punzi, S., Cassito, M. G., Castellini, G., Costa, G., & Gilioli, R. (2007). Mobbing and its effects on health: The experience of the "Clinica del Lavoro Luigi Devoto" in Milan. *La Medicina del Lavoro [Workplace medicine], 98*(4), 267–283.

Quigg, A. M. (2003, March). Bullying: End the Nightmare. *Stage Screen & Radio: The Journal of the Broadcasting Entertainment Cinematograph & Theatre Union,* pp. 1, 8–9.

Quine, L. (2003). Workplace bullying, psychological distress, and job satisfaction in junior doctors. *Cambridge Quarterly of Healthcare Ethics, 12*(10), 91–101.

Quinn, R., & Cameron, K. (1983). Organizational life cycles and shifting criteria of effectiveness: Some preliminary evidence. *Management Science, 29,* 33–51.

Raine, A., Dodge, K., Loeber, R., Gatzke-Kopp, L., Lynam, D., Raynolds, C., et al. (2006). The reactive-proactive aggression questionnaire: Differential correlated of reactive and proactive aggression in adolescent boys. *Aggressive Behavior, 32,* 159–171.

Randall, P. (1997). *Adult bullying: Perpetrators and victims.* London: Routledge.

Rayner, C. (1997). The incidence of workplace bullying. *Journal of Community and Applied Social Psychology, 7*(3), 199–208.

Rayner, C. (1998). Workplace bullying: Do something! *The Journal of Occupational Health and Safety—Australia and New Zealand, 14*(6), 581–585.

Rayner, C. (1999). From research to implementation: Finding leverage for prevention. *International Journal of Manpower, 20*(1/2), 28–38.

Rayner, C. (2002, August). *Round two: Redefining bullying at work*. Paper presented as part of a joint session, "Workplace abuse, aggression, bullying and incivility: Conceptual integration and empirical insights," at the American Academy of Management meeting, Denver, Colorado.

Rayner, C., & Hoel, H. (1997). A summary review of literature relating to workplace bullying. *Journal of Community and Applied Social Psychology, 7*(3), 181–191.

Rayner, C., Hoel, H., & Cooper, C. L. (2002). *Workplace bullying: What we know, who is to blame, and what can we do?* London: Taylor & Francis.

Rayner, C., & McIvor, K. (2006). *Report to the Dignity at Work Project steering committee: Research findings*. Portsmouth, UK: University of Portsmouth Business School.

Reed, G. E. (2004, July-August). Toxic leadership. *Military Review*, pp. 67–71.

Reinhold, R. (1990a, January 24). The longest trial - A post-mortem; collapse of child-abuse case: So much agony for so little. *The New York Times*, p. A1.

Reinhold, R. (1990b, January 25). How lawyers and media turned the McMartin case into a tragic media circus. *The New York Times*, p. D1.

Reitz, S. (2008, December 12). Bullying at school prompts lawsuit. *The Miami Herald*, p. 23A.

Richards, J., & Daley, H. (2003). Bullying policy: Development, implementation, and monitoring. In S. Einarsen, H. Hoel, D. Zapf, & C. L. Cooper (Eds.), *Bullying and emotional abuse in the workplace* (pp. 247–258). London: Taylor & Francis.

Rigby, K. (1994). Psycho-social functioning in families of Australian adolescent schoolchildren involved in bully/victim problems. *Journal of Family Therapy, 16*(2), 173–189.

Rigby, K. (1996). Peer victimization and the structure of primary and secondary schooling. *Primary Focus, 10*(7), 4–5.

Rigby, K. (2004). Addressing bullying in schools: Theoretical perspectives and their implications. *School Psychology International, 25*(3), 287–300.

Rigby, K., & Johnson, B. (2006). Expressed readiness of Australian schoolchildren to act as bystanders in support of children who are being bullied. *Educational Psychology, 26*, 425–440.

Roberts, D. R., & Davenport, T. O. (2002). Job engagement: Why it's important and how to improve it. *Employment Relations Today, 29*(3), 21–28.

Rosenthal, S. A., & Pittinskya, T. L. (2006). Narcissistic leadership. *Leadership Quarterly, 17*, 617–633.

Rothschild, B. (2000). *The body remembers: The psychophysiology of trauma and trauma treatment*. New York: Norton.

Sackett, P. R., & DeVore, C. J. (2002). Counterproductive behaviors at work. In N. Anderson, D. S. Ones, H. K. Sinangil, & C. Viswesvaran (Eds.), *Handbook of industrial, work, and organizational psychology*. Vol. 1 (pp. 145–164). London: Sage.

Salin, D. (2003). Bullying and organizational politics in competitive and rapidly changing work environments. *International Journal of Management and Decision-Making, 4*, 35–46.

Salmivalli, C. (1999). Participant role approach to school bullying: Implications for interventions. *Journal of Adolescence, 22* (4), 453–459.

Salmivalli, C. (2010). Bullying and the peer group: A review. *Aggression and Violent Behavior, 15* (2), pp. 112-120. doi:10.1016/j.avb.2009.08.007

Salmivalli, C., Lagerspetz, K., Bjorkqvist, K., Osterman, K., & Kaukiainen, A. (1996). Bullying as a group process: Participant roles and their relations to social status within the group. *Aggressive Behavior, 29*(2), 1–15.

Salmivalli, C., Lappalainen, M., & Lagerspetz, K. (1998). Stability and change of behavior in connection with bullying in schools: A two-year follow-up. *Aggressive Behavior, 24*, 205–218.

Salimivalli, C., & Nieminen, E. (2002). Proactive and reactive aggression among school bullies, victims, and bully-victims. *Aggressive Behavior, 28*, 30–44.

Salmon, G., James, A., & Smith, D. M. (1998). Bullying in schools: Self reported anxiety, depression, and self esteem in secondary school children. *British Medical Journal, 317*, 924–925.

Santavirta, N., Solovieva, S., & Theorell, T. (2007). The association between job strain and emotional exhaustion in a cohort of 1,028 Finnish teachers. *British Journal of Educational Psychology, 77*(1), 213–228.

Santos. F. (2009, March 22). At a prep school the gloves are off. *The New York Times*, pp. ST1, ST-7.

Scaer, R. (2005). *The trauma spectrum: Hidden wounds and human resiliency.* New York: Norton.

Schreiber, N., Bellah, L. D., Martinez, Y., McLaurin, K. A., Strok, R., Garven, S., & Wood, J. M. (2006). Suggestive interviewing in the McMartin preschool and Kelly Michaels daycare abuse cases: A case study. *Social Influence, 1*(1), 16–47.

Schuster, B. (2001). Rejection and victimization by peers: Social perception and social behavior mechanisms. In J. Juvonen, & S. Graham (Eds.), *Peer harassment in school: The plight of the vulnerable and victimized* (pp. 290–309). New York: Guilford Press.

Scott, B. R. (1971). *Stages of corporate development-Part 1. Case No, 9–371-294.* Boston: Intercollegiate Case Clearing House.

Seigne, E., Coyne, I., Randall, P., & Parker, J. (2007). Personality traits of bullies as a contributory factor in workplace bullying: An exploratory study. *International Journal of Organization Theory and Behavior, 10*(1), 118–132.

Serantes, N. P., & Suárez, M. A. (2006). Myths about workplace violence, harassment, and bullying. *International Journal of the Sociology of Law, 34,* 229–238.

Shallcross, L., Sheehan, M., & Ramsay, S. (2008). Workplace mobbing: Experiences in the public sector. *International Journal of Organisational Behaviour, 13*(2), 56–70.

Shapiro, C. (2005). *Corporate confidential: 50 secrets your company doesn't want you to know–and what to do about them.* New York: St. Martin's Griffin.

Shapiro, F. (1995). *Eye movement desensitization and reprocessing: Basic principles, protocols, and procedures.* New York: Guilford Press.

Shapiro, F. (1999). Eye movement desensitization and reprocessing (EMDR) and the anxiety disorders: Clinical and research implications of an integrated psychotherapy treatment. *Journal of Anxiety Disorders, 13,* 35–67.

Sharp, S. (1996). The role of peers in tackling bullying in schools. *Educational Psychology in Practice, 11*(4), 17–22.

Sheehan, M. (2004, October). Workplace mobbing: A proactive response. Paper presented at the Workplace Mobbing Conference, Brisbane, Australia. Retrieved from http://www.lindas.internetbasedfamily.com/f/MobMS.pdf

Sheehan, M., & Barker, M. (1999). Applying strategies for dealing with workplace bullying. *International Journal of Manpower, 20*(1/2), 50–57.

Siegel, D. J. (2003). An interpersonal neurobiology of psychotherapy: The developing mind and the resolution of trauma. In M. F. Solomon, & D. J. Siegel (Eds.), *Healing trauma: Attachment, mind, body, and brain* (pp. 1–56). New York: Norton.

Smith, J. D., Schneider, B. H., Smith, P. K., & Ananiadou, K. (2004). The effectiveness of whole school antibullying programs: A synthesis of evaluation research. *School Psychology Review, 33*(4), 547–560.

Soares, A. (2010, June). Organizational dimensions and bullying at work. Presentation at the 7th International Conference on Workplace Bullying and Harassment, University of Glamorgan, Cardiff, Wales.

Sonnenfeld, J. A., & Ward, A. J. (2007, January). Firing back: How great leaders rebound after career disasters. *Harvard Business Review,* pp. 76–84.

Sourander, A., Ronning, J., Brunstein-Klomek, A., Gyllenberg, D., Kumpulainen, K., Niemelä, S., et al. (2009). Childhood bullying behavior and later psychiatric hospital and psychopharmacologic treatment: Findings from the Finnish 1981 birth cohort study. *Archives of General Psychiatry, 66*(9), 1005–1012.

Spector, P. E. (1997). *Job satisfaction: Application, assessment, cause, and consequences.* Thousand Oaks, CA: Sage.

Sperry, L. (1993). *Psychiatric consultation in the workplace.* Washington, DC: American Psychiatric Press.

Sperry, L. (1996a). Leadership dynamics: Character and character structure in executives. *Consulting Psychology Journal, 48,* 268–280.

Sperry, L. (1996b). *Corporate therapy and consulting.* New York: Brunner/Mazel.

Sperry, L. (1998). Organizations that foster inappropriate aggression. *Psychiatric Annals, 28*(5), 279–284.

Sperry, L. (2002). *Effective leadership: Strategies for maximizing executive productivity and health.* New York: Brunner-Routledge.

Sperry, L. (2004). *Executive coaching.* New York: Routledge.

Sperry, L. (2009a). Workplace mobbing and bullying: A consulting psychology perspective and overview. *Consulting Psychology Journal: Practice and Research, 61,* 165–168.

Sperry, L. (2009b). Mobbing and bullying: The influence of individual, work group, and organizational dynamics on abusive workplace behavior. *Consulting Psychology Journal: Practice and Research, 61*(3), 190–201.

Sperry, L., & Duffy, M. (2009). Workplace mobbing: Family dynamics and therapeutic considerations. *American Journal of Family Therapy, 37*(5), 433–442.

Sperry, L., & Larsen, R. (1998). Aggression in the workplace: An overview. *Psychiatric Annals, 28*(5), 243–244.

Spurgeon, A. (2003). Bullying from a risk management perspective. In S. Einarsen, H. Hoel, D. Zapf, & C. L. Cooper (Eds.), *Bullying and emotional abuse in the workplace: International perspectives in research and practice* (pp. 327–338). London: Taylor & Francis.

Srabstein, J. C., Berkman, B. E., & Pyntikova, M. S. (2008). Antibullying legislation: A public health perspective. *Journal of Adolescent Health, 42,* 11–20.

Strandmark, M., Lillemor, K., & Hallberg, R. (2007).The origin of workplace bullying: Experiences from the perspective of bully victims in the public service sector. *Journal of Nursing Management, 15*(3), 332–341.

Sutton, R.M., & Douglas, K.M. (2005). Justice for all, or just for me? More evidence of the importance of the self-other distinction in just-world beliefs. *Personality and Individual Differences, 39,* 637–645.

Sutton, J., Smith, P. K., & Swettenham, J. (1999). Bullying "theory of mind": A critique of the "social skills deficit" view of anti-social behaviour. *Social Development, 8*(1), 117–127.

Sutton, R. I. (2007). *The no asshole rule: Building a civilized workplace and surviving one that isn't.* New York: Warner Business Books.

Taylor, F.W. (1911). *The principles of scientific management.* New York: Harper.

Taylor, S., Thordarson, D. S., Maxfield, L., Federoff, I. C., Lovell, K., & Ogrodniczuk, J. (2003). Comparative efficacy, speed, and adverse effects of three PTSD treatments: Exposure therapy, EMDR, and relaxation training. *Journal of Consulting and Clinical Psychology, 71*(2), 330–338.

Tehrani, N. (2004). Bullying: A source of chronic post traumatic stress? *British Journal of Guidance and Counselling, 32*(3), 357–366.

Tepper, B. J. (2000). Consequences of abusive supervision. *Academy of Management Journal, 43*(2), 178–190.

Tierney, P., & Tepper, B. J. (2007). Destructive leadership [Editorial]. *The Leadership Quarterly, 18,* 171–173.

Tigrel, E. Y., & Kokalan. O. (2009). Academic mobbing in Turkey. *International Journal of Behavioral, Cognitive, Educational and Psychological Sciences, 1*(2), 91–99.

Tomei, G., Cinti, M. E., Sancini, A., Cerrati, D., Pimpinella, B., Ciarrocca, M., et al. (2007). Evidence based medicine and mobbing. *Giornale Italiano di Medicina del Lavaro ed. Ergonomia [Italian Journal of Workplace Medicine and Ergonomics], 29*(2), 149–157.

Topix. (2008, December 10). Miss Porter's School sued over expulsion [Msg. 478]. Message posted by 1catlover to http://www.topix.com/forum/source/the-morning-call/T09EAVFG1RPGNLMVC/p19

Topix. (2008, December 10—2009, July 27). Miss Porter's School sued over expulsion. Messages posted to http://www.topix.com/forum/source/the-morning-call/T09EAVFG1RPGNLMVC

Torbert, W. (1974). Pre-bureaucratic stages of organization development, *Interpersonal Development, 5,* 1–25.

Toufexis, A. (2001, June 24). Workers who fight firing with fire. *Time Magazine.* Retrieved from http://www.time.com/time/magazine/article/0,9171,1101940425-164280,00.html

Tracy, S. J., Lutgen-Sandvik, P., & Alberts, J. K. (2006). Nightmares, demons, and slaves: Exploring the painful metaphors of workplace bullying. *Management Communication Quarterly, 20*(2), 148–185.

Tuchman, G. (Interviewer). (2007, November 16). [AC 360, CNN] Megan Meier story: Interview with Tina and Ron Meier. Video retrieved from http://www.youtube.com/watch?v=HFsfDLCkfQU

Uris, A. (1964). *Techniques of leadership.* New York: McGraw-Hill.

Vaknin, S. (2001). *Malignant self love: Narcissism revisited.* Czech Republic: Narcissus Publications.

Vanderckhove, W., & Commers, M. S. (2003). Downward workplace mobbing: A sign of the times. *Journal of Business Ethics, 45,* 41–50.

Van der Kolk, B. A. (1994). The body keeps the score: Memory and the emerging psychobiology of post traumatic stress. *Harvard Review of Psychiatry, 1,* 253–265.

Van der Kolk, B. A. (2003). Posttraumatic stress disorder and the nature of trauma. In M. F. Solomon, & D. J. Siegel (Eds.), *Healing trauma: Attachment, mind, body, and brain* (pp. 168–195). New York: Norton.

Van der Kolk, B. A. (2006). Clinical implications of neuroscience research in PTSD. *Annals of the New York Academy of Sciences, 1071,* 277–293.

Van der Kolk, B. A., Roth, S., Pelcovitz, D., Sunday, S., & Spinazzola, J. (2005). Disorders of extreme stress: The empirical foundation of a complex adaptation to trauma. *Journal of Traumatic Stress, 18*(5), 389–399.

Van der Kolk, B. A., & van der Hart, O. (1991). The intrusive past: The flexibility of memory and the engraving of trauma. *American Imago, 48,* 425–454.

Van der Wal, M. F., De Wit, C. A. M., Hirasing, R. A. (2003). Psychosocial health among young victims and offenders of direct and indirect bullying. *Pediatrics, 111*(6), 1312–1317.

Vartia, M. (1996). The sources of bullying—Environment and organizational climate. *European Journal of Work and Organizational Psychology, 5*(2), 50–57.

Vartia, M. (2001). Consequences of workplace bullying with respect to the well-being of its targets and the observers of bullying. *Scandinavian Journal of Work Environment and Health, 27,* 63–69.

Vartia, M., Korppoo, L., Fallenius, S., & Mattila, M. -L. (2003). Workplace bullying: The role of occupational health services. In S. Einarsen, H. Hoel, D. Zapf, & C. L. Cooper (Eds.), *Bullying and emotional abuse in the workplace: International perspectives in research and practice* (pp. 285–298). London: Taylor & Francis.

Vickers, M., H. (2002). Researchers as storytellers: Writing on the edge and without a safety net. *Qualitative Inquiry, 8*(5), 608–621.

Weber, D. (2008, November 14). Tough new policies in Florida schools target bullies. *Orlando Sentinel.*

Weber, M. (1947). *The theory of social and economic organization.* A. M. Henderson, & T. Parsons (Trans.). New York: Oxford University Press.

Weich, S. (2008, December 3). Cyber bullies spread hatred despite lesson of Drew trial. *St. Louis Post-Dispatch,* p. B1.

Westhues, K. (1998). *Eliminating professors: A guide to the dismissal process.* Lewiston, NY: Edwin Mellen Press.

Westhues, K. (2002, December). At the mercy of the mob. *Occupational Health & Safety Magazine Canada, (18)*8, 30–36.

Westhues, K. (2004). *Workplace mobbing in academe: Reports from twenty universities.* Lewiston, NY: Edwin Mellen Press.

Westhues, K. (2005a). *The envy of excellence: Administrative mobbing of high-achieving professors.* Lewiston, NY: The Tribunal for Academic Justice/Edwin Mellen Press.

Westhues, K. (2005b). *The pope versus the professor: Benedict XVI and the legitimation of mobbing.* Lewiston, NY: The Tribunal for Academic Justice/Edwin Mellen Press.

Westhues, K. (2005c). (Ed.). *Winning, losing, moving on: How professionals deal with workplace harassment and mobbing.* Lewiston, NY: The Edwin Mellen Press.

Wheatcroft, D. J., & Price, T. D. (2008). Reciprocal cooperation in avian mobbing: Playing nice pays. *Trends in Ecology and Evolution, 23*(8), 416–419.

Williams, K. R., & Guerra, N. G. (2007). Prevalence and predictors of internet bullying. *Journal of Adolescent Health, 41,* S14–S21.

White, M. (2007a). *Maps of narrative practice.* New York: Norton.

White, M. (2007b, October). *Addressing the consequences of trauma.* Workshop conducted for The Narrative Therapy Institute, Cocoa Beach, Florida.

Wilson, C. B. (1991, July). US businesses suffer from workplace trauma. *Personnel Journal, 70*, 47–50.

The Workplace Bullying Institute (n.d.). *How employers pay*. Retrieved from http://bullyinginstitute. org/education/bbstudies/econ.html

The Workplace Bullying Institute (n.d.). *Legal advocacy for workplace bullying laws*. Retrieved from http://workplacebullyinglaw.org/

The Workplace Bullying Institute/Zogby International. (2007, September). *U.S. workplace bullying survey*. Retrieved from http://bullyinginstitute.org/zogby2007/wbi-zogby2007.html

Wrzesniewski, A., McCaukley, C. Rozin, P. & Schwartz, B. (1997). Jobs, careers, and callings: People's relations to their work. *Journal of Research in Personality, 31*, 21–33.

Yamada, D. C. (2004). Crafting a legislative response to workplace bullying. *Employee Rights and Employment Policy Journal, 8*, 475–521.

Yamada, D. (2007, June). *Potential legal protections and liabilities for workplace bullying*. Retrieved from http://www.newworkplaceinstitute.org/docs/nwi.web.bullying&law2.pdf

Yildirim, A., & Yildirim, D. (2007). Mobbing in the workplace by peers and managers: Mobbing experienced by nurses working in healthcare facilities in Turkey and its effect on nurses. *Journal of Clinical Nursing, 16*, 1444–1453.

Yildirim, A., Yildirim, D., & Timucin, A. (2007). Mobbing behaviors encountered by nurse teaching staff. *Nursing Ethics, 14*(4), 447–463.

Young, L. (2008). Bullying worse than sexual harassment: Study. *Canadian HR Reporter, 21*(7), 9.

Zapf, D. (1999a). Mobbing in organisationen. Ein überblick zum stand der forschung [Mobbing in organizations. A state of the art review]. *Zeitschrift für Arbeits- and Organisationspsychologie, 43*, 1–25.

Zapf, D. (1999b). Organizational, work group related and personal causes of mobbing/bullying at work. *International Journal of Manpower, 20*, 70–85.

Zapf, D., & Einarsen, S. (2003). Individual antecedents of bullying: Victims and perpetrators. In S. Einarsen, H. Hoel, D. Zapf, & C. L. Cooper (Eds.), *Bullying and emotional abuse in the workplace: International perspectives in research and practice* (pp. 165–184). London: Taylor & Francis.

Zapf, D., Einarsen, S., Hoel, H., & Vartia, M. (2003). Empirical findings on bullying in the work-place. In S. Einarsen, H. Hoel, D. Zapf, & C. L. Cooper (Eds.), *Bullying and emotional abuse in the workplace* (pp. 103–126). London: Taylor & Francis.

Zapf, D., Knorz, C., & Kulla, M. (1996). On the relationship between mobbing factors, and job content, the social work environment and health outcomes. *European Journal of Work and Organizational Psychology, 5*, 215–237.

Zimbardo, P. G. (1974). On "obedience to authority." *American Psychologist, 29*(7), 566–567.

Zimbardo, P. (2008). *The Lucifer effect: Understanding how good people turn evil*. New York: Random House Trade Paperbacks.

Index

ABC model, 82
abuse
    child sexual, 17–19
    emotional, 28, 39
    employee-abusive organizations, 80–81
    interpersonal, 4, 23
    *Mobbing: Emotional Abuse in the American
        Workplace*, 27
    in school, 48*f*
    verbal, 57–58
    in workplace, 39, 48*f*
abusive leadership styles, 100–103
abusive managerial behavior, 102–3
abusiveness
    awareness of, 93
    organizational, 89–90, 213–14, 213*f*
abusive supervision, 39
academic mobbing, 29. *See also* school mobbing
accountability, anti-mobbing policy, 266
ADA. *See* Americans with Disabilities Act
Adams, Andrea, 27
Adizes model, 113–14
administrators
    organization, 156–57
    school, 63–65
ad numerum fallacy, 16
adolescents. *See also* children
    as mobbing victims, 97–98
    as perpetrators of mobbing, 99–100
    victims, protecting, 203–7
aggression
    behaviors, 41, 43–44
    bullying and, 29, 41, 244–45
    childhood, 24–25
    electronic acts of, 58
    mobbing and, 68–69
    occupations and, 85
    organizational, 85, 89–90
    performative acts of, 58
    physical, 29, 57–58

proactive, 97–98, 245
reactive, 97–98
in workplace, 39
written acts of, 58
aggressive passivity, 27
airline industry, 150–53, 234–35
allegations of mobbing, 250
American Psychiatric Association, 44.
    *See also Diagnostic and Statistical
    Manual of Mental Disorders*
Americans with Disabilities Act (ADA), 237
animals, mobbing and, 24, 35–36
antecedents
    ABC model and, 82
    of mobbing, 93–107, 117
anti-bullying laws, 227
anti-bullying policies, 11
    Olweus Bullying Prevention
        Program, 254–56
anti-harassment policy, 223
anti-mobbing policies, 215
    accountability and sanctions, 266
    appeals process, 266–67
    complaints and, 265–66
    confidentiality and, 266
    developing, 249, 259–61, 260*f*
    due process and, 266
    mobbing behaviors and, 263–64
    mobbing defined in, 263
    organizational, 262–67
    prevention and, 264–65
    purpose of, 262–63
    reporting of findings and, 266
    sample, 262–67
    school, 224–35, 259–61, 260*f*
    time frame of, 266
    workplace, 261–62
appeals process, 266–67
Arendt, Hannah, 44
assertiveness, 167

Printed in the USA/Agawam, MA
November 7, 2013

581740.068